Ashbel P. Fitch

The New York Times.

ILLUSTRATED MAGAZINE SUPPLEMENT.

THE NEW YORK TIMES COMPANY.

SUPPLEMENT TO THE NEW YORK TIMES.

SIXTEEN PAGES. JULY 16, 1899. PRICE, FIVE CENTS.

Photograph by Wilhelm, New York.

ASHBEL P. FITCH,

EX-CONTROLLER OF THE CITY AND NOW PRESIDENT OF THE TRUST COMPANY OF AMERICA.

Ashbel P. Fitch

CHAMPION OF OLD NEW YORK

David F. Remington

With a Foreword by Joanne Reitano

The Adirondack Museum

Syracuse University Press

First Edition 2011

11 12 13 14 15 16 6 5 4 3 2 1

∞ The paper used in this publication meets the minimum requirements of the American National Standard for Information Sciences—Permanence of Paper for Printed Library Materials, ANSI Z39.48-1992.

For a listing of books published and distributed by Syracuse University Press, visit our Web site at SyracuseUniversityPress.syr.edu.

Library of Congress Cataloging-in-Publication Data

Remington, David F.

Ashbel P. Fitch : champion of old New York / David F. Remington ; with a foreword by Joanne Reitano. — 1st ed.

p. cm.

Includes bibliographical references and index.

ISBN 978-0-8156-0988-9 (cloth : alk. paper)

1. Fitch, Ashbel P. (Ashbel Parmelee), 1848–1904. 2. Legislators—United States—Biography. 3. Legislators—New York—Biography. 4. United States. Congress. House—Biography. I. Title.

E664.F535R46 2011

328.73'092—dc22

[B] 2011013584

Manufactured in the United States of America

In loving memory of my two cousins, descendents of Ashbel P. Fitch:

Rennie Roberts, to whom family history was a beacon
and Ragged Lake was a sacred place,
and
Kitty Egan, who treasured and nurtured the Fitch family legacy.

DAVID F. REMINGTON is a retired investment banker, volunteer, Adirondacker, cyclist, and amateur historian. He is a great-grandson of Ashbel P. Fitch. He lives with his wife, Chelsey, on the rocky coast of Maine.

Contents

Illustrations

Foreword

JOANNE REITANO

Nothing is so difficult as shedding light on an unknown historical figure, but Dave Remington has rescued Ashbel P. Fitch from obscurity. Not colorful like James G. Blaine or corrupt like William M. Tweed, Fitch was notable for being independent and principled. He was dedicated to his city and his standards despite the odds. Using primary sources, Remington has illuminated the career of steady and significant public service in an unsettling, unsavory time of rapid change.

The concept of an "honest Tammany man" seems like an oxymoron, but it became a reality in the curious career of Ashbel P. Fitch, who served New York City as a four-term congressman and a one-term city controller during the late nineteenth century. Although unrecognized today, Fitch was well respected in his own day and played a constructive role on both national and local stages. In an era known for party loyalty, he switched from Republican to Democrat, managing to accept Tammany's endorsements while rejecting their patronage demands. Finally, as a gold Democrat, he ended his own political career by supporting the Republicans in 1896. Fitch was a complex character whose apparent inconsistencies were defined by his consistent commitment to integrity.

In Congress, Fitch was an ardent defender of New York City. His support of tariff reform reflected an appreciation of the city's dependence on trade. His efforts to have New York City chosen as the site for an 1892 World Exposition reflected boosterism. Both issues engrossed him in the dilemmas of industrialization and urbanization, as did his defense of immigrants. A lawyer for New York City's German brewers, Fitch opposed the xenophobia of the times and championed cosmopolitan diversity. Consequently, he criticized the intemperance behind the temperance movements in Washington, D.C., Albany, and New York City itself.

As New York City controller, Fitch's record was impeccable, so impeccable that it embroiled him in vitriolic conflicts with police commissioner Theodore Roosevelt and street commissioner George E. Waring, Jr. In fact, Remington's research raises questions about the policies of these supposedly model reformers. So, too, it critiques the leadership of reform mayor William L. Strong. Through it all, Fitch emerges as the most forthright public servant of all. His career is worth recording because it offsets so many of the negative stereotypes of the Gilded Age and shows how one person can make a difference in a democracy. If Tammany men were, as they put it, always at a loss trying "to explain Fitch," Remington has succeeded.

Brooklyn, New York

Preface

I have been living with Ashbel Fitch since my childhood. He was an ethereal presence at the Adirondack estate that my cousins and I frequented and that Fitch had acquired years before. I remember my father talking about his grandfather's friendship with Grover Cleveland. But as time passed and Fitch's children and grandchildren passed away one by one, memories of who Ashbel Fitch was and how he had lived faded and details of his remarkable career were lost, leaving only sporadic curiosity in their place.

Fifteen years ago, I was enjoying Edmund Morris's marvelous story *The Rise of Theodore Roosevelt,* and to my surprise I encountered, on page 530, Morris's account of Roosevelt's 1896 confrontation with Ashbel Fitch in Mayor Strong's office. Although Morris devoted three pages to the altercation, his story centered on Roosevelt, not Fitch, and Morris's Fitch was vacuous, one-dimensional, and without purpose. Knowing the whereabouts of nearly fifty ancient volumes of Ashbel Fitch's memorabilia, and assuming that if Morris devoted his few pages to the encounter there must be more in those volumes, I sought them out. I was not disappointed. In fact, I was captivated by what I discovered, and at that moment, uncertain as to just what I would find, I embarked on my long journey to identify the real Ashbel Fitch. My predominant sources were authentic newspaper accounts of events that occurred more than one hundred years ago, told in the reporters' own words. I spent hours, days, weeks, and years on end sifting through the Ashbel P. Fitch archives, mostly newspaper clippings and hundreds of letters to his wife, doggedly coaxing Ashbel Fitch's story from the mountain of words. I loved every second of it.

Nineteenth-century New York newspapers opened a new world to me. Of course there were the *Times, Tribune, Herald, Daily News, Sun,* and *World* of modern vintage, but there were also the *Commercial Advertiser, Post, Mail and Express, Telegram, Journal, Mercury, Recorder, Star, Globe, Brooklyn Eagle, Harlem Reporter,* and more. Across the country there were the *Boston Daily Traveler, San Francisco Examiner, Jacksonville Times-Mirror, Kansas City Times, New Orleans Picayune, Chicago Inter-Ocean,* and *Springfield Republican,* among many others. Their reporting was fresh, sometimes naïve, but earnest, aggressive, and generally accurate with respect to facts. Opinions, however, were notoriously slanted toward the editorial objectives of the newspapers, and more than once I've placed today's reader in the same position as his or her nineteenth-century counterpart, that is, whether to believe what was written. It's not always clear—today, or one hundred years ago. But after several years plumbing the depths of these nineteenth-century journals, Ashbel Fitch began to emerge, and this book, about the man and his time, took shape.

The endless fascination of history lies in the spirit of "discovery." To discover something familiar, something that relates to the present, or to solve a once-unfathomable mystery is one of life's underappreciated joys. In the middle of the health-care debate, in December 2009, opponents of the bill appeared on CNBC to point out that as the health-care bill was nearing passage in the Senate, over the "opposition" of the health insurance companies, their stocks were trading at their all-time highs. I was at once reminded of Ashbel Fitch who, in 1891, was locked in debate over a shipping subsidy bill that he believed would benefit the shipping companies, not the public. On the floor of Congress he said, "Pacific Mail Steamship Co. was yesterday quoted at 38; this afternoon it is 40 3/8. . . . The stockholders of the Pacific Mail Steamship Co. are the honest laboring men whom Congress is going to help." Having heard so often how history repeats itself, I now find myself watching presidential politics in search of similarities with the Gilded Age, and there is no lack of opportunities to draw upon.

After more than a dozen absorbing years, the story of Ashbel Fitch has now been told. Fitch is no longer a one-dimensional figure to me, and he will not be to readers of this volume. He was a citizen politician whose various positions, while surely not always right, were based on principles that he would not discard. As he once said after casting a difficult vote that was not in line with his political party, "you have to use your head . . . even in Congress."

Over the long course of researching and writing this book I've encountered new friends and old friends who have helped me in surprising ways. I am particularly grateful to Joanne Reitano, professor of history at LaGuardia Community College, for her insightful commentary on my manuscript and for her delicate but forceful prodding. She is a teacher, and there is no higher calling. I am equally indebted to my cousin D. Brenton Simons, president of the New England Historic Genealogical Society and a great-great-grandson of Ashbel P. Fitch for his guidance, encouragement, and sound advice. I am also grateful to Mark Bartlett, head librarian, and his library staff at the Society Library of New York, and to Jean Ashton and her library staff of the New-York Historical Society. I am appreciative of the advice and encouragement I received from many friends, who included Ken Ackerman; Gabor Boritt, retired professor of Civil War studies at Gettysburg College; Ann Campbell Cahill; John Collins; John Ernst; Grace Friary; Neal Garonzik; Thavolia Glymph, associate professor of African and African American studies and history at Duke; Greg Goodell, director of museum services at the Gettysburg National Military Park; Judy and Jay Keyes; Dan and Michelle Page; Jerry Pepper, librarian at the Adirondack Museum; Phil Olsson; Ginger Plexico; Jay Remington; Rennie Roberts; K. Jacob Ruppert; Rebecca Read Shanor; Nancy Clark; Addie Shields, Clinton County historian; Adam Sonnenschein; Scott Steward, director of publications, New England Historic Genealogical Society; Pieter Verbeck; Peter Welsh; Bob Wilburn, formerly president of the Gettysburg Foundation and now distinguished service professor and director at Heinz College of Carnegie Mellon University; and Tony Wood, executive director of the Ittleson Foundation.

Of course I have saved the best for last. The entire staff of Syracuse University Press has assisted in the development of this work, and I am indebted to them all, especially Mary Selden Evans, Mona Hamlin, Kay Steinmetz, and my ever-watchful editor D. J. Whyte. The encouragement of Caroline Welsh, retired director of the Adirondack Museum, was critical to the success of this project. And I am eternally grateful to my family—my children, Jay and Chelsey, and Chelsey, my wife of forty-nine years—who every day gave their unqualified support to this undertaking.

Fitch and Parmelee Ancestry

John Mason (1600-1672) — Anne Peck

Priscilla Mason — **James Fitch** (1622-1702) | **Parmelee, John** (1620-1687) — Hannah

Mindwell Higley — **Nathaniel Fitch** (1679-1759) | **Parmelee, Joel** (1675-1748) — Abigail Andrews

Susannah Blackman — **Isaac Fitch** (1734-1791) | **Parmelee, Hezikiah** (1712-____) — Mehitable Hall

Mary Bosworth — **Jabez Fitch** (1752-1837) | **Parmelee, Simeon** (1740-1820) — Jemima Hopkins

Anna Manning — **Jabez Fitch, Jr.** (1794-1876) | **Parmelee, Ashbel** (1784-1862) — Fanny Brush

Edward Fitch (1821-1887) — **Parmelee, Fanny** (1822-1893)

Ashbel Parmelee Fitch (1848-1904)

Ashbel P. Fitch

Introduction

> New York always was the place for the man from somewhere else. There is always ready here a gold box and the freedom of the city for any man from anywhere who can earn them. The question the city asks of the latest comer is not "where do you come from?" but "where are you going?"
>
> —ASHBEL FITCH, 1898

Mayor William L. Strong slammed the top of the solid oak table. Everyone jumped. The mayor cried "Gentlemen stop it or I'll have you both arrested." It was early May 1896 in New York City at a Board of Estimate meeting in the mayor's office at city hall. Police commissioner Theodore Roosevelt arrived unannounced to strong-arm city controller Ashbel Fitch into authorizing payment of expenses that the Police Department had incurred, and the controller refused to pay.

Fitch's recalcitrance was just the tip of the iceberg of a highly symbolic, long-standing and quietly resentful relationship between two forceful men. Their clash of wills, certainly dramatic, disruptive, and in some quarters entertaining, had a deeper meaning than would a schoolboy tussle. They were alike in many ways. Both were New Yorkers. Both loved the outdoors. But Roosevelt symbolized the reactionary, Republican America that resented the escalating foreign influence in New York City. Fitch, a socially liberal Democrat, following an enviable seven years in Congress where he made a splendid record, was nominated by Tammany Hall to be controller of New York City. In Fitch and in Tammany Hall, Roosevelt saw all that was wrong with New York.

The older of the two by ten years, Fitch belittled Roosevelt and that, no doubt, added to Roosevelt's temper. Roosevelt thought Fitch was "a contemptible unscrupulous scoundrel."[1] Fitch thought that Roosevelt acted like a belligerent spoiled child, lacking judgment and petulant when he did not get his way. Roosevelt was idealistic and politically ambitious, but he was also a snob,[2] a publicity-seeker and a reformer, always lecturing and scolding. Fitch was pragmatic and almost without political ambition.

Roosevelt was born and raised in New York. He was dismayed at the surging immigrant tide engulfing New York and the controlling, corrupt power of

Tammany Hall. Fitch came to New York City as a ten-year-old from rural upstate New York. He learned to speak perfect German at the University of Jena and made his considerable fortune as the German brewers' lawyer. To Fitch, New York was a shining city of opportunity.

New York City voters elected Fitch to preside over a sprawling, yet widely respected, New York City Finance Department, which had been at the epicenter of the Tweed scandal twenty-five years before.[3] Since then, it had grown into a model municipal department, conducting its affairs professionally and without a hint of scandal. Only inveterate Tammany haters, and there was no shortage of those, expected bad things from the Finance Department. Roosevelt was a political appointee who shared power with three other police commissioners atop a demoralized Police Department that had no public respect and a badly tarnished image.

The duty of the city controller was to administer the city's financial affairs and to oversee departmental expenses. Roosevelt was all too familiar with the responsibilities of an "overseer," as they had been his when years before he chaired a State Assembly committee that was formed to investigate New York City.[4] It was more difficult for Roosevelt to be "overseen" than it was for him to "oversee," and it was not likely when his overseer represented Tammany Hall.

Before Mayor Strong's outburst, each man had made his point, but Fitch was gaining the upper hand. Roosevelt was furious. An impatient Fitch dismissed Roosevelt, saying all he liked to do was fight. Roosevelt said Fitch would run away from a fight. Fitch answered "maybe, but not from you." The mayor's hand descended when the verbal exchange escalated to a choice of weapons.

Theodore Roosevelt at thirty-eight had not yet begun his miraculous, meteoric rise to the presidency. But he had made headlines as a young assemblyman at Albany more than ten years before. He ran unsuccessfully for mayor in 1886, finishing a distant third behind Abram Hewitt and the socialist Henry George. Roosevelt's western exploits were chronicled locally.[5] He was civil service commissioner in the Benjamin Harrison administration. Roosevelt was well known in New York. No one doubted his courage. Fitch was equally well known but in the days that followed, and as the city learned that he was the unscarred veteran of more than thirty sword fights at the University of Jena, it became clear that he, too, was not to be trifled with.

Ashbel Fitch was a man of countless contradictions. He was a New York City lawyer and politician who was born on New York State's wilderness border with Canada, the northern frontier. His university years were spent in Germany, where his liberal German education gained the upper hand over his conservative rural roots. He ran for office twice as a Republican and four times as a Democrat, winning five New York City elections. He was well known in New York as a Tammany-backed politician, one who was trustworthy and above-board. Tammany Hall nominated him four times for office, yet because he did not share Tammany's values, he was never a member of Tammany Hall. He was often assumed to be German, although his forebears were the earliest Pilgrims and Puritans. He was a quintessential New York American who both loved New York and admired Europe.

Fitch was a recognized authority on the works of his hero, the immortal German poet Johann Wolfgang von Goethe. Goethe's writing was generally out of reach for all but the most expert German linguists, which Fitch was. Insight into Fitch's character and beliefs emerge from even the most basic understanding of Goethe's philosophy. Goethe believed that happiness was life's goal. No romanticist, he recognized full well the wide range of life's tragedies, evils, and disappointments. Said Goethe biographer John Armstrong, "One of [Goethe's] principles is that we need to master ourselves. To live well we need to be able to say 'no' to ourselves—but this is not a life denying, fearful attitude to pleasure. On the contrary, it is a discipline that allows us to do the larger things that are important to us, to allow our more worthwhile projects to be undertaken and to enjoy what pleasures we can without being ruined by them, without finding that all of our time is taken up with them, or that we are endlessly combating the ill consequences of our moments of gratification."[6]

"Moving on," "growing up," and "getting over it" rather than indulging in self-pity were essential. It was clear-eyed self-assessment, "facing facts" that provided satisfaction and happiness. Fitch's paradoxical life experience gave birth within him to a tolerance of difference, even foreignness, a cheerful acceptance of ambiguity that was uncommon in the nineteenth century, and a marked sympathy for individual freedom.

His good humor and affability masked a keen intellect, determination, and a willingness to fight. When Theodore Roosevelt sniped that Ashbel Fitch was acting "in the interest of the criminal classes,"[7] Fitch, his sense of honor secure, retaliated. He had successfully gone before New York voters on five separate occasions during the preceding ten years. He was determined to do the job he was elected to do, and he would not be deterred by Roosevelt's accusations or innuendo. Roosevelt had been soundly beaten ten years earlier in his attempt to become New York's mayor, and in 1896 he was simply marking time.

Fitch was born a Republican. His father was a founder of the Republican Party in northern New York in 1856 and remained a Republican his entire life. His family was Republican. Fitch grew up in New York's Republican Party during the 1870s and early 1880s, when he spent nearly all his time practicing law and building his fortune. He first ran for Congress as a Republican in a Democratic district where his liberal views on temperance, home rule, and tariff reform were political assets.

Yet they were not assets in the national Republican Party, and it was not long before Republicans drove him out.

Following his father's death, Fitch turned to the Democracy,[8] the ostensible result of his dynamic speech before Congress attacking the high-tariff policy of Republicans. His transfer from Republican to Democrat was done with some forethought and ample conviction. Still, Republicans had offered him no good choice and, as is usually the case, he would pay a political price for his conversion. Some Republicans had no use for him, and some Democrats did not trust him. His political success following his party transfer is made even more remarkable by the obstacles he overcame.

There were two major political parties, although in New York State there were effectively three: Republicans, Grover Cleveland or "swallow-tail" Democrats,[9] and Tammany Hall Democrats. Both sorts of Democrats prided themselves, as they do today, on being the party of the people. To Cleveland that included honesty in government, civil service reform, pension reform, tariff reform, and hard currency. Tammany Democrats were in politics to make money, and they lived in New York City.

Cleveland is especially notable because he was the only Democrat elected president in the fifty-six years between James Buchanan in 1856 and Woodrow Wilson in 1912. He won the popular vote in three consecutive presidential elections, 1884, 1888, and 1892. His hold on the public was remarkable. His enormous popularity was a by-product of the jagged-edged integrity that he so publicly demonstrated as mayor of Buffalo, governor of New York, and president of the United States. From the outset of his political career, Tammany Hall was anathema to Cleveland. His unwillingness to compromise with Tammany gained him followers in upstate New York and across the nation, and it earned him enemies in New York City, the "tipping point" in presidential elections. Whether Tammany Democrats would support Cleveland was always an interesting calculation and, in any election in which he ran, a topic of intense speculation.

Fitch became a Cleveland Democrat, nominated, nevertheless, four times to public office by Tammany Hall before finally being turned down by Tammany in 1897. His political success as a Cleveland Democrat in a city controlled by Tammany Hall can be credited to his independence, both financial and willful, the former provided by his large law practice and German connections and the latter by his political skill and his German education, in no particular order. Throughout his political career he remained a practicing attorney, and his successful New York law firm provided most of his income. His time in elective office spanned a dozen years, wherein it can be argued that the groundwork for modern New York was laid, modern American liberalism was born and nurtured, and the uneasy relationship between conservative America and her liberal metropolis, with Tammany Hall as the lightning rod, was given root.

Consider the scope of the liberal agenda in the 1880s. There were no "entitlements" and no progressive income tax, popular advances that would come later and have a direct economic impact on all Americans. But the liberalism that grew up in Gilded Age New York City, nurtured by immigrants and with its emphasis on individual freedom, gained favor in the nation's metropolis, in its most populous state, which had the most votes in the electoral college. For whom those electoral votes were cast was generally determined by the size of the Democratic plurality in New York City, that is, whether it was sufficient to overcome the large, reliable Republican plurality upstate, and it generally determined who would be president.

Beyond New York City, Fitch, Roosevelt, and the rest of the political figures of the Gilded Age performed on the uniquely American political stage that followed the Civil War. One analysis of the period was provided by Elihu Root, secretary of war under McKinley and Roosevelt, secretary of state under Roosevelt, United States senator, and Nobel Peace Prize winner in 1912 in his introduction to Robert McElroy's biography of Grover Cleveland. A lifelong Republican, Root called Cleveland's presidencies "a very critical period in American history," saying further:

> The readjustment . . . to the conditions created by the Civil War . . . involved . . . the great reconciliation between the peoples of the two sections, who, after four years of fighting, of killing and wounding each other, were to try the experiment of living together again as parts of the same people sharing in the conduct of the same government. It was a reconciliation which had to be effected by the same generation which fought the war, because if that generation died unreconciled, bequeathing its resentments and hatreds to a younger generation, the undertaking would have been almost hopeless. . . . That the reconciliation was effected within the life of that generation and that survivors of the Union and Confederate Armies came to work together with harmony and mutual confidence in the government at Washington, is one of the greatest American achievements.[10]

That fact alone, a sectional imperative for the good of the country, imparts a conceptually simple yet complex gravity to the history of the Cleveland era. One of the thorniest questions was the issue of race relations that the Civil War only began to address. Another was marked by the arrival of New York's immigrant population, many of whom were Fitch's constituents, who gained in numbers after the Civil War and were an easy target for the nation's xenophobes. Some of the most intolerant of those were Fitch's contemporaries in Congress, many of whom were former Confederate soldiers. Several, not all, of the issues they debated were argued in Congress before the Civil War, but secession and war were no longer options. It was critical then, that legislators with sharply divided points of view move forward and, at the same time, find ways to get along with one another.

Historians assessing the politics of Gilded Age New York City tend to highlight the 1870 Tweed Ring scandal, wherein millions of dollars were stolen from the city through its Finance Department, and the 1894 Report of the Lexow Committee that revealed corrosive corruption in the city's Police Department. The twenty-four years between the two scandals is often bridged and connected by the ever-present corruption of Tammany Hall. By overlooking kaleidoscopic political story lines and subplots, such cursory analysis, not wrong as far as it goes, fails to reveal what actually took place. Tammany's corruption, though widespread, was not everywhere. "Evidence" of Tammany's corruption was made up, exaggerated, sometimes proven, but every Democrat was not a Tammany Democrat.

Fitch's liberal devotion to individual rights was honed on the tip of his sword on the dueling fields of Jena, where students stood ready to defend their rights and privileges at a moment's notice. In the confrontation with Roosevelt it found its expression in a citizen's right to buy a beer on Sunday and to enjoy it as he saw fit, in a saloon, at home, or in a beer garden, without fear of being spied upon or otherwise harassed. It also found its expression in 1886 in his defense of those boycotted by socialists and in several congressional debates: in 1888 on the unfairness to ordinary New York consumers of the added costs of living resulting from the tariff; in 1891 on the unfairness to American authors of the absence of international copyright protection; and in 1893 on the unfairness to New York voters of the heavy-handed enforcement of the Federal Election Law.

When Fitch spoke for tariff reduction in Congress, he spoke for the businessmen of New York as well as for his individual constituents who were "unprotected" from the higher prices for consumer goods that the tariff caused. His words on their behalf carried across the land and made his national reputation. The *New York Times* said that more than one million copies of his speech were circulated nationally in the succeeding two presidential campaigns.[11]

He argued that the Columbian Exposition, which would be held in Chicago in 1893, should be held in Harlem in 1892. Rural Republicans opposed anything in New York that might reflect well on the Democratic city that was ruled by Tammany Hall. He bridled when western congressmen labeled New York a "foreign city," inferring anti-Americanism because of its steady stream of immigrants, or referred to its bankers, who financed America's growth, as "Wall Street bandits" or "servants of Rothschild." His many defenses of gold-backed currency were not only a plea on behalf of New York's bankers and businessmen, but for all those who relied on fixed incomes or owned savings accounts whose financial assets were diminished by the inflationary consequences of massive injections of silver into the nation's money supply.

As city controller from 1894 through 1897, Fitch remained steadfast during the final three years of his term, a bulwark between Tammany's insatiable appetite for patronage and the self-righteous, free-spending of Mayor Strong's reform administration. Tammany had nominated him for the office and would have turned the city's Finance Department into a patronage office had he allowed it. On the other hand, Republican reformers would have effectively dismantled time-tested budgetary practices devised by Andrew Haswell Green out of the wreckage of the Tweed fiasco. The story of Gilded Age reform in New York City that emerges from a study of Ashbel Fitch's term as controller is less about the failures of Tammany, of which there were many, and more about the public disappointment in reform that had its roots in Republican hatred of immigrant New Yorkers and the reformers' obsession with Tammany Hall.

The miracle of the reinvention of the Finance Department placed New York in a position of financial strength and at the forefront of municipal finance only twenty-odd years after Tweed. When viewed as one component of a much larger city government, the Finance Department was an island that Ashbel Fitch occupied, situated between two warring forces, reform and Tammany Hall. He defended it with courage and vigilance, earning equal numbers of Republican and Tammany enemies along the way, and in so doing he protected the city's credit and enhanced its well-earned reputation for fiscal integrity. While Fitch's two predecessors in office had been equally effective in keeping Tammany at bay, only Fitch was called upon to defend the Finance Department from threats on two sides.

He was one of several leaders of the city's gold Democrats who, at considerable political cost, bolted their party to vote for the Republican William McKinley for president in 1896. Tammany used Fitch's support of McKinley as an excuse for turning him down for a second term as city controller in 1897. He was heavily involved in the financial planning that preceded the consolidation of the city's five boroughs in 1898. He sat on the Brooklyn Bridge Commission and the Rapid Transit Commission, and he excoriated them both for their ineffectiveness and careless management.

Having made such a notable public record during his time, the question becomes why Gilded Age historians have overlooked Ashbel Fitch. Whatever the reason, students of German-American history would not have been surprised by his anonymity if Fitch had been, in fact, of German origin. He was not, but his politics were. Albert Bernhardt Faust's monumental two-volume work entitled The German Element in the United States includes a chapter entitled Political Influence of the German Element in United States. Faust concludes that "real influence is a different matter from the ins and outs of the political game; and while the German element has not been conspicuous in the latter,"[12] he offers several examples of German-American politicians who, while not well known, were at hand when the time came to improve and transform American politics, essentially the contention of this volume as it pertains to Ashbel Fitch. If Fitch were German, Faust would likely have included him on his list of influential German-American citizens.

It might be that Fitch's association with Tammany Hall marked him as unworthy of historical attention. Or maybe historians' lack of curiosity or expertise regarding financial matters causes them to oversimplify or even trivialize late-nineteenth-century New York. In this respect, Kenneth Ackerman's account of Samuel Tilden's[13] reconstruction of Controller Richard Connolly's 1870 Finance Department in his *Boss Tweed* is unusually descriptive.[14] Or perhaps the events surrounding Tweed's enormous theft from the city's Finance Department simply overshadows the straightforward and professional Finance Department that emerged from the ashes. Whatever the reason, the fact remains that Fitch was, in every respect except his ancestry, a German politician who practiced politics without ever abandoning his law practice or becoming a "career politician."

There is no question that Tammany Hall's corruption dominated New York politics during the late nineteenth century. Whatever corruption there was after Tweed, however, thanks to Green and a succession of upright city controllers, went on away from the city's revenue stream, assessments, budgets, financings, or other business of the Finance Department. It must have been difficult for the prideful, stubborn Theodore Roosevelt to preside over a Police Department that was riddled with corruption while the "Tammany controller" Fitch's department was a pristine model of good government.

Ashbel Fitch received four nominations for public office from Tammany Hall in spite of the fact that his relationship with Tammany was tenuous at best. His values were not Tammany values. His incorruptibility, both in office and on the particular issue of hard currency, not doubted by his peers, was never so evident as it was in the municipal election of 1897, when Tammany Hall refused to renominate him for the second term as controller that he sought and so richly deserved. His relationship with Richard Croker, the crooked, dictatorial boss of Tammany Hall, was distant and sometimes antagonistic.

During Fitch's term as New York's controller, the nation was crippled by unemployment and its worst depression perhaps ever. Still, the city borrowed when it needed to at home and abroad and financed its expansion at a cost to taxpayers equal to or lower than that of any other American city and occasionally the federal government, hardly a sign of a corrupted city. From a historical distance such niceties may be difficult to discern. But Ashbel Fitch's classification as a Tammany politician sitting astride New York's Finance Department does him and the department an injustice in the eyes of history. Its significance is easily misunderstood, and its meaning is undeserved.

And there may be other more subtle factors behind Fitch's historic anonymity. His multidimensional activities and affiliations, sometimes on the wrong side of history, may have blurred his image. He was the brewers' lawyer, so by definition he was on the wrong side of the temperance movement that steadily gained ground until it peaked in 1920 and Prohibition became law. While Prohibition failed, its opponents, including Ashbel Fitch, speaking for the rights of the individual well ahead of their time, never gained the high moral ground during Fitch's lifetime.

Then, too, virtually everything Germanic that could be either diminished or erased by America's entry into World War I was diminished or erased. Sadly, this included the works of the immortal poet and philosopher Goethe, whose life Fitch cherished and whose writings he studied, translated, and interpreted.[15] The winners write history. Too much of what Fitch stood for was out of vogue within fifteen years of his death.

Ashbel Fitch had two separate public careers: as a four-term congressman (1886–93) and as city controller (1894–97), both of which were in the considerable service of New York City. Historians who come upon him as controller may not realize they can find him in Congress. Those who find the Republican congressman may not identify the congressional Democrat, the "Tammany controller," or the man whom the arch-Republican Chauncey Depew placed in nomination as Republican candidate for New York City controller in 1897 as the same man.[16] Much like his German constituency he was less interested in political parties than he was in consistent principles. He ignored "party discipline." When under intense political pressure from Republicans, his wry response was "You have to use your head . . . even in Congress!" While America and New York faced rampant change, his independence and his consistency appealed to both parties at different times and for different reasons, all of which renders Ashbel Fitch an impressive character.

Whether these or other aspects of Fitch's career explain his relative anonymity, we cannot know. As Elihu Root observed, the late nineteenth century was a decisive period for the nation's extraordinary development and its essential healing. Ashbel Fitch stood tall in a position of political leadership during that time and at a place where crosscurrents and momentous events shaped New York's and the nation's history. Fitch's political career provides a window on the politics of America and New York City in the late nineteenth century. And there was no time in the nation's history when New York City had more influence on the political affairs of the nation than it did during that period.

In November 1893, after Fitch's powerful speech in Congress to repeal the Federal Election Law, the *New York Uptown Visitor* exclaimed, "Our metropolis has never had, either in Congress or elsewhere, a bolder or more eloquent *champion* of her good name than Ashbel P. Fitch. His speech . . . has forever endeared his name to New Yorkers [emphasis added]."[17]

Fitch's performance in elective office for twelve years, as well as his many public statements and speeches, demonstrate without a doubt that he was the foremost champion of the nation's metropolis during those last years of the nineteenth century: of its luster, its excellence, its immigrant cultures, its opportunity, its tolerance, its personal freedoms, and its finances. In this he easily surpassed all of New York's other political leaders. In this he had no rival.

1

Forebears and Early Years, 1848–1885

> Mr. Fitch's steady adherence to a course which he deemed right, though it involved the alienation of political associates, and his conscientious performance of public duty with no other motive than the fulfillment of his trust, justly entitles him to the respect of his fellow citizens and to the esteem and affection of his personal friends.
>
> —GROVER CLEVELAND, December 1890

Ashbel Parmelee Fitch was born on October 8, 1848, in Mooers, New York, the first child of Edward and Fanny Parmelee Fitch. James K. Polk was president, American expansionism was at its height, gold was discovered at Sutter's Mill in March, and the Civil War was twelve years away. The tiny hamlet of Mooers reposes at the northeast corner of New York, about three miles south of Canada and ten miles west of Lake Champlain. Located north of the Adirondack Mountains, on the flat southern shelf overlooking the St. Lawrence River Valley, it was a wild and lonely outpost when Ashbel Fitch was born, bleak and desolate during the long, cold winter months.

On his father's side Fitch was descended directly from the Pilgrims of the *Mayflower,* through six generations of his paternal line, from the Puritan minister Reverend James Fitch (1622–1702), a founder of both Norwich and Lebanon,[1] Connecticut, and through James Fitch's wife, Priscilla (1641–1714) from Major John Mason (1600–1672), a colonial military legend, "a hero and a statesman . . . a fit founder of a great nation"[2] and a first citizen of Connecticut.

James Fitch's great-grandson Jabez (1752–1837) fought in the Revolution. After the war he moved his family west to Spencertown, New York, and then north to Champlain, New York. A scarcity of good farmland in New England drove Jabez to the Canada border, where he found the cheap and abundant land that he sought. Large New England families had too many children to provide land for all. Great-grandfather James Fitch, for example, who gave land generously to his children,[3] had fifteen grandchildren through just one of his fourteen children, his seventh son, Nathaniel.[4]

On his mother's side Ashbel Fitch's lineage ran to John Parmelee,[5] who arrived in Connecticut in 1635. John's great-grandson Simeon (1740–1820) fought for the

British in the French and Indian War (1754–60) and fought in the Revolution under General Anthony Wayne. Simeon's son, the legendary divine Ashbel Parmelee, (1784–1862), born in Stockbridge, Massachusetts, was for fifty years among the northern frontier's best known and most influential clergymen. He played an outsized role in north country life and his sermons were widely circulated.[6] Middlebury College conferred honorary A.M. and D.D. degrees upon him in 1853.[7] He is believed to have been an organizer of the Underground Railroad, although for obvious reasons there is no known evidence to support that. About the time that Jabez Fitch first reached Champlain, Ashbel Parmelee, then in his late teens, was entering into a distinguished frontier ministry in Malone, New York.

After nearly two hundred years of Parmelees and Fitches in America, the paths of the two pioneering Connecticut families crossed in the early 1800s on the northern New York frontier. They each shared the other's experience of life's struggle in one of the most unforgiving wilderness backwaters that America would ever know. And both were exemplars of self-reliance, integrity, and community values. Ashbel Fitch's character and values were founded on the lives of these New England ancestors.

In politics Parmelee was a Whig and then a Republican. He never discussed politics from the pulpit but never hesitated elsewhere. Years later President Rutherford B. Hayes's vice president, William A. Wheeler, a native of Malone and lifelong friend of Parmelee's son, recalled as a boy, "wending my way to the old church where Father Parmelee, perched ten feet above his hearers in a pulpit shaped like the turret of a monitor, hurled the hot shot of divine law into the rebellious hosts of the 'adversary of souls' at close range with a fuse cut short."[8] It was for Ashbel Parmelee that Ashbel Parmelee Fitch was named. The uncommon name Ashbel (meaning "man of Baal") came from the Bible and was the name of one of the several sons of Benjamin.[9]

Parmelee's contemporary, Jabez Fitch, town supervisor of Mooers for most of the twenty years between 1817 and 1837, when he died, secured a modest place in regional history by standing firm, though to no avail, against payment of town funds for bounty services that were either not intended under the law or were falsified.[10] His great-grandson Ashbel Fitch, a future controller of New York City, would surely have approved. One day he would be well-known for standing firm against the wasteful expenditure of taxpayers' money.

Although the values inherent in these men's lives were very much a part of Ashbel Fitch's upbringing, Ashbel Parmelee's earnest religious conviction gave way to Goethe's secular philosophy within the young Ashbel Fitch. Parmelee sought eternal salvation, while Goethe sought happiness on earth. As an amateur historian Ashbel Fitch had an abiding interest in his genealogy. His roots gave him self-assurance. He knew where his family had lived, and he was not so far removed from their frontier hardships not to appreciate just how they had lived. He knew why his

1. Reverend Ashbel Parmelee, circa 1850. Ashbel B. Parmelee, *Biography of Rev. Ashbel Parmelee, D.D.* Philadelphia: J. W. Lewis & Co., 1880.

father and mother had so determinedly turned their back on the hardscrabble life of their parents' frontier for the city of opportunity that was New York. And he would never forget his debt to the big city for the opportunities he found there.

Ashbel B. Parmelee (1816–1886), the only son of the Reverend Parmelee, was born in Malone. Five years later, Edward Fitch (1821–1887), the son of Dr. Jabez Fitch Jr.[11] (1794–1876) was born in Mooers. In 1846 Edward Fitch married

Parmelee's sister Fanny, and by 1849 Parmelee and Fitch had established a law partnership in Malone. Between Edward's marriage and his partnership, Ashbel Fitch arrived, Edward and Fanny's first child of three, who no doubt provided additional motivation, if any were needed, for the young family to leave Mooers for Malone and a larger law practice for Fitch.

While Parmelee found life in Malone satisfying, Fitch, the more ambitious of the two partners, was restless and determined to leave. Both men were politically well connected. Parmelee and the aforementioned Wheeler were lifelong friends. Wheeler had served as an assemblyman, state senator, and congressman, before serving as vice president under Hayes. Fitch was friendly with Wheeler, too, and that friendship helped him find opportunities in New York City.

Young Ashbel Fitch spent his first ten years in Malone. His grandparents, the doctor and the minister and their wives, lived nearby and no doubt loved their grandson's company. The northern frontier was primitive, farms and forest, wild animals and rutted dirt roads traveled by horse and wagon. He learned to fish at an early age in the Chateaugay River, the sparkling, fast-moving Salmon River that runs through the center of Malone, and in the other surrounding lakes and streams that teemed with native brook trout. He acquired a sportsman's love of the outdoors in his earliest childhood. In a letter to Fitch in 1900, Arthur Fitzwilliam Tait, the noted British-American painter of sporting scenes, recalled his "vivid remembrance of our first meeting at your home in Malone, and your enthusiasm as a fisherman. Long may you live to enjoy it."[12]

In 1854 Edward Fitch's election to the New York State Assembly put him in contact with then senator William H. Seward[13] and New York governor Myron Clark.[14] Known as a good speaker, Fitch's election to the assembly placed him near the center of the founding of the Republican Party in northern New York State[15] and, as a Seward ally, for the latter's reelection by the assembly to the United States Senate in 1856.[16]

Fitch left Malone in 1858 for New York City and a law practice in partnership with Clark. Edward and Fanny Parmelee Fitch, with their three small children, Ashbel and his younger sisters Ella and Alice, along with so many others from all over America and the world, saw their opportunity in New York. America was bursting, and New York was at its center. Fanny's and Edward's move no doubt was painful, probably mystifying, and even frightening to the grandparents who would lose contact with their grandchildren. But Edward Fitch was ambitious. He would seek his fortune along with countless other Americans, and he would chart the path for his son's future, which he, Edward, saw as boundless.

The lives of Ashbel Parmelee and Edward Fitch, intertwined by marriage and linked professionally, were also joined through their sons, cousins Morton Parmelee

2. Edward Fitch, ca. 1850. Photographer unknown. Courtesy of D. Brenton Simons.

(1850–1897) and Ashbel Fitch. Born two years apart and raised together for eight years, each was the brother the other never had, but there were marked differences between them. Parmelee's bachelor life was that of small-town success in the lumber business, leadership, good works, and a life spent outdoors. Ashbel Parmelee Fitch, the grandson and namesake of the Reverend Ashbel Parmelee, and the son of Ashbel B. Parmelee's sister Fanny and Edward Fitch, became a New Yorker. He performed on the national stage in a competitive milieu. While he clearly had a gift for politics, in the end family and financial success drove him. He shared qualities with each of the colonial and frontier Americans who came before him; a common touch, a strong work ethic, a sharp intellect, sensitivity, pragmatism, and some rigidity regarding matters of principle.

Young Fitch's move to New York brought him under the tutelage of Dr. Thomas Hunter, the remarkable young Irish immigrant for whom Hunter College is named. Born in 1831, Hunter arrived in America around 1850 and began at once his life's profession of teaching young people, in this instance at Grammar School No. 35 on East Thirteenth Street. He had obvious gifts of vision, originality, and discipline.

3. Watercolor portrait of Ashbel P. Fitch, ca. 1858. Artist unknown. Courtesy of D. Brenton Simons.

Within four years he was vice principal of the school and was made principal in 1857 at the age of twenty-six.

Hunter's tenure as principal of "the Thirteenth Street School," as it was known, lasted twelve years, spanning the "War of the Rebellion" and the New York City draft riots. Ashbel Fitch would later recall waiting in line all night with his classmates to see President Lincoln's body lying in state.[17] Hunter was known as "an excellent pedagogue and strict disciplinarian."[18] At the time of his accession "three hundred pupils were in the school. . . . He soon made it the banner school, with more than a thousand pupils, and with applicants from all over the city on the waiting list. One of Hunter's most celebrated innovations was the abolition of corporal punishment that the Board of Education later legislated out of all of New York's public schools."[19] Thomas Hunter was one of the most influential figures in New York City education and he was a lasting inspiration to Ashbel Fitch.[20] Fitch attended the Thirteenth Street School until 1864 and graduated from Williston Academy in Easthampton, Massachusetts, two years later in 1866.[21]

Edward Fitch, in his late thirties in 1858, was establishing himself in New York and forging relationships in the large bustling German community known as "Kleindeutschland" or Little Germany. Eric Homberger, in his *Historical Atlas of New York City,* notes that the enclave covered "a 400-block area east of the Bowery, north of Division Street and south of Fourteenth Street along the East River . . . Avenue B, known as the 'German Broadway,' was," he said, "lined with small shops and basement factories. Everywhere there were goods piled on the canopied sidewalks [while] nearby Avenue A was lined with large beer halls, oyster saloons, and grocery stores."[22]

Within that lively community were businessmen needing legal advice in their new country. Perhaps it was a German client who spoke no English, and Fitch spoke no German. For whatever reason, Edward Fitch recognized a career opportunity for his son. He encouraged him to train for the law, and he pointed him toward Germany for his college education. His efforts were rewarded when Ashbel Fitch sailed for Germany and the University of Jena in the autumn of 1866.

Before leaving, he paid a visit to his grandfather Jabez in Plattsburgh, New York. When Fitch returned to New York, Jabez wrote him that "[t]he true way to succeed in any business life is to have a liking for it and I hope in your case it may excite in you that diligence in your profession which will make you successful and eminent in it." His assessment of the German character was undisguised and unflattering, warning his grandson to go to Germany "fortified against German philosophy and infidelity."[23] The conflict between Fitch's conservative rural roots and the liberal education that lay before him was seldom more apparent. Yet he would go through life happily revering his grandfather[24] and at the same time nurturing a strong affinity for German culture.

Fitch was bright, and presumably he did well at Jena, although we know little of his initial attempts at German and the early challenges he must have faced. His oldest daughter, Bessie, related that on his first Atlantic crossing, an elderly German gentleman sat down beside him at dinner. Upon finishing, the gentleman murmured "a blessing on the meal" in a low German voice, to which the eighteen-year-old Ashbel Fitch was supposed to have responded "Damn you too sir!"

Fitch spent three years in Germany, two at the University of Jena and then one year at Berlin, to complete his undergraduate education. Jena had a particularly rich history, and the mere mention of its name stirred powerful emotions in German hearts. In the early nineteenth century the University of Jena[25] was at the forefront of German universities in its liberal acceptance of new ideas, some of which survived and plainly rubbed off on the youthful Ashbel Fitch. It was home for the Jena Romantics, the earliest Romantic poets of Germany. More than twenty years after he was a student at Jena, in March 1891 Fitch, by then a recognized authority on the life and works of Goethe, delivered a lecture entitled *Goethe in Youth and Old Age*. With memories of Jena still fresh in his mind, Fitch said,

> During all the last years of [Goethe's] life he was occupied, among many other things, in the development and assistance of the University of Jena. He had watched over it in good and evil days, sent Schiller to its Chair of History and arranged himself its library and museums. The magic of his enthusiasm, the force of his example was felt alike by the faculty and the students. His impetus is not yet lost. No one who has learned to love the quaint little city on the Saale and has lived in its atmosphere of culture and academic freedom, no one of the many to whom the mention of Jena brings back memories of youth . . . can fail always to be grateful to Goethe. There, at all events, his memory will always be sacred. As long as the University stands, calling around her, as she does now, the flower of Germany's youth, full of aspiration and ambition, so long will the echoes of Goethe's footsteps be heard in the streets of Jena, and his songs be sung in the shadow of the old *Schloss* [castle], where he wrote so many of them.[26]

Fitch visited Jena whenever he had the chance. Goethe's warm feelings toward the little city were reason enough for him to return.

His work ethic, discipline, and sense of honor were forged at Jena, where he was a member of the Corps Franconia, the fighting corps of the university to which Bismarck belonged. Years later, in 1896, Fitch described the Corps Franconia to a *New York Journal* reporter:

> The Corps Franconia and the *Burschenschaft*[27] are the standing armies of the German universities. They are ready to defend against the official class, against a

> class of military nobility, against any comer in or out of uniform, the rights and privileges of the student and of his alma mater; and to insist upon the doctrine of personal responsibility on the part of every man, however high his office, for all that he does or says. They have their place and object, and those who understand why they exist and the high sense of honor which they enforce are always ready to defend their existence. Every man who has done anything great in Germany in the last fifty years, if he was a student, wore the colors of a fighting corps or *Burschenschaft*.[28]

The *Burschenschaft* had its roots in the Napoleonic Wars when students learned to defend themselves from persecution for their political activities. The reporter continued, "If a student were insulted by an officer in the late 1860s, eighty students fought duels with eighty officers simultaneously . . . at least thirty duels during a three-year course, literally fighting their way through college. Some of the duelists came out without a scratch. They were the premier swordsmen. Young Fitch was one of those. His face was unmarked."

Fitch's German education was not all sword fighting. Quite apart from things military, Fitch at Jena would begin his avocation as a student and admirer of Goethe. While Goethe has been impenetrable for some audiences, owing largely to the difficulty of translating German, he possessed boundless vision and creativity, and his mode of thought tempered the rigorous military aspects of Fitch's education. Fitch flourished during those years, and he remained attached to all that he learned during that early stage of his life.

After three years of the best German education, he returned home in 1869, eagerly looking ahead, filled with a sense of duty, discipline, and honor, tempered by tolerance, liberalism, and a zest for life. His German education had a meaningful and lasting impact on his career and on every aspect of his life in New York. In business or in politics, his distinctly American roots, his vitality, his cheerful outlook, and his German fluency were among his chief characteristics. He joined his father in a law partnership, which under some circumstances, might have been stressful, but Fitch and his father were successful partners professionally, affectionately and constructively allied.

Organized religion was never prominent in Fitch's life, but he was immersed in German culture. His friends were German, and he was often assumed to be German. He spoke the German language perfectly, but it would be less than accurate to mark the impact of Fitch's German education solely by his acquired German fluency, although it was, of course, critical. When he returned to New York from Germany, he built his social circle and his law practice around New York's German society, and the two complemented and reinforced each other. These were German–Americans, some of whom spoke little or no English, and they were probably delighted to hear news of the homeland from an engaging young American.

German immigrants had been arriving in America since the origin of the nation and before. But the first large wave came in 1848, prompted by political upheavals, demands for new freedoms, and poor living conditions in Germany. There was an even larger immigration in the 1880s. Germans were politically sensitive and sophisticated, and throughout the mid-1800s Germany spawned a wide range of political philosophies, some of them revolutionary. After the American Civil War, as industry replaced agriculture as the nation's burgeoning occupation and ushered in an era of urban concentration and development, New York's largest-in-the-nation German community became a hotbed of discontent. Some German-Americans looked for their future in labor organizing activities and other forms of political activism.[29]

Nonetheless, other German immigrants adapted to America's capitalist society and were notably successful. In New York, the brewers Jacob Ruppert and Maximillian Schaefer and the piano manufacturer Henry Steinway were conspicuous examples, but their success may have stimulated the class consciousness of New York's German-Americans. Anarchists such as Johann Most[30] inspired violence and revolutionary activity. Samuel Gompers's American Federation of Labor was effective in organizing workers. Seeing this, Henry Steinway's son, William, escaped the organizing activity in the late 1860s by moving his company to Astoria, Queens, where he created a piano city, a peaceful, stable, and conservative German community with steady employment.

Politically, the Republican Party appealed to mid-nineteenth-century German immigrants. Their yearning for liberty attracted them to the party of Lincoln. But eventually Republican temperance and nativism lost most Germans-Americans to the Democracy. Yet New York City's German-American voters, in light of their well-known political independence, while rejecting Republicans, failed to give their unqualified support to Tammany Hall to the same extent that the Irish did. Their political preferences were generally unpredictable.

Into this mixture of fast-paced change and frantic political activity in 1870s New York came Ashbel Fitch, actively courting business and personal relationships with German capitalists and at the same time forging a reputation with their workers. As one indication of his success, the socialist mayoral candidate Henry George told the *New York World* in 1886 that he voted "for the Republican Fitch" for congress.[31]

Fitch joined the two great German social and musical societies in New York, the Arion and the Liederkranz, both of which kept interest in the German language, music, and literature alive. The Liederkranz had a handsome clubhouse and concert hall on Fifty-eighth Street between Lexington and Fourth Avenues. The Arion, an offshoot of the Liederkranz, not wanting to be outshone, purchased building lots in 1885 on the southeast corner of Park Avenue and Fifty-ninth Street and built a beautiful concert hall in the Italian Renaissance style in plain sight of the Liederkranz. Arion was well known for its elaborate masked balls, which were arranged by hundreds of members for thousands of guests at Madison Square Garden. There were two classes of Arion members—"active" members who sang in the chorus and "passive" members, like Fitch, who were simply expected to appreciate good music, which he did.[32] He was not a singer, but he liked music and he was eager to meet new people and expand his business circle.

The Arion and the Liederkranz societies held their summer night's festivals in mid-June a week apart. Both were held at Washington Park, Sixty-ninth Street on the East River, which for the Arion "was [in 1888] brilliantly illuminated by Chinese lamps and colored gaslights, and was handsomely decorated with German and American flags."[33] The Liederkranz festival was equally radiant. "Between four and five thousand ladies and gentlemen were in the grounds" on a "warm and sultry" night.[34] Steamers passed on the East River, slowing down to enjoy the glittering scene, the best of German society of New York, the ladies in elaborate summer costumes, and the gentlemen in full dress.

He often went riding, although he never owned a rig. In later years he wrote to his wife, "if I can get away I'm going to ride with Jake [Ruppert] this afternoon."[35] "I'm going to ride with Ed [Schaefer] tonight." "Ed & Emil Schaefer and I rode out on the road last evening together, had dinner at Hupfel's & went afterwards to the Hessian Summer Nights Festival at Hamilton Park." And "I rode out with Ed Schaefer about seven o'clock. . . . Before our dinner was ready Jake Ruppert drove in and joined us and we had dinner together . . . we had a pleasant time there until about 10 o'clock when we broke up, & had a race home."

Weekends were for long walks, outings, or other recreational activities. One summer Sunday when his wife, Lizzie, was away visiting her family, they "all had breakfast at seven and then went on board the *City of Chester* at the foot of Ninety-third Street." Seventy-eight "duffers" of the Terrace Bowling Club ate lunch and drank sixteen kegs of beer before arriving at a farm, where the "Mouquin's people" had set up tables for dinner. They "played ball or laid quiet under the shade" and then had dinner. Beer drinking was an integral part of socializing, and even family activity, in German New York.

Throughout the city's history, some of its most prominent German-American citizens were brewers, including William Beekman, for whom both William and Beekman Streets are named; Jacob Kip; and Oloff von Cortlandt. George Ehret, born in Baden, Germany, in 1835, was another. His father, Anselm Ehret, emigrated to America in 1852 and advised his son to do likewise. Five years later, George Ehret arrived. He, too, was a brewer, and he began plying his trade at Hupfel's Brewery on Thirty-eighth Street between Second and Third Avenues. Within three years he rose to be Hupfel's foreman, and after another six years he was ready to start out on his own, just two years before Fitch began practicing law.

Ehret began the Hell Gate Brewery in 1867. He built his first plant on the lower part of the block between Ninety-second and Ninety-third Streets and Second and Third Avenues. Hell Gate Brewery was known from the beginning for its good water and modern equipment and methods. In September 1870, Ehret's brewery burned to the ground, but within four months, he rebuilt it at the same site. In that first year (1871) Hell Gate Brewery produced more than 37,000 barrels, which grew to more than 220,000 in 1880 and to nearly 300,000 barrels by 1885.[36] By 1886 Ehret employed about three hundred men, with a weekly payroll of between four and five thousand dollars. He was the cornerstone of Ashbel Fitch's law practice and political career. It was through Ehret that Fitch became counsel to the Lager Beer Brewers' Association of New York, effectively the city's twenty-eight or so major brewers, and later began his political career. If the brewers wanted Fitch to represent them privately, they would surely be happy to have him represent them publicly.

Fitch spent many evenings, on business or for recreation or both, in Ehret's or Ruppert's *bierstube*. The brewers' bierstube was where social beer drinking was first brought into into the basic fabric of German society. The brewers' custom of entertaining all visitors, even strangers, and of furnishing free beer to brewery employees, was introduced by the brewing monks of the Middle Ages. In his book, *Twenty Five Years of Brewing,* Ehret said:

> The *Bierstube* in Hell Gate Brewery is a very large square room decorated and furnished in genuine old German fashion, filled with quaint cabinets, high-backed chairs and solid oaken tables, crudely carved and ornamented with antique drinking vessels, and many rare objects of great interest, for which an antiquarian might envy their possessor. The walls are covered with suggestive paintings, on which falls a warm light, softened by multicolored panes of glass in the roof and walls. Many verses apostrophizing the drinker, or relating to beer, beer making, malt, hops, drinking-customs and the like, are distributed all over the room, usually on scrolls underneath pictures, or placed so as to fill up artistically the interstices between the mural decorations. Everything tends to render the visitor reluctant to leave the place, and this evidently is the impression which the host intends to make upon his visitor.[37]

Years later Fitch, Jacob Ruppert Jr., George Ehret's son Frank, and several others formed the "Green Turtle Club," which became the entertainment fad du jour. Members needed to "prove themselves able by actual test to get away with eleven

4. King, Moses, 1899. *Notable New Yorkers, 1896-1899*. New York: The Orr Press.

Schoppen of beer within an hour, the same prescribed in German university towns with regard to admission to the local *Kneipen* or social clubs." Dinner meetings of the Green Turtle Club, always in Ruppert's *Bierstube,* opened with a first course of green turtle soup. Every member was asked "to sing a new song, tell an original story or cook an original dish."[38]

Throughout those years, Ashbel and Elizabeth Fitch became pillars of New York's German society. They would enjoy dinner meetings of the Goethe Society as a couple, an unusual practice during their time.[39] He was always drawn to German history. On a business trip to Europe in 1884 he wrote her,

> We went . . . to Weimar where we stayed over night & visited Goethe's house & other places connected with him, then we drove over to Jena Saturday over the battlefield & reached there towards night.[40] I sent my card to my old organization and a committee called at once to welcome me back & escort me to the headquarters. Of course I did not know any of them but we had a bond of union in the colors and I was made thoroughly at home. On the whole I had a warm welcome & a good time at Jena. Still I came away sorry that I went there. The fellows who were my friends there were very good to me & I missed the "old familiar faces" very much. Several of them fell in the war with France & I found their names on the monument which has been raised to the student soldiers who were killed.[41]

Although there were feelings of euphoria in Germany in 1871, only thirteen years later Fitch, still bathed in German culture, was solemn, saddened by memories of old times and old friends killed in battle.

In a revealing public display of his comprehensive knowledge and devotion to German culture, Fitch was a featured speaker at a Liederkranz dinner in the early spring of 1891 to honor Edmund C. Stanton and Anton Seidl for their contributions to German opera in America. William Steinway presided, and he introduced Fitch's speech on "the influence of German music and art upon American progress."[42] Steinway said, "Mr. Fitch went to Europe—to Germany—as a thorough American, to study music and some other things there. He studied at the universities of Jena and Berlin. . . . We all know that he is a great admirer of our great immortal German poet, Goethe. He has become thoroughly familiar with German music, from the time of Sebastian Bach until the present time of Wagner, and I assure you, gentlemen, if you have anything to translate from German into English or from English into German, he is your man."[43]

Germans also supported Fitch's political career not only because he spoke perfect German, but because they knew him. They were his friends. And there were other reasons, too. "During the 19th century, in all the most important issues that made for political betterment in the United States," historian Faust states,

"Germans played a leading part. Such were (1) the question of slavery; (2) civil service; (3) sound money; (4) party reform; (5) temperance and personal liberty; (6) independent voting,"[44] a virtual synopsis, as we shall see, of the issues that defined the political career of Ashbel P. Fitch. While Fitch was not German, his liberal politics were German, and he was influential in the debates that surrounded every issue that Faust identified, save the question of slavery that preceded him.

In his first try for elective office, the Ashbel P. Fitch Independent Association featured all German names such as Schaefer, Hupfel, Gillig, Ruppert, Ehret, Diel, Haslocher, Henes, and Opperman on its letterhead. A political advertisement in an unidentified newspaper made note of his support among both Republican and Democratic businessmen. It was signed by five members of the Liederkranz Society, including William Steinway, the piano maker; six members of the Arion Society, including George Ehret, the brewer; three members of the Central *Turnverein;* and four members of the German Society. The *New York Advertiser* said, "Mr. Fitch is more popular than any other politician among the Germans. He belongs to every German society from Seventy-sixth Street to Yonkers, either as a regular or honorary member, and, although he is not a remarkable singer, he figures conspicuously in the German singing organizations."[45]

Long before he was established in New York, but shortly after his return home from Germany in 1869, Fitch's raison d'être appeared in Morrisville, New York, a tiny Central New York village located thirty miles southeast of Syracuse, where Edward Fitch and his family spent summers.[46] How and why the Fitches chose Morrisville in the hill country of central New York for their summer retreat is unclear, when they could easily have been closer to New York City or further north with both their families in Malone. Proximity to the city would be one obvious advantage of Morrisville over Malone, but there may have been others.

Who will ever know, for example, whether the young Cross girl somehow caught the eye of Edward or Fannie Fitch, and if she was one of the reasons the Fitches were conveniently situated at Morrisville when their son returned from Germany. But when he came to visit, describing Elizabeth "Bessie" or "Lizzie" Cross, as the "belle of the village," he was immediately smitten. He would sit in a lawyer's office on Main Street pretending to study for his law examinations while on a clandestine lookout for Lizzie, who wore a bright red feather in her hat and passed by his perch on her way to the post office.

Elizabeth Adelia Cross was born in 1850 in Morrisville. Her father, George Cross, a jovial, heavyset man with a twinkle in his eye, owned an iron foundry and manufactured stoves. His granddaughter Bessie recalled his pockets full of

5. Elizabeth Cross Fitch, ca. 1890. Photographer unknown. Photograph from the Ashbel P. Fitch archives.

peppermint candies, which made him a favorite of his grandchildren. His wife, Julia, was a "perfect cook" who always kept two stone crocks full of cookies in the basement. When George married Julia in 1850 they took their wedding trip on a slow boat to Albany on the Erie Canal.

After spending most of his summer in Morrisville, Fitch returned to New York to enroll at Columbia Law School. He passed his examination, was admitted to the bar several days after his twenty-first birthday, and entered into an enduring law partnership with his father. He made rapid inroads into the brewers' legal work, and there was more to his progress than his ability to speak German. Although Fitch's liberal German education conflicted with his ancestral Puritanism, his awareness of his poor, honest ancestors, and their time and toil in America may have provided common ground between him and his immigrant friends. Fitch's parents left the northern frontier, just as his German and Irish friends had forsaken their homelands. His immigrant friends fortified him against the more elegant families of some of his peers. And his willingness to lead, to speak out, and to run for office fit well with his German friends, who often preferred to remain in the political background.

Fitch was solid, educated, and smart. But to Theodore Roosevelt or Joseph Choate, to name just two men whose families had established themselves in New York or Boston before they flourished in New York, Fitch, with his natty dress, his immigrant friends, and his enthusiastic outspokenness, may have seemed "foreign" to them, and "foreigners" in their eyes epitomized what was wrong with New York. On the other hand, to the brewers Jacob Ruppert or George Ehret, who spoke accented English, perhaps Fitch's three-hundred-year ancestral history in America had meaning. Ironically, he seemed to have more in common with his German and Irish friends than he did with the Yankees.

Although Fitch fell in love with Lizzie Cross during that summer of 1869, when fall came they parted. He wrote her flirtatious and passionate letters full of gossip, teasing, and some posturing. As time passed, he wrote about his business and their future plans together. She wrote him in April 1870, "what a blessing that we are allowed the privilege of communicating otherwise than verbally. I fear that you and I would have derived much less pleasure during our short acquaintance, could we not have addressed each other in this manner."[47]

His work absorbed him, and his letters were not all passion and flirtation. In the early months of 1872 he wrote Lizzie, "I love my work," and "I am as busy evenings as through the day and graceless enough not to forget my work even on Sunday." He told her, "My business grows beyond all my hopes," [I am] "weighted down by a pressure of work, which I can't honorably avoid," and "[I am] overwhelmed with work and in trouble on some of it."

By early 1873, the year of a disastrous financial panic, his law business was booming. He wrote her exuberantly, "My calendar showed twenty-four engagements in court alone for this week beside my office and real estate practices." And three months later, "I have nine cases on the calendar and am commencing three times as much new work this month as a year ago." By 1874, "there is more business in the office every day then there was the day before," and he claimed "a rush of new business." His commercial sense was keen and he watched his book of clients carefully. He wrote her, "the ledger shows one hundred fifteen new accounts . . . and not only is this an increase in the volume of business, it improves in quality." He summed it all up in early 1872, "Do you wonder that I am happy over the increase of my business when I can see in it the possibility of a thousand comforts and luxuries for my darling, and a provision for the time when we can, perhaps, do no more work. I have a thousand happy fancies darting through my head in regard to our future when I look over my papers and can see a trip to Europe in the new register which I opened on the New Year."

He told her how he hated summer's heat. Of a divorce case, he said, "anything more disagreeable in the way of work seldom comes into my hand, and I came out today, although successful altogether disgusted . . . more so perhaps, than I would have been if I had been beaten." He was energetic, as in "I am in a half dozen lively fights in court."

Returning from Morrisville on the late train to New York, he discovered that there was no stop for dinner, but his "cigar case and brandy flask" led to "an introduction to the baggage master, conductor & brakeman, who invited him to share in the contents of their tin dinner cans." He described a "merry party seated on pails around an old chest, eating cold meat and bread & butter." Trains were the best mode of transport in the late 1800s. Railroad tracks ran everywhere. Fitch wrote Lizzie from Albany, Baltimore, Philadelphia, and Indianapolis, going from one eastern or midwestern city to another just as we fly today, on a moment's notice but in considerably more comfort.

Fitch lived well, spending all of what he earned, and he worried constantly about collections. In early 1874, he talked about "need[ing] all that there is," and "financial trouble of which I have spoken." In February, he told Lizzie that he "succeeded in paying off one of the debts which have been on my mind." He solved the debt problem by expanding his income, paying his creditors and avoiding more debt.

He also wrote her about politics. The Crosses were Democrats. Typically good-natured, Fitch wrote Lizzie, "I suppose you are rejoicing over the Democratic victory of last Tuesday," but he went on to say that the Republicans had not "done the square thing" in his district and deserved to be beaten. As early as 1873, Fitch's interest in politics, especially his sensitivity to Republican arrogance or indifference to New York City, was evident, but he was unconcerned about political differences with his prospective in-laws.

Temperance was another matter. The movement was strong in upstate New York and across the country, electing Edward Fitch's former law partner, Myron Clark, New York governor in 1854 and passing a Sunday blue law in New York in 1857. By 1881 both Maine and Kansas were dry. Fitch's business with the large German brewers provided the cornerstone of his law practice and rendered anything other than his strong disagreement with the excise law that mandated Sunday saloon closings untenable. Nevertheless, Fitch was a social drinker and he based his opposition on the liberal view that the law violated personal freedom. Some unknown question from Lizzie regarding temperance elicited a stern admonishment from Fitch. "About the temperance question you know well enough what my ideas and my practices are. I shouldn't say anything to hurt any feelings of yours on the subject, but I hope you'll consider a little before you take any decided step on any such matter."

In 1873, almost four years after they first met, Fitch, who regularly wrote loving, respectful, and often romantic letters to Lizzie, for some unknown reason lost his temper. "Lizzie!" said he. "Your letter has just reached me. As if I had not enough to take care of already it brings me a fresh installment of trouble. It must be answered very briefly, and indeed I have not much to say in reply. With all the kindness possible toward you, I must say to you that if you doubt my intention to stand by my words written and spoken, the sooner we close our accounts the better . . . for your part, you have my word and promise, repeatedly spoken and written. Either they are sufficient for you or they are not. . . . Take your choice, Lizzie, but make it final. We must end this sort of thing right here *at once* and *forever*." And then it was gone, whatever it was, into the ether of time and forgotten memories. Three weeks later, she was his "own darling little girl" who sent his "whole love" to his "Dearest." He seldom displayed a temper.

By 1874, they had been courting for five years. He wrote her, "You are my best friend, and my partner as well as my sweetheart." His letters, still replete with expressions of his love, were decidedly more grounded than they were several years before. Upon returning to New York from a two-week business trip to Indianapolis, Fitch reported that his associate George Fuller "came in with my letters and papers and stayed till midnight while over cigars and glasses we went over the business of the fortnight of my absence, and planned the work of the new month. Things were not altogether in as bad shape here as I had feared they would be and today I have got the threads picked up again which were dropped. No one can see ahead very far, but I hope for a good fall and have anyhow a good start already."

He had matured quickly. His first ten years in Malone had given him a solid preparation in life's lessons. His years at the Thirteenth Street School must have provided the best transition to urban New York that a young man raised in rural America could have had. His years in Germany, his courtship of Elizabeth Cross, and his partnership with his father added up to a solid preparation for his life's plan. He was ready for the next adventure. He presented Lizzie with a single pearl engagement ring in an antique gold setting. They were married on November 12, 1874, in Morrisville, and they left for Philadelphia on their honeymoon and then for married life in New York.

Calling herself an "unsophisticated country girl,"[48] Lizzie Fitch must have approached New York with some apprehension. Yet with Fitch busy and gushing confidence, she had no time to worry. They returned from their honeymoon, possibly to live briefly with Fitch's parents, and Lizzie was soon pregnant[49] and the young couple's dreams, written over five years of love letters, began to materialize.

New York's complexity, a rich, turbulent, popular tapestry, defied description. Every aspect of how the big city was managed was changing. The city was still recovering from Tweed's massive theft. Urban problems, never seen before, dogged New York. There were no precedents or guidelines, no lessons to be learned from the experience of other cities. It was all trial and error. New York had everything: a growing population, urban problems, vast wealth, and enormous opportunity. Its society fit easily onto a matrix, stratified along lines of wealth with yawning gaps between rich and poor and divided vertically among Dutch, English, German, Irish, Jews, Protestants, Catholics, and numerous other religious or ethnic groups. Deep divisions between Republicans and Democrats were rooted as much in ethnicity or religion as they were in politics.

Everyday New Yorkers faced an array of hardships in America's first and only American metropolis, but unlike London, Paris, or Rome, New York's explosive growth was fueled by uneducated immigrants. By 1874 the city's population surpassed one million, and it would reach more than 1.2 million by 1880. The life of the city was still centered below Fortieth Street,[50] but well-to-do German immigrants were moving from Kleindeutschland to Yorkville, the upper eighties,[51] the new home for upper-class German-Americans, where Fitch would feel at home.

On the bottom rung of New York society's ladder, life was a matter of abject survival. A ghoulish snippet in the *New York Sun* told of a boatman in the East River near Mill Rock at Hell Gate, a narrow turn in the East River near Ninetieth Street where currents ran strong, creating rough water, and dangerous whirlpools.[52] The boatman complained about floating dead bodies, which he tried to avoid. "Chances are that somebody's gone through their pockets already,"[53] making it hardly worthwhile for the man to take the body to the coroner and go through the paperwork.

The *New York Times*[54] reported that as workmen began demolishing a cooperage at First Avenue and Thirty-ninth Street, residents of surrounding tenements gathered and joined the work by tearing off planking and clapboard and carrying it off for fuel. Patrolman Meyers of the Twenty-first Precinct was called but each time he turned away, women and children swarmed around battling workmen and each other for the prized firewood. At noon the workmen retired for lunch, and Patrolman Meyers left for Saint Gabriel's Parochial School at Thirty-sixth Street, which was his duty. Crowds then overran the place resulting in the collapse of the roof. John Laws, age fifty-five, an unemployed laborer, and Eliza Burns, nine, were killed. "She was quite dead when got out and she still clasped in her hands the firewood she had gathered." Louis Lacomb, eight, had severe internal injuries. This was New York in the Gilded Age.

It was becoming a city for the very rich and the very poor, as the middle class migrated to northern Manhattan and across the East River to Brooklyn. While societal risks from a downtrodden population were generally downplayed or ignored, Tammany Hall saw opportunity in the masses. As Kenneth Ackerman wrote in *Boss Tweed,* "Tweed viewed the immigrants not as charity cases to pity . . . instead, he respected them as voters to bargain with. . . . He won their loyalty by providing tangible service when government 'safety net' programs barely existed."[55] "The Hall" had always welcomed immigrant Americans as new customers, and they asked for their votes in exchange for the warm welcome. Laws, no doubt, were overlooked in the process, but the feeling of belonging that Tammany Hall provided to new citizens was often the jumping-off point for an immigrant family's integration into American society, to be celebrated, not regretted.

Lizzie Fitch, of course, was sheltered from the meaner side of New York life. Her interest and occupation were to provide a warm home for her husband and her children. Fitch's letters to her, generally written when she was visiting her parents in Morrisville, were forlorn. "You can scarcely imagine how desolate the rooms looked nor how each bit of furniture had some new touch to give my heart ache."

Ashbel and Elizabeth Fitch first lived on East Sixty-first Street, assuming a lease from his father. There Bessie (1875) and Ashbel Jr. (1876) were both born. They next moved to East Ninety-third Street, near George Ehret's Hell Gate Brewery, where their third child, Ella, was born in 1878. A year later they moved to 1388 Lexington Avenue at Ninety-first Street, where they would remain for the next sixteen years. They were thirty and twenty-eight years old in 1879. They had been married five years, and they had three children; the oldest, Bessie, was four.

The first street address of the building at 1388 Lexington Avenue was 1376. Fitch was not pleased when the address changed because 1376 held two "13s," his lucky number. But his luck held. The house at 1388 was well built, a four-story-and-basement brownstone with a mansard roof and high dormer windows on the top floor, built among wooden frame houses—an imposing home. The typical brownstone stoop and doorway entered a front hall with a marble floor. Lizzie's piano sat in the parlor that opened off the hall amid plush, carved-ebony furniture. Behind the parlor, separated by sliding doors, was a library filled with books, elegant woodwork, and a large center table. Next to the library was a small office that Fitch put to good use. The dining room was in the basement front, as was customary at the time, with a large kitchen to the rear. The upper floors were bedrooms. Outside, the yard was generous, graced with a variety of flowers and a fertile, flourishing vegetable garden.

Lexington Avenue, opened in 1870, was still being developed in 1879 when the Fitch family moved there. Vacant lots remained. George Ehret, New York's largest brewer and Fitch's most important client, leased Fitch the stately brownstone until he purchased it in 1882 for twenty-three thousand dollars, five thousand of which was a downpayment paid in cash. Ehret sold the property to Fitch and took back notes without recording the debt, with the understanding that Fitch would repay it when he could. Fitch's practice was to bill Ehret for legal services, receive Ehret's payment, and then return Ehret's check in payment of the debt. In that way the eighteen-thousand-dollar debt was extinguished in four years.

As more children arrived (Morton in 1881, Littleton in 1883, and Doris in 1887) Lizzie needed domestic help, and of course she had it. There were cooks and maids coming and going under her watchful eye and that of the quite indispensable Lizzie Petrie, who had joined the Fitch household in 1876 when she was nineteen. Of French and West Indian descent, Petrie functioned as nurse, domestic servant, and adjunct family member. She spent as much time raising the Fitch children as anyone, surely a godsend to their parents. By all accounts she was strict but loving, sympathetic to the sunshine and black clouds of children's daily lives, and she had a keen sense of right and wrong. She was recalled by Bessie, the oldest, as "thoroughly and powerfully scrubbing their every inch in the bathtub," giving out "vigorous early instruction in brushing teeth," and a strong brusher and comber of little girls' long hair.[56]

Fitch made friends easily across class and ethnic lines, a rare talent in New York in 1875, and he skillfully turned it to his advantage. His education, quick wit, and German fluency combined with a youthful appearance and good humor, made him a favorite in any group. His routine when Lizzie was home was work, meals, and out many nights on business or not. But it was really all business. When she was away in the summer months, he dined at Handrich's, the Arion, Heim's, and Mouquin's and spent evenings at Ehret's or Ruppert's breweries, working, drinking beer, or playing cards.

His letters were replete with news and opinions, too, at times about the labor turmoil that wracked the nation. Midwestern railroad strikes of the late 1870s attracted his attention. In July 1877, Fitch wrote that "the strike . . . has grown into an insurrection in many places. Here the militia is all under arms . . . in order to be ready to be sent away if needed. I don't anticipate any trouble here." And "the strike . . . has grown to serious proportions. Nobody talks of anything else here." He told Lizzie of "conflict between the military and the mob in Chicago in which a large number were killed and wounded."

The midwestern railroads overbuilt in the 1870s, and a deteriorating economy led to a horrific collapse. Thousands of workers were left without jobs. The military was called out to put down riots in St. Louis, Chicago, and elsewhere. Matthew Josephson, in his classic history *The Robber Barons,* said, "During the summer of 1877 the workers of the Baltimore & Ohio Railroad struck against wage cuts and their strike spread quickly to . . . the Pennsylvania system. The most destructive labor war the nation had ever known was now seen in Baltimore and Pittsburgh, with militant mobs fighting armed troops and setting in flames property of great value in revenge for the many deaths they suffered."[57] It was a tumultuous, violent time in America as business and labor were becoming acquainted with one another for the first time, and no one knew what the lasting effects might be.

Fitch also told Lizzie that "news came that all the miners in Paris—50,000—or more have struck. It is becoming clear that the strikes were all planned before hand by some secret organization." Karl Marx had written *Das Kapital* only ten years before. Germany was a hotbed of revolutionary activity. Newly arrived German immigrants were pouring into New York every day to join thousands of German-Americans already there. Samuel Gompers, the founder of the American Federation of Labor, was organizing laborers in New York, and his and other labor organizations were tinged with socialism and anarchism. The combination of labor unrest, violence and rising European immigration into New York City contributed to a xenophobic distrust of New York on the part of many Americans. Joanne Reitano, in her 2006 study *Restless City,* noted that by 1886, "labor activism peaked across the country, with twelve hundred strikes in New York City alone."[58]

Fitch had seen the turmoil and unrest too, but he was unable to grasp the extent of the dislike of New York it caused. Nor had he any idea of how America's distrust and dislike of his home city, which to him was unfair and illogical, would capture his heart and his mind as he found himself, time and again, advocating for New York City.

2

Politics and the Road to Washington

> There is no story of modern development more striking than that which has taken place . . . on the island of Manhattan, and there is nothing in that story so interesting as the manner in which the different elements of this curiously constituted population have grown to respect and like each other and live and work together.
>
> —ASHBEL P. FITCH, 1887

By the mid-1880s, Fitch's flourishing law practice was unusually diverse, running the gamut from estate and divorce law to reorganizations, liability, bankruptcy, and other corporate matters that were strictly commercial. For the brewers, children were mangled by beer wagons as they played on New York's teeming streets, and Fitch defended the accused. Eugene Sullivan, age seven, had his skull crushed under the wheel of a Schaefer brewing wagon.[1] An Abbott Brewing wagon ran over and killed another boy, whose father sued Abbott for $5,000 and was awarded $750.[2] Charles Durant, six, sued Catharine Lipsius of the Lipsius Brewery after the Lipsius wagon hit him. Another six-year-old, Abraham Bulkin, was standing on the curb of Chrystie Street near Hester Street, when one of George Ehret's beer wagons came dashing along and a wheel hub struck him, throwing him under the wagon and crushing one of his arms, which was amputated immediately. Bulkin was awarded $6,000.[3]

Fitch's legal work went well beyond liability cases. He represented a group that acquired the Lauer Brewing Company of Reading, Pennsylvania. He liquidated estates. He auctioned a parcel of "unimproved" real estate on the west side of First Avenue between Forty-third and Forty-fourth Streets.[4] He was elected a trustee of the Brooklyn Elevated Railway, representing George Ehret.[5] The *Brewers Journal* reported that Frederick Opperman had purchased an interest in the Turtle Bay Brewery from the estate of his late partner, John Muller.[6] Fitch conducted the negotiations for both parties, an unusual measure of mutual trust in their attorney.

He often handled divorce cases; one in particular, *Herman Spahn vs. Maria Louise Spahn,* would be publicized for its intrigue and titillation, and it was an early indicator of Fitch's skillful handling of the press. Herman Spahn bought and sold silks for an importing house, earning commissions of ten thousand dollars a year. Spahn, who was about forty years old, wanted his marriage to the twenty-five-year-old Marie Louise Spahn annulled. The case required that both parties and their legal counsel travel to Europe to gather evidence.

When the December 18, 1885, *New York Times* ran a thinly disguised and amusing article headed "Monsieur and Madame" describing a bizarre European odyssey in June and July of 1884, part of a fictitious divorce trial ("Moreau vs. Moreau"), Fitch could have been the only source for the story. He made himself available to reporters, he was quotable, and when he needed to he seemed able to get his views into print. His press relations were part and parcel of his political success. The *Times* story, though minor, was an early effort. The reaction had to have been favorable, and 1886 was an election year.

More than a year before, Fitch wrote to Lizzie, "politics are booming. . . . I am requested to speak at a West Side district next week and to preside Thursday night in the district. There is a large desertion of Independents to the Democrats, and the Irish Democrats to the Republicans & things are very much mixed. Thank heavens there will be but three months of it!" In October the Republican Committee nominated him to run for Congress in the Thirteenth District, basically northern Manhattan north of Fifty-second Street and east of Eighth Avenue to Eighty-sixth Street and the northern tip of Manhattan. It was by all accounts the nation's wealthiest, largest, and fastest-growing congressional district. The *New York Times* described him as "a lawyer, forty years old, and counsel for the Brewers' Association."[7] The *New York Tribune* added, "Mr. Fitch . . . is a prominent lawyer of this city, with a large practice. He has never held any political office and has not heretofore taken any prominent part in politics."[8]

The Democrats nominated Egbert Viele, a self-important West Point general with a good war record and at best only loose ties to Tammany Hall.[9] Viele's interests, skills, and commitments were toward large public improvements. An engineer by education and training, he claimed to be the original designer of Central Park and he may have been.[10] He was also a ceaseless, dedicated promoter of Harlem River improvements such as dredging, widening, and the construction of new port facilities. His sought-after result was to enable shipping traffic heading south on the Hudson River to access Long Island Sound without rounding the tip of Manhattan Island. Ships headed toward New England and Europe would gain considerable savings in time and money.[11]

Years later, with Fitch in Congress, the Harlem River Ship Canal became a legislative test of wills between Fitch, representing business interests of Harlem, and an alliance of railroads, New England congressmen, and certain other real estate interests in Harlem, with Fitch getting the better of it. The railroads resisted spending large sums of money to raise tracks and build bridges so that shipping companies could become stronger competitors. New Englanders and some upstate New Yorkers seemed to think that the canal would cut them off from New York City and points west, and even suggested that the Harlem River should be filled in and built upon.[12]

Nevertheless, on June 17, 1895, the improved Harlem River Canal opened to a parade, speakers, a three-mile long flotilla, a banquet, and fireworks.[13] General Viele chaired the commemoration committee and described the ship canal as "a continuation" of the Erie Canal that will save "the grain trade a distance of twenty-four miles and very large expense in its exportations and gain readier access to the ocean."[14] Viele's enthusiasm aside, the Harlem River never became the New York port that its backers envisioned. Beset by obstacles, both navigational and political, the waterway was finally overtaken by other forms of transportation.

Returning to October 1884, Fitch's short formal note[15] thanking the committee but declining the nomination—"I regret very sincerely that I cannot accept the nomination"—was less than revealing and shed no light on what lay behind his refusal. Years later he would point to tariff reform as the controlling issue, there being little or no difference between his un-Republican reformist views—that is, more, not less international trade and lower, not higher, consumer prices—and the Democratic platform that included tariff reform. Without a defining issue, Fitch did not run; Viele did, he won, and he took his seat in Congress.

While Fitch's business and political activities continued to expand, so did assorted health problems, his clients' and his own. He spoke seriously with Ehret concerning Mrs. Ehret's recent attacks "of bleeding from the lungs. He is I think alarmed about her & asked me very fully about the pine forests in the Adirondacks—their affect on the lungs etc." Fitch's health, too, was a concern, as it would be for the rest of his life. He tried, with only limited success, to watch his weight, and he suffered painfully from gout when he was only in his forties. In August 1885 he wrote Lizzie that he had been taken quite ill on his way home from the office "with cramps in the stomach, kidneys etc. and got with difficulty to the Belvedere Hotel where I went to bed & sent for Dr. Spannhake who came at once."

Recovering quickly, his mind never strayed far from business and politics. He wrote to her in September 1885, "I have been appointed without my suggestion chairman of the committee on appeals in the county committee which is new evidence that everything will be solid for the nomination [for Congress] next fall if I want it. *And I shall want it fast enough if there is a fair show to win*" (emphasis added).

From the time he returned from Germany in 1869, Fitch concentrated his efforts on building his legal practice. By all accounts his work, much of it for the German brewers, was lucrative. In his late thirties, with more than enough money coming in to satisfy the needs of his large family, the wealthy young lawyer began to look for higher mountains to climb. Unlike 1884, and with the enthusiastic support of George Ehret and the other large brewers who had little use for Viele, Fitch set his sights on a serious run for Congress in 1886. He was thirty-eight years old, at the top of his profession, and obviously had political ambitions. He had participated in Republican activities for years, and was, at that time, president of the Twenty-third Assembly District Republican Committee.

Cosmic change was rumbling across America in 1886, as it had, unabated, since the end of the Civil War. An array of governance issues for the young, burgeoning industrial power were also bubbling to the surface. Tariff, silver coinage, civil service, women's suffrage, temperance, and the threat of socialism were among the questions that were patiently and persistently sorted out. They all affected New York, and temperance in particular was the brewers' issue. A temperance bill was introduced in Congress in 1875, and although it failed for eleven years, the brewers had no doubt that it would be brought forward again.

In the mid-1880s, stoked by appalling living conditions as well as German immigration and organizing activity, the specter of socialism had New York and several of Fitch's clients in a state of high anxiety. Socialism was the dominant issue of the 1886 New York mayoralty race. The newly formed Labor Party nominated Henry George, a well-known and popular socialist, for mayor. Labeled "the most powerful radical in the world" by Theodore Roosevelt biographer Edmund Morris, Morris also described George as "balding, red-bearded, and runtlike." According to Morris, "George argued that because it takes many poor men to make one rich man, progress in fact creates poverty."[16]

When George announced that "if thirty thousand workingmen pledged to support him, he would run on an independent Labor ticket"[17] and thirty-four thousand pledges flowed in, New Yorkers noticed, and they were afraid. George was popular with the lower classes to the extent that Tammany Hall's uncharacteristic nomination of the anti-Tammany swallow-tail Democrat Abram S. Hewitt attests. Hewitt, the industrialist son-in-law of Peter Cooper,[18] had a good reputation, and with Tammany's endorsement he won the election. Republicans nominated Theodore Roosevelt in the vain hope that a divided Democratic/socialist vote might elect him, but he finished a distant third. Fearful Republicans and swallow-tail Democrats voted for Hewitt, the Tammany-backed Democrat, in order to defeat the socialist.

Socialism was an intangible nineteenth century "foreign" import to America from Europe, much of it from Germany. Some five million Germans came to America during the nineteenth century, and like other immigrant populations they found their way to their settling places throughout the country. But the largest German community[19] was in New York City where there was a total German-American population in 1900 of more than three-quarters of a million citizens.

Says Homberger, "There were German 'trades' in New York in the nineteenth century (tailors, boot and shoemakers, cabinet and piano makers, upholsterers), and Germans played a major role in creating the trades union movement of the city,"[20] which from time to time went out on strike and flirted with socialism. There were brewery workers and drivers unions, too. Midwestern and upstate rural Republicans blamed the labor turmoil on German and other foreign immigrants; they feared that socialism would follow on the heels of the organized labor activity that was in plain view.

Fitch would have been among the first to see socialist activity in the German community. His clients would have seen it and felt it. Socialism was meant to benefit the working classes, yet it would have seemed to some of his clients more like a blunt instrument used to bully and intimidate those it was supposed to benefit. Fitch's law practice provided a narrow bridge from the German business community to the American legal system. While representing his German clients, Fitch's opposition to socialism advanced his political career.

His opposition began with George Ehret. Ehret's practice, and that of most other big brewers, was to lend money to saloon owners to expand their businesses and, as a further consequence, sell more beer. The custom, which many years later would be prohibited by antitrust laws, was commonplace at the time. One of Ehret's customers, Mr. Theiss, had operated a saloon on Canal Street for years, served a good clientele, and managed a nice business. Theiss hoped to build a second place where men and women could be served and music played, similar to beer gardens in Europe. Ehret agreed to loan Theiss one hundred thousand dollars for ten years at 5 percent, terms apparently not dissimilar to what a bank might offer. The "place was fitted up elegantly" and "business was conducted on an entirely respectable plan."[21]

Difficulties arose when the new beer garden became the target of a Central Labor Union boycott. The "CLU," as Reitano points out, "endorsed a wide range of strategies including strikes, boycotts and political activism."[22] The boycotters demanded that Theiss fire his orchestra leader, Mr. Eschert, which, after several years of harassment, Theiss reluctantly did. Later on Eschert said "for 143 weeks I got fifty dollars a week and I was well satisfied with my pay when these four defendants [the boycotters] demanded my discharge because they said I worked for less than union wages. Mr. Theiss refused their request, and then they boycotted his place until he was compelled to discharge me, and he paid $1,000 to the boycotters. The fifteen other members of the band were also discharged and a new band, consisting of union men, was employed."[23]

Before he gave in to the boycotters, a badgered, distressed Theiss asked his friend Ehret for advice. Ehret advised paying the thousand dollars. After Theiss took Ehret's advice, both men thought the matter resolved. But it reappeared when Eschert, the bandleader, sued. The judge hearing the case sent the CLU boycotters to jail for extortion "for terms ranging up to four years in Sing Sing prison."[24] Ehret claimed[25] that it was the boycotters who had originally asked him to intervene. After Eschert sued, the boycotters believed that Ehret could have persuaded the judge not to send them to prison. That was the reason, not—as some historians have claimed, because Theiss served Ehret's beer—that the CLU began boycotting Ehret with some considerable effect.

Ehret unwittingly became a principal in a public sorting out of right and wrong. The *New York Times*[26] told the story of ten men who walked into a saloon, each calling for a beer. Glasses were filled and each man took a sip, stopped, looked at one another, and asked the bartender if that was "George Ehret's beer." The bartender nodded and at that the ten made for the door saying they didn't drink Ehret's beer. Ten filled glasses each worth five cents and the proprietor lost fifty cents. Saloon owners who suffered most removed their Ehret beer signs. A far larger number of boycotters than those who once boycotted Theiss's beer garden were now boycotting Ehret's beer. A week after the boycotters' conviction, Ehret admitted that the systematic movement "to leave alone" his beer had injured his business.

The situation was further confused by disagreements among the boycotters. One CLU delegate said that workingmen were wasting their time diverting dollars from George Ehret's coffers into somebody else's. "I'm against all this. It is nasty and mean and does the cause of labor no good. If we want to do anything that will stand by us, why not do it at the polls?"[27]

An Ehret driver, at a Knights of Labor meeting, declared, "Just because a half dozen of the socialistic societies get up and cry 'outrage' at fancied misconduct is no reason that all the workingmen of New York should raise their hands against a man and . . . three hundred employees should be thrown out of employment. Mr. Ehret is a good boss. He pays good wages. He takes as much interest in his workingmen, if not more, that any other of the big boss brewers."[28]

The other brewers, no doubt enjoying an increase in beer sales, nonetheless "manfully joined in a protest against the boycott,"[29] concluding that they "cannot believe that fair-minded American citizens will sustain a boycott based on such injustice, and for this reason they protested publicly against it."[30] Fitch, as counsel to the Brewers' Association, told the *New York Sun,* "while a number of saloons [near] factories and near labor union meeting rooms have given up Ehret's beer, others had ordered it just because it was boycotted." He added that he wouldn't reveal their names because that "would be certain to draw upon them the vengeance of the boycotters."[31]

As the Ehret boycott dragged on, a Bohemian society began boycotting one Mrs. Landgraf's bakery, and it appeared that the boycott might force her to close her prosperous business. Overnight though, the public mood changed, and the widowed Mrs. Landgraf began receiving sympathy and support from unions and customers alike. The dismissed bandleader Eschert's declaration, "this is a free country," fired the German spirit.

Fitch was at the center of it, the place to be for a young man planning a run for Congress. The *New York World* said, "the Executive Committee of the Master Bakers Association held a meeting" at his office. "Resolutions were adopted sympathizing with Mrs. Landgraf. . . . It was also decided to retain Mr. Fitch as counsel of the association, and he was requested to ascertain what legal steps could be taken to prosecute the boycotters in Mrs. Landgraf's case. The meeting denounced 'boycotting' and 'boycotters' in round terms. The committee represented nine hundred master bakers in New York and vicinity,"[32] many, if not most of whom, were German and might be expected to vote for Fitch if he were ever a candidate for public office.

While socialism was dominating the political headlines, other questions, such as tariff, silver coinage, temperance, women's suffrage, and civil service were also argued and negotiated, one at a time. And they were settled, in the Congress, in the courts, and in the newspapers sometimes only until the succeeding election. For many years, alliances were formed and dissolved while interests shifted and positions hardened or softened according to which way political winds were blowing. This is how and this is when the foundation of America's modern, liberal society evolved, and Ashbel Fitch was heavily engaged in many of those contests.

Coincidentally, while the boycotts of Fitch's German clients were proceeding and he was gaining political recognition as a victim's representative, a tariff bill was wending its way through committee and onto the floor of the House of Representatives. It was the Morrison Bill, a tariff reform measure named for Ways and Means chairman William R. Morrison, Democrat of Illinois. Burgeoning federal surpluses that deflated the economy were causing anxiety on both sides of the House, but the Democrats had been complaining most and they were in power.

The Morrison Bill incorporated additions to the "free list" and lower duties on several products.[33] The uncertainty was caused by a large block, thirty-six with the benefit of hindsight, of protectionist Democrats, led by the legendary former Speaker and chairman of the House Appropriations Committee, Samuel J. Randall, Democrat of Pennsylvania. When the Morrison Bill to revise the tariff downward was voted on the House floor, it was defeated 157 to 140 by a combination of Republicans and Randallite Democrats. Grover Cleveland was irate. "Do you call yourself a Democrat?" he demanded of a New Yorker who voted against the bill.[34]

Out of nowhere Egbert Viele had voted with the high-tariff Randallite Democrats against the bill. Why he voted with Republicans and protectionist Democrats against the will of his constituents, for a bill that was of national significance but had not previously attracted his attention, was inexplicable. Tariff reform was a leading-edge Democratic issue. It was sufficiently powerful that a Republican running on tariff reform could defeat a protectionist Democrat in a Democratic district. Fitch, on the strength of his personal popularity within the German community, might have beaten Viele without Viele's high-tariff vote. But Viele's vote against the Morrison Bill created an opening for Fitch—a powerful defining issue for a reform-minded Republican to run on in a reform-minded Democratic district.

Meanwhile, three hundred miles to the north, Fitch's uncle, Ashbel B. Parmelee, died in August 1886. Fitch prevailed upon his cousin Morton, the executor of his father's estate, to sell him a "lucky" thirteen acres on the eastern shore of Ragged Lake, near Owls Head in the northern Adirondacks. Fitch, frustrated and increasingly unhappy with Lizzie's long summer absences in Morrisville, dreamed of owning his own place in a rustic setting where he could entertain in style and be alone with his family. Ragged Lake was sixteen miles into the woods on a notably rough, rutted, and rocky dirt road. The spot he chose to build his camp was on the far side of the lake where no road ran, on a gentle rise from the shoreline with a panoramic view of the wilderness and stunning sunsets.

Six months later, on February 7, 1887, Edward Fitch also died. One of his obituaries captured an insightful perspective on his son's career: "Ashbel Fitch was his father's pride and appreciating the value and great advantage of a first-class education he did what he could do in this direction, afterwards sending his son to Europe where with distinction he graduated at [Berlin and Jena], thus becoming a fine German scholar and quite a linguist,—a decided advantage as it proved to him in the practice of his profession subsequently. At present Mr. Fitch is doing business for no less than twenty-eight prominent brewers in this city, from which an idea may be formed of the enormity of the business he is doing."[35]

For Ashbel Fitch, Edward Fitch's passing was more than the loss of his father, which was considerable. Edward and Fanny Fitch's unconditional love forged the very foundation of Fitch's self-esteem. Ashbel Parmelee and Edward Fitch were the senior links to Fitch's Republicanism, to William Wheeler and William Seward and the northern frontier. Within a matter of months, both Ashbel Parmelee and Edward Fitch were gone, and the urban lawyer, with his own mind, his own business interests, and his own politics continued to emerge.

An October 22, 1886, a printed notice endorsing the nomination of Ashbel P. Fitch, Esq., for member of Congress from the Thirteenth Congressional District declared that Mr. Fitch was long known as "an able, successful, and upright member of the bar of this city."[36] The notice was signed by eight Republicans of some note, including Levi Morton, Elihu Root, and Joseph Choate. Morton served in Congress, was vice president under Benjamin Harrison, and later was governor of New York. Root became secretary of war under McKinley and Roosevelt, secretary of state under Roosevelt, United States senator, and he won the Nobel Peace Prize in 1912. Choate, an eminent attorney, became US ambassador to Great Britain.

Fitch had worked within the Republican organization since 1871, when he was elected a general committee delegate by the Republican Association of the Twentieth Assembly District, but his nomination grew out of his business and personal relationships with the prominent German brewers, most of whom were Democrats and on good terms with Tammany Hall. Their positive disposition toward the Republican Fitch was undoubtedly enhanced by their dislike of Viele.

After the Democrats renominated General Viele for Congress in spite of his vote on the Morrison Bill, Charles Dayton, president of the Harlem Democratic Club, paid a call on Ashbel Fitch. Dayton wanted to know Fitch's position on the tariff. Fitch told him that he was for "lower duties and a revision." The tariff was crucial, so the Democrat Dayton quickly put aside his party allegiance in exchange for the Republican Fitch's promised vote for tariff reform. "Good," said Dayton. "Take the Republican nomination. I and many other Democrats will support you openly on that issue."[37]

One week later, at the Republican district assembly, Fitch was formally nominated, and the *New York Uptown Visitor* reported that "A committee of five was appointed to escort Mr. Fitch into the hall. On his entrance there were in rapid succession a series of such violent earthquake shocks of applause that the proprietors of the Harlem Hall if not fully insured, must have grown pallid with alarm. Mr. Fitch thanked the delegates, his address being remarkable for clearness, comprehensiveness of thought and simplicity of diction."[38]

His nomination was well received. Fitch was described as "magnetic,"[39] "a particularly good nomination,"[40] and "a man of clear and decided views."[41] The *New York Times* said that "The brewers of the city are indebted to him for much valuable service to which is attributable their general conservative course in public affairs."[42] Friends and business associates gathered around, many of them Democrats, to express their support. They worked through the Young Men's Independent Club, organized in 1884 to support Grover Cleveland for president,[43] and the Ashbel P. Fitch Independent Association.

Fitch was an energetic, aggressive campaigner, making several speeches each night in both English and German. He was well organized; his posters went up, and he assembled an array of endorsements from Democrats, Independents, merchants, and Republican newspapers. One newspaper reported that one hundred sixty of

Ruppert's and Ehret's "workmen met this week and organized for Mr. Fitch. Of that number only three had ever voted the Republican ticket."[44] Five days before the election, Roosevelt, campaigning for mayor, and Fitch appeared together on the podium at Harlem Hall.

Fitch's canvassing message was comprehensive. He favored "the deepening and preservation of the channels to the port, the necessity of speedily carrying out the scheme of the Harlem Canal, of restoring and promoting American shipping and shipbuilding, and the necessity of revising the tariff (so that while protecting American industries, too great a tax shall not be imposed upon necessities)."[45] The former was Viele's issue, the latter his own on which Viele, by his vote against the pro–tariff reform Morrison Bill, was vulnerable. Fitch added, in what years later would turn out to be the essence of understatement, "I am opposed to the compulsory coinage of silver."[46]

Viele's message was imperious, stiff, and narrow, aimed squarely at workers on public projects, appropriations for which he had inserted in the Rivers and Harbors Bill. He named more than half a dozen projects with total appropriations in excess of $2 million and their consequent positive impact on job creation, most of which was true and to his credit. But by all accounts he was an inept politician. In addition to his extraordinary vote on the Morrison Bill, Viele had managed to make himself unpopular with segments of the Democratic Party that included Tammany Hall as well as with working men and average citizens.

If Viele gained any sympathetic Republican votes for his vote against the Morrison Bill, they were negligible. Instead, Fitch went on the offense, attracting a variety of working, German, and other Democrats to his cause. When the results were counted, they showed that Viele, a seven-thousand-vote winner in 1884, had lost by four thousand votes in 1886. The voters also elected seven other congressmen, all Democrats, to the New York City delegation to the Fiftieth Congress, including Amos Cummings,[47] the amiable newspaper reporter for the *New York Sun* and a longtime member of Tammany Hall; Bourke Cockran, the eloquent, articulate, Irish Tammany sachem; Samuel S. "Sunset" Cox, one of the more able legislators to ever grace the House of Representatives; and four lesser lights. Cox was elected to Congress sixteen times from Ohio and New York. Statewide, there were nineteen Republicans and fifteen Democrats.

Congressional representatives were the sole legislative voice of the people in the Gilded Age, senators being appointed then by state legislatures. As a consequence, congressmen attracted more public attention then than they do today, as they are now often overshadowed by popularly elected senators.

Ashbel Parmelee Fitch, born thirty-eight years before in a rural upper New York State hamlet on the Canada border, was elected to the House of Representatives in his first run for public office. His diverse background served him well in a metropolis that was a collection of narrow interests. He was born in the country, educated abroad, and lived in the city. He traced his ancestry to the *Mayflower,* but he seemed German, and he had a common touch. He was raised a Republican, but his wife and many of his friends were Democrats. He was a gifted speaker in two languages, and he had an active and successful law practice of extraordinary scope. His personality quite naturally transcended and embraced the inherent divisions that were New York.

His political influence was magnified by New York City's impact on New York State, and New York State's impact on the nation. In the presidential elections of 1880, 1884, and 1888 the winner's margin of victory in the Electoral College was smaller than New York State's electoral vote. And whether New York State went Republican or Democratic was largely determined by the size of the Democratic plurality in the city. In those days New York City was a lever to the presidency.

Along with many others of his generation, Fitch was now engaged in what Abraham Lincoln may have suggested at Gettysburg twenty-three years before when he proclaimed that "it is for the living, to be dedicated here to the unfinished work which today those who fought here have thus far so nobly advanced." Whether Lincoln spoke to the hard fighting that lay immediately ahead or possibly to a broader sweep of the advancement of American democracy that would follow the war, we cannot be sure.[48] Whether Ashbel Fitch read those words when they were uttered or was motivated by them, for twelve years he was an active participant in "unfinished work." And his work occurred during a formative period and at a central place, late-nineteenth-century New York City, that, barring wartime, was one of the more significant political milieus in the nation's history.

The generation of political leaders that followed Lincoln, so flawed, living in a time of peace and cyclical prosperity, were heavily engaged no longer in war but in healing and in the day-to-day "unfinished work of the living." As a wag once said "neither making laws nor making sausages are pretty sights," and that was especially so in New York City and in the Congress in 1886. But they brought passion to a raucous political stage that at times was dangerous. Between 1864 and 1901, only thirty-seven years, seven men were elected to ten presidential terms and three of the seven, Abraham Lincoln, James Garfield, and William McKinley, were murdered.[49]

Grover Cleveland, one of the four presidents whose life was spared, dominated the politics of the era. His two nonconsecutive presidential terms (1884-88 and 1892-96) spanned a twelve-year period that fell halfway between the end of the Civil War and the outbreak of World War I. As we have learned, no less an authority than the arch-Republican Elihu Root referred in 1923 to the time of Cleveland's presidencies as "a very critical period in American history."

Much of the great reconciliation between North and South to which Root pointed took place in the House of Representatives, where elected representatives of the South, and then the West, prolonged the sectional arguments that were prevalent before the Civil War. Southerners were especially successful at adapting to the new order, that is, accomplishing in Congress what they had failed to accomplish on the battlefield twenty years before. The newer versions of the old debates often had powerful flavors of individual rights blended into the mix. With the tariff it was nascent consumerism, as it was with silver coinage. And as will be described later, a debate about the Federal Election Law literally revived the idea that southern blacks could be prevented from voting, which many believed had perished at Appomattox Courthouse.

Ashbel Fitch participated in, and sometimes led, these debates in the House of Representatives. While conservative on financial matters, he added large dollops of social tolerance to a reactionary stew that needed it. His was a progressive voice that helped urge America toward a more popular and tolerant democracy. Yet Republicans would make it increasingly difficult to reconcile Fitch's voice with their own. On any issue, he would fight for New York City in Congress whenever the situation demanded it, and he would prove to be a formidable vote getter in the competitive world of New York politics.

Congressmen elected to office in November 1886 took their seats in Congress thirteen months later in December 1887. The relaxed schedule, which originated in the earliest days of the Republic, was first intended to allow office holders sufficient time to wind up their affairs and travel by horseback to the capitol from distant parts of the country. Fitch, a few hours by train from Washington, had more than enough time to prepare his office for his absence, and to lay the political foundation for his future in Congress.

His prominence was enhanced by his solid victory over a Democratic incumbent in a Democratic district, the only Republican congressman in New York City. While Viele dismissed Fitch's victory as an accident, Fitch used it as inspiration to encourage the city's Republicans in future elections, a move toward "party reform" that may have appealed to his German constituents. He worried that it would become impossible for Republicans to carry the state in national elections if upstate Republicans wrote off the city. He urged the party to unbend, to make New York City a comfortable home for Republicans. And he worked at building Republican strength as chairman of the Committee on Appeals of the Republican County Committee under Elihu Root's chairmanship.[50]

Before the Fiftieth Congress convened, a long-standing struggle that had occupied New Yorkers for years erupted anew. Home rule, the right of the city to govern itself free from domination by Albany, became entangled with the socialistic fervor that gripped New York. As historian Joanne Reitano recounts in *Restless City*, the Republican-controlled legislature at Albany passed several bills in 1857, one of which was an Excise Law that regulated liquor sales and mandated Sunday saloon closings in New York. Says Reitano, "A direct attack on the drinking traditions of German and Irish immigrants, the liquor law was part of the larger nineteenth-century temperance movement . . . immigrant voters readily saw the connection between nativism and temperance."[51]

From their beginning, the blue laws were either cursed or applauded by almost every New Yorker and enforced or not enforced by politicians who tried to discern which way the political winds were blowing. Responding to temperance pressure, new mayor Abram S. Hewitt, in early 1887, initiated a campaign to intensify the enforcement of the excise laws, going so far as to apply the "law to those places where German singing societies met [forbidding] them to rehearse in rooms off the saloons"[52] without a license.

The German community responded immediately. Out went a public announcement of a "monster mass meeting"[53] at Cooper Union on Saturday evening May 7, 1887. There would be "Two Grand Stands Out Doors" to accommodate the crowd. In the meantime, state senator Jacob Cantor, a city Democrat, introduced an amendment in Albany authorizing the mayor "to permit wine, beer and liquors to be sold 'while concerts consisting of vocal or instrumental music only, are being given in a place duly licensed by him.'"[54] When, before the monster meeting, the amendment passed, it deflected whatever political pressure the protest generated off Albany and onto the mayor, but it hardly resolved the matter. To German-Americans, Sunday beer was a serious matter. They had come to America to be free.

Hewitt's enforcement of the blue laws raised obvious questions such as temperance, individual liberty, and home rule and, as would become apparent, some others that were not so obvious, such as musicians' employment and socialism. Through it all ran the fears and suspicions of "real Americans" toward immigrant cultures.

Apart from those questions and crosscurrents that gained attention, the spectacle of protest in 1887 in New York City was remarkable—glittering, intense, chaotic, and, for some in the crowd, exhilarating. And immigrant protests of any kind provided fertile ground for socialists and anarchists. The monster meeting was one such display. Citizens began gathering near Cooper Union on Eighth Street as the gray afternoon lengthened into dusk under a light rain. There were colored lights, flags, and a brass band from the West Side Wirthshutz Verein,[55] a local German-American social club. The two grandstands were on Eighth Street, one near Third Avenue for German speakers and one near Fourth Avenue for English. Calcium lights illuminated platforms that were trimmed with bunting.[56]

Eagerness and excitement mounted as the crowd assembled. Some estimates reported a crowd of five thousand protesters, including a "large sprinkling of females."[57] They all came ostensibly to assert their right to hear music and drink beer at the same time, but they were unemployed musicians and others with political and social agendas of their own, eager to take advantage of the crowd. The *New York World* reported that "there were plenty of people there who cared little for either beer or music. Their purpose may properly be described as a strike of the citizens of the metropolis, against the management of metropolitan affairs by a company of largely rural, upstate lawmakers, who were unfamiliar with the requirements of the big city."[58]

When the doors swung open, the band played "Skyrockets," and the early arrivals moved across the hall. They were followed by small processions of the Maltsters Union No. 1 marching up from East Fourth Street, the Brewers' Union in a full regiment, and the German Cooks' Union, which formed the line at Houston and Forsythe Streets. Quickly, the hall was filled, "a light colored sea of faces and bald heads rising up on all sides and splashing against the walls and a surf of black coats where the unlucky ones stood up."[59] The band played on, protesters struggled for a last chance to get inside, policemen patrolled the aisles, lights went up, and hats came off.

When the crowd settled down, the German-speaking congressman Ashbel Fitch was unanimously elected chairman of the assemblage. One reporter described him as "looking exceedingly like a German, only hesitating between Hesse-Darmstadt or the northwest corner of Bavaria in determining his local nativity. But the Honorable Ashbel P. Fitch is in reality a chip from Plymouth Rock."[60] Fitch congratulated Senator Cantor, his schoolmate in Thomas Hunter's classrooms, on his legislative triumph and expressed his hope for home rule in New York.

Fitch introduced the evening's speakers. The names of moderates Oswald Ottendorfer, editor of *Staats Zeitung,* the leading German newspaper, and Carl Schurz, a Civil War general, friend of Lincoln, editor, politician, and civil rights activist were hissed; Samuel Gompers, a founder of the American labor movement, and Henry George, the socialist, were cheered. As the speakers were introduced, loud cries arose for "Shevitch, Shevitch," and it became even more apparent that beer and music were not the focal point of the rally. Under mounting pressure, Fitch finally yielded the floor to the socialist M. Shevitch.

Shevitch spoke in English in support of organized labor, reform, and home rule, messages for an English-speaking public. Then in German he told the crowd that the large mayoral vote for Henry George[61] had been a "terrible dynamite bomb thrown in New York" that was the "beginning of the tearing down of the temple of corruption and hypocrisy. Not until a Sampson should tear asunder the pillars of that rotten structure would organized labor cease its agitation"[62] The authors of *Gotham* describe the 1882 immigrant Johann Most as a European anarchist whose favorite panacea was dynamite, and Shevitch, may have been one of his disciples.[63] His oral attack in German no doubt repelled New Yorkers and played into the hands of the city's xenophobes. Following Shevitch, Fitch adjourned the meeting, in the judgment of the *Kansas City Times* his "shrewdest move of the evening."[64]

After the chaotic protest meeting, Fitch left for a well-earned vacation. He spent most of August 1887 visiting his new place in the Adirondacks, fishing and camping with friends and his son Ashbel. He returned to the city in the early autumn of 1887, then turned around and headed north again to Saratoga for the Republican state convention. Grover Cleveland's election to the presidency in 1884 had broken a string of six consecutive victorious Republican presidential campaigns beginning with Abraham Lincoln in 1860. Cleveland, the former mayor of Buffalo and New York governor, carried New York in 1884, and he would surely make a strong run in 1888. Republicans were intent on recapturing the White House.

A total of 693 delegates met in Saratoga at a cavernous wooden skating rink that was well past its prime. The upper beams sported Japanese parasols, festoons of Chinese lanterns, bunting, and American flags. A platform was set three feet above the ground, behind which "were hung handsome engravings of Abraham Lincoln and General Grant in heavy oak frames" still imagined to be exercising their moral authority over the party.[65] The New York City delegates numbered 115 and included Senator William Evarts,[66] Levi Morton,[67] ex-governor Alonzo Cornell, and Congressman Fitch as well as "Frederick Finck, one of the indicted aldermen of 1884, Shed Shook, the protector of Republican saloonkeepers and professor of political 'fine work' and other 'boys of the machine.' A few respectable figureheads won't change the character of that crowd" opined the Democratic *New York World*.[68] Seth Low,[69] the youthful Brooklyn mayor, was made temporary chairman as the 1887 Republican convention came to order.

Low spoke for twenty minutes[70] addressing what were, in his view, the foremost statewide questions of the day. Prohibition, after at least thirty-five years, still topped the list. More than a century ago, Republicans grappling with temperance remind us of Republicans today struggling with abortion: an emotional issue framed by moral positions on one side and individual freedoms on the other. Low, groping for a solid center, positioned prohibitionists at one end of the argument, with "impossible demands" for shuttering the liquor trade and Democrats at the other end, offering "limitless yields" to the free consumption of alcohol.

As general counsel to the Brewers' Association, Fitch was already an irritant to Republican prohibitionists. Two years later, in August 1889, an article appeared in the Democratic *New York Sun* under the headline "Liquor Men in Politics."

Temperance disciples complained that the liquor and beer industry's direct influence in the legislature subverted their achieving their prohibitionist objectives. Assemblyman Ernest H. Crosby, Republican from New York County, said,

> The brewers' . . . immense wealth gives them opportunities for wholesale bribery. They raise the enormous funds for use in all canvasses in which the temperance issue is raised. But [they] have [even] greater power. . . . Each brewery has a large number of beer shops under its direct control. They select men of straw, provide the money to establish them in business, and take back chattel mortgages on the saloon fixtures. They thus gain absolute possession of the mortgagor, body and soul, and he follows their directions in politics. . . . Two years ago the brewers in a strong Democratic district determined to send an attorney of theirs, Mr. A. P. Fitch to Congress. They secured the Republican nomination for him. The Democratic barrooms were ordered to support him, and he was elected.[71]

Crosby's overwrought understanding of the brewers' control of voting as well as his understanding of Fitch's nomination was contradicted by the *Sun*. The newspaper pointed out, "for the most important offices . . . connection with the liquor business or the saloon interests in New York . . . is and has always been within recent years, an insurmountable barrier to election. During the twenty years intervening between 1869 and 1889, sixty-two elections have been held in the various districts of the city for state senators to Albany, and . . . no liquor dealer or saloon keeper has in a solitary instance been chosen. . . . During the twenty years a large number of saloon keepers have been candidates, but in no case has one been successful."

The *Sun*'s survey found further that only two members of Congress had any connection to the liquor or beer industries in the prior twelve elections—more than one hundred candidates—one of whom was Fitch, and the Democratic paper concluded that there were other reasons for his election. The article concluded that saloonkeepers generally rivaled each other for business and failed to act in concert, and that voters seemed reluctant to vote for candidates from the liquor or beer industries.

When Low completed his list of issues, Fitch spoke again in support of home rule. His comments both at the Cooper Union "monster meeting" and at the state convention were harbingers of things to come.[72] In spite of his deep Republican roots, Fitch was becoming a dissenter within his own party for home rule and tariff reform.

Regarding home rule, and following another dismal Republican showing at the New York City polls, Fitch addressed a moderate but critical letter (Appendix A) dated November 27, 1887, to state senator Cornelius Van Cott, simultaneously mailing it to every Republican member of the legislature and surely to several newspapers. Since his election the previous fall, Fitch had said very little about New York City, but that would change.

In his letter, Fitch observed that the city's Republican vote had plummeted from "ninety thousand in 1884 to fifty-eight thousand in 1887."[73] "There does not seem to be any reasonable probability of success for the party at the future elections in this state," he said, yet at the same time he provided an eloquent, optimistic, even affectionate portrait of New York.

> All the world has been freely invited to come [to New York City], just as our ancestors came, and people from almost everywhere have accepted the invitation. The German, the Irishman, the Frenchman, Swiss, and Italian have each been gladly received, and each has earned his right to a cordial welcome and a fair chance with the rest of us. . . . There is no story of modern development more striking than that which has taken place, in the last quarter of a century, on the island of Manhattan, and there is nothing in that story so interesting as the manner in which the different elements of this curiously constituted population have grown to respect and like each other and to live and work together.
>
> Any one who may claim that there is in this great population any larger percentage of vice or ignorance than exists anywhere else in the country, is misinformed or is prejudiced. In this city there is as much local patriotism as exists anywhere else in the state.[74]

According to Fitch, New York City's larger problem, larger than vice or ignorance, was Republican abuse. In his view, New York's welfare "ought to be a matter of interest to every citizen of the state" but "it has come to be believed here that the Republican Party cares nothing for the interest or sentiments of the city." More specifically he added, "The large German vote which former candidates of the party received has been entirely turned against us" and then asked why this was so. Answering his own question, he pointed to unfair underrepresentation in the city's delegation at Albany, unfair distribution of the tax burden to the disadvantage of the city, and legislation that aims at improving New York City's morals, like the excise laws.

It seemed that the state legislature's abuse of New York was accompanied by an upstate Republican dislike of foreigners, which found its expression in its hatred of Tammany Hall. To illustrate the point, when Republicans gained control of New York City in 1895, the Republican legislature and the Republican governor came to the aid of the Republican mayor at once.[75] Fitch concluded his letter with a plea to the Republican Party and a promise that "More votes can be got in this city by common fairness than can be got by any combination or by the nomination of any particular candidate."

Reaction to the Fitch letter was immediate if not universal. While Republicans were defensive and Democrats remained silent, several newspapers added their opinion. The *Kingston Leader* acknowledged that "New York has been punished because it has persisted in being Democratic," that Republicans are profiting from their control of the city, and that "the legislature is chiefly composed of men who have no more idea of the needs of a great city like New York then they have of Sanskrit."[76]

The *New York Times* called Fitch's letter "timely" in the sense that it was "high time" someone said it, but in another sense it was "not timely. It comes too late." It went on, "The Republican Party cannot . . . retrace its steps, or free itself from the policy which it has so long pursued. That policy is dictated by the immediate personal interests of the small politicians into whose hands the party has committed itself. They will not abandon it voluntarily."[77]

Eight days after writing his letter to Van Cott, and thirteen months after his election in 1886, on the first Monday in December 1887, Fitch took his seat in the Fiftieth Congress. He had invested more than a year establishing his reputation as an independent Republican, particularly on the major issues of home rule and tariff reform. He wrote Lizzie on his House of Representatives stationery: "The first letter which I write on this paper is of course to you. Any little success which I get I always care for most because it is yours as well as mine." He was happy with his seat "on the front row on the aisle just where I wanted to be."

3

National Prominence, Tariff Speech

Fiftieth Congress, 1886–1888

> The tariff debate in the House yesterday was distinguished by one of the most remarkable speeches delivered since the debate commenced. It was eloquent, logical, liberal, enlightened and original. It was a strong plea in favor of the tariff bill and it was made by Mr. Fitch, the Republican, who represents the district in the northern part of New York City.
>
> —*Washington Post,* May 17, 1888

The next day, December 6, 1887, Grover Cleveland, with no warning and to the astonishment of many, utilized his entire annual message to Congress to focus the nation's attention on the tariff. A full year before the presidential election of 1888, Cleveland initiated an intensive effort to raise the nation's awareness of the cruel inequities of the tariff system. Reitano, in her book *The Tariff Question in the Gilded Age,* titled her first chapter "The Spirit of 1888, Cleveland Defines the Issues."[1] Likewise, Allan Nevins, in a major chapter heading in his epic two-volume biography of Cleveland, called it "The Great Tariff Message of 1887." Said Nevins, "the message was a sweeping arraignment of a tariff system by which protection had been raised to a ridiculous extreme, continued upon many articles long after it was needed, and used as an excuse for viciously unjust burdens upon the poor. The tariff, as Cleveland pointed out, was precisely the system of taxation under which the ill-paid workingman and hard-pressed farmer bore the heaviest burden."[2]

Retired newspaper man David S. Barry made a spirited attempt, in his 1924 reminiscence, *Forty Years in Washington,* to impart the excitement and fervor of nineteenth-century tariff arguments. Said Barry, "In the present day and generation the people of the United States refuse to get excited about a prosaic subject like the tariff; they have been tuned to more sensational topics and fail to get a thrill on anything less exciting than war, or a question that might lead to war. But before the Spanish-American War days a subject like that of the tariff could and did stir the people into a frenzy of political discussion, and it is hardly putting it too strongly to say that the fight between Cleveland and the tariff reform element of the

Democratic party on the one hand and [protectionists] on the other literally set the country on fire."[3]

The tariff, the duty placed on foreign-made goods entering the country, was one of several of the nation's most compelling and most contentious political questions for the same reasons that taxation and globalization are today. Fitch was a rare Republican who campaigned for tariff reform. In fact he believed that his views on the tariff would differentiate his first candidacy in such a way as to win his election, and it did.

The tariff had its roots in the founding of the Republic. Its original purpose was to raise revenue, and the first tariff, enacted in 1789, produced sufficient revenue to launch the fledgling government.[4] Another more contentious purpose of a tariff, however, was to protect American industry, infant or otherwise, from competition—lower-priced imported goods that would lower prices and profits for American manufacturers and might cost jobs. The purpose of a "protective" tariff, as opposed to a "revenue" tariff, is to raise prices on foreign goods in the domestic or "home" market. Higher prices on competing foreign goods consequently were said to "protect" both owners of businesses and the jobs of workers who manufactured domestic goods. At the same time higher prices for protected goods raised the cost of those goods to consumers.

The nation's first protective tariff, which placed duties of 30 to 40 percent on a "protected list" of goods, was enacted in 1816. Henry Clay of the Whig Party, the Republican Party before the late 1850s, was a passionate supporter of protection through high tariffs. Clay's argument provided the basis for the northern imperative—to protect manufacturers by limiting imports and maintaining the domestic pricing structure. Democrat John C. Calhoun debated Clay, arguing for the South that Congress had no constitutional power to subsidize industry and that a protective tariff was a subsidy. High tariffs limiting foreign imports also limited foreigners' capacity to buy American exports. Calhoun's southern position promoted increased exports of cotton and lower prices for domestic consumers.

Seeds of the Civil War were sown in these debates. After the war, Republicans cut tariff duties by 10 percent, in 1872, but restored them in 1875. After they lost control of the House of Representatives in 1882, they appointed themselves the party of the tariff and insisted that tariff reform could not be considered until they were restored to power.

The 1880s tariff was comparable to today's income tax in terms of the percentage of the federal government's revenue it produced. There was no income tax until 1913.[5] The tariff generated about two thirds of the nation's revenue, most of the remainder coming from internal revenue taxes on liquor, beer, and tobacco. Unlike today, there was no federal budget deficit; in fact, there was a bulging surplus that curtailed the amount of money in circulation, lowered the nation's productivity, and limited growth. There emerged therefore, after Cleveland's tariff message, an intense national debate about tariff policy, its purpose, and what goods or industries should be protected. In the heat of political battle the term "free trade" was bandied about, generally by Republicans to describe Democrats who favored tariff reduction. In fact, very few Democrats supported free trade and no tariff.

As a practical matter, the tariff could be even more vexing than its theory. Senator George F. Hoar, Republican of Massachusetts, whose interest in the tariff was piqued by complaints in the Boston customhouse, sponsored a resolution in early 1886 that empowered the Senate Finance Committee to investigate the customhouse, particularly with regard to chronic undervaluations of imported goods. A *New York World* article observed that the subject of "under-valuations" was an old one.[6] The adjustment of values on foreign merchandise was a delicate task. The government employed a large staff of appraisers, and whichever way the values were fixed someone complained. If the invoice value was accepted, domestic manufacturers complained that it was too low; if the invoice value was advanced, the importer "cried out in indignation."

A good illustration of the practical difficulties of levying a fair tariff was found in acting Port of New York collector E. L. Hedden's[7] ruling on a complex case before him.[8] A New York firm imported a large shipment of silks that the firm claimed to have bought as subdivided lots, at prices averaging about half the cost of such goods sold in the regular way. The examiner saw nothing in the outward appearance of the samples to indicate that the goods were any less valuable than the goods behind hundreds of invoices entered at nearly twice the cost of this particular lot. He was convinced that the dutiable values should be sharply increased.

The importers disagreed and demanded a reappraisal. They proved that the label tags and piece wraps were defaced, as though they were shopworn. Shopworn goods often could not enter the commercial trade until they had been through the hands of a repacker, if not a redyer. Consequently, there was ample commercial justification for a lower price. One expert said that he would have given the purchaser only 25 percent, not 50 percent, for his bargain. The merchant appraiser, arguing for an increase, and fearful of the potential market impact of goods dumped at half price on a thin market, demanded a rate of duty that would measurably protect the men who bought their silks at higher prices.

The general appraiser, upon reappraisement, found a dozen men willing to swear that they could buy the goods abroad at the low invoice price. Collector Hedden finally agreed and barely increased the goods five centimes per ounce, or about 1½ percent ad valorem or "to the value." In just this manner, government appraisers, each exercising their best judgment and whatever political or other bias they had, carried out the administration of the tariff schedules with respect to thousands of items across the country. This was the tariff "system" that America relied upon for two-thirds of its revenue.

While not technically a tax, the tariff surely amounted to the most regressive tax in the nation's history[9] measured by its size, its significance in funding government expenditures, its pervasiveness, its effect on the cost of the necessities of life, and its impact on ordinary Americans. The tariff produced unneeded revenue that in turn created a large and growing government surplus. The surplus, by reducing the money supply, added to financial pressures on strapped citizens everywhere. And it had a greater impact on urban than on rural voters because rural voters, who produced much of what they consumed, generally paid less tariff than urban voters, who produced next to nothing. To a friendly critic, trying to persuade Cleveland to be cautious and to avoid arguing the tariff directly, Cleveland said, "What's the use of being elected or reelected, unless you stand for something?"[10]

Never before had an entire annual presidential message been devoted to a single issue. Cleveland spoke of crippling economic injury that the expanding budget surplus would do if it were left unchecked and to the tariff as the cause of the surplus. He rejected suggestions to reduce internal revenue taxes, and he refused, as some had suggested, to limit his attack exclusively to tariffs on luxury goods. Lowering the tariff on luxury goods paid by the well-to-do would only increase the tax burden for average citizens. "It was the tariff on necessities which he attacked."[11]

Grover Cleveland's courageous campaign to modify the tariff helped lay the groundwork for the nation's turn from regressive to progressive taxation during the next several decades. In that sense, and in some others, civil service for example, Cleveland and his supporters were forerunners of modern American liberalism. Republicans across the country took heart. Cleveland was popular. Before he delivered his tariff message he was hard to attack. His tariff message provided his opponents with an opening, a core issue to fight about, and they responded with relish.

The tariff had been the cornerstone of American economic policy since the nation's beginning. In some quarters, Cleveland's attack was seen as un-American. James G. Blaine, the 1884 Republican presidential nominee, in an interview with a *Tribune* correspondent that was telegraphed to America from Paris, called Cleveland's message a "free trade manifesto."[12] Blaine's way of dealing with the surplus was to maintain high tariffs and to eliminate the tax on tobacco. Of the seminal issues that were to dominate Congress in the next several years, a few of which set America's course for decades, the tariff was the first of these to engage Fitch. It was seen to be odd, and in some quarters traitorous, for Fitch, a Republican, to appear to agree with the Democrat Cleveland, yet Fitch would soon gain a national reputation for his principled position.

The *Boston Globe,* in January 1888, in a long article that led with "Their Maiden Efforts" said this:

> Many new members of the House of Representatives are beginning to attract public attention. . . . One of these men has a face peculiarly pleasing. He sits on the front row of seats on the left of the Speaker. He has regular features, full blue eyes, and a forehead that reaches to the nape of his neck. He wears the stiffest of choker collars and dresses in exquisite taste. His full face is trimmed with a trim brown beard and a Germanic mustache beats time to the music of his voice. No client ever watched his lawyer more earnestly than this gentleman watches the business of the House. Whether in his seat or meandering behind the low screens at the back of the hall, his ears are always open, and he never seems to lose the thread of legislation.
>
> This man is Honorable Ashbel P. Fitch, the Republican congressman from New York City, who overcame a sixty-five hundred Democratic majority at the late election. He likes fun but he loses much of it in the House by going to New York once a week to attend to his law business. He is probably the only Republican representative between Passamaquoddy Bay and Key Biscayne who favors the president's tariff reform message.[13]

Fitch attracted attention. His letter to New York Republicans put them on notice before the tariff debate began. The *New York Times* wrote that he had "a habit of thinking for himself,"[14] which in some political quarters might mean that he was vulnerable to being abandoned by the Republicans at the next election. The first speculation that Fitch might leave his seat in the House to run for mayor of New York was caused by the imminence of the 1888 election as well as by his seemingly precarious position as the lone Republican in the city's House delegation from a Democratic district. "Fitch for Mayor" boomlets would pop up intermittently for years to come but for reasons that would become increasingly apparent with the passage of time he was never interested in becoming mayor of New York.

In Washington, he made friends with Democrats, sitting as a member of "a Sub-Committee on National Defense and Armament" and listening to Democratic "Representatives Charles Tracey and Edward Greenman of New York . . . on the subject of establishing a plant and building guns at Watervliet, New York."[15] Tracey, who had been with then governor Cleveland in Albany, soon emerged as one of Fitch's closest confidants and an ally in future silver coinage debates.

Republican newspapers attacked him. The *Albany Express* reported that he "was the only free trader . . . in the east who did not [in 1884] make his escape from the Republican Party boiling over with righteous indignation at its moral decadence" and that "His failure to escape at the proper moment has soured him . . . he has become a nuisance."[16] The commentaries were a prelude to the great tariff debate of May 1888, which might determine the winner of the next presidential election. The debate would center on the Mills Bill, named for Texas representative Roger Q. Mills, chairman of the House Ways and Means Committee, which was responsible for originating tax legislation.

Mills, one of many former Confederate soldiers in Congress, was in his mid-fifties in 1888, and in his eighth consecutive term. A homespun Texan, he had made himself an expert on the tariff—how it damaged southern exports by limiting imports and how it carelessly burdened average to poor Americans who were forced to pay it. The bill he crafted with Cleveland's Treasury secretary, John G. Carlisle, was originally intended to reflect Cleveland's tariff message. But it was criticized for favoring the South,[17] and its rate reductions, averaging about 7 to 8 percent, were modest. The raging debate and the national attention it garnered, however, were far from modest. One Republican congressman said, "If Mills of Texas does not shut up, most of the other mills of the country will have to."[18]

From 1872, when Congress rescinded the income tax that paid for the Civil War, until 1913, when Congress again passed a progressive[19] income tax, a war raged, and it continues today, about who would pay for America. The Mills Bill debate was a major episode in that intricate, drawn-out contest during which arguments on both sides were refined and public understanding of a complex issue was enhanced.

Fitch found the cornerstone of his arguments for tariff reform in past Republican platforms. Both Republican presidents James Garfield and Chester Arthur had been sympathetic to tariff reduction, although they were pulled in the other direction by powerful Republican protectionists. Nevertheless, Fitch insisted that past Republican platforms had pledged tariff reform. Some Republicans, adamantly opposed to tariff reform, argued that the way to reduce the federal surplus was to reduce revenue taxes on tobacco and alcohol. The distinction Fitch drew between the two, tariff and revenue taxes, was that revenue taxes were paid by those who chose to smoke tobacco or drink liquor or beer, while the tariff was forced upon all citizens who needed to pay for the necessities of life.[20] He believed that the tariff was a discriminatory tax on his "unprotected" constituents and that the surplus would ruin the nation's economy. As Winston Churchill would say many years later, "for a nation to try to tax itself into prosperity is like a man standing in a bucket and trying to lift himself up by the handle."

The Mills Bill debate began on April 17, 1888. Congressman William L. Wilson, Democrat of West Virginia, was one of the first to speak. Wilson, a bookish former college professor, had made himself a serious student of tariff legislation and a passionate advocate of tariff reform. His learned, brilliant speech on the House floor in May 1888[21] rested on the immutable proposition that "The great rule that those who pay taxes, and they alone, should impose taxes" was a "test of free government," and it was being tragically violated by the existing tariff laws. In Wilson's view, private interests that controlled tariff legislation were overriding the public interest. In describing the distressing effect of the tariff, Wilson declared, "In this manner, sir, we have seen the pressure of taxation in this country removed from its income, removed from its property, removed from its luxuries, and fastened upon those articles of general consumption that meet the primary wants of all the people."

Wilson linked the tariff to the powerful and sometimes violent movement to organize labor, because tariff protection, which was supposed to enable business owners to "protect" labor through higher wages, failed to do so. He pointed to "the growing antagonism between labor and capital that has marked the recent history of our country, unsatisfactory relations between employers and the employed, long industrial depressions, twenty and odd thousand strikes, and twenty and odd hundred lockouts in our industrial establishments during the past six years alone."

He also linked the emerging domination of the business trusts to the tariff by asserting that "the law steps in and confers special privileges on certain parties whereby they may dictate or largely dictate their own terms to consumers. . . . The government says to the protected industries, 'I will add 47 percent to the value of all articles made abroad and thus shield you against competition from without' and the protected industries are now saying 'let us combine to shield ourselves against all competition from within'" too. It was a powerful speech, set against a sweeping historical backdrop of labor unrest and laced with relevant, current statistics.

As interest in the tariff debate rose, eastern newspapers sensed Fitch's importance as the only elected Republican representative of New York City who appeared to be sympathetic to the Democratic position on tariff reform. Since his election to the Fiftieth Congress in November 1886, Fitch had established himself as an independent voice on the left wing of the Republican Party, particularly regarding home rule, which was of peculiar interest to New Yorkers, and tariff reform, which interested all Americans. Tariff reform was a consuming political issue wherein the interest of his constituency contradicted the politics of his party. Tariff defenders and reformers alike began attacking or defending him, although no one was sure what he was going to say.

His moment arrived on May 16, 1888;[22] he was "the first tariff speaker of the session from the metropolis and the first Republican to come out boldly for tariff reform."[23] It was the surprising spectacle of a wealthy New York lawyer boldly standing up for the fair treatment of ordinary Americans that caught the nation's attention. He spoke in plain language that was easily understood by the man in the street. He mixed politics with logic and moral outrage. Contrary to custom, he was uninterrupted, either by Republicans who were still hoping he would support the Republican position and so avoided antagonizing him, or by Democrats who enjoyed his attack on the new Republican dogma. He openly assailed the Republican Party with cutting irony that, while common in nineteenth-century debates, was seldom directed at members of one's own party (see appendix B).

He referred to Representative Richard Guenther, Republican of Wisconsin, for example, as "the guardian of the American infant." Guenther had proposed "a duty of four cents per dozen on the 14 million dozens of eggs which are now imported free of duty, and which we in New York eat and are obliged to pay for in order to protect the American hen and her rural owner against the combined poultry of Europe." Putting his evident sarcasm aside, though, his comments were firmly grounded on past Republican platforms that promised tariff reform and on the words of the last two Republican presidents, James Garfield and Chester Arthur, which did likewise.

He attacked the anti–New York xenophobia that he routinely encountered in House debates—and this debate was no exception. Representative Charles O'Neill, Republican of Pennsylvania, speaking in opposition to the bill, had said that "New York is in large measure a foreign city." Answering O'Neill's slight, Fitch allowed that it was "true of course that New York has many foreign-born citizens, and among them are a large number [of O'Neills]. All of us in this country are foreign-born or are descendants of European immigrants. Whoever speaks deprecatingly of the patriotism of the citizens who come to this country by choice and not by accident throw thereby a doubt on the integrity of that ancestor of his who first took the oath of allegiance to the United States."

He defined his constituents in plain language. He listed them as "architects, artists, clergymen, clerks in banks, insurance and law offices, journalists, musicians, lawyers, physicians, teachers, bookkeepers, railroad employees, drivers, conductors, policemen, firemen, telegraph and telephone operators, salesmen, mechanical engineers, civil engineers, stenographers, printers and skilled mechanics of all sorts not employed in industries which have protection under the present tariff."

"In [my] district lives, too," he said, "an army of deserving women who earn their living by unprotected labor, and often that of others dependent upon them. Somebody should say a word for these people." He used firemen and letter carriers as examples of unprotected workers who were not overpaid. "The money," he said, "which they draw at the end of every month is not more than they need and they are often sorely pinched to buy even the taxed doll to fill the taxed Christmas stocking or to pay for the taxed medicine necessary for any member of the family."

He paused to ask his Republican friends in the House to consider how the present tariff affected the people he described and then answered his own question. "They pay upon everything," he said. "Look for a moment at what they eat. There is a tariff duty on beef, on pork, hams and bacon, butter and lard, cheese, molasses, grapes, wheat flour, oats, corn meal, rye, barley, potatoes, raisins, vinegar, honey, rice and rice meal, sugar, extract of meat, pickles, currants, apples, salt, and condensed milk. The list is substantially an inventory of the stock of the grocery store at which they buy. There is a duty on the coal which warms them, on their cooking and household utensils, on their entire clothing from their hats to their stockings, on the medicine given them when they are sick, and on the roofs over their heads."

Twisting the knife for emphasis, he rhetorically posed the question, "Is it unreasonable to ask that a tariff which puts jewelry at 25 percent and oil cloth for tenement-house floors at 40 percent ad valorem; which brings in silver-plated harness at 35 percent and children's cotton stockings at 40 percent; under which India shawls of the finest quality pay 40 percent and common woolen shawls 86 percent should be modified?"

He attacked the "endless" stream of objections to lowered tariffs from farmers, wool growers, manufacturers, mine owners, and planters. "They seem to think that they are to have a monopoly of objections." Frustrated, he exclaimed, "Well, for one, I, for my district of consumers, object to this chorus of objection. We do not own sheep; we can not raise rice or vegetables or sugar; we mine no coal in the Thirteenth District of New York."

He acknowledged that the Mills Bill was not ideal. He said that he would offer amendments to it, adding that if the Republicans would offer the tariff reform bill they promised, he would support that instead. He avoided for the moment any promise that he would vote for the Mills Bill, not wanting to remove himself from the contest when he most wanted to be relevant, perhaps to help move the party in his own direction, and to enhance the prospects for his amendments.

Reaching a pinnacle of outrage he concluded, "There is something better than Republicanism or Democracy, and that is common honesty . . . if I am asked to oppose this bill, not so much on account of its contents as on account of its history [that is, Democrats originated the bill], I must decline to do so, even if I stand alone on this side of the House." At this point and on this issue, Fitch had in effect declared himself a Cleveland Democrat. It remained to be seen whether it was an aberration or a conversion.

Reactions to his speech were immediate, widespread, and in a few instances dramatic. The *New York Herald* led with "Mr. Fitch Makes a Sensation—Although a Republican He Declares Emphatically for Tariff Reform."[24] The *New York Times* sub-headline read "Mr. Fitch Tells What New York Wants."[25] The *New York Evening Telegram* called it "the most convincing and consistent [speech] heard yet."[26] Republican papers such as the *New York Mail and Express*[27] and the *New York Tribune* were restrained in their complaints, the former castigating Fitch only for straying from the Republican Party line, not for his reasoning. The latter's reportage was so muted as to appear complimentary. "The speech of Mr. Fitch of New York," opined the newspaper, "was a rather ingenious plea in behalf of the people of his district, who, he stated, are engaged in avocations in which they derive no benefit from the protective system, but are taxed to support it. He indicated his purpose to vote for the Mills Bill if nothing better is offered, although he declared that the bill is imperfect and needs much amendment. He also declared that he favors the continuance of the protective policy."[28]

Editorial comment echoed beyond New York and across the country. The *Lancaster Intelligencer* called it "the most sensible speech that has been made."[29] The *Jacksonville Times-Mirror* reported, "Mr. Fitch has proved himself possessed of sufficient nerve to boldly array himself against the present policy of his party."[30] The *Galveston News* said that Fitch "recently delivered a speech of much vigor and striking pertinence in favor of the Mills Bill."[31] The *Washington Post* wrote, "The tariff debate in the House yesterday was distinguished by one of the most remarkable speeches delivered since the debate commenced. It was eloquent, logical, liberal, enlightened and original. It was a strong plea in favor of the tariff bill and it was made by Mr. Fitch, the Republican who represents the district in the northern part of New York City."[32]

Within a week he received "over six hundred letters and despatches" in response to his speech.[33] The Reform Club of New York wanted "fifty thousand copies of your speech at their expense."[34] The *Nation,* an independent weekly published in New York, intoned that "Mr. Fitch, by thoroughly exposing the [Republican] dog-in-the-manger policy has made a national reputation by so doing."[35]

What may have pleased Fitch most was an *Albany Argus* editorial under the headline "A Blow Vigorously Dealt."[36] The *Argus,* controlled by Daniel Manning, Cleveland's first secretary of the Treasury, declared Fitch to be fearless of the party lash, then pronouncing, "Mr. Fitch measures up to heroic proportions" when he said that if asked to oppose the bill he would "decline to do so even if I stand alone on this side of the House."

While lacking the amplitude of other notable messages, such as Mills's or Wilson's, Fitch's speech had an impact on public opinion that few others had because of who he was and how he spoke. He was a Republican from the wealthiest congressional district in America, and he argued for lower taxes on working people and lower taxes on life's necessities. His argument was plainspoken, rooted in fundamental fairness. He listed the kinds of people who were hurt by the tariff, and it turned out they were every man and, remarkably, every woman. He listed the taxed items, drawing sympathy to his constituents, who were "often sorely pinched to buy even the taxed doll to fill the taxed Christmas stocking." This was a speech that was easily grasped by ordinary Americans, coming from a man and a place from which it was least expected. To those who thought he was a traitor to his party, Fitch's response was, "You have to use your head . . . even in Congress."[37]

The *New York Times* said that Fitch's rousing speech "attracted national attention" and that "some hundreds of thousands of copies were circulated by the Reform Club of New York." Continuing, the *Times* said, "In the two presidential campaigns which followed, Mr. Fitch's speech was reprinted in German and in English by the Democratic National Committee and more than one million copies were distributed."[38]

In fewer than eight months Ashbel Fitch had made his name at home and across the nation by taking two strong stands against his own party and for his city, one for home rule in his State, and the other for tariff reform. No one knew just what it would mean, but it would not be long before Republican intolerance of foreigners, of New Yorkers, or even of respectful dissent within their own party would be directed toward Ashbel Fitch.

He was at once the outspoken Republican darling of Democrats, and either a puzzle or a pariah to his fellow Republicans. Some were bitter. The *Brooklyn Eagle* said that he was "to be burned in effigy."[39] The *Chicago Journal* declared that he had "betrayed and violated"[40] Republican sentiment and set a "scandalous example." The *Burlington Free Press* said that Fitch had "recently acquired some little cheap notoriety."[41] The *New York Tribune*[42] called him "adrift." The *Troy Times*[43] asked for his resignation. The *Troy Press* pointed to "radical divisions in the Republican ranks upon the tariff question."[44]

Seldom in American history was party loyalty paid more homage or were political parties so fragmented. Most Republicans favored the protective tariff. But they disagreed on how to reduce the dangerously large, burgeoning surplus, two-thirds of which was generated by the tariff. A very few such as Fitch favored tariff reform and reduction, while most others preferred reductions in internal revenue taxes, either on cigarettes (Blaine) or on whiskey and beer (Depew). Republicans backing a reduction in whiskey taxes were opposed by temperance voters who were also mostly Republicans. The *Omaha Herald* snickered, "Congressman Ashbel P. Fitch has not left the party but the party has left him. He stands on the platform of 1884, while the party now straddles a whiskey barrel."[45]

The Harlem Republican Club knew exactly where it stood. Within a few days it held a special meeting "to determine what should be done" about their congressman. The club's members were inveterate protectionists who would quash reformers in their midst. Several members were hostile and wanted to censure Fitch personally, but moderates prevailed. The club adopted three resolutions that (1) were protectionist; (2) were anti–Mills Bill sentiments, calling it a "free trade measure"; and (3) "earnestly requested our representative in Congress to use his influence and vote against the passage of [the Mills] bill."[46]

The debate that opened in the House in mid-April closed by mutual consent on May 19, but the vote on the Mills Bill was not scheduled until July of 1888. The *Philadelphia Times* told its readers that after carrying the speeches of Speaker John G. Carlisle and congressman and future president William McKinley "the paper would reprint Mr. Randall's Democratic high tariff speech against the Mills Bill and Mr. Fitch's Republican tariff speech supporting it, [each] independent utterances at variance with the policy of their respective parties."[47] Newspaper advertisements appeared for copies of the printed tariff speeches of Carlisle, McKinley, Thomas B. Reed of Maine, Fitch, and William C. Breckenridge of Kentucky. Fitch was subjected to daily persuasion by Senator Matthew S. Quay of Pennsylvania, a Republican organizer and peerless fund-raiser. Some observers anticipated a close vote.

While attention was directed toward the independent Republican congressman, the *Albany Journal* reported an interesting letter to the editor from a North Country reader, Fitch's Republican cousin Morton Parmelee. Parmelee began with a plea to the paper, "Will you please allow me in all courtesy to say a word in response to your short and sharp editorial devoted to Congressman Fitch's position on the tariff question?" Parmelee pleaded for upstate Republican understanding of his wayward big city cousin. He wrote, "Mr. Fitch is as good a Republican, by inheritance and instinct and choice, as ever sat in your editorial chair. . . . Do we not want at least one Republican congressman from New York City?"[48] Morton Parmelee's thoughtful, serious plea for less partisanship fell on deaf ears.

Two weeks after Fitch delivered his tariff speech in Congress, an eager reporter from the *New York World,* hoping to cause a stir, found Fitch at the Terrace Garden[49] on Fifty-eighth Street and must have been disappointed by the patient and restrained Ashbel Fitch whom he found there. In a reasoned, tolerant statement, Fitch complimented the Harlem Republican Club on the "courtesy of their tone," explaining that he didn't expect that his friends would always agree with him on every issue. He stood firm on the doctrines that Republican presidents Garfield and Arthur had "maintained and defended." But, he said, "I consider the question [of tariff reform] to be a business one, beyond the control of any party, and having been elected aside from party lines in a district very strongly Democratic by businessmen's support, I shall treat this question from that and not from a party standpoint."[50] At that point the matter might have been dropped, but it was not.

A week later, the West Side Republican Club also held a heated meeting to draft another set of resolutions to rebuke their congressman. Fitch's defenders argued that he "has always been a Republican [and] the club ought [not] now to jump upon him and consequently drive him and his large German following into the Democratic Party."[51] Coincidentally, the *New York Sun* reminded voters that "New York City will choose its eight members of Congress in November 1888." There is, the paper observed, "no opposition to the return of any members of the present delegation except Ashbel P. Fitch, the free trade Republican."[52] Some newspapers thought he was vulnerable.

A week before Congress was scheduled to vote on the Mills Bill, Charles Dayton visited President Cleveland in Washington. Dayton, a Brooklyn-born lawyer, graduated from Columbia Law School the year before Fitch graduated and was elected to the New York Assembly in 1881. Along with several other young men, including Daniel Lamont, Cleveland's private secretary and secretary of war in the second Cleveland administration, and Congressman Charles Tracey, Dayton worked with Cleveland in Albany when Cleveland was governor of New York. In 1882 the lifelong Democrat Dayton joined the citizen's movement against Tammany Hall and helped organize the Harlem Democratic Club. Since his call on Fitch of nearly two years before, Dayton and Fitch had become friends and political allies.

In the summer of 1888, Dayton, still president of the Harlem Democratic Club, sat down with Cleveland. He may have mentioned to the president the Republican congressman from New York who was for tariff reform and with whom he (Dayton) by then had a warm relationship. Afterwards Dayton and Fitch met for an hour with Treasury Secretary Fairchild. That evening, Fitch hosted a dinner for Dayton at Chamberlin's.[53] It was for him a typically eclectic group that included Lamont; Henry Watterson, the irascible owner of the *Louisville Courier-Journal* and aggressive tariff reformer; Democratic congressman Charles Tracey; Roger Mills; "Sunset" Cox, the twelve-term member from New York; and the legendary Thomas Reed of Maine, the Republican Speaker of the House. In that gathering Reed was no doubt the sole defender of Republican protectionism, and he surely held his own with ease. The *Sun* posed the question, "What's in the wind?"[54]

Fitch resigned from the Harlem Republican Club that day, prompted he said, by two more club resolutions, the first calling for the abolition of all internal revenue taxes and a total reliance on the tariff for government revenue. The second described the Mills Bill as a "free trade measure" and said that "its passage would be destructive to the industrial interest of the country." In his typically moderate and even lighthearted resignation, Fitch held that the repeal of the whiskey tax "would increase its consumption enormously," and that a tariff reduction of 7 percent as provided in the Mills Bill should not cause anyone to fear the "destruction of the industrial interest of the country."[55]

After two months of negotiating amendments, the eagerly awaited vote on the Mills Bill was scheduled for July 21 at 11:30 A.M. It followed a vote on a protectionist motion to remove wool from the "free list" that was defeated 122 to 93, a sign that the reformers had the advantage and that the vote on the Mills Bill might not be as close as many had predicted. By 11:00 the galleries were filled. President Cleveland's striking young bride of two years was there with her mother, eager to report back to the president. Representatives of the British Embassy and other foreign legations were there "ready to pounce upon the richest market in the world if free traders succeeded in their schemes. The other galleries were packed almost to suffocation and hundreds of persons were unable to gain admission."[56]

Tension mounted as Mills methodically laid out his case. At 1:18 P.M. the voting began. When Democratic Congressman Bliss of New York voted against the bill there were "rounds of Republican cheers . . . when the name of Mr. Fitch was called . . . the Democrats howled with delight."[57] The final tally was 162 to 149 in favor, registered amid a chorus of cheers and backslapping on the Democratic side. A great victory for tariff reform was then left to languish in the Republican-controlled Senate and never became law. The Mills Bill would have left the tariff "at upward of 40%, [still] higher than any tariff this country had before the Civil War."[58] Nonetheless, the taxation issue that Cleveland had brought to the fore, so critical to the nation's economic well-being, was framed by the exhaustive, extraordinary House debate on the Mills Bill and would be put before the country again in the upcoming presidential contest.

With just a few months remaining before the election, Fitch's political future remained unclear. His rumored mayoral candidacy, which was based on assumptions that Republicans would turn him out of his House seat as a consequence of his tariff heresy, had been discussed for months. What was not well understood was that although he was a Republican, his district was heavily Democratic. By definition he was elected by Democrats, and he had little to fear from Republicans.

His supporters included a large number of German Democrats, led by the wealthy German brewers. Throughout the years Fitch developed an influential and loyal following among immigrant Germans. German-Americans were more often than not reluctant to run for office. It was well known that they voted independently[59] and were less likely to be swayed by party labels than were other immigrant groups. While many Germans had followed Lincoln's Republicans into the Civil War in the 1860s, in succeeding years they joined more recent German immigrants who were uncomfortable in a xenophobic Republican Party wherein some elements preached temperance. Beer drinking was an integral part of German culture.

German-Americans were connected to Fitch by nearly twenty years of experience, loyalty, and trust. If the brewers trusted Fitch to negotiate financial transactions between them and to speak publicly on their behalf, and they did, they could certainly find no better candidate to represent their interests in Washington. He was one of them. The fact that he was a Republican meant little to these independent-minded Germans, even though many of them were more comfortable in the Democratic Party. Were Fitch a Democrat, so much the better.

In late July, the presidential yacht *Susquehanna,* returning from a fishing trip in New England with Cleveland on board, anchored off Fire Island, where the Fitch family was vacationing. There were rumors[60] that Fitch had gone on board to visit with the president, although Fitch denied it, calling it "a wicked invention of the enemy."[61] A day later, the Republican *New York Press* reported that "Republicans of the Thirteenth are after Mr. Fitch's scalp."[62]

Four days later, the Harlem Democratic Club, sensing an opportunity to gain a convert, allowed that the Republican "Ashbel P. Fitch is entitled to the admiration and respect of his constituency."[63] As the Democrats were paying homage to the Republican maverick, campaign literature was accumulating at Democratic Party headquarters. The *New York Tribune* said, "The number of documents, including Cleveland's messages, R. Q. Mills tariff orations and Ashbel P. Fitch's speech which have been sent out since Monday, is stated at one million of which 500,000 were for distribution in the state."[64]

In the midst of rumors and speculation, Fitch resigned from the Republican Party on August 13, 1888. Two months before, he told the *New York World,* "if the party desires to get rid of [me] there is always a way. If I go of my own free will, however, I shall not leave like a thief in the night, but with a band of music and a torch light procession."[65] It was a stunning development that drew national attention, as it would today. In his letter to Donald MacLean, the new president of the Republican Twenty-third Assembly District, Fitch laid out again his well-publicized views on the tariff before elevating the tenor of his discourse well beyond his belief in tariff reform to his core beliefs as an American citizen. He wrote,

> The Republican Party leaders have determined to make a campaign in which the expression of views . . . shall be described as "free trade attacks upon American industry," and those who hold them shall be credited with a burning desire to aid the British workingmen, whom they have never seen, as against their own friends and countrymen. Mr. Blaine's keynote for the campaign, applied to our District, is that we are from now till November to accuse the Democratic and revenue-reform businessmen in Harlem, who in private life, are in partnership with us in all commercial, charitable, social and religious affairs, of being engaged in a conspiracy, inspired by England, to ruin their own country and degrade their fellow citizens. I have no desire to take part in such a campaign. . . . I very much prefer, if necessary, to be in a minority for the rest of my life rather than to make a successful campaign on what seems to me to be ridiculous and unfounded misrepresentation of the efforts and motives of my neighbors.[66]

Although he would have preferred a different ending, he could not have been discouraged. The nation's newspapers, from San Francisco to Portsmouth, Kansas City to Chicago, and all points in between, carried the news of his resignation. Politicians seldom change parties. Most newspapers treated it as a noble gesture of a principled politician, but some called him a traitor. One newspaper, commenting on his "lonesomeness" said, "there was no other pervert to furnish similar Democratic material."[67] Theodore Roosevelt on his way home from his Dakota ranch called Fitch a "traitor."[68]

On the other side, one southern newspaper referred to Fitch as "the hero of the hour,"[69] and yet another noted that he "has not left the party, but the party has left him."[70] That was the crucial point. Fitch's 1888 views on the tariff were consistent with earlier Republican platforms, of 1880 or 1884. The 1888 platform reversed course on tariff reform. Some newspapers, the *Utica Observer* for one, linked Fitch to Seth Low, who had also recently left the Republicans, by commenting, "The secession from the Republican Party of men of intelligence like Seth Low and Congressman Fitch cannot be neutralized by smears in Republican organs. Though as late as last fall Mr. Low was elected Chairman of the Republican state convention at Saratoga, yet he is now condemned as a 'free trader' and an exponent of 'Sunday school politics.' Similar treatment is doubtless in store for Mr. Fitch."[71]

Fitch and his family left Fire Island in August for his Adirondack retreat. The wilderness property that he had acquired two years before, the rugged outdoor fishing camp for men only, had become a snug new family cottage, a shingled two-story building with a center chimney. Before he was finished, the original building would be flanked by two others of comparable size, all connected by a single porch more than 150 feet long. A fourth building housed a kitchen and servants' quarters. And there was a woodshed, icehouse, boathouse, and lakeside tennis court. During the next twenty years his original thirteen acres would grow to more than two thousand.

Fitch's next few weeks were spent with his family, surveying their new wilderness home. They ate dinner when it was too dark to cast a fly. Evenings were spent around a blazing fire in front of an open camp telling stories or singing songs. One can only imagine his mood, possibly one of contentment with his family's new camp, probably not of regret for his principled stand, possibly of relief for his decision to leave the Republican Party, and surely of some apprehension for the political turmoil that he knew lay ahead.

While Fitch relaxed in the Adirondacks, the *New York Times* commented editorially on his resignation. Said the *Times,* "No wonder that Mr. Fitch is unwilling to take part in a campaign based upon 'such ridiculous and unfounded misrepresentations of the efforts and motives' of honest and patriotic citizens. The

6. Fitch family at Ragged Lake. August 1892. *Clockwise:* Morton standing at left, then (seated) Bessie, Ella, Ashbel Jr., Lizzie, and Littleton. Ashbel Fitch standing at right. Photographer unknown. Photograph from the Ashbel P. Fitch archives.

defection from his party of such a man is a most significant incident. He is forced, in order to adhere to his opinions and be faithful to his convictions—in order to be consistent in his record and true to himself—to leave a party that has abandoned its own ground, that has announced a new doctrine upon the most important issue before the country, and that has entered upon a campaign of misrepresentations and false pretense."[72]

Fitch turned abruptly from Republican to Democrat, but his controversial tariff reform speech was not the only reason for his conversion. His education and immersion in German culture and politics, which embraced personal freedom and political independence, formed a solid liberal foundation for his personal comfort in the Democratic Party. Republican temperance, xenophobia, arrogance, and insensitivity toward people and habits he valued made him uncomfortable. His tariff views and his strong conservative opposition to silver coinage were perfectly aligned with the Democratic president. And he was finding common political ground and becoming fast friends with Charles Dayton, Charles Tracey, and Daniel Lamont, the young members of Cleveland's coterie. While tariff reform was the immediate cause of his conversion, it was hardly the only one.

Gaining the acceptance of his new fellow Democrats would be a challenge for Ashbel Fitch. Political parties, suspicious of converts, tend to wonder whether their new friend can be relied upon. For the same reason the rejected party will never forget the snub, always regarding the convert as a traitor. It would take years, but Fitch would learn painfully that he was no exception on either count. The *New York Times* in mid-September reported that "Mr. Fitch will probably have to stay at home though this is not certain. He has a large personal following in Harlem, and may run, whether any of the great political organizations nominate him or not."[73]

While he was unwinding in the Adirondacks, reflecting on the swirl of recent events, it was all politics in New York. The *Chicago Times* said, "Four hundred thousand documents were sent out. . . . The speeches of Mills, Carlisle and Ashbel P. Fitch were in greatest demand."[74] In "Spirit Lake, Iowa—speeches of Fitch and Mills are in greatest demand; Hartford, Connecticut—President's message and speeches of Fitch, Carlisle and Mills we find very effective; Philadelphia, Pennsylvania—we want more copies of Fitch's tariff speech which takes well here."[75]

Returning from the Adirondacks, Fitch began laying the groundwork for his political future as a Democrat. He resumed his verbal joust with the Harlem Republican Club in order to set the public record straight on "free trade." Said he, "I am not in favor of free trade . . . the Mills Bill is not a free trade measure; that my vote for it was a vote in the direction of higher wages, more steady employment, and more comfortable living for the working men and women in our city."[76]

Democrats running for office in New York City in 1888 were nominated by the County Democracy, essentially Cleveland Democrats, Tammany Hall, or both (called "fusion" candidates).[77] The anti-Tammany County Democracy, established in 1881, was founded by such swallow-tail Democrats as Abram Hewitt, industrialist, former congressman, and mayor of New York, and William C. Whitney, former New York City corporation counsel, secretary of the navy, urban transit entrepreneur, and political operative. It is worth noting that Whitney in 1875, was Tammany's candidate for corporation counsel and following his victory, as noted by law professor and author William E. Nelson in *Fighting for the City,* "he built the law department. And, by creating a bureaucratic entity [the law department] capable of resisting parochial political pressures, Whitney helped give New York City the liberal, cosmopolitan and European style that it possesses today."[78]

Charles Dayton was a County Democrat. These Democrats, including Whitney, had by then left Tammany Hall and were working hard to defeat it. One can only wonder if Fitch's efforts to seek Tammany's support caused consternation among the County Democracy. While it may have, the County Democracy had battled

Tammany for seven years with no success, and their prospects were not improving. For Fitch to continue in elective politics as a Democrat with any hope of success would require some rapprochement with Tammany Hall.

From May until November of 1888, only five months, Fitch engineered his transformation from an outspoken, principled Republican to an outspoken, principled Democrat, comfortable both personally and politically with his new party. At the same time he had dramatically expanded his political horizons because in 1888, notwithstanding German or brewer backing, there was a limited political future for a Republican in New York City.

Thomas F. Gilroy,[79] the Irish-born Tammany sachem and future mayor of New York, proposed Fitch for membership in the Harlem Democratic Club, and when the time came, Gilroy, along with state senator Jacob Cantor, escorted him to the club. When it was his turn to speak, Fitch "thanked the convention for its endorsement of his official life. He said that he had always endeavored to perform his duties in the interest of the greatest number of people, *without regard to party affiliation,* and [he] gave them his assurances that if elected he should continue to pursue the same policy" (emphasis added),[80] which was just about what he always told Republicans.

Fitch's tariff speech, his renouncement of the Republican Party and his exodus, his unwavering support from the brewers, and his proven ability as a campaigner not surprisingly overcame Tammany pride, but not without hesitation. Seen through Tammany eyes, he was a Republican lawyer who had drawn voters away from Tammany in the latest election. Now that the Republicans were rid of him, Tammany members would want to nominate one of their own. They failed because the German brewers were important financial sponsors of both Fitch and Tammany.

The brewers were not corrupt, but they lived in a new country in which they were made welcome by Tammany, not by Republicans. Upstate Republicans, many of them pro-temperance, would put them out of business if they were able to stop, or at least interrupt, the flow of their Sunday beer. Tammany ran New York, and the city worked. Who would the brewers support if they didn't support Tammany? Many Germans, it was true, were Cleveland or County Democrats. But new citizens of New York City, especially those with payrolls to meet, just like businessmen today who support both parties, supported Tammany because Tammany's opponents were irrelevant.

Expressing its uncertainty about Fitch's future, the *New York Times* said, "In the Thirteenth [District] Ashbel P. Fitch was placed in nomination. Trouble was expected as the true-blue Tammany Hall men never did like a convert so they decided Fitch was not their man."[81] Whoever their man was though, quickly withdrew and Fitch was the Tammany Hall nominee.

"The Hall" had its roots in the Tammany Society, founded in 1787 as a patriotic fraternal order named for a legendary Indian, Tamanend, who "supposedly paved the way for a peaceful settlement of the American colonies."[82] There were "braves," "sachems," and "sagamores" in Tammany Hall and the accompanying rituals that usually distinguish secret societies. By 1820, and without leaving all the mumbo jumbo behind, Tammany had become a political organization and, by the 1880s, following the 1870s Tweed Ring debacle, quite sophisticated and very disciplined.

While Tammany's rightful reputation for corruption is well-known, "to get out of it what was in it," it was often exaggerated by its frustrated opponents. As they lost again and again, they became more strident, as one might speak louder in order to add logic to an argument. Tammany's political discipline was ahead of its time. Its distinctive asset was its raw ability to mobilize voting power. Tammany could consistently turn out a vote like no other political organization could, and it did so routinely for the purpose of electing its candidates. Key to Tammany's discipline was its laserlike focus on local issues and local action.

The instruments of Tammany's power were public or private, formal or informal popular institutions such as the police and fire departments or even saloons, where bartenders could spread the word or maybe even steal a ballot box. Its influence was enormously magnified by the weight of New York City's population in the state and by the electoral weight of New York State in the nation. Stated in these terms, Tammany seems evil, and it was. Graft, bribery, and being alert when streets were opened or contracts let were commonplace and enabled Tammany to extract its "rightful" share of the "boodle."[83] But there was an underlying egalitarian Tammany philosophy that had an appeal in New York and helped sustain it. As Alfred Henry Lewis said in his book *Richard Croker,* "Tammany Hall, be assured, would not have lived almost a century and a quarter, were it not of vitality inborn and of itself. . . . Tammany was from its birth bed a disturber of . . . aristocracy."[84] Tammany resisted entrenched elite interests, and as long as those remained, New Yorkers tolerated its dark side.

Albany's repudiation of home rule for New York and the persistent high tariffs were two examples of such entrenched interests, and they were Republican. And Republican machine politics were every bit as corrupt as Tammany Hall. While to some Tammany might be forgiven for such an immoral equilibrium, even that was not the whole story.

Tammany made things happen in New York City. Tammany members built sewers, laid pipes, built transit systems, and paved streets. The infrastructure of New York, the nation's singular metropolis, was built brick by brick and pipe by pipe by Tammany, its leaders, and its members. Not many Republican hands were dirtied doing that work.

Tammany Hall also welcomed millions of the nation's new citizens from abroad, and they were a sorry-looking lot. Tammany made them into Americans. A Tammany Fourth of July was a celebration to behold. Tammany Hall on Fourteenth Street was one of the nation's loudest patriotic trumpets, blaring the meaning of America by sight and sound to everyone who heard it or saw it. Inside the Hall, gold spangled blue-and-red plush drapery and blue brocaded silk curtains matched the bunting, flags, and tassels that emblazoned the Hall outside. Brilliantly polished bronze figures and floral displays of national colors made the multitude's spirits soar. Every window was decorated with a shield, a flag, and a big brass eagle.

The crowds, dressed in their finest clothes, came early and filled the Hall. At midmorning the band began to play, raising the already high level of excitement. Between the Sousa marches and other patriotica were tunes like "Slide, Kelly, Slide" and "Maggie Murphy's Home." New York's most prominent politicians were there, and after the Declaration of Independence was read, the Tammany Glee Club joined in with "The Sword of Bunker Hill."[85]

This was how Tammany manufactured Americans out of the "tired and poor," "the huddled masses yearning to breathe free," the "wretched refuse"[86] that arrived in New York generally illiterate and often penniless. Tammany, more than any other American organization connected these people to America. One might ask rhetorically, "what would one pay to have someone do this job?" As are so many things in America, it wasn't always pretty. But to judge Tammany only as a corrupt political machine, which it was, is to overlook its very special function in New York City, especially during the last twenty years of the century, when foreign immigration was at its peak.

By mid-October 1888 the County Democracy tried urgently to negotiate a fusion ticket with Tammany, which paid little or no attention. On its own Tammany nominated "Sunset" Cox, Ashbel Fitch, and two others in sure Democratic districts. The *New York Sun* said, "Their system of division seemed to be like that of the Irishman who quarreled with his wife and divided the house. He took the inside and he gave her the outside."[87]

Fitch spoke every night at least once and generally more to tariff groups, rallies, and ratification meetings in two languages. Some members of the County Democracy felt that with the help of anti-Fitch Republicans they might elect a County Democrat to Congress.[88] Tammany men were both for and against Fitch, as were County Democrats. Before it ended though, there was union on certain candidates, including Cox, Fitch, and Roswell P. Flower, but not all. Flower, a Watertown, New York, native, was a Wall Street power and a future governor of New York.

As a Democrat, Fitch was speaking to new, unfamiliar groups of voters. For example, the County Democracy of the Twenty-third Assembly District (comparable to the Thirteenth Congressional District) sponsored a grand parade of two thousand Democrats followed by a mass meeting and an ox roast at Sulzer's Harlem Park at Second Avenue and 127th Street. "The parade formed at the foot of East Ninety-second Street at 7:00 p.m. It consisted of the Twenty-third Assembly District Association, the Murphy Legion, the Timothy J. Campbell Association, August Strassburg Association, J. A. Butler Association and the J. J. Carney, B. O'Rourke, James Mee, Peter Miller, William Hall's Sons and Michael Gearon Association, the Young Men's Democratic Social Club, the Elevated Railroad Employees Democratic Club, the Seventeenth Election District Cleveland and Thurman Club, the Butchers' Association, the Tonawanda Club in Indian costumes, Beattie's Battery,"[89] among others, not the groups that Fitch spoke to when he was a Republican. But he was at home at any political gathering.

With the election just weeks away, his reelection campaign was buoyed by the news that "more copies of his [tariff] speech were circulated by the Democratic National Committee than any other document except the Mills Bill and the President's message."[90] His canvass, which he operated from two headquarters at Ehret's and Ruppert's breweries, was energetic and distinctive. Both offices busily distributed campaign literature. Whereas most candidates used the United States mail, Fitch deployed fifty brewery workers to deliver his message personally. His speeches stressed tariff reform, reelecting Cleveland, and home rule for New York City.

On the Republican side, Fitch's acceptance of the Tammany nomination was a blow. Republicans had no obvious nominee in waiting, but after some consideration they settled on James Otis Hoyt, a forty-two-year-old lawyer. Hoyt was a prominent member of the Union League Club and was said to be motivated by Fitch's "betrayal of the party."[91] The *New York Press* described Hoyt as a "doughty antagonist" insisting that "because of his strong protective tariff views, he will draw heavily from the wage workers."[92] The *Press* predicted a "nip and tuck struggle" in his political combat with Fitch and said Hoyt was "confident of victory." The Democratic *New York Sun,* described Fitch as an "avowed and unregenerate Republican" and groused that he was "at the head of the Republican machine in Harlem" and "is not a Democrat" and that "a nomination such as Mr. Fitch's tends to break down the party lines."[93]

Opposition to Fitch's candidacy appeared in some quarters to stiffen as the election drew near. The Republican *New York Tribune* ran a long article under the headline "Fitch's Canvass Going to Pieces."[94] The reasons, it turned out, were twofold: first that "the remarkable Mr. Hoyt" was developing wide and deep support, and second that Democrats were unhappy with their own nomination of a renegade Republican. The paper reported that "neither Tammany Hall nor the County Democracy wanted Fitch, but Grover Cleveland insisted upon it."

When the campaign concluded, Fitch garnered about 60 percent of the votes cast, a modest landslide. The final tally was Fitch 28,580, Hoyt 19,412. Fitch returned to the Fifty-first Congress on the Democratic side of the aisle, a sweet result indeed. But he was in the minority again because the Republicans regained control of both houses of Congress and the White House in 1888.

Cleveland's late 1887 tariff message, in which he boldly attacked a system of taxation by tariff that was the cornerstone of the nation's tax policy for most of the century, came too late for a sufficient number of Americans to digest its meaning against a determined and well-financed Republican opposition. The irrefutable logic of Cleveland's message notwithstanding, the protective tariff was advertised as "America first," and its defeat, when viewed in that light, was hard to engineer on less than a year's notice.

Some onlookers blamed Cleveland's loss of New York, his home state, on Tammany's lack of support. Whether that was true, Cleveland's New York City plurality was insufficient to offset the upstate Republican vote. While he won the popular vote nationwide, without New York's electoral vote, he was beaten in the electoral college.

Republicans, armed with an enormous war chest filled by protectionist businessmen and the Grand Army of the Republic that was in open revolt because of Cleveland's pension vetoes, ran a polished campaign and still lost the popular vote.[95] They would return, determined to have their way, with majorities in both houses of Congress and a Republican in the White House. Tariff increases and black voting rights in the South[96] would be near the top of their list.

Notwithstanding Cleveland's disappointing loss in the electoral college, there would be no accusations, no lawsuits, no recounts, and no bitterness. Fitch, in a remarkable turnabout, began the year as an unknown Republican congressman and finished it as a Democratic congressman in the national spotlight. Political events of 1888 that propelled him to prominence reverberated across the nation for more than a decade. Democrats seemed unfazed by their colossal losses, buoyed as they were by Cleveland's popular vote, by their liberal convictions that they knew were right, and by an overall feeling that the nation was moving in their direction. There was no complaining, and no apologetic self-analysis of their failure, or of a new need to "find their voice" because they had "lost their way." They were like a football team whose rally had fallen short, but all that they would concede was that time had expired.

4

New York's World's Fair Lost

Fifty-first Congress, 1888–1890

> But I say to you, gentlemen, whenever you get a chance resent this notion that New York is un-American and a foreign city. She is American in the highest sense, because she welcomes every foreigner; she puts his children in her schools; and she makes good American citizens of them; and the time will never come, until the tide ceases to go up to the battery, until the Hudson ceases to go down to the Hook, that New York will not be as patriotic—as American in every sense of the word—as any city in the United States.
>
> —ASHBEL P. FITCH, March 1890

On the last Saturday in 1888, Fitch was in Boston at the Hotel Vendome as a featured speaker at the Massachusetts Tariff Reform League. Three hundred disciples of tariff reform were there, their first such gathering since the election, and where there might have been defeat or discouragement in the air there was excitement and optimism. Cambridge mayor and future Massachusetts governor William Russell presided. When Russell introduced Fitch as the "distinguished representative from New York who, to be true to himself and his conscience, broke all party ties and stood forth as the fearless, able champion of tariff reform,"[1] the reformers were on their feet, and the applause was deafening.

Fitch told his audience that Republican leaders threw principles aside in order to form a strong opposition to the Democratic president. They offered a choice between party discipline and the closely held principles on which some of them were elected, "to join with them in a campaign of hypocrisy," "to appeal to the lowest depths of selfishness and fear."[2] And what, he asked rhetorically, was to be the punishment of those who failed to join? "To be beaten at the polls; to be in a minority. To these gentlemen that sentence is the most severe that can be imposed. . . . They believe that the brains and the belief of a man in public life should be a piece of clockwork of which the national committee should hold the key."[3] The *New York Post* called it a "rattling speech," and the audience responded with glee.

President Eliot of Harvard pointed out to the assemblage that college professors were universally in favor of tariff reform. "How did the college professor 'get there'?" he said with droll humor. "In the first place he is an intelligent man, generally of large reading. He knows how he is taxed, and that is what you have got to teach the great majority of American farmers, mechanics, fishermen and clerks . . . you have got to carry home to them how they are taxed."[4]

Returning to Washington, the excitement of Fitch's whirlwind entrance onto the national stage in the spring of 1888, less than a year before, gave way to the prosaic, sometimes tedious routine of legislative service. He was by all accounts responsive to his constituents, and that combined with a weekly New York-to-Washington commute wore him down. He wrote Lizzie that his "mail is something immense again" and that he worked well into the night to get part way through it. In early 1889, a scant two and a half years after his initial election to office, Fitch first began considering his retirement from politics. He dreamed of a return to the full-time practice of law and to the enjoyment of his young family, now six children, three boys and three girls, all between the ages of two and fourteen.

And he was undoubtedly preoccupied by his plans to remove his entire family to Germany for the following year—Germany, where he had left his heart and soul as a youth twenty years before. His affinity for German culture was never stronger. He read Goethe and he socialized with his German clients. When he was in Washington, the *Brooklyn Eagle* described him as "a devoted adherent of good beer," who would "get up pleasant little parties to go out to one of the breweries [and drink] the best beer in such quantities as they desire."[5]

In a similar vein, the *New York Evening Sun* carried a story about a section of "Brewersville" in the east nineties, a miniature park hidden at the corner of Third Avenue and Ninety-first Street that was concealed "like a jewel hidden in green, a small house that reminds one of an old German knight's castle." This explained Fitch to a reporter, was Old Homestead. Here Washington Irving [seeking a secluded spot on the island] wrote his book *Astoria*. Old Homestead was owned by Jacob Ruppert, who generously offered it as a sort of Union or Knickerbocker Club for Germans. The occasion was the club's grand opening. The sweet strains of merry music were overheard played by Lieboldt's band and the tables were placed around the trees in the good old Vienna prater style.[6]

Fitch's enthusiasm for German education and culture and his long view and good judgment trumped whatever self-inflicted pain he would cause himself by sending his family abroad. He hoped his wife and children would learn to speak German, and he believed to his core that an educational year in Germany would be the best, most responsible good deed he might do for his children. Lizzie apparently went along gamely, because it would be a treat, a challenge and an enormous responsibility for her.

On the last day of July, the hour of the much-anticipated Fitch family pilgrimage had almost arrived. Before it did though, Fitch's enthusiastic and playful friends from the Old Homestead Club surprised him with a late-night serenade. Several hundred members and two German bands formed in the darkness at the ancient castle and marched to Fitch's Lexington Avenue home. When they arrived, the blaring bands woke the neighborhood, and a committee rushed into the house and carried Fitch off to the club. George Ehret, Jacob Ruppert, and others made speeches to which Fitch responded, toasts were drank, and "three cheers and a Tiger were given to Mr. Fitch, all hands wishing him a bon voyage."[7] Carl Schurz was among the well-wishers.[8] He and his family, too, would board the Hamburg American packet ship *Columbia* on her maiden voyage to Europe the next morning.

The *Columbia* cleared Sandy Hook at 9:50 A.M. on August 1, 1889, arriving at Southampton at 11:30 A.M. on August 8, an adjusted time of six days, twenty hours, and forty-nine minutes, besting the former record by thirty-three minutes. Traveling over the North Sea and then overland, the Fitch entourage arrived first in Hamburg, where they spent several days, then traveled south to Hanover. Continuing south they spent two days in Frankfurt, visiting among other places, the Goethe family home. After a three-day stop at Heidelberg, they wound up at Stuttgart on August 20.

They were on the road again almost immediately, this time headed east to Wildblad, a famous family resort in the Black Forest of Wurtemburg. The published record of Hotel arrivals at the Hotel Bellevue read, "Fitsche, Mr. Ashbel P., Membre of Congress, U. St. A. with wife, family and servants, Amerika, U.S.A." The party included Grandmother Cross, Lizzie's mother, as well as the indispensable Lizzie Petrie. After two weeks, the family returned to No. 51-A Kronenstrasse in Stuttgart, where they were joined by "Fraulein" a governess, to spend the year. Fitch returned alone to New York.

From Southampton, he traveled on the *Augustus Victoria, Columbia*'s sister ship, and reached New York on October 12, cleared quarantine, and went to his office, which was "full of flowers. The office staff sent an immense 'Welcome' in white & red pinks." Then he was off to see his mother and sister with some of the flowers in hand.

While Fitch was in Europe, Samuel Sullivan "Sunset" Cox died. The senior member of the city's congressional delegation, Cox was a nineteenth-century giant among House legislators. Born in Ohio in 1824, he graduated from Brown in 1846. He studied law and began his Ohio practice in 1849, before moving to New York City after the Civil War. A Democrat, Cox served most of sixteen terms in Congress from Ohio and New York during a period of thirty-three years, through nine presidencies, the Civil War, Reconstruction, a brokered presidency, and all that went on in New York City from 1865 to 1889. Cox was said to be the only New York congressman with a "national reputation for statesmanship"[9] and an honest reputation among friend and foe alike. Speaker Reed, Republican of Maine and a Cox opponent in many debates, said, "Mr. Cox was not an orator, hardly a leader, and perhaps not a wit; but in action he was a whole skirmish line, and has covered more movements of the Democratic party, and led it out of more parliamentary pitfalls than any of its orators and all its leaders put together."[10]

The loss of "Sunset" Cox threw new light on the mediocrity of the New York congressional delegation, a collection of Tammany hangers-on such as General Francis Spinola and "The Iceman," Charles Turner.[11] The *New York Evening Telegram,* bemoaning Cox's loss, opined that New York needed representation "beyond a mere ward politician and local leader of heelers."[12] In the same breath the paper concluded, "with his [Cox's] leadership silenced, who have we left? In the entire city delegation, Mr. Ashbel Fitch stands almost alone, and he is far from the equal of Sam Cox."[13] The *New York Herald* said that most of the delegation had no national reputation and that "Ashbel P. Fitch and Roswell P. Flower[14] are about the only ones whom the businessmen of New York know."[15] Fitch could not have felt demeaned in his second term in Congress by being ranked behind "Sunset" Cox, especially as Cox himself had "pronounced Fitch one of the brightest young men in Congress."[16] From that time on, most observers regarded Fitch as the leader of the city's congressional delegation.

Alone in New York, Fitch never became accustomed to being separated from his family. He wrote from the Manhattan Club, "It is ten o'clock. I have had my dinner, talked law with half a dozen judges and politics with a dozen candidates for office and I'm going to send you a line before I take my solitary walk over to the elevated and go home." He told her that he dined there almost every evening because it was close to the Brewers' Association and the cooking was good, well served, and less expensive than restaurants. Besides, he said, "I find pleasant company to meet with & meet the people who govern the town and state & who are and can be of use."

He was still considering withdrawing from public life. "With politics I have as little to do as possible," he said. And this was only October 1889. "I may speak once or twice" he continued, "to oblige some people who helped me out. [I] mean to keep out for this year & perhaps for some years to come. With one large family to care for I fancy sometimes I ought to keep strictly to business & give up the political fancies which I have had." The idea would grow on him during the coming year. He told her that "Business comes in steadily. The only difficulty is getting it done," which only fueled his frustrations.

Preparing for his return to Congress in December, he told Lizzie, "No, we don't believe that Chicago will get the fair. With their customary western brag and walk

7. *From left:* Amos Jay Cummings, Samuel Sullivan "Sunset" Cox, and Ashbel P. Fitch, ca. 1888. Photographer unknown. Photograph from the Ashbel P. Fitch archives.

they have claimed a majority in Congress etc. but I don't think anybody much outside of Illinois will want to go to a fair in Chicago. Still they are at work with all their might. Next week when the House gets together we can see something of the situation. I go over Sunday afternoon." Fitch referred to the Chicago World's Fair of 1893 that he and most New Yorkers believed would be held in New York in 1892.

It seems that in July of 1889, official New York realized that the four-hundredth anniversary of Christopher Columbus's discovery of America was on the horizon. The *New York Herald,* among the first to take credit for that realization, called for a "grand international exposition" and assumed "that the proper place for such a World's Fair would be New York, the financial and commercial metropolis of the New World; the natural, central and the best and highest representative of the civilization of the continent which Columbus discovered."[17] A bitter congressional fight loomed ahead that as much as any other highlighted America's animosity toward New York. Had it been resolved differently, Harlem's development might have taken a remarkably different turn than it did.

In those days Harlem was a well-situated upscale New York suburb that attracted some of New York City's wealthier residents. Fitch's friend Charles Dayton lived in Harlem. Fitch referred to Harlem as a "city," and he made note of the fact that Harlem had more voters than either of the states of Rhode Island or Nevada.[18] Fitch vigorously promoted a World's Fair, easily recognizing the benefits that would flow to New York if a fair were located in northern Manhattan, where in his view it "probably" would be.

When asked about potential opposition in Congress to a New York fair, Fitch was sanguine. He linked the opposition to those who would oppose the Harlem River Improvement. He attributed it to "small minded men in Congress whose dislike of New York comes from the fact that New York is the creditor of many of the people in the Western and Northwestern states," and to "loose talk about the mysterious influences of Wall Street and so on."[19]

Nonetheless, newspapers and politicians supported the idea, and within a week Mayor Hugh J. Grant invited five hundred of New York's most prominent men to his office "to consider the advisability of holding an international exposition at New York in 1892."[20] Jay Gould, Collis Huntington, Henry Marquand, J. P. Morgan, Levi Morton, Joseph Pulitzer, John D. Rockefeller, Whitelaw Reid, Charles Dana, James Gordon Bennett, P. T. Barnum, August Belmont, Grover Cleveland, Theodore Roosevelt, and Cornelius Vanderbilt were all invited. Thomas Edison said he was "only too glad to do everything in my power to assist." Samuel Gompers wrote a strong letter of support, as did Morgan.[21]

The meeting started promptly, and what an assembly it was. "There sat Jesse Seligman, the millionaire banker, nearby the grizzled but good-natured face of

General William Tecumseh Sherman, the bright features of ex-Secretary of the Navy William C. Whitney, William Steinway in a shabby office coat which one of his fifteen-dollar-a-week clerks wouldn't have worn."[22] Congressman Ashbel P. Fitch, William R. Grace, and Isador Straus were there, and on it went, a gathering perhaps unique in the annals of the nation and only remotely possible in the city of New York.

The final item on the agenda was an adopted resolution to appoint four committees of twenty-five, one each on permanent organization, finance, legislation, and site and buildings. When the meeting adjourned and the distinguished citizens of New York went their independent ways, there could not have been more than a few who were not anticipating that the New York Exposition would be held in Harlem in 1892. Five months later, however, Chicago was hard at work to land the fair, while the New York committees had done next to nothing.

As the curtain rose in December 1889 on the Fifty-first "Billion Dollar" Congress, the first congress to authorize more than $1 billion in spending, Fitch was seen "gravitating naturally to his old seat on the Republican side then changing his mind and strolling across the chamber to sit down with the Democrats."[23] He was the "envy of many of his colleagues"[24] for his election, triumphant after being given up on by his party. Whatever glory was his, however, was short-lived, as the World's Fair was close upon him. He was "deeply interested"[25] in it, but he knew it would be an uphill battle.

In order to win the fair, New Yorkers would have to prove they wanted it and would have to persuade Congress that they should have it—no mean feat. Fitch watched the other cities compete, notably Chicago and St. Louis. He noticed well-organized, well-equipped, community-based lobbying efforts, energetic and determined, that were not relying on their congressmen alone to do the job. Chicago had a World's Fair headquarters in Washington. These were all indications of a hard fight for New York.

Fitch observed pointedly that Congress was not convinced that New York was sufficiently committed to the fair to make it successful. Upstate and New England Republicans were afraid of a World's Fair in New York City that might redound to the credit of Tammany Hall and the Democrats in a presidential election year. It did not escape him, or anyone, that the city voted Democratic and that Republicans controlled Congress. By this time, a New York World's Fair guarantee fund, begun in September to raise $5 million, had already reached $2 million.

The mayor's Legislation Committee, one of the four committees formed in the mayor's office during the summer, referred "the shape and manner that New York would present its claims for the World's Fair before Congress"[26] to its own executive committee, an inauspicious beginning. That committee, whose members included ex-mayor Abram Hewitt, Elihu Root, Chauncey Depew, William C. Whitney, and, ironically, Senator Thomas C. Platt, met at Depew's office in the Grand Central Station. Fitch, included by special invitation and liking nothing better than to ask for a piece of business, argued strenuously that New York should send "representative men" to Congress immediately to urge the city's claims and blunt her rivals' contention that New York had little interest in the fair. He called attention to the inexperience of the congressional delegation, especially since Cox's death, and its inability to carry the day without help. He had told the *New York Evening World,* "If such men as Chauncey M. Depew, Thomas C. Platt, William C. Whitney, ex-Governor Cornell, John C. Calhoun and John Inman would go to Washington and urge upon Congress the claims of this city, the good it would do is incalculable."[27]

Before the meeting, and fearing its outcome, he had done his best to encourage the committee to make the right decision. On the day of the meeting, the *New York World, New York Herald, New York Journal,* and *New York Times* ran headlines that Fitch may even have helped write, such as "We Must Act," "On to Washington at Once," "We've Got to Work," and "New York Must Rush Its Claims Speedily." The committee, comprising men who were not used to going anywhere "hat in hand," least of all to Congress, considered its options and determined that it would do nothing. Whitney's resolution was to the effect that "until the matter shall have been taken up by Congress . . . the appearance of delegations from this committee . . . would simply result in personal lobbying which is not within the scope of the duties of this committee."[28] The following day's headlines in several New York newspapers told a different story[29] from the day before—"No Lobbying for The World's Fair," "New York Won't Lobby," and "New York's Dignified Attitude."

Faced with the intransigence of the committee that should have wanted to land the fair, the New York delegation canvassed the House by pairs, one Republican and one Democrat. Fitch and Moffitt from Chateaugay were assigned to Ohio and Oregon. After visiting with most of the twenty-one members from Ohio, they realized that most members favored Chicago. "The plain fact is," he wrote his wife, "that New York *because* she is richer and better situated than her sister cities is not popular with them. And then we have such a delegation! Dunphy, Quinn & McCarthy are new men of no social or political standing & can't reach anybody. Turner 'the ice man' who has been sent from the lower Dist., we don't even know ourselves. That leaves Spinola who is ill, Flower, Cummings[30] & I. We shall do the best we can but we need help from N. Y." (emphasis in original). And two weeks later, he wrote, "The New York Committee on Legislation [still] has done nothing."

To illustrate the challenge facing the city's delegation, one might consider some of the immigration proposals that were before the House and the Senate, proposals that shed light on the likely outcome of the fair debate, or at least on the likely attitudes of some members toward New York City. For instance, Congressman William C. Oates of Alabama, the same Oates who, at Gettysburg, heroically led the Confederates' 15th Alabama up from the base of Little Round Top to his ill-fated rendezvous with Joshua Lawrence Chamberlain's 20th Maine, sought to restrict from entering the country any alien "who is an idiot, a pauper or liable to become a public charge or has been legally convicted of a felony or who is afflicted with any loathsome or contagious disease."[31] Oates also hoped to restrict anyone from entry who could not speak English, or was a polygamist, anarchist, socialist, or communist. Oates would later become governor of Alabama.

Senators John H. Mitchell of Oregon and Henry W. Blair of New Hampshire had restrictive ideas of their own. Mitchell wanted to exclude all political offenders and all persons not in favor of the home government. Blair's idea was to restrict anyone who for five years had not behaved as a person of good moral character, as well as Catholics. There could be no mistaking that New York's surging immigrant tide would slow to a trickle if it were left up to Oates, Mitchell, or Blair, and the World's Fair would be held elsewhere.

Of separate but related interest, The *Philadelphia North American* carried a newspaper article under the headline "The Educational Advantages of the Senate and House," which read, "The advocates of collegiate and university education will be surprised, no doubt to learn that the college bred men are in a minority in either branch of Congress . . . one hundred thirty-seven members describe themselves as having had common school education, and seventy describe theirs as 'academic.' Eight avow themselves self-educated, and thirty-five make no allusion whatever to their manner of education, leaving it to be inferred that . . . they 'simply growed.'"[32]

It was among these men that Fitch and his colleagues would have to win votes if the World's Fair were to be held in New York City. He could not have been optimistic. On a day that was devoted to the introduction of bills, he sat and listened to the monotonous reading by the clerk of resolutions and laws "which members send up & which will never be heard of again. Meantime the House talks & laughs and tells stories so that it sounds like a schoolroom when the teacher has stepped out. The galleries are deserted & the whole aspect of the place is one of careless disorder."

The formal presentation of the New York World's Fair Committee took place on Saturday, January 11, 1890. More than fifty resolute New Yorkers made the journey to Washington, led by Chauncey Depew, who would at last make the presentation. On Friday night, the congressmen met about seventy delegates who made a considerable impression from their time of arrival to departure.

On Sunday Fitch described the scene at the train station Friday night. "New York came over in great shape night before last. We were all at the depot to receive them, Mr. Depew, Mr. Vanderbilt, the Mayor, ex-Secretary Whitney, Mr. Steinway. . . .

Friday evening I entertained [some of] them at Chamberlin's. Yesterday the hearing was had." Depew's presentation, delivered with his respectfully arrogant aura of noblesse oblige intact, argued that World Fairs should only be held in the metropolis of the host country; lesser cities, while very nice, wouldn't do. The *New York World*'s headline the following day was "Ours! Now We'll Surely Get It."[33] The *New York Times* led with "In the Lead for the Fair."[34]

Fitch, no doubt disingenuously, declared that "the work of the city's congressional representatives had been lightened by [the delegation's] splendid work of Saturday."[35] Although he was "encouraged,"[36] he had to know it wasn't enough. Help had been too long coming, and New York was too far behind. He wrote to Lizzie "I'm afraid we won't get it but we shall try very hard."

While the New Yorkers appealed to Congress, a bill prepared by Depew, Whitney, and Root that authorized $10 million in city bonds for land takings for the fair made its way to Albany. The bill provided, too, that the city's "Board of Estimate may appropriate any portion of the proceeds of the bond offering not already expended to erect extensions to the Metropolitan Museum and the American Museum of Natural History."[37] To New Yorkers, the clause made perfect sense, that is, efficient legislation to deal with a roster of projects. To New York's opponents, unused to so many options, it was odd and hardly indicative of a burning desire to host a World's Fair.

The House debate that followed, characterized by desperate nit-picking and mind-numbing procedural motions, first turned on whether the fair should be under the aegis of a special committee or remain with Foreign Affairs. Aside from the usual relevant arguments to the effect that Foreign Affairs had dealt with the fair for several months, Congressman Robert R. Hitt of Illinois chaired it, and New York wanted a special committee with a chairman who was not from Illinois. Speaker Reed said that it made no difference who chaired the committee because the fair's location would be voted by the entire House and would not be under any committee jurisdiction. McKinley, however, for the Rules Committee, reported a resolution that created a special World's Fair Committee and that carried by a narrow margin. Carlisle, voting for New York, appeared in the House for the first time in several days and caused House Republicans for Chicago to shout, "Look how Tammany Hall is rallying her vote. Of course she wants the fair so as to elect a Democrat president in 1892."[38] New York was a lever to the presidency. Republicans would avoid lending Democrats a helping hand.

Fitch, never giving up on the fair, continued to lobby through the press. He waxed eloquent on "Depew's masterly presentation," claiming that "everyone was charmed with Depew, particularly the southerners" and that he was "much encouraged." Fitch dismissed Chicago's claims that New York had no place to hold the fair, publicly singing Harlem's praises:

> Harlem has become known throughout the United States. They had an idea . . . that the fair was to be held a way out from the city—a journey. . . . I said to them, "why we have two cities there and the fair is to be between them. One is the city of New York and the other is the city of Harlem. Harlem is a city in itself, bigger than most any you have in the South and the West and the East. It has its own clubs and churches and newspaper and as much local pride as Buffalo or Boston or Chicago." . . . They said "you haven't a cable railroad in New York." I said, "but we have in Harlem, and all the fine parks are in Harlem and in fact everything that is desirable in the city is located in Harlem, while we are free from all the objectionable features of the city." You know those people think that New York and Wall Street are one and the same thing, and they have a great prejudice against Wall Street. I tell them that we haven't any Wall Street in Harlem. Harlem is a place quite different—a place of charming homes, of fine avenues, beautiful drives and magnificent views.[39]

As January 1890 turned to February, Chicago continued its relentless lobbying. The New York State legislature, owing surely to Republican boss Thomas Platt's efforts, which he denied, moved slowly on the $10 million fair funding bill, thus providing additional reason for Chicago to claim that New York was not sufficiently interested in hosting the fair. The legislation passed just a few days before the House voted on the fair's location, and that only because of another "monster rally" at Cooper Union, where Platt was publicly pilloried for managing the delay in Albany.[40] Nonetheless, together with the now fully subscribed $5 million guarantee fund, New York had $15 million earmarked for the fair. Chicago had nothing.

By late February the opposing sides were set for debate. Congressman William M. Springer of Illinois, laid out his case that "the people of New York did not want the fair, that it could not be had in New York without it being turned into a political machine, that New York would have to spend several millions [to acquire land] before she would be as ready for the fair as Chicago is now without spending a dollar."[41] Turning to Chicago's financing, there was one direct exchange:

> Mr. Springer: I hold in my hand a statement to this effect signed by Sam W. Allerton, C. B. Farwell and Potter Palmer each of whom is able to pay the whole sum in itself. . . .
>
> Mr. Fitch: Read it!
>
> Mr. Springer: I will.[42]

After doing so, Springer triumphantly declared what would prove to be a hollow promise: "Chicago will ask no money from Congress!"[43]

Roswell Flower, the first speaker for New York, constructed his argument on the proposition that only New York had the facilities to house, feed, transport, and entertain visitors from all over the world. He said that New York was "the only city prepared to undertake the enterprise, complete the buildings by March 1, 1892, and close the fair by November 1, 1892 . . . the only place where the fair can be held in that year, where politics will be debarred, for we will finish the building two months before a president is nominated and close the fair before the election."[44] He also claimed that a New York fair would be the only fair free from "appropriation except for your own exhibits."[45]

Fitch's brief speech was thinly clad in a gracious appeal to what he hoped would be the universal recognition of New York's hegemony. No matter how hard he tried, it was a thin veneer that covered the personal disgust he felt and the offense he took at New York's abuse by Congress. He was seldom offended and never intemperate, but he took the abuse, especially the slurs on foreigners, personally.

He said New York should be "well satisfied" with two features of the debate, first that the friends of New York had "said no unkind word, used no malignant expression on her behalf." He referred to New York's rivals as "her younger sisters," of whom New York was very proud, pointing out, "Not one new acre of corn can be planted in Dakota; not one new bale of cotton raised in the South; not one new mine opened or vineyard laid out on the Pacific Coast without adding to the value of real estate on the island of Manhattan," and "The wealth which you have helped us to get goes freely through every channel of business, through every avenue of investment, through every effort of philanthropy or charity from one end of the country to the other."

The second satisfactory aspect of the debate was the reciprocal of the first, that is, her rivals' treatment of New York. At this point, though, he would not restrain himself from mentioning one "insignificant exception," to whit, the comments of Congressman Bishop W. Perkins of Kansas. Perkins produced a New York telephone directory in which he found "names of Europe," that is, "foreign" sounding names, but no real American names of honor.[46] Fitch retorted wryly,

> My friend from Kansas (Mr. Perkins) . . . insists that New York is not an American city, because it has no hotels named after . . . Grant and Sherman . . . he failed to remember that both Grant and Sherman chose this city which he calls un-American as their permanent residence after having tried Chicago and Washington. We [New Yorkers] do not share the peculiar notion of patriotism which leads my friend from Kansas to think that the highest honor that can be paid a statesman or a soldier is to name a hotel after him. But if my friend will withdraw his opposition to the selection of New York . . . in my district some grateful citizen will erect a substantial and elegant building and name it "The Perkins" in his honor.[47]

Having thus vented his frustration, he proceeded to give real form to his enduring love for his home city. He claimed that New York was "the most agreeable city of residence in the United States," adding,

> It has been well said that New York is a fair in itself. Broadway is a fair—there is no other street like its nine miles in the world. Fifth Avenue is a fair, from Washington Square to Fifty-ninth Street. Central Park with its thousands of children is a daily exhibition of health and happiness. The art galleries and libraries and operas—the fifty theaters, on the boards of which masterpieces are given in half a dozen languages—are a continual entertainment.
>
> In the harbor of New York on any bright afternoon is a grand naval exhibition. Eighty thousand strangers are every day in New York in attendance—at this fair . . . there is no language which civilized man speaks which is not heard on its streets. There is no section of our country or of any other which is not represented in its business and social life, and there is no faith which has not built itself a place in which to worship in the city of New York. . . .
>
> In fact although not in legal name there are two cities on the island of Manhattan between which is proposed to place this exposition. At the upper end of the island, where a very few years ago Harlem Lane ran through the meadows between the farms of the old Hollanders, a new city has been built, than which there is none more lovely in the world. The windows of its homes look out upon the Hudson and the Palisades to the west, to the Harlem River on the north, and on the east to the white sails which cover Long Island Sound. It has its own churches and schools, and its own newspapers and club houses and social life, as charming as can be found anywhere in the country.[48]

It was a good speech that would appeal to New Yorkers but change no votes. Indeed one Chicago newspaper reported that "the speeches were made in a House where not one member in five was present, and besides, they were all addressed to a jury of men who have already made up their minds, or who at all events are not to be converted by speech making."[49]

The vote came a few days later, and people entered the Capitol early to witness the anticipated drama. The crowded galleries saw noisy demonstrations as excitement pulsated through the House. As the vote progressed, and argument, pleading, and consultation increasingly occupied the floor, deals were made or not made, and the crowd grew silent as the suspense rose and the outcome remained in doubt.

The previous week, Flower had predicted that New York would lag by 20 votes on the first ballot, St. Louis would support New York on the second or third ballot, and Washington would follow. He thought that Chicago would never top 137 votes. In fact, New York "lagged" by 43 votes on the first ballot, not 20, drawing 72 votes to Chicago's 115, and peaked at 116 on the sixth ballot. Washington and St. Louis never did come over to New York, together controlling 43 votes on the eighth and final vote when Chicago won.

It was a momentous vote for the city of Chicago, a seminal reward for an enthusiastic, almost frantic, extraordinarily intensive and effective marketing effort put forth by the sons of Chicago. The incredible result was the Chicago World's Fair of 1893, which literally remade that small midwestern city that badly needed remaking into one of the country's most beautiful and influential cities.

For New York it was a reversal, in part self-inflicted, but in part a setback delivered by its enemies. The effect of the loss of the fair on New York's development will never be known. Considering the subsequent evolution of northern Manhattan, it is difficult to conclude that this was not a staggering blow to New York's fortunes and future. Given the enormous impact of the fair on Chicago, it seems reasonable to assume that New York, too, would have emerged as a different place had it won the fair.

Who was to blame? Fitch's responsibility was to represent his district, the interests of which he saw early and clearly. In spite of his considerable efforts to persuade others to the urgency of his views, they were not persuaded, and they were not open to persuasion. New York's rivals said that New York did not want the fair, and the committee's unwillingness to organize a congressional effort early lent credence to their claim. It was critical, as was the delay in Albany to pass the fair funding bill. These were failures of New York that Chicago exploited.

But the damage was not all self-inflicted. Chicago misrepresented her financing, and the untruth was critically effective in debate. The Republican Party, as Fitch had pointed out in his letter to state Republicans four years before, was hostile to New York City, and it acted on its hostility. Eight votes from New England, about one-third of the total, and sixteen of twenty-six Pennsylvania votes went to Chicago in what one would suppose should have been a vote largely dictated by geography, that is, the closer the fair was to one's constituency, the more one's constituents would be able to attend. New York's failure to land the World's Fair could be traced to the efforts of New York's and Pennsylvania's Republican senators Platt and Quay. At least for Platt, it would not go unnoticed, and there would be repercussions.

A week or so later, Fitch spoke at Delmonico's to the lumber trade of New York, whose members had planned on building the World's Fairgrounds and were seriously wounded by the World's Fair vote. The dinner was quiet, and Fitch's resentment, now two weeks old, remained close to the surface. He began with a story that he attributed to Joseph Choate. A lawyer who was planning to go to Europe the succeeding day gave a farewell dinner, packed his bags, and was at the steamer the following morning. Later in the day he ran into a friend who had been at dinner the night before. The friend said he thought the lawyer had gone to Europe. The lawyer said "my trunk was on board when I learned that a rich client of mine had died. I was afraid that if I went away the heirs would get the property."[50]

That was the spirit, he said, by which New York lost the Fair. He then turned to the congressional nativism that offended him most:

> The only thing that was said against us—something I want to resent here, and which I hope you will all resent, wherever and whenever you have the opportunity—was that this town of ours is a foreign city—is un-American. Over and over in that debate it was said to us that New York has nothing in common with the rest of the country, that New York is a foreign city . . . when they meant, as they did, that New York was a foreign city in feeling, they issued a slander on this town that every honest man who is here ought to resent. When did New York become a foreign city? When did it become unpatriotic? Was it when Alexander Hamilton spoke here in the fields—a young student in Columbia College . . . ? Was it any time during the war when the men and money of New York were poured out to carry on the war?
>
> . . . I say to you, gentlemen, whenever you get a chance resent this notion that New York is un-American and a foreign city. She is American in the highest sense, because she welcomes every foreigner; she puts his children in her schools; and she makes good American citizens of them; and the time will never come . . . that New York will not be as patriotic—as American in every sense of the word, as any city in the United States.[51]

Eighteen months later, in the autumn of 1891, Roswell Flower captured the Democratic nomination for governor to succeed David B. Hill.[52] In those days, New York governors were elected in odd years for two-year terms. Flower's Republican opponent, state senator J. Sloat Fassett, was Republican leader in the state senate and led the Albany delays that held up the fair funding bill and gave credence to New York's opponents' accusation that New York "doesn't want the fair." The political impact of the fair's loss would not soon go away.

One reason it continued to make headlines was Chicago's ultimate plea to Congress for federal funds to build the fairgrounds. The *New York Sun* carried an editorial[53] in early September 1891 recounting the House fair debate in the context of Chicago's subsequent request to Congress for federal funding for the fair. The *Sun* recalled Representative Candler of Massachusetts, an author of the fair bill, asking for federal funding only for the national exhibit. Representatives Covert, Cummings, and Tracey of New York, with $15 million committed to the fair or in the bank, had reaffirmed that New York would ask for no funding from the national treasury.

Springer of Illinois, responding to Fitch's order to "read it," had boasted, "We will ask no money from Congress!" Then Senator Cullom, also of Illinois, later vowed in a speech to the Senate that Chicago's pledges would be "carried out." It was on the strength of these promises, observed the *Sun*, that Chicago won the fair. But this was another day, and the group from Chicago was back in Washington with their collective hands out, in the *Sun*'s words "all on their knees on the shore of Lake Michigan, stretching out their hands toward the national treasury for cash with which to dig the foundation of the Columbian Exposition." There was no Chicago money for the fair, yet another insult to New York.

In a letter to the *Sun* Fitch noted, "It is perhaps worthy of mention that Senator Fassett's speeches in Albany were quoted very largely and with great delight by the advocates of Chicago. . . . We shall have a chance in Harlem this fall to have another ballot between the friends of Chicago and those of New York, and the result will be well worth watching."[54]

Still recuperating from a dangerous summer illness, Fitch cabled Flower after his nomination for governor, "accept my sincere congratulations. No district in the state has so close an interest in the fair as the Thirteenth. . . . When I recover from my illness will be glad to speak anywhere for you."[55] One month later Flower advanced on Harlem with political revenge on his mind. Thousands turned out in the rain to greet him, a "brilliant scene inside of the Belmont Riding Academy at St. Nicholas Avenue and 124th Street,"[56] of flags, bands, and eager, excited Democrats. The meeting opened with a series of resolutions accusing Republicans of hostility toward New York City, of unfair legislative apportionment, for home rule and especially denouncing the cost to the region's economy of the loss of the fair.

Said Flower, "Had the World's Fair been located at Morningside Park it would, according to Chauncey Depew, have been worth $300 million to the business and trade of New York and the surrounding county" to say nothing of what it might have meant to the New York Central Railroad. He named the farmers, the tradesmen, the real estate owners, and the artisans, all of whom would have shared in the benefits of the fair in addition to the millions of people around New York City and in New England who would have taken it in. All this to say nothing of the lasting impact that an 1892 Columbian World's fair would have had on the permanent development of northern Manhattan.

Flower said that the Harlem site was selected because it "overlooked the Harlem River, the Hudson River, the East River and Long Island Sound. It was accessible to thirty nations that would have been represented here, and it was nearly in the center of the densest population in the country within a ten mile radius." As to Fassett, Flower told his audience that the "delay he caused in the state senate, lost the fair to us. Congressman Fitch looked pale from his illness but was in excellent voice and his speech had much of the ring about it which is so welcome to his constituents." After his oft-repeated indictment of Republicans in Congress and in Albany, he insisted that the citizens of New York City would "punish them for interfering with their interests."

Flower was elected governor handily. Republican obstruction in Albany of a World's Fair for New York City was a key to his victory. The Democracy continued to gain momentum, rumbling on toward the momentous presidential election of 1892. Historians may have lost track of the World's Fair debate, its long-term impact on New York, and its role in the New York elections of 1891 and to a lesser extent 1892. But it was a disappointment that some New Yorkers could and did remember. It became part of the arsenal used by Grover Cleveland's supporters to increase his vote in New York City in 1892 when and where he needed them. For Ashbel Fitch, the gubernatorial election of 1891 renewed his energy to work for New York and for Cleveland and to oppose those who would injure New York. But in the summer of 1890 he was preoccupied by his thoughts of reuniting with his family and of the 1890 election that would be soon upon him.

5

Republican Overreach, Democratic Momentum

Fifty-first Congress, 1888–1890

> Mr. Fitch is in fact the only man that we have had in the House during the past year who was able to speak with intelligence and ability for the interests of the city.
>
> —*New York Evening Post,* September 23, 1890

In early May 1890, the tariff retook center stage in the Fifty-first Congress under the skilled leadership of Ohio Republican William McKinley, chairman of the House Ways and Means Committee and the nation's twenty-fifth president-to-be. Republicans controlled the House. There was decidedly less public interest in the tariff because Republicans, having no interest in tariff reform, allowed a quarter of the time for debate than the Democrats had allotted for the Mills Bill two years before. McKinley and Mills, for and against the McKinley Tariff Bill respectively, led the debate. The *New York Sun,* describing them said:

> Major McKinley opened the debate. . . . The Major wore a black frock coat, unbuttoned, and looked more like Napoleon then ever. . . . As he warmed up . . . his voice became clear. . . . Every word was distinctly uttered and the points were sent home with graceful gestures. As [McKinley] began his remarks Mr. Mills crossed to the Republican side of the chamber and sat down ten feet away from the speaker. He rocked to and fro in a pivotal chair with his eyes fastened on the Major and seemed deeply interested. . . .
>
> [When it was Mills's turn, he] stood in the middle aisle of the Democratic wing of the House. . . . Mills has white hair and a silvery mustache. His eyes are bright and sunny, and he has an extremely pleasant face. His voice is clear and resonant. He spoke off hand, with hardly a reference to a note or an authority. His argument was clear and exhaustive. It abounded in classic allusions and metaphors. . . . At times his comparisons were so droll that they set everybody laughing. He ridiculed the idea of protecting the farmer by placing of duty upon wheat. He said that last year we exported 90 million bushels of wheat and imported only 1,946 bushels; the

> same with corn; the same with rye. The importation could all have been raised in a turnip patch . . . implying, from what are we protected?[1]

Fitch led off the third day, and he would say later that McKinley paid him the compliment of moving closer to hear him.[2] The central point of Fitch's remarks was his description of the tariff's impact on his New York constituency. He said,

> Your plans are openly hostile to us. The metropolis is largely a commercial city. To you commerce is a crime, and importation an impertinence. New York is largely, too, a city of consumers. . . . You have no sympathy with these consumers. . . . In all your legislation in this session you have shown your dislike for New York, and your disregard of her interests. . . .
>
> There has always been a love of liberty in the cities by the sea. There is in the salt air a breath of defiance of wrong and injustice. We in the city of New York are of different blood and of many races, but we have in us, above all, the American love for "fair play," and will try to convince you that the questions which are raised by this bill of yours can not be settled adversely to us and to all the interests of our city until the tide ceases to come up to the Battery and the Hudson down to the Hook.

New York has been at the center of the nation's banking and commerce since its time as a Dutch colony, and it was an international city since its beginning. New Yorkers earned their living from international trade and businesses that supported it, and they have not produced quantities of goods for their own consumption for years. Southerners and Westerners especially earned their living from the land, and they consumed much of what they produced. To these men, the interests of New York were not something to be protected, nor were its "foreign" population.

The *New York Times* opined, "We do not envy the nature of any citizen of New York who could read the manly, logical and eloquent words of Mr. Fitch without a thrill of sympathetic pride. They were a fitting declaration of independence from a man who worthily represents this great, busy city of commerce, manufactures and labor."[3]

The McKinley Bill passed the House by a vote of 164–142. The *Boston Globe* wrote, "McKinley gained a victory, but a dearly purchased one. . . . He looked anxious."[4] Attitudes had changed since Cleveland delivered his 1887 message arguing for tariff reform. Perceptive Republicans saw trouble ahead, but the bill passed the Republican-controlled Senate and became law, albeit an unpopular one that helped lead the nation toward economic catastrophe. Years later Fitch gained some small satisfaction when McKinley, then president and free from the confines of his rural Ohio district, where protectionism was equated with Americanism, altered his stance on the tariff. With broader responsibility, McKinley's views grew more sophisticated. Historian Margaret Leech wrote, "The home market was no longer central in McKinley's thoughts of prosperity. He had come to a decision that logically invalidated the exclusive doctrine of high protection, and conceded that the United States had outgrown the defensive confines of the tariff wall,"[5] essentially Fitch's position.

Fitch's congressional year was devoted to the fair, the issue that had the largest immediate impact on his district, and to a lesser extent to other misguided Republican pieces of legislation. His participation was limited by his minority status under Republican Thomas B. Reed, the most dominating Speaker the House had ever known. Nevertheless, he had spoken against the McKinley Tariff, and just before he was scheduled to leave for Europe to retrieve his family, the House came alive.

The Silver Bill, later known as the Sherman Silver Purchase Act, passed both the House and the Senate and became law.[6] A conference committee working on the bill fixed the Treasury's new purchase obligation at four and one-half million ounces of silver monthly at market rates, nearly twice as much as required under the Bland Allison Act that it supplanted, almost the entire output of the western mines. The Sherman Act added significantly to the debasement of the nation's currency. Coupled with the McKinley tariff, it had a calamitous impact on the American economy.

A second bill, which passed the House by a vote of 155–149 but would not become law, was Henry Cabot Lodge's Federal Election or "Force" Bill as its opponents named it. The *Philadelphia Times* called it the "Lodge-Davenport-Reed Force Election Bill after the sponsoring congressman, the Supervisor of Elections in New York and draftsman of the bill, and the Republican Speaker of the House."[7]

The Lodge Bill incorporated the enforcement provisions of the Election Law of 1871,[8] yet the earlier law and the bill of 1890 were two entirely different pieces of legislation, drafted by the same people for two different purposes. Both benefited Republicans. The Federal Election Law of 1871 was aimed by its sponsors at preventing New York immigrants from voting. Fitch was duly familiar with it and with its author, John I. Davenport.

The alleged purpose of Lodge's "Force" Bill of 1890 was to protect the voting rights of black citizens in the South. It would have brought most congressional elections in southern states under direct federal supervision, which they were not under the 1871 Law. The defeat of the Force Bill in the Senate marked, in one author's opinion, "the exact point in time that the federal government abandoned the cause of finding a solution to the South's race problem . . . [for] more than a half-century."[9] Fitch did not speak on the Force Bill but he would lead the effort to repeal the 1871 law in the Fifty-third Congress.

While the Fifty-first Congress did its work, Grover Cleveland, at home in New York, watched anxiously. Historian Allan Nevins wrote that Cleveland believed "the Harrison Administration [two years into its term] was making . . . one dangerous blunder after another. The Force Bill, the McKinley Tariff, the Sherman Silver Purchase Act, the expenditures of a billion dollar Congress ruled with a rod of iron by Thomas B. Reed . . . all this struck Cleveland as a record in which perversity and weakness were equally mingled."[10]

Nearing the date of Fitch's departure for Europe, it became clear that he had conquered his loneliness by throwing himself into his work. The fair was lost, Reed had made congressional life miserable for Democrats, the tariff was raised, more silver was diluting the nation's money supply, and he had less time for his law practice. He was exhausted, and he had worked himself into dangerously poor health while he half decided to retire from politics. Many of the New York newspapers, either as fact or speculation, mentioned that Fitch would not be returning to Congress.[11] On Thursday, July 3, 1890, the *Normannia* under Captain Hebich left her Hoboken pier with Fitch, Mr. and Mrs. Chauncey M. Depew and their son Chauncey Jr., William Steinway, and hundreds more on board. He was finally away, having barely survived a forlorn year separated from his family.

The *Harlem Reporter* published an interview with Fitch's doctor[12] in which the doctor said, "Congressman Fitch went abroad upon my advice and because I thought the journey and its enforced rest an absolute necessity if he desired to save himself from a complete physical collapse." "Do you consider Mr. Fitch's condition dangerous?" asked the reporter. "Not if he gets rest," answered the doctor, implying that travel arrangements were made at the last minute upon the doctor's advice, which was not the case. But Fitch clearly needed to rest.

His Atlantic crossing was uneventful. He arrived in Stuttgart nine days after leaving New York, reunited with his family after a ten-month separation. The family excitement was palpable. The Fitch boys were in soldier suits, the girls in their best dresses. Little Bessie wrote in her diary "Talked. Evening—Ella and I played on the piano and Ashbel on the violin. Talked, talked." Family life overcame his loneliness and restored him.

At home Fitch was not forgotten. The undistinguished New York City congressional delegation continued to draw attention, Fitch being an exception, along with Flower or Cummings, depending on the writer and the newspaper. The *New York Advertiser,* referring to Fitch as "the most prominent of the New York City representatives," said, "During this Congress Mr. Fitch has been undoubtedly the strongest man among the New York City Democrats. He has not done much speaking, but whenever the occasion arose, he was looked up to as the leader of the delegation. No man in it has anything like his knowledge of tariff matters and none can present his views as forcibly. He was opposed, of course, to the McKinley Bill, and made a strong speech against it. He is an excellent parliamentarian and has figured as a lieutenant of Judge Crisp and Benton McMillin, the ablest of Democratic parliamentarians on the floor."[13]

He was also recognized as the leading spokesman for the city of New York. The *New York Evening Post* said, "Mr. Fitch is in fact the only man that we have had in the House during the past year who was able to speak with intelligence and ability for the interests of the city."[14] In this regard he was unique. None of the other stars of the era, certainly not Cleveland, Roosevelt, Croker, Choate, Depew, Hewitt, or anyone else utilized their public platform to speak passionately about New York City and in particular the tolerant, very positive, unique benefits of foreign cultures to the city.

He returned from Europe in late August of 1890, arriving in New York in early September with Lizzie and family securely in tow. Within days he read that "Col. John Fellows[15] is practically in Tammany and is a candidate for Congress from Mr. Fitch's district,"[16] and in the *New York Star,* "In the Thirteenth it is taken for granted that Congressman Ashbel P. Fitch does not want to go back."[17] There was no word from Fitch until Gilroy declared, "I favor the nomination of Ashbel P. Fitch."[18] That settled it. Fitch was the Democratic nominee from the Thirteenth District.

One can only speculate on whether something particular changed his mind. It seems most likely that his renewed family life was an invigorating tonic that gave him back his health and his positive, spirited, cheerful outlook. He must have concluded that to continue his political career was not only the right thing to do at the time, but in the long run, it would be most satisfying and good for business. A likely Democratic victory in November 1890, the ouster of Tom Reed as Speaker, and a position in the majority for the first time, would make his congressional service more palatable than it had ever been. Besides, the great battle, in the short term for control of the White House in 1892 and in the long term for the economic future of America, was just beginning, and he was in the midst of it.

Charles Dayton summed it up at the Harlem Democratic Club: "Mr. Fitch has faithfully and manfully withstood the appeals of his party on the tariff question. In the 1888 campaign his speeches had great weight, and today, whenever weak-kneed tariff reformers need strengthening, our distinguished congressman is sent for from all parts of the United States. I happen to know that to return to Congress is an injury to Mr. Fitch in his private affairs; but I also know that he has consented to take this nomination because as a matter of principle, he believes it is his duty to the people of this district to represent them for the third time."[19]

Nominations for New York's congressional delegation were less predictable than usual owing to the delegation's mediocrity and to shifting perceptions of both candidates and parties. The County Democracy clung to its hope of relevance and a balanced agreement with Tammany Hall, while the weaker Republicans reached out to them in the unrealistic hope of a fusion ticket that could conquer Tammany. It was soon apparent that Tammany was capable of ignoring them both. Richard Croker was approaching the zenith of his and Tammany's influence. His organization was superb. He was alert, attempting to improve the stature and prestige of the city's congressional delegation, which, after all, had a limited impact on the municipal business that he cared most for.

Immediately before the election, there was a dispute about the accuracy of the New York City census. Fitch called it a "deliberate steal."[20] Mayor Hugh Grant wrote the Secretary of the Interior formally requesting a recount, accompanied by statistical evidence to support his claim. In a short speech before Congress, Fitch said, "New York is a step-child whose existence would be gladly forgotten by the gentlemen in charge of legislation in this House. They took from us, for partisan purpose alone, the chance to give a creditable representation of the anniversary of the discovery of the country. They have, for partisan purposes alone, diminished our weight here and in the electoral college by admitting states into this Union which had not got half the population of the district which I have the honor to represent. And they have followed that up by a census taken in such a careless and partisan manner as to be a gross injustice which New York will always resent."[21]

New York's immigrant population provided a tempting target for rural American politicians to strike in order to increase the relative size of their congressional and electoral college delegations. One way to do that was to admit new states to the Union. Another way was through the census. Fitch knew that, and he drew attention to it to protect the Democratic vote in the city and by definition in the State. Both sides recognized that the New York vote, decisive in three previous presidential elections, would again be critical to the outcome of the election of 1892.[22]

Fitch's 1890 campaign message was crisp and straightforward, stressing tariff reform, a permanent improvement of the Harlem River and her harbor, strong fortifications, a readjustment of the congressional districts, so that one vote in Wyoming or Washington may not outweigh five in Harlem and a Democratic Congress because the Republicans dislike New York and will always strike at and injure her.[23]

McKinley's tariff, which had become law earlier in the year, inspired and energized Democrats. The *New Haven Register,* pointing to Fitch's Mills Bill speech of two years before, stated, "The *Register* published his speech during the last national campaign, and it was given general circulation. Wherever it went and was read, it helped the cause of tariff reform, for the question was clearly and ably argued."[24] Three years later, the vehement tariff argument that began with Cleveland's 1887 message still simmered and showed no signs of abating. In the defense of New York Fitch stood virtually alone. But he had also joined the Cleveland team on the crucial issues of tariff reform and silver coinage.

When Fitch and five other congressmen,[25] were asked to contribute to the *North American Review*,[26] it was widely assumed that he would direct his remarks to the tariff, which he did, but not before he said a few words about Speaker Reed's dictatorial rule over the House of Representatives. Thomas B. Reed,[27] a six-term Republican congressman from Maine, had emerged as Speaker of the House in the Fifty-first Congress. Reed had long fought House rules, claiming that they were "a systematic outrage on government by a majority," and that "the object of the rules appeared to be to prevent the transaction of business." Reed cut through the rules, arguing that "the only way to do business inside the rules was to suspend the rules."[28] If a member were present and failed to respond to a roll call, Reed would count him, thus preventing silent members from sabotaging a quorum. At one point he asked, "Will the gentlemen who say they are not here please take their seats?"[29]

As Fitch pointed out, "In this House the Speaker has governed the majority as well as the minority." He characterized Reed as "the second person of importance" in the government, which assessment evoked considerable notice. It was a novel idea in 1890 and marked Reed's expansion of the Speaker's role from that of a passive parliamentarian to the active framer of the legislative agenda that it is today. Reed once said, "Whenever I walk through the streets of . . . New York . . . my gorge always rises."[30] He was no friend of New York City, but when he retired from politics, he too chose to live there.

Every night that Fitch spoke he attacked the tariff. His district was the largest district by area in New York City, and the largest by population in the country. As Tammany grew stronger and tightened its grip on the city, calls for reform of the city's governance grew louder. Ex-Treasury secretary Charles Fairchild, former mayors Grace and Hewitt, and others, notably Seth Low, groped blindly for ways to unite effectively against Tammany. But they failed continually as their individual agendas wilted before Tammany's superior organization, and they would not unite. While reformers assailed Tammany, Fitch lived above the fray, successfully avoiding risky positions and focusing on national, uncontentious New York issues upon which most Democrats could agree. When the 1890 election results were tallied, he polled 28,494 votes while his opponent, Percy D. Adams, drew 12,596 votes, the largest margin of victory in the country and the largest ever given to a New York City congressman.[31]

His success was part of an overall Tammany sweep in New York City and a Democratic landslide in New York State and throughout the country. Both county candidates, Tammany opponents, lost. Voter disgust with the manipulative designs of Lodge's Force Bill, the greed evident in McKinley's tariff, Reed's arrogance, and other Republican misjudgments erupted, and even McKinley lost his House seat and was sent home to Ohio.

Cleveland remained silent throughout the election, although he was quietly inching toward his third presidential campaign. Mayor Grant, having survived the Fassett Committee's[32] threatened indictments and aided in part by the perception of a crooked Republican census, trounced the reform contender. Senator and Republican state party boss Thomas C. Platt no longer controlled the legislature, in part because of his not so stealthy hand in the city's loss of the World's Fair. Nationwide, Democrats gained 179 seats in the Fifty-second Congress, advancing from a deficit of 27 seats to a majority of 152.

The election of 1890 set the stage for the presidential election of 1892. Each party staked out its position regarding the great issues of the day (temperance, tariff, and silver among others), but it was silver that after years of debate and legislation would suddenly emerge as the national lightning rod. Silver reached beyond the whips of political party discipline because it divided both major parties. Silver separated rich and poor, east and west, and borrowers and lenders, but not Republicans and Democrats. Silver had been an important political issue for more than a quarter century. But by 1890 it was an enormous pyre, set but not yet lit. It soon became the popular symbol for what was wrong with America, and it would shake the nation's political foundations well into the following century. All it would take was the spark of a tragic depression to ignite it.

To celebrate Fitch's electoral victory, several of his close friends, including William Steinway, Thomas Gilroy, Jacob Ruppert Jr., and Charles Dayton gave a dinner in his honor at Delmonico's. The illustrious restaurant, by then operating at four locations, "had become so entwined in the city's life that the restaurant, and the people seen and heard there, drew almost as much public notice as did the capers of politicians at Tammany Hall."[33] Fifty covers were laid for an intriguing combination of New York's Cleveland and "machine" (that is "Tammany" or "Hill") Democrats. Because of the difficulties involved in bringing the two political groups together, it was understood that the dinner was a personal affair to honor Fitch and that there would be no political speeches. Newspapers reported that the evening was all joviality, marked by laughter and good humor. Grover Cleveland, unable to attend, wrote a gracious letter of regret that read in part:

> The honor thus tendered to Mr. Fitch is preeminently deserved. His steady adherence to a course which he deemed right, though it involved the alienation of political associates, and his conscientious performance of public duty with no other motive than the fulfillment of his trust, justly entitles him to the respect of his fellow citizens and to the esteem and affection of his personal friends.

> As one of his warmest friends,[34] I feel that my enforced absence on the occasion you contemplate is a real deprivation, but I am glad that I can congratulate him upon the proof which has been furnished him by the suffrages of his constituents that his efforts in behalf of good government have been fully appreciated. I am sure he never hoped for, nor could he have received, better rewards. Yours very truly, Grover Cleveland

Fitch, with a few well-chosen words, expressed his gratitude and credited his massive mandate to "his avowed opinions as a protester against an unjust and unfair treatment" of New York City.[35]

Several days later, newspaper articles describing the dinner appeared under headlines such as "Wouldn't Cheer for Him."[36] The story had leaked that William Steinway, succumbing to the good fellowship of the evening and unable to restrain himself, had burst forth with a jubilant pro-Cleveland speech finishing with "three cheers for Grover Cleveland, our next president." According to the *New York World,* "many of those present stood up and cheered. Most of the Tammany men remained in their seats."

Eastern newspapers, including one in Governor Hill's native city of Elmira,[37] strained to find out who stood and who sat. Hill, who had been lieutenant governor under Cleveland, had his eye on the Democratic presidential nomination in 1892. Cleveland stood in his way, and if Tammany opposed Cleveland, which it did, that was sufficient reason for Hill to cooperate with Tammany.

Most reports held that the dinner ended swiftly and awkwardly after Steinway's comments in support of Cleveland. Two days later, trying to make amends, he recreated his speech to the *New York Sun*[38] as an honest exposé of the probably not believable but according to Steinway indefatigable effort that Governor Hill had expended in 1888 on Cleveland's behalf and of Cleveland's recognition of Hill's effort. Steinway blamed Cleveland's loss of the city on protectionist German Democrats who voted for the Republican Harrison for president.

Further fallout came two days later, when the *Sun* reported Charles Dayton's extraordinary "County Democracy" remarks that probably followed Steinway's.[39] "This fall's election ended it," said Dayton. "We [the County Democracy] have made two big fights against Tammany with the forces of fusion. We have failed to defeat Tammany Hall, and we are now determined to recognize it as the people's choice for the Democratic organization of the city. And that it will continue to be as long as it meets public expectation in the conduct of the city's affairs."[40]

After nearly ten years opposing Tammany, the County Democracy was finished. Tammany, its disciplined antithesis, now reigned supreme. But even Tammany's stunning success, gained in the face of very determined County opposition, would be harder to duplicate without it. A dinner to honor a congressman had stirred the city's politics. Tammany's escalating dominance of New York affairs was alarming to its opponents, who imagined a return to the tragic days of Tweed. They were quick to see the similarities, but they were equally slow to see the differences, and there were many, one of the most important of which was the integrity of the city's Finance Department, which had been at the epicenter of the Tweed affair.

When Fitch returned to Washington in early February 1891, a Republican-sponsored bill to benefit the shipping industry was being debated in Congress. Fitch and most other Democrats opposed it because it subsidized ship owners; they laid any reduction of shipping on the doorstep of the tariff. Republicans, they said, wanted to reimburse shippers for the damage they inflicted on the shipping industry by their own tariff. But Republicans still held the House, and the outlook for swift passage of the bill was good. The Democratic Fifty-second Congress, elected in November of 1890, would not convene until December 1891.

Fitch, with Democratic control of the House on the horizon, promised that if the shipping bill passed, he would sponsor an inquiry in the next House into just why it did pass,[41] the implication being that he knew of corrupt practices in the sponsorship of the bill. Several newspapers hinted that his threat had found its mark.[42] Free passes on European steamers were mentioned as possible inducements for congressional support of the subsidy bill. Firing back, lobbyists for the bill asserted that Fitch may have been employed by the steamship companies, but it was not effective.

During the bill's debate the *New York World* reported,

> The most convincing argument of the day was a rattling little three-minute speech by Representative Fitch of New York . . . he said. . . . Whenever an important measure is brought into the House . . . which it is alleged will greatly benefit the laboring man we find upon close examination that it is a proposition to give a large amount of money to the friends of the other side of this House. It is a scheme to take money out of the pockets of the people and put it into the hands of those who have contributed large sums to insure the continued success of the Republican Party. . . . The stock in the Pacific Mail Steamship Co. was yesterday quoted at 38; this afternoon it is 40⅜. . . . The stockholders of the Pacific Mail Steamship Co. are the honest laboring men whom Congress is going to help. Even the galleries joined in the hand clapping that followed Mr. Fitch's well-directed thrusts.[43]

Congress careered toward its adjournment and the end of Republican rule. Before it ended, Fitch spoke on the International Copyright Bill to extend copyright protection to foreign authors. The nonpartisan bill had failed earlier in the session, but persistency on the part of a staunch group of senators and congressmen, including Henry Cabot Lodge, William McAdoo of New Jersey, and Fitch, again brought it to the floor. House debate took place on March 2, after which the bill passed, 127–77.

Congress adjourned on March 3, 1891, without voting on the shipping bill, thus defeating it in the Republican-controlled House, and Fitch had led the opposition. He returned home to look after the legal affairs of his clients and to attend a flurry of social, business, and political dinners and meetings. The Fifty-first Congress was a failure if measured by progress on the Democratic agenda, but it was an equally clear strategic success. Democratic morale was sky high because they had placed themselves on the right side of important issues, especially the tariff, and they were in a position to win. Republicans, in a classic triumph of greed over fear, in control of both houses and the presidency, had overreached. In hindsight, Democrats had both the issues and the candidate. It would be a matter of execution as to whether they could retake the White House.

With Fitch's victory over the shipping lobby as a backdrop, the Harlem Democratic Club held its semimonthly meeting on the day Congress adjourned. Charles Dayton, commenting on his recent trip to Washington, where he witnessed "the gallant fight against the Ship Subsidy Bill," said, "I know that I am justified in saying that it was under the leadership of our own congressman, Ashbel P. Fitch, that the Democrats gained one of the greatest triumphs over one of the largest and most formidable lobbies that ever existed." He went on to suggest that the club "tender him a reception" in recognition "of Mr. Fitch's glorious record in this matter."[44]

The extraordinary reception was held in early April at the clubhouse on 125th Street. Fitch arrived smiling, with Lizzie on his arm. They were greeted warmly with cheers of support and congratulations from 150 of his friends. After several speakers recognized his work in the Fifty-first Congress, Charles Dayton presented Fitch with a magnificent Tiffany sterling silver punch bowl one and one-half feet high and six feet in circumference. "May your household, wife and children," said Dayton, "and those who shall come after them, ever treasure this bowl as a symbol of friendship, love and duty."[45] The enormous bowl was rolled into view amidst enthusiastic applause.[46]

Fitch was overwhelmed by the rare gift. "On rising to respond, he was received with loud cheers and waving of handkerchiefs." Cordially taking Dayton's hand he said, "There is nothing in the world that feels so good as the grasp of the hand of an old friend." In a tremulous voice, nearly overcome with feeling, he continued, "I assure you it is not so hard to speak to a hostile Speaker or an insolent majority in the House as it is to speak to a party of men like you. . . . I feel here tonight as if I were in my own house and I feel as if I were in the circle of my own family."[47] He thanked them profusely for their gift and for their loyalty. Fitch's son Morton recalled, "No one event in Father's political career gave him greater pleasure than the presentation to him of the silver punch bowl by his friends in the Thirteenth Congressional District."[48]

A dinner to celebrate the passing of the International Copyright Law, attended by numerous authors from both political parties, was held in the second week of April. On the night that Fitch received his splendid silver bowl, he had said a few words about copyright: "The fight to get for the author who has written a book the same protection as is given to a patentee has lasted for forty years. To me it seems impossible how anyone could say that the man who wrote *Hiawatha* was not entitled to the same protection as the man who invented a mousetrap and yet there were men who defended that course."[49] The dinner at Sherry's was a grand celebration mingling politicians, educators, and authors from across the country.

Three months later, on the Fourth of July 1891, Congressman Benton McMillin of Tennessee came to New York for the dedication of the "Sunset" Cox monument on Astor Place, since removed to Tompkins Square Park. McMillin was one of three contenders for the House speakership in the upcoming Fifty-second Congress, the other two being Judge Charles F. Crisp of Georgia and Texan Roger Q. Mills of Mills Bill fame. McMillin thought his chances were good, although he noted that all three contenders were southerners, the implication being that a split vote might open the door for a northerner.

Fitch, on good terms with each hopeful, offered only that "McMillin will get the majority of the New York delegation, although after speeches from both Crisp and McMillin at the dedication, maybe Crisp will be stronger."[50] This would be an important contest when Congress convened in December, for Cleveland and for Fitch. For Cleveland, in biographer Nevins's words, the election of Crisp "[struck] a blow at Cleveland and [opened] a Pandora's Box of evils."[51] For Fitch, his votes for Crisp seemed to be anomalous, a deviation from the otherwise remarkable success he had both placating Tammany and supporting Cleveland. While the truth cannot be known, it is difficult to follow the trail of Fitch's checkered relationship with Tammany and Richard Croker without acknowledging the possible personal significance of his votes for Crisp for Speaker of the House in December 1891.

As the year came to a close, Democrats, who only the year before were a minority in Congress, regained control with a vengeance in the autumn of 1890, and in late 1891 they were eagerly looking forward to recapturing the White House in 1892.

6

Silver Beckons

Fifty-second Congress, 1890–1892

We do not envy the nature of any citizen who could read the manly, logical and eloquent words of Mr. Fitch without a thrill of sympathetic pride.

—*New York Times,* May 11, 1890

Although the 1892 presidential election was still a year away, the election of a new House Speaker marked the substantive beginning of the race between Cleveland and David B. Hill for the Democratic presidential nomination. Cleveland had not yet declared his candidacy, and no one was sure if he could be nominated and win if he did. In 1888 he had believed he could win the presidency without winning New York, but three years later he knew that was not true.

The two leading candidates for House Speaker were Crisp of Georgia and Mills of Texas. Charles F. Crisp was born in Sheffield, England, in 1845. Historian Allan Nevins described him as a man with "picturesque antecedents. His parents had been roving English actors,"[1] although Crisp was raised in Georgia. He joined the Confederate Army in 1861 at sixteen and fought for three years before being taken prisoner in May 1864. Following his release in 1865, he studied law, became a judge, and was first elected to Congress in 1882. Mills, raised in Texas, was twelve years Crisp's senior. He too fought in the Confederate Army throughout the war and was first elected to Congress in 1872. He was the Democratic Party's leading expert on the tariff, having devoted his nearly twenty years in the House to understanding the pain the tariff inflicted on his constituency.

The similarities between the two southerners went well beyond their shared experience as Confederate soldiers. Both said they were for tariff reform and both supported the free coinage of silver, as did many southern and western Democrats. Silver was inflationary. Silver was the debtor's friend. Silver expanded the money supply, helped ease credit, and stimulated exports by cheapening the dollar. These features of silver coinage favored the southern economy. It was in their relative emphasis that differences between the two men emerged.

To Mills, nothing was more important than tariff reform, and that endeared him to Cleveland. Cleveland knew that politically a new Democratic-controlled Congress should deal with the tariff quickly and successfully before it dealt with silver because the tariff united Democrats. Democrats from the north, south, and west favored tariff reform, and it appeared that Democrats had the votes to pass tariff legislation if they would organize to do so. Silver, on the other hand, divided Democrats, and for that matter it divided Republicans too. People with money to lend wanted to be repaid what they lent, not something less valuable. Landlords with apartments to lease wanted their rent paid in gold, and, increasingly, they insisted on it. Any congressional effort to deal with silver before dealing with the tariff might sabotage later attempts at tariff reform. Cleveland, out of office, edging toward another presidential run, looking more and more like a candidate, preferred Mills to Crisp if only for his dedication to tariff reform.

Crisp, the pragmatist, prized the minimum of five votes that Tammany could deliver for any House bill and for his own race for Speaker. Crisp wanted to be recognized as the Speaker of the House who delivered the free coinage of silver to America more than he wanted tariff reform. Tammany supported Crisp not for his views on silver or the tariff, but because Crisp was willing to bargain with them. Crisp let it be known that he sought Tammany support, and that was another reason for Cleveland to be attracted to Mills. Outgoing New York governor David B. Hill, who at that moment had presidential aspirations, knowing Tammany's aversion to Cleveland and seeing Tammany allied with Crisp, embraced them both. His enemy's enemies were his friends.

There was no motivation for Fitch to take sides in the Speaker fight. By his public statements, all the candidates appeared to suit him. His unwavering support of Cleveland suggested a preference for Mills. But Fitch was a New York Democrat who was publicly allied with Tammany. While he had overcome the growing distaste for congressional life that had gripped him eighteen months earlier, the roots of his discontent lingered. He commuted weekly to Washington for nearly five years, and he spent lavishly. His professional practice did well, but not as well as it might, and his six children, now ages four to sixteen, were growing up too often without him. Fitch valued the grateful support of his friends and surely enjoyed his leadership of important debates in Congress, but he needed to return to New York for his health and his peace of mind.

Resigning from Congress was one way to exit, but if he wanted to remain active in New York politics, Richard Croker held the key to his future. Croker's sudden interest in House affairs added to the delicacy of Fitch's situation. Croker could deliver votes in Congress for the speakership or anything else. He knew that he would get nothing from Cleveland, and that put him at odds with Mills. All of this worked to align Tammany with Hill for president, Crisp for Speaker, and probably a list of favors for Tammany from both Hill and Crisp.

As an example of what went on, when Fitch decided preliminarily against running for Congress the year before, Tammany planned to replace him with Fellows. When Fitch reconsidered, Charles "Ice Man" Turner from the Sixth District was directed to step aside for Fellows. Turner was told to attend the convention, decline to run, and nominate Fellows, all of which he did. He was told that he would not be forgotten.

After the election of 1891, Francis B. Spinola of the old Tenth District died, and Croker replaced him not with Turner but with Bourke Cockran, a Tammany sachem, Irish-born, educated in France, articulate, a superb orator, and well connected. Concurrently, Thomas Coakley, another Tammany Democrat who had been Assistant Doorkeeper in the House of Representatives, launched his personal campaign to become Doorkeeper. Before it went too far, Croker told Coakley to make a losing fight because he had decided to bring Turner back as Doorkeeper. Thus, the former congressman from the Sixth District of New York in the Fiftieth Congress became Doorkeeper of the Fifty-second Congress.[2]

As Tammany was booming Crisp for Speaker, many papers, the *Washington Post,* for instance, supposed that Fitch would support Mills.[3] The *New York Tribune* said that John DeWitt Warner would also vote independently from Tammany if both he and Fitch thought that electing Mills would improve Cleveland's chances for the nomination.[4] The *New York Sun* said that Bourke Cockran and Fitch "will not obey instructions" and that Croker was on his way to Washington to see that his "orders are carried out."[5]

Various newspapers put forth several lesser issues as they tried to develop proprietary insights into the Speaker's race. The *Harlem Reporter* said that Crisp would be more supportive of the "finishing of the Harlem Ship Canal"[6] than would Mills. The *New York Evening Post* declared that "Crisp is too much of a prohibitionist to suit Mr. Fitch."[7] But the *New York Mail and Express* pronounced, "The Speakership fight has now passed from a contest between Mills and Crisp and represents solely the battle between the Cleveland-Carlisle and Hill-Gorman factions. It is a battle . . . which the leaders are going to fight to the bitter end, . . . which does not look at all bright for Cleveland and Mills."[8] This was a Washington fight that Croker wanted to join because he could see that if Crisp prevailed, Tammany would be rewarded.

Fitch, ordinarily talkative, was unusually subdued. When he was cornered he was careful. "They are four [Mills, Crisp, Springer, and McMillin] very eminent gentlemen, and whether they get to be Speaker or not they are [each] bound to be a power in the House,"[9] or "The Democratic Party would be perfectly safe with either of the four."[10]

The *New York Tribune* said that Cleveland's attempts to feign his lack of interest in the fight for Speaker failed to deceive anyone. There were rumors of Daniel Lamont's "shameful errand" to see Brooklyn "Boss" McLaughlin, to "end-run" Tammany on Cleveland's behalf. One of Mills's lieutenants was quoted, "If we win, it will be a great victory over the anti-Cleveland combine led by David B. Hill, 'Boss' Croker and the Tammany organization."[11]

The polling began on Saturday, December 5. The party caucus was held on the floor of the House, with the candidates and their followers occupying adjoining committee rooms, Mills in Ways and Means and Crisp in Appropriations. An hour before, the rooms and corridors began to fill with members, as well as with the idle curious. The *New York World,* two weeks before the vote, predicted Crisp winning by 107 to Mills's 54. The first ballot in fact showed Crisp considerably weaker (84 votes) and Mills stronger (78 votes) than predicted, but Crisp led nevertheless.

On the seventeenth and final ballot of the day, Crisp's lead stood at 94–91. Feverish counting and strategic moves and countermoves by each of the leading candidates marked the voting. Visits to restaurants and anxious on-and-off deliberations about whether to adjourn were calculated to entice one of the also-rans to withdraw. Amid tactical speculation about losses, gains, and momentum, or who was ready to drop out, all the participants were defending the future of the Republic as they saw it. The caucus ran ten hours, to eleven o'clock that night, when it was adjourned and scheduled to reconvene at ten o'clock Monday morning.

When the voting resumed, there was little movement and no letup in the tense struggle. On the twenty-second ballot Crisp led Mills by 2 votes. But on the twenty-third Crisp led by 5, which became 6 after the twenty-fourth. When Crisp managed 2 more votes on the twenty-eighth and another on the twenty-ninth, he had 104 votes, with only 114 needed to win. The end was near. Springer's total had been eroding while McMillin's had held steady at 19. On the thirtieth ballot, 15 of McMillin's 19 votes moved to the Crisp column and the contest was ended.

Fitch voted for Crisp on every ballot. The *New York Times* was rancorous and vengeful in defeat. About Cockran and Fitch, the latter whom it had always admired, it grumbled, "The New York congressmen who obeyed the orders of Tammany and Hill are for the most part of the sort who are fit only for such work, but Messrs. Fitch and Cockran are making a gratuitous sacrifice of such a future as manhood can command."[12]

The next day was no better. After pronouncing that "the policy of the Democratic Party has changed," the *Times* observed with some sarcasm that "Tammany Hall received a part of its reward at once in the election of Turner as Doorkeeper. Of course the House may be assumed to know what it wants by what it does. But it is a rather expensive thing to compel the Democratic Party to elect a Speaker representing a reactionary and perhaps fatal policy, as the price of the gift to the Congress for two years of Turner's society."[13]

Mills was crushed. When he left the House floor, "his face was flushed and his manner [was] that of a thoroughly angry as well as terribly disappointed man."[14] He retreated to his hotel room at Willard's, where he became seriously ill, delirious with malaria. When he recovered he sulked, as Crisp assembled his new Democratic team. In spite of recurrent reports that Crisp would reappoint Mills chairman of Ways and Means for the Fifty-second Congress, the position Mills held in the Fiftieth Congress under Speaker Carlisle, he did not. Mills realized that he would no longer be a power in the House, and his nineteen-year House career, always aimed directly at the Speakership, was effectively finished.

Judging what was behind Fitch's votes for Speaker is an intriguing exercise. Why did Fitch vote for Crisp? On the surface he should have preferred Mills to Crisp. On the other hand, Croker supported Crisp, and Croker controlled Fitch's political future in New York. It appears that Fitch would not want to antagonize him. There are other possible reasons, though, that Fitch might have voted for Crisp. He might have disagreed with Mills on the tactical aspects of tariff reform; Crisp had devised what he called a "piecemeal" policy that supposedly constituted tariff reform by adding taxed items to the "free list." Or, having worked with Crisp on parliamentary matters he might have been closer personally to Crisp than he was to Mills, and he might have believed that Crisp would be a more effective Speaker than Mills. There is no way of knowing. But it seems possible that Fitch's votes for Crisp were one half of a bargain with Richard Croker, perhaps made, perhaps implied or most likely simply hoped for, that would ultimately return Ashbel Fitch to New York. Whatever the reason for his vote, Fitch would continue to support Cleveland without confronting Tammany, if that were possible, for as long as possible.

Crisp, speaking later to reassure his opponents while extending thanks to his supporters, said, "I beg to say to you now, when I speak the first words to you since I am your selection for Speaker, that my election means no step backward on tariff reform. I desire to say that there is in our party today no man who more earnestly believes in the Democratic doctrine of tariff reform than I do."[15]

The *New York Herald* spoke with Fitch in January about tariff reform. Said Fitch, "The free list . . . is the tariff reformer's hope. The way to accomplish permanent reform . . . is to place articles on the free list. Once there, they are not likely to be disturbed in time of peace . . . but [if left off the free list] with a considerable duty the rate is likely to be shoved up and down by successive congresses without attaining permanent relief from taxation for the people. . . . I believe that Mr. Crisp is a consistent tariff reformer and that [the] committee will carry out the wishes of the Democratic Party expressed in the elections of 1890."[16] Regardless of his statements to the contrary, it is hard to believe that Fitch was not aware of the obstacles that a piecemeal policy would face.[17]

Crisp then did exactly what the *New York Times,* Cleveland, and Fitch would have preferred he not do, that is, along with Bland of Missouri, ignite another silver war before effectively dealing with tariff reform. Cleveland was far from defeated, though, as the *Times* had fretted, and Fitch would redeem himself if redemption were called for and play a fascinating, perhaps decisive, role in Cleveland's resurgence.

Immediately after the vote for Speaker, Fitch's stalwart defender, the *Harlem Reporter,* offered this gratuitous advice to the *Times,* "The *Times* wonders whether 'any of Mr. Fitch's constituents in the Thirteenth District have taken the trouble to write to him a letter of censure for his support of Mr. Crisp?' . . . The *Reporter* regrets as much as anyone that the congressman . . . could not view the speakership contest as it did and that he voted against Mr. Mills. We do not believe, however, that anything Mr. Fitch did warrants the abuse the *Times* has visited upon him. . . . The congressman has proved his devotion to tariff reform . . . Mr. Fitch used his judgment . . . and believing Judge Crisp was sound on the tariff, gave him his vote . . . The *Times* should stop its scolding."[18]

As the cheering, congratulations, and chants of "Crisp, Crisp, Crisp" subsided, there began the slower, more drawn out days of what either "might have been" or "should have been" and the even more derogatory celebrations of the "free-trader" Mills's defeat. Attention moved away from the result of the caucus to the new Speaker's appointments.

It was widely assumed that Fitch would be named to the Ways and Means Committee. The *Brooklyn Standard Union*[19] held that line, as did the *New York Recorder.*[20] The *Washington Post* said there would be a New York man on Ways and Means "probably Mr. Fitch,"[21] as did the *Chicago Times.*[22] The *Herald* said that "Mr. Fitch is likely to be one of five northern Democrats on Ways and Means,"[23] and the *New York Mail and Express,*[24] *Boston Daily Traveler,*[25] and *New York Times*[26] all reported Fitch on Ways and Means as fact. The *New York Journal,* raising a cautionary flag, said that Cockran and Fitch both wanted Ways and Means but that "Fitch's absenteeism is proving a handicap to him in the fight for the place."[27] The *New York Sun* carried a similar story with Cockran having the inside track, presumably not because he had better attendance, because he did not, but because he was a Tammany sachem and Fitch was not.[28]

Crisp announced his committees the next day, and Cockran was named to Ways and Means. It was supposed that one reason Crisp did not pick Fitch for Ways and Means was that his attendance record was not good, and a committee such as Ways and Means, which authors the nation's tax laws, needed its members to attend meetings. In this respect Fitch's dual life took its toll. As an offset to his attendance record, however, he was accessible and responsive to his constituents, he dutifully answered his mail, and he participated in important debates that affected New York or when great national issues hung in the balance. His enormous capacity for work preempted constituent complaints. But the day-to-day tedium of House procedural debate and the resolution of rules were beyond his patience. The startling irony of Cockran's appointment, however, was not lost on the *New York Telegram,* which took great pains to point out that Cockran's attendance was no better than Fitch's.[29]

Notwithstanding press speculation that Fitch sought Ways and Means, it is doubtful that he did or that he was disappointed with his assignments. Ways and Means would have required important changes in his life, most notably in the time that would be available to him to manage his law practice, changes that he might have been unwilling or unable to make. The *New York Telegram* said that Tammany wanted a chairmanship for Fitch and that Crisp opposed it because of Fitch's attendance record.[30] Crisp seems to have slated Fitch for the Appropriations Committee. When Fitch learned of it, he reportedly asked one of his brewer friends to intervene, which if they were asked they probably did, the result being a chairmanship of the Committee on Private Land Claims[31] along with his familiar and most welcome place on Foreign Affairs. The *New York Sun* noted that "both were very much to his liking."[32] The *New York Tribune* pointed out that Private Land Claims was "of slight importance since the establishment of the Land Court, but the Chairman enjoys the benefit of clerical assistance at public expense,"[33] surely no small matter of either convenience or expense to Fitch, and it must have pleased him.

Cockran's assignment to Ways and Means illustrates, as did the Turner appointment, the quid pro quos that went on between Crisp and Croker. Cockran, a brilliant orator, bon vivant, and life of any gathering with his tuneful Irish brogue, was, according to the *Philadelphia Ledger,* a "remarkable selection."[34] Only the overbearing influence of Tammany, where Cockran was one of the "Big Four," could have provided him with such a platform.[35] The *Ledger* added, "This is only his second term in Congress. He is an able man but he has devoted his life to local politics and criminal law, and has, so far as anyone here knows, never devoted a day's study to the tariff question." The *New York Press* more succinctly added, "Bourke Cockran is on the Ways and Means Committee, an utterly absurd place for him."[36] The *New York Times* called it "either impudent trading with Tammany or incredible folly."[37]

With all eyes in Washington beginning to turn toward the fall election, Fitch's public face appeared in both the Hill camp, probably for his votes for Crisp, and the

Cleveland camp. In that, though alone, he was on familiar ground, at ease with ambiguity. For six years, through three House elections, both Tammany and the County Democracy, bitter antagonists themselves, either formally or informally endorsed his candidacy, the latter even when he was a Republican. With the County Democracy in demise and Tammany in its ascendancy, he needed all his political skills to remain on good terms with both the Hill and the Cleveland contingents. In short interviews with the New York World, seven New York City congressmen were asked whether Cleveland or Hill would have the New York delegation. Six of the seven gave short answers; four supported of Hill and two declined to comment. Said Fitch, "it seems to me that all of us in Congress who desire Democratic success next year will do better to spend our time in attacks on the Republicans and their policy than in attacks on each other. . . . There has been more than enough talk about our differences."[38]

The *New York Telegram* said, "It is very clear that . . . there is an organized Tammany effort to boom Senator Hill . . . Congressman Fitch [and others] does his share of Hill booming."[39] *Puck* ran a large colorful cartoon[40] showing Hill and Croker driving an engine with a trailing car full of supporters, rather prominently including Fitch, driving toward Chicago and presumably a Hill nomination for president. Fitch learned from Goethe to face the fact of Hill's opposition to Cleveland and, irrespective of his votes for Crisp, to move on without otherwise yielding in his support of Cleveland.

When, for example, in early February, Roger Mills arrived in New York as the guest of the Reform Club,[41] Cleveland people to the core, "in the Club House were Carl Schurz, Charles S. Fairchild, Ashbel P. Fitch, Francis Lynde Stetson" and several others.[42] The *New York Tribune* reported that Fitch was in a group at dinner with Mills before the reception to which "All of the Democratic members of Congress from New York City were invited, but the Tammany Hall delegation was conspicuous in its absence. In fact the whole meeting was strongly flavored with anti-Hill feeling."[43]

In January 1892, the Democratic National Committee set the time and place for the national convention as June 21 in Chicago. The New York committee then set the time and place for the state convention as February 22 in Albany, well before upstate roads were cleared of snow. The public reaction to the much-too-early date reinforced the perception of many voters that Hill was slippery. It was seen as a way for Hill to try to gain an advantage for his urban supporters over his rural opponents and as an attempt to spawn a national Hill bandwagon. The convention had never before been held before mid-April. The public response was immediate. The Reform Club of New York fastened the label "snap" on the premature convention. The name stuck, and it hurt Hill. His supporters became "snappers," and Cleveland's were "anti-snappers." The "snap convention" marked the initial slowdown and ultimate wreck of the Hill campaign. But it was not so clear at the time, and Cleveland's men had work to do.

While presidential politics heated up in early 1892, the *New York Telegram* carried a small, probably little-noticed item, reporting that "Cong. Ashbel P. Fitch is making a tremendous opposition to the proposed [Bland] Free Coinage Bill. He argues that New York cannot be carried by the Democrats [in the next election] on a free coinage measure. He is credited with having converted five Congressmen inside of an hour to his views on the silver question."[44] Fitch believed that if a free, that is, unlimited silver coinage law emerged from the Fifty-second Congress that was controlled by Democrats, New York State and, if the recent past were any guide, the presidency would probably be lost to Democrats in 1892.

Silver coinage was a quintessential American political issue, a proxy for other great issues wherein vital interests are often opposed and for the means by which they are decided in the American democracy. On the pro-silver side stood the special interests of wealthy silver-mine owners allied conveniently with an array of hard-working ordinary citizens who may have borrowed money to help meet their goals in life or who were otherwise struggling to make ends meet. These citizens believed in the unlimited coinage of silver. Lined up in opposition were the country's major lenders and another array of hard working citizens who had saved their money or who were dependent on fixed incomes or both. Unlimited coinage of silver would probably cause these people serious economic injury or even financial ruin, and many of them were Fitch's New York City constituents. The moral trump card in the contest was the sanctity of contracts that Americans prized, as well as the country's unwillingness to turn its back on the old saws, such as "a man's word is his bond" and "a deal's a deal."

The *New York Mail and Express* published a pithy history of the complicated topic of silver, the central idea of which was that the value of a commodity depended on its relative supply and demand.[45] In the twenty-five years since 1848, when gold was discovered in California, the United States had produced about six times as much gold as silver. This large, incremental supply of gold depressed its price and sent silver to a premium, whereby it was held (or better said, "hoarded") for as long as the premium prevailed, just as Sir Thomas Gresham (1519–1579) said it would be more than three hundred years before in his famous "law." Gresham said in 1558 that when two coins are equal in debt-paying value but unequal in intrinsic value, the one having the lesser intrinsic value tends to remain in circulation and the other to be hoarded.

The pre-1873 premium, therefore, that took silver out of circulation preempted its coinage. Silver was demonetized in 1873 when the price of gold was approximately sixteen times the price of silver. But from then on, until 1889, the relative production of the two metals reversed. Silver production was double that of gold. In other countries around the world, production trends were similar, although the disparity between the two metals was not as great as it was in the United States. The Bland-Allison Act of 1878[46] that mandated a 16:1 silver-to-gold ratio meant that silver coins, with the same debt-paying value as gold coins, would weigh sixteen times more than the gold coins and would have had a similar intrinsic value in 1873. By 1878, the same amount of silver would have had an intrinsic value of about 90 percent of the gold, and the "holding back" of gold would have begun.

The government's gold reserves, established for the purpose of redeeming greenbacks, were generally considered to be adequate at $100 million.[47] In order to appease the silver interests, however, the Bland-Allison Act forced the federal government to purchase and either coin or issue greenbacks for $2 to $4 million of silver bullion per month, all of which was backed by the gold reserve. As the amount of silver and greenbacks in the money supply increased, and the price of silver declined, more people began hoarding more gold. While the government continued paying its obligations in gold, its revenue increasingly consisted of silver and greenbacks, not gold, so the combination of the two, silver and greenbacks coming in and gold going out, produced a net gold outflow that drained the nation's gold reserves.

For years the pro-silver forces in Congress worked to "liberate" silver from what they viewed as the confines of the Bland-Allison Act, which, while mandating silver coinage, limited the amount coined. An article in the *New York Commercial Bulletin* that added fuel to the fire had appeared two years before in early April 1890 under the headline "Opposing the Silver Bill—Eastern Members of Congress Beginning to Realize the Danger." The hard-money men wanted to repeal Bland-Allison, to rid the nation's money supply of silver forever. But faced with a new silver bill that many in Congress apparently believed would carry, the article described the eastern members' growing disputation of the "proposition that a silver bill must be passed. The young reform Democrats, especially Mr. Andrew of Boston, Mr. Fitch and Mr. Flower, both of New York, are beginning to consult on the subject both in its fiscal and political relations."[48]

The ill-considered, indeed disastrous new bill became the Sherman Silver Purchase Act of 1890. A conference committee fixed the Treasury's purchase obligation at four and one-half million ounces of silver monthly at market rates, nearly twice as much as required under the Bland-Allison Act it supplanted, and almost the entire output of the western mines. Although the Sherman Act magnified the silver folly, as the price of silver was by then roughly 80 percent of the price of gold at 16:1, it was still not free coinage. Coupled with the McKinley Tariff, however, it would have a calamitous impact on the American economy.

By 1892, at 16:1, silver traded at about 70 percent of the price of gold. The inevitable conclusion was that "free and unlimited" coinage of the less valuable silver would drive the more valuable gold out of circulation and would significantly repudiate outstanding debt and other contractual obligations. Why would one repay a one dollar debt with one dollar if it were possible to repay it with seventy cents? One would not, and that was the sought-after opportunity for western and southern farmers and businessmen, to engineer an enormous wealth transfer away from the nation's banking centers and across rural America.

In February of 1891, a year before the little-noticed item describing Fitch's anti-silver activity appeared in the *New York Telegram,* Cooper Union was the site of a major anti-free coinage rally to issue publicly a policy statement for the anti-silver forces to support and defend. Fitch, probably in Washington, sent a letter of regret, as did Grover Cleveland. Cleveland at the time was only haltingly becoming publicly reengaged in politics. Cleveland's letter was, on one hand, one of gratitude, "that the business interests of New York are at last to be heard on this subject," but on the other hand ("the dangerous, reckless experiment of free unlimited and independent silver coinage"), it was an aggressive attack on free coinage.[49]

Former Treasury secretary Charles Fairchild, building on Cleveland's attack, added, "I am here tonight because I once held a high office, in which I was immediately preceded by a good man, and immediately followed by another good man.[50] Both are gone, and both owed their death, in no small measure, as I believe, to the excessive anxiety which they felt from the evils that they feared this issue [silver coinage] might cause the country."[51] After years of debate and legislation on the fringe of the American consciousness, in February 1891 silver was fast becoming the farthest-reaching and most talked-about economic issue of the day, supplanting even tariff reform.

Five resolutions were adopted at the Cooper Union rally, one of them "That the first requirement of a sound metallic currency is that its value shall be permanently stable." A second resolution accurately and succinctly summarized the reasons New Yorkers opposed free coinage:

> That the proposed debasement of our currency . . . will impair private and public credit; it will confuse and hamper our commercial relations with gold paying countries; it will curtail legitimate business; it will violate the obligations of existing contracts and disastrously affect many industries; it will fall with peculiar severity on the depositors in savings banks, and trust companies and those holding life insurance and mutual benefit policies; it will lessen the purchasing power of the money in which are paid the earnings of laborers and of the salaried classes.[52]

That resolution held the essence of the argument for gold-backed currency for the citizens of New York.

So in February 1892, two years after passage of the Sherman Act and one year after the Cooper Union rally, Congressman Richard Parks "Silver Dick" Bland, Democrat of Missouri, introduced another in a long line of silver bills[53] to provide for the "free and unlimited coinage of silver," precisely the bill that Speaker Crisp's opponents feared. This bill would go beyond the Sherman Act, replacing mandated amounts of silver purchase with the free and unlimited coinage of silver, limited only by the available supply of silver.

The *New York Evening Post* under the headline "Silver Heresy" outlined Fitch's view that to dilute the nation's currency with silver would "practically wipe us out if carried far enough."[54] Historians have pointed to slavery as the first major issue to divide the nation on a sectional basis.[55] Silver divided America, too. Silver was fast emerging as the single sectional economic issue that could and would dominate the nation's political landscape for the next decade.

Because Democrats controlled the House, a fight about silver coinage could only hurt them. Republicans, as divided on silver coinage as were Democrats but out of power, gleefully watched the turmoil in the Democrats' ranks. While silver coinage split both parties, generally on a sectional basis, with much of the South and West for and the Northeast against, it was the common view of Fitch and others that if the Democrats, the party of tariff reform, passed a silver bill prior even to reporting a tariff bill out of committee, then recent Democratic gains, especially in the northeast, would be placed at risk, as would Democratic control of the House and the election of a Democratic president in 1892.[56]

The still gloomy *New York Times* went so far as to say that if the new Bland Free Coinage Bill passed, "the nomination of Mr. Cleveland will be made extremely doubtful, if not impracticable."[57] For all those reasons, Fitch thought the Bland Bill was worth fighting. For his part, Bland believed that his bill would pass easily in the House. He seemed to have assumed that the gold Democrats lacked strength and leadership, which they did not, and that he would gain a few Republican votes, which he did. He was assisted in his work by William Jennings Bryan, the first-term Democrat from Nebraska, who was in his first silver fight. Fitch watched Bryan and did not like what he saw.

With Democratic divisions on presidential politics, tariff reform, and silver coinage as a bewildering backdrop, the House opened for business on Monday, March 7, 1892. Before the chaplain had added his "amen" to the opening prayer, Thomas Catchings, Democrat of Mississippi, one of Crisp's top aides and chairman of the Rules Committee, leapt to his feet. Catchings offered a resolution that set March 22–24 as the date for debate of the Bland Free Coinage Bill, which date was a significant deviation from the normal legislative sequence. Catchings caught the anti-silver men off guard. Rallying quickly, floor leader Charles Tracey objected. Tracey said that the prior day's journal had not yet been read, so the resolution was out of order.

Crisp replied that the Rules Committee was always in order. Tracey, alertly recognizing a chance to filibuster Crisp's ruling, declared that no business could be done before the journal was read. Within a few minutes, preserving the remainder of his time, he yielded the floor to Fitch, who compared Catchings's report to Hill's "snap" convention, implying duplicity and deceit. Fitch claimed that every parliamentary body in the world corrected its journal before it proceeded to the business of another day, and if the rules authorized the Speaker's ruling, they should not. Unfortunately he paused at a moment of Tracey's distraction, so in an instant of silence between the two, Crisp recognized Bland. A furious Charles Tracey protested to no avail that he still had the floor.

Bland seemed surprised at the filibuster, claiming that Bourke Cockran and John Andrew, Democrat of Massachusetts, had promised Bland there would be no filibuster. This set off another uproar—Cockran and Andrew were on their feet at once with about fifty other Democrats crying foul. From that point on, the day was lost to short speeches, rules requests, clarifications, points of order, amendments, and the like, but at five o'clock the journal was finally read and March 22 was set as the date for debate, an initial victory for the silver men.

When the debate resumed, arguments on both sides revolved around conflicting, sometimes speculative, understandings of the economic impact of free coinage. Fitch, preferring to avoid the murky waters of economic theory, offered instead of his own analysis the petition of the New York State Chamber of Commerce. The chamber "states with such clearness and accuracy the views which I hold on the subject that, after reading it, I prefer to present no further argument . . . but to say simply that the statement . . . covers completely the case against the free coinage of silver as we in New York understand it."[58]

The Chamber petition read, "any change in the existing standard of value affecting outstanding contracts necessarily changes the amount to be paid by debtors and to be received by creditors . . . any degradation in the standard of value simply confiscates a portion of the income of all who derive support from wages, salaries, loans, pensions, savings bank deposits or accumulations in the form of life insurance and annuities." That argument, in spite of its overpowering logic, had for years fallen on the deaf ears of silver men who profited from silver mines and silver coinage. Fitch, waving the Chamber's report as he endorsed it, wrapped his position not only in the Chamber's economic terms but in his own political terms, hoping to gain Democratic converts.

Party members on both sides were influenced more by where they lived than by their political party. But there was too, in Fitch's view, an unbecoming class aspect of the debate that he would not ignore. Said he,

> It is interesting to notice from the advertisements in the New York daily papers that whenever gentlemen, like the member from California, in any part of the country, desire a new system of waterworks, or of lighting by gas or electricity, or new communication through their streets or with other cities—when, in fact, anything is to be done which needs any money they come to these "bandit chiefs of Wall Street," as my friend describes them, for help and assistance. Even the "honest farmer," Mr. Speaker, in the West or the South when he needs a little money to improve his farm, seeks a good-natured, accommodating "bandit of Wall Street" who lends it to him, and then often finds both principal and interest paid only in abuse of New York City and of the so-called "creditor class."[59]

The *New York World* said he "scored the first hit of the day,"[60] and the *New York Sun* enthused, "the most interesting and spirited speech was made by Rep. Fitch."[61] But try as they might, the anti-silver men failed to enlist Republican leaders Reed and Lodge in their battle to derail the bill. Both men made no secret of the fact that they would vote against it, but in the meantime they enjoyed watching the Democrats fight with each other.

Late in the afternoon on the third day Bland, who with Crisp remained confident of the bill's passage, moved the question. The vote was whether the bill would be brought forward on the House calendar or taken up in its proper order, which would probably kill it for the session. Crisp, with a tight grip on his gavel, was nevertheless unprepared for the action of Republican congressman Julius Caesar Burrows of Michigan, who moved to table the bill. Crisp reluctantly admitted that Burrows's motion took precedence over Bland's and everyone knew that if Burrows's motion carried, the Bland Bill was dead.

This time the silver men were on the defensive. As daylight faded, the Capitol's gaslights glowed in the gathering darkness and spurred interest and excitement as the crowd continued to grow. Every seat was filled. The aisles were "packed like an immense bank of flowers far into the corridor and beyond."[62] The crowded House floor made it difficult for members to move around and stay in close touch with one another as the drama unfolded. Burrows's action inspired the Democrats, who were looking for any sign from the Republicans that help was at hand, and this was the sign they were looking for.

The vote to table, 148 in favor and 147 opposed, put the anti-silver men on the edge of ecstasy. But Crisp asked for a recapitulation. He asked the clerk to call his own name and the Speaker's "no" vote created a 148–148 tie. Then, with the anti-silver men led by Tracey, Fitch, and Bourke Cockran moving to recess, moving adjournments, calling the role, and creating whatever other delays they could, the filibuster began.

There was a loud argument about whether Dennis D. Donovan of Ohio, recorded as voting against tabling the bill, was even in the hall. The sergeant at arms was asked to restore order, and he did so "bearing the mace and passing about the hall to see that members resumed their seats."[63] According to the *New York Tribune*, "cries of order and a tremendous increase in the turbulence drowned all coherent remarks. The scene was one the like of which old members of the House cannot recall, and the proceedings were indescribable in detail. When 'Ike' Hill seized the mace and strode down the main aisle, members fell back as he approached. Tremendous applause and laughter greeted him and good nature was temporarily restored."[64]

The evening wound down as members "paired"[65] and left while some others were excused for reasons of ill health. Cockran left and at 12:25 A.M.; Bland surrendered, moving adjournment, which carried. The free coinage bill, yet again, was dead.[66] But silver, early on in a House where Democrats had earned a euphoric electoral victory the previous autumn, proved again what would soon become evident. The argument about the gold or silver underpinning of the nation's money supply could destroy Democratic Party unity and make it hard for the party to prevail. The leadership of the New York Democrats, though—Fitch, Tracey, Cockran and Warner—registered an important victory for gold-backed currency.

The performance of the anti-silver Democrats shocked the silver men. Only one week before the vote, Bland had predicted an easy forty-vote victory.[67] Other of his allies had referred to "a lack of ability of the youngsters" who were "playing at leadership."[68] The *New York Times* said, "Mr. Fitch (D-N.Y.) came in for praise as a new manager who kept his temper, did not lose track of the Speaker, and always had his hand on the lanyard when the moment came for a shot. Mr. Cockran (D-N.Y.) and Mr. Warner (D-N.Y.) who stood by and joined in when needed were extremely helpful."[69] Several papers joined the *Albany Argus* in recognizing that "for the present at least, the charge will not be brought that New York is represented by mediocrity without influence in the House."[70]

Four months later, in early July 1892, the Stewart Bill, named for Congressman William M. Stewart of Nevada, more legislation for free coinage, was put forth, and the anti-silver Democrats resumed their filibuster. This time, by doing so, they prevented the bill from being referred to committee. Off the House floor, Crisp, Bland, and Catchings showed their frustration by inviting Fitch "to step into the room of the Committee on Rules."[71] Catchings persuaded Fitch that the anti-silver men would erode their own support in the House if they continued to filibuster a bill that was not yet even out of committee. Crisp asked Fitch to use his influence "to put an end to it." Seeming to agree, Fitch spoke with Tracey, who called a meeting of the sixty or so anti-silver Democrats, who decided that the bill would face determined opposition on the floor if it reached the floor, and they agreed to stop their filibuster. A few days later the Stewart Bill was reported out of committee. Reed, perhaps persuaded by Fitch and Fellows,[72] or perhaps simply tired of the positive publicity that the New York anti-silver Democratic cabal were generating, played a more active role opposing the bill. When it came up it was voted down 154–136, thus again finishing silver coinage for the session.

The genius of American democracy lies not as much in the ability of its leaders to compromise on the great issues as in the capacity of its losers either to surrender or to persist peacefully. With the Civil War as the lone exception, losers have always calculated that it was in their interest to fight another day within an accepted governing framework than to fight outside it. In the long run, losers in the American democracy either lose, continue the fight, or ultimately prevail. Great questions are not decided in days, weeks, or months, but in decades wherein minorities work to become majorities.

That is how throughout one hundred years the tariff was reduced to next to nothing, how the progressive income tax became law, how temperance won and then lost, and how women gained the vote, and so it was with silver. Ultimately, but not without a fight, the gold standard was abandoned, beginning the dollar's slide that continues today.[73] In America, great questions are decided by the winners of elections or legislative votes after hard-fought campaigns or debates. The losers lick their wounds, retool their issues, continue the fight, and wait for their time to come. In the final twenty years of the nineteenth century, a period generally free from American military combat, the ideological foundations of many of the great issues of modern American society were laid out at a dizzying pace. These great questions needed to be resolved in order for America to take its place at the head of nations.

7

New York and the Election Law in Cleveland's Victory

Fifty-second Congress, 1890–1892

> My friend says that we have nothing to do with Europe. . . . That is not true of New York. . . . Her sidewalks are crowded with a stream of sturdy immigrants . . . on their way from Europe to develop the West and the South . . . and to raise up families of children who will be as good and loyal Americans as any of the men who sit in this House.
>
> —ASHBEL P. FITCH in Congress, 1892

Early in 1892, the tender stalks of political plans and aspirations began to shoot skyward just as flowers bloom in the spring. Hill's candidacy for president reached its zenith in February of that year and then fell precipitously during the next few months. His "snap" convention awakened doubts in voters' minds, doubts that lay below the surface but were thrust to the fore when aroused.

With Hill's popularity in decline, Cleveland's road to the presidency appeared open. Yet Fitch observed in the *Washington Star,* "it will take a great deal of self-control [at the national convention] to prevent its being a great injury rather than a benefit to Mr. Cleveland . . . there is certainly nothing to be gained by forcing the nomination of Mr. Cleveland in such a way as to insure his defeat. If we want Cleveland nominated . . . we want him elected."[1] He referred to the Democrats' internal divisions, specifically Tammany's dislike of Cleveland and Cleveland's failure to carry New York City by a sufficient margin in 1888, thus failing to carry New York State and failing in the electoral college to gain the presidency. It could not be allowed to happen again.

Finishing the *Star* interview, Fitch said, "There are many of Cleveland's most devoted friends in New York, however, who think there may be some doubt about his ability to carry New York [State]. Mr. Cleveland himself has doubts on this subject and has no desire to force his nomination on the party. The situation is a very delicate one."[2] It was imperative that Cleveland carry New York. In this enterprise

Fitch would be totally absorbed in a way that he may not have anticipated, but which may have been decisive.

The Democratic convention opened on Tuesday, June 21, in Chicago. It seemed like Whitney[3] was everywhere, coldly eyeing the delegates. He was optimistic, claiming Cleveland's nomination was a "matter of fact,"[4] but his Tammany opponents for Hill thought they had a better sense of the delegates' emotion, and they believed in their own dislike of Cleveland. Convention speeches that started at five o'clock droned on until two in the morning. Tammany's last chance came in the person of the eloquent and persuasive Bourke Cockran. Cockran took the podium to deliver a forceful speech aimed at driving a wedge between Cleveland and the assembled delegates. Whether or not the speech was his best ever, as some have claimed it was, it failed in its purpose. The vote was taken early Thursday morning, and the result left no doubt that Democrats wanted Grover Cleveland to lead their ticket in 1892 for the third consecutive time.

With 617⅓ votes, Cleveland triumphed over David Hill's 114 votes on the first ballot. Tammany Hall was again at odds with their party's standard-bearer, but they needed his victory. Cleveland, with his wife and a small circle of friends, heard the news at sunrise over a special wire to Gray Gables, Cleveland's Cape Cod retreat.[5] He was again atop America's political landscape just as he had been four years before. Cleveland Democrats, who had fought for good government, tariff reform, and hard currency in the past, were eager to do political battle once more.

But uniting New York Democrats behind Cleveland was a delicate proposition. Fitch delivered a "vigorous ratification speech" at the Harlem Democratic Club, basically instruction on how to be a graceful winner. Said he, "The Democrats of Harlem have all got together to renew the fight for Cleveland. Our differences were fought out manfully at the convention and after the ballot was taken, all dissensions vanished. We are all loyal. Let there be reciprocity in this loyalty and when our [Tammany] friends come back from Chicago, let us receive them in a conciliatory spirit. The Democracy is not a limited partnership. We must all get together." "We will! We will!" called the audience.[6]

A few days later, when asked if Tammany would support the ticket nominated at Chicago, he said, "I have no doubt of it whatever. I know it is true . . . that there is a class of voters who ordinarily vote with Tammany Hall but who have a prejudice against Mr. Cleveland . . . much, however can be done to get that vote"[7] and he fully intended to do what he could.

He began in May 1892 when a story in the staunchly Republican *New York Tribune* reporting that "Democrats" were "fighting appropriations to enforce the law,"[8] was ultimately converted into an extraordinary triumph for New York Democrats. Election laws, written by Republicans when Tweed was manufacturing voting rights for immigrants as they came ashore,[9] were being used twenty-five years later in New York to hold down the Democratic vote in the city. The *Tribune* continued sarcastically, "it was natural that the provisions for the support of the judiciary and the enforcement of the laws should provoke Democrats." While the newspaper gave several examples of what it believed was misguided Democratic recalcitrance, it finally directed its attention to an amendment to the Sundry Civil Bill that was offered in Congress by Congressman Joseph D. Sayers, chairman of the Appropriations Committee.

Sayers's amendment "provided that no person who holds an office or employment under the government shall receive compensation for discharging the duties of any other officer or employment, nor shall such person hold more than one office of profit at the same time except as expressly provided." It ended with "and this limitation shall also extend to the District Attorney for the southern district of New York."[10] Sayers, a Texas Democrat, paying no particular attention, innocently introduced the amendment as an expense control initiative.

Amos Cummings alertly began questioning Sayers about the southern district. How did Sayers learn about the southern district? Sayers, not knowing, asked the clerk to read the letter he received from the first controller of the Treasury Department, a Republican. After the reading, Fitch moved to strike a portion of the amendment that he, Cummings, and others in the New York delegation knew were aimed directly at New York City Democrats. Attempting to explain New York politics, he said,

> Mr. Chairman, we have in the city of New York a state of affairs which you gentlemen do not have in the eastern district of Texas. At every Presidential election a large number of deputies are sworn in in the city of New York, and placed under the direction of Mr. [John I.] Davenport, whose . . . deputies make hundreds or perhaps thousands of arrests. If this amendment is adopted it will leave in Mr. Davenport's control the trial of all these cases.
>
> The Clerk of the Circuit Court in the city of New York is Mr. John A. Shields. There is not a better lawyer in these matters, or a fairer man connected with the bar of the state of New York. We try, if we can, all our election cases before him . . . we say to you gentlemen, without wishing to go into our personal troubles in New York City with Mr. Davenport, that you will inflict upon us a great wrong, and you will endanger the interest of justice and fair play if you pass [this] amendment, which will legislate Mr. Shields out of office and which I believe has been cunningly conceived in the apparent interest of economy, but for an entirely different purpose.

After further debate Cummings offered another amendment that excluded the southern district of New York from the bill.[11] The debate grew more contentious as old wounds from federal interference in state affairs and state interference in city affairs dating back to the beginning of Reconstruction were reopened. Cummings recalled that "in 1868 thousands of naturalized voters were arrested at the polls . . . and their papers [confiscated] because a few fraudulent papers were discovered." John Raines from upstate New York exclaimed "A few?" then answered his own question with "a few thousand."

Spoiling for a fight, Cummings rejoined, "Not so. Every man who held a certificate issued in the year 1868, whether fraudulent or not, was arrested when he went to the polls, his papers taken from him, and in hundreds of instances never returned to him. At that time John I. Davenport had appointed eleven thousand[12] United States marshals in [New York City] to drag men from the polls, imprison them on false charges, and rob them of their votes."

Cummings was a reporter for the *New York Sun,* congressman from the Ninth District of New York and a Congressional Medal of Honor winner. His passionate statement on the floor of Congress marks an interesting counterpoint to the accepted historical record of massive Tammany election fraud during the Tweed era. As a long-time Tammany Hall stalwart, Cummings is far from an unbiased witness. On the other hand, in the face of other exaggerated anti-Tammany rhetoric of the 1890s, Cummings's testimony seems worth noting.

When Cummings' time expired, Fitch asked that it be extended; it was, and he continued until Republican representative Sereno Payne of upstate Auburn, New York, came to the floor. Payne, coyly denying that he knew what was being discussed, said that he did notice that "my colleague from the city of New York [Mr. CUMMINGS] was considerably excited, and I was not surprised to hear the name of John I. Davenport, because there is nothing that makes the average Democrat so red in the face as the name of John I. Davenport."

Payne said that the naturalization papers

> were seized because they were fraudulent papers issued by a fraudulent naturalization mill to swell the Democratic vote in the city of New York. We had dishonest elections . . . and the reason John I. Davenport is not popular with our friends on the other side is that he has succeeded in cutting down the fraudulent vote in the city of New York. . . . Tammany Hall has control of the whole thing from beginning to end, and now if they can get rid of Davenport, if they can get rid of federal supervisors, if they can get rid of federal marshals, then they can reopen their naturalization mills and the minute a foreigner plants his foot upon American soil in the port of New York he can be made a voter and can walk up to the polls and cast his vote to counteract the effect of the vote of an American citizen.

As Payne persisted, both Fitch and Cummings tried to interrupt him, but he refused to yield. When Fitch finally regained the floor he began, "as the gentleman

[Mr. PAYNE] would not yield, and as somebody might possibly, not being acquainted with him as well as we are in New York, imagine that he had given some accurate statement of what happened . . . [laughter]"; then, rebutting Payne, he finished with an echo of his Republican past, "The main reason why the Republican Party in the state of New York has been of late so signally defeated is [not because of Tammany Hall or naturalization mills but] because of the injustice which it has inflicted over and over again upon the city of New York."

The debate wore on. Cummings' motion passed but Payne had aroused Fitch when he said that Democrats "want to get rid of [Davenport] . . . [and] they will have to do it, if they do it at all, in the old-fashioned way—by passing a law legislating him out of office." The lines were drawn. Fitch, his eyes on the New York City vote in the presidential election only five months away, would act on Payne's suggestion in the next session.

Meanwhile, a spate of newspaper articles in mid-July again suggested Fitch's name for the New York mayoralty, this time with some apparent effect. Most of the newspapers reported that he sought the job, which was never true, but in this instance they made a statement of his considerable electoral value in the political marketplace. Articles appeared as far away as Boston, Buffalo, Washington, Charleston, Baltimore, and Savannah. The *New York Evening Advertiser*[13] was first with the news, under the banner headline of "Fitch for Mayor." "He Is a Firm Friend of Grover Cleveland and Has Many Admirers among the Republicans and Germans—It Is Said Prominent Tammany Men Favor His Nomination." The newspaper explored the positive electoral dynamics of a Fitch candidacy, which it said would head off the Tammany nomination of a pure Tammany man, and called him "a popular congressman, a good lawyer, and his views on many questions are sound and satisfactory to the business community."[14]

Other newspapers followed, some of them adding an original thought or two. The *New York Herald* referred to Fitch's work as counsel for the Brewers Association, "the twenty members of which are enormously wealthy. They own mortgages on about five thousand of the eight thousand saloons in the city. They are large contributors to the Tammany Hall campaign fund."[15] The *New York World* asked the most interesting question, to wit, "no one appears to know how Richard Croker feels toward Congressman Fitch. He [Fitch] jumped into the wigwam about four years ago on the tariff issue, coming fresh from the Republican Party."[16]

The *New York Tribune* called Fitch an "uncompromising Cleveland man who sympathized with the anti-snappers in their attack upon Hill. His supporters urged that his nomination would be accepted as an omen of harmony by the anti-snapper element and aid in solidifying the Democratic Party in the campaign."[17] The *Springfield Republican* called him "an honest man and a good speaker."[18] The *Baltimore Sun* said, "he would be a candidate of much broader political experience than it is usual for Tammany to put up"[19] and his local paper, the *Harlem Reporter,* said, "his vote would be one of phenomenal proportions. During his congressional career Mr. Fitch has made a record that would be a tower of strength."[20]

It was not all positive. Republican papers, the *New York Globe* for example, called him a "turncoat," saying he was "first elected to Congress as a Republican, and then turned his coat and was reelected as a Democrat . . . he is a very popular man, although not so great a one as his political successes would seem to indicate, unless in politics slyness and greatness are identical."[21]

The mayoralty was always within Fitch's reach, but it would have been financially ruinous, and he knew it. As for Croker, Fitch was independent, not what he wanted. Commissioner of Public Works Thomas Gilroy, a solid Irish immigrant, a great friend of Fitch's, a grand sachem in Tammany Hall, and a hard worker who came up through the system, wanted to be New York's next mayor, and he would be.

During the third week in July, Fitch turned his attention to the New York campaign, citing "gross abuses in the administration and supervision of the election laws in the city and county of New York."[22] Recalling his dispute on the House floor with Sereno Payne two months before, he introduced a resolution in Congress "authorizing the Speaker to appoint a special committee of five members to investigate the election laws and methods so far as they relate to the election of Congressmen and to report back to the House at the [first session of the Fifty-third Congress],"[23] which was not then scheduled to convene until December of 1893, more than one and one-half years away.

The Federal Election Law of 1871 was born out of New York City politics. It was the brainchild of John I. Davenport, who, as chief supervisor of elections for the southern district of Manhattan, an appointment for life under the law he had drafted and with the assistance of the Union League Club, nurtured the operation of the law for twenty-three years. Davenport began his career on the staff of General Benjamin Butler.[24] In 1868 he turned up as counsel for the Union League Club in a congressional investigation of alleged naturalization fraud by the Tweed Ring in New York City, which was petitioned by the club. The report of some thousand pages pointed to election fraud that required preventive legislation. Davenport drafted the legislation, which was brought to a Republican Congress, passed in 1871, and became known as the Federal Election Law.

The law was an ingenious combination of political dirty tricks and self-perpetuating self-enrichment decked out in the full moral regalia of election-fraud prevention. It was a very unusual piece of legislation. Because it was only applicable to congressional elections in cities with populations of twenty thousand or more, and because it could not be enforced without citizen complaints, it was narrowly applied and unnoticed in most sections of the country. But it was energetically enforced, notoriously but not exclusively, in New York City.[25] Under the direction of an entrepreneurial supervisor such as Davenport, the law became a permanent executive tool to enhance his income as well as his personal prestige among Republicans.

It was a long, intricate statute under which supervisors as well as special deputy marshals were appointed and their duties defined.

> Supervisors were "to attend to the registration of voters . . . and scrutinize the registry and supervise the voting for Members of Congress." They "must attend at all times and places for holding election of Representatives and counting of votes. They must challenge the vote of any person whose qualifications they doubt. . . . They must personally inspect and scrutinize the manner of voting and the way and method in which the poll books, registry lists and tallies . . . are kept. . . . They are authorized . . . to take, keep and remain in such position from time to time, whether before or behind the ballot boxes, as will in their judgment best enable them to see each person . . . offering to vote, as will best conduce to their scrutinizing the manner in which the . . . voting is being conducted . . . and at the closing of the polls . . . they are required to place themselves in such position in relation to the ballot boxes for the purpose of engaging in the work of canvassing the ballots."[26]

In sum, the law provided for an aggressive, heavy-handed, federal presence at the polls that facilitated direct intervention and was offensive to New Yorkers.

As the debate about the repeal of the election law began, the *Harlem Reporter* compared it to the Lodge Force Bill of two years before that passed the House, failed in the Senate, and never became law. Both pieces of legislation, designed for different purposes at different times, were crafted by Davenport. It was no coincidence that both shared the same enforcement mechanism and both shared an intrusive Federal presence at the polls. Of the Force Bill the *Reporter* said,

> It is a mistake to suppose that the Force Bill is a sectional measure intended to be enforced in southern states. . . . It would apply to the entire country. . . . Under the proposed act Republican judges could appoint for New York City . . . thousands of federal marshals and supervisors to take charge of the polls and practically control them. . . .
>
> Another section of the bill creates a returning board with power to reject in the count any ballots it sees fit, without hindrance from either state or city election

> officers. A certificate of election from this returning board is given precedence over a certificate signed by state authorities, and the clerk of the House of Representatives is compelled by the bill to place on the role of members the name upon the certificate emanating from the returning board.[27]

The reasons the Force Bill failed to become law are numerous and complex. At its core, if it had become law, it would have encouraged black suffrage in the South and in those days blacks, still loyal to the memory of Abraham Lincoln, voted Republican. The bill contained the same enforcement mechanism as the law of 1871, but that law in New York was used by the appointed-for-life election supervisor Davenport to hold down the immigrant vote that most often voted Democratic. "In 1890, the number of federal officers at the polls in New York City was over ten thousand."[28] The law of 1871 was used in New York to benefit Republicans. The bill of 1890 was intended to benefit Republicans, too.

Although Republicans tried to delay Fitch's resolution to appoint an investigating committee, it finally carried 187–0 when Republicans refused to vote. Fitch asserted that "the object of the resolution is to ascertain the part that John I. Davenport plays in the elections for the representatives at public expense." One article described Davenport, whose

> favorite method of interfering with the suffrage among Democrats has long been to arrest as many as his cage would hold . . . and keep them locked up until the day after the election. . . . It made no difference to him that there was no grounds whatever for the suspicion; the object was to prevent them from voting, and so long as that was accomplished, [Davenport] was deemed by Republicans to have earned his money. Last year when he renewed this trick and had over one hundred men under arrest on suspicion and their cases were brought into court, it was found that there was only one, if recollection serves, but certainly not more than three, in which he had any evidence whatever that even seemed to sustain the charge, and he was severely rebuked by the judge on the bench for such an audacious abuse.[29]

If the account is to be believed, the "rebuke," probably delivered by Judge Shields, could easily have motivated Davenport to attempt to have him removed. Sayers's amendment, had it become law, would have insured Davenport's continuing ability to operate freely in the southern district.

From the moment that Amos Cummings noticed the details of Sayers's expense-control amendment, Fitch realized that he had a powerful political issue in hand that had the potential to increase Cleveland's vote in New York City and his chances to win the presidency. Expanding on the objective of his resolution, Fitch added,

"John I. Davenport . . . is an ardent Republican partisan who occupies an important office of a semi-judicial character. As the author of the Force Bill he and his views on elections are pretty well known, and the entire machinery of his federal office is operated in the interest of the Republicans. It has even been said that when the appropriations for his work fail, the Union League Club makes up the deficit, and his partisan work goes on."[30]

Whitney, meanwhile, never losing sight of New York's influence on the national election, was "arranging to make the ceremony of notifying Grover Cleveland and Adlai E. Stevenson[31] of their nomination an affair of wide interest."[32] The ceremony was to take place on July 20 at Madison Square Garden. When the day came, Cleveland was formally notified of his nomination amid great fanfare and celebration, after which he made his way to a reception at the Manhattan Club, where an enthusiastic crowd awaited him. Fitch and Croker were among hundreds of supporters. Encountering Croker in the receiving line, Cleveland was met with a warm greeting and Croker's wish that Cleveland's good luck at fishing "will presage what is to occur next November."[33] They cordially exchanged fish stories for a few minutes until Croker moved on.

The next evening Cleveland and his coterie were at the Sagamore Club at Mount Morris Park in Harlem attending another splendid recreation. Before the candidates arrived, a brilliant fireworks display lit up the sky, Bayne's Sixty-ninth Regiment Orchestra played "Ta-ra-ra-boom-de-ay" and the crowd sang along "with various appropriate additions of a political sort." Cleveland's party arrived from Whitney's home on Murray Hill preannounced "a few minutes before nine o'clock by a band of bicyclists with twinkling alarm bells."[34] After a few short speeches, a smaller group retired to a second-floor room for dinner, then to a front parlor for an after-dinner social and related conversation where Fitch "and the ex-president had a confab of some length,"[35] possibly regarding the Davenport investigation. Within a week the Fitch family left for Ragged Lake for their first visit in four years.

On August 5, 1892, Speaker Crisp of Georgia, hardly disinterested in election laws, rang down the gavel on the final session of the Fifty-second Congress after a customary flurry of last-minute legislation that included "the appointment of a five man committee [chaired by Fitch] to investigate the alleged violations of the election law in New York and to operate in the interim before the Fifty-third Congress is seated."[36] Davenport was widely believed to have been the author of the election law.[37] Democrats referred to his methods in New York City as "Force Bill methods." The next step was to determine what role, if any, the Fitch Committee would play in Cleveland's New York election strategy.

When Fitch returned from the Adirondacks, he, Whitney, Don Dickinson,[38] and several other prominent New York Democrats held a long dinner meeting at

8. Grover Cleveland is at center right; Ashbel Fitch is facing away from Cleveland and to Cleveland's left, and Adlai Stevenson is second from left. *New York Staats Zeitung,* July 23, 1892.

Whitney's home to discuss Fitch's committee. The question was whether to pursue the investigation before the election or to set it aside temporarily. Anything relating to federal elections was risky because of the national implications in a presidential election. If the Fitch Committee pursued its investigation and nothing came of it, the failed effort could damage Cleveland's campaign, especially in New York, where Cleveland needed to win by a wide margin. Alternatively, a successful investigation might make a positive difference in the city where Cleveland usually struggled for votes. "They were together for nearly ten hours,"[39] "to discuss ways and means to thoroughly expose the methods of Davenport."[40] Every aspect of it "was thoroughly discussed, the evidence was gone over, and [in the end] it was decided to push the investigation without delay."[41] Davenport had already announced that he "would appoint three deputy marshals [as] supervisors for each polling place in the city."[42]

Whitney saw the political potential of the Davenport investigation for Cleveland's New York campaign, and he must have given the order to move ahead before the election. Without Whitney's approval Fitch could easily have delayed the investigation until after the election. Whitney's (and Fitch's) "argument was that the election will depend upon New York" and that they had to find ways to increase Cleveland's majority in New York and Kings Counties "over [their] original estimates in order to give any hope of carrying the state."[43] The Davenport investigation was the sort of thing Whitney needed. The next day Dickinson left for Gray Gables to see Cleveland. Fitch met with the Democrats on his committee, who seemed determined to begin their investigation before the end of September.

The *Chicago Herald* said, "It is uniformly admitted that New York State is to be the real battleground." The paper also reported another meeting in "Don M. Dickinson's parlors at the Hoffman House. . . . Mr. Dickinson presided at the gathering of Mr. Cleveland's friends and plans for raising funds were discussed by Mr. Whitney, ex-Secretary of the Treasury Charles Fairchild . . . Thomas Fortune Ryan, treasurer of the Broadway Railroad Company, and Congressman Fitch."[44]

The presidential campaign began in earnest in mid-September. Fitch was a featured speaker at a procession through his district "numbering at least four thousand with three bands of music making a very imposing and brilliant display with fire works, red fire and torches."[45] From that night on he was speaking in English and German almost every night.[46] And with six weeks to go before the election, his investigating committee met, and while no actions were taken, the *New York World* reported that it "sat in secret and had a discussion which must have been lively, judging by the ring of voices which filtered through the door."[47]

A smiling John Davenport said, "Pshaw. That's all right. I have been investigated about nine times already and I'm none the worse."[48] The *World* carried its description of a "serenely confident" John Davenport who believed, because he had not been subpoenaed, that the Fitch investigation had been abandoned.[49] Fitch told the paper that the investigation would begin the following week. A cat-and-mouse game was taking shape, as Davenport refused to testify and Fitch was temporarily without subpoena power while Congress was in recess. He told the *World,* "the committee can get along famously without the presence of Mr. Davenport, and already it has evidence of a most important character in its possession."[50]

Through September and into October Fitch maintained his intention to pursue Davenport, finally notifying him on October 8 that the committee would meet on October 14. Davenport, answered that "he did not intend to be present."[51] He said that if Fitch had asked him to testify earlier, he would have testified. But with the election so close, his testimony would have to wait until it had passed. Said he, "I am charged . . . with numerous duties of the most trying and intricate character . . . to enforce the National Election laws, and to prevent and punish violations of the same. . . . To do this requires of me every moment of my time. . . . I therefore suggest and request that the committee adjourn its hearing until November 16 when I will appear."[52]

Newspapers across the state and in the city reported Davenport's rejection of the committee's invitation, many under the headline "Davenport Refuses." The Republican *New York Mail and Express* said "Good for Davenport,"[53] while the *New York News* said "Davenport Afraid."[54] The *New York Evening World,* reacting in mock horror said "Defied by John I."[55] Davenport apparently believed that Fitch could not or would not go forward without him.

Fitch scheduled the October 14 meeting at the Post Office building just one floor below Davenport's office. When Davenport failed to appear, Fitch sent the assistant sergeant at arms to his office to give him "one last chance,"[56] but to no avail. From that moment on, with only three weeks to go before the election, "questions" about the details of Davenport's activities began appearing in the press. Davenport, by refusing to appear, provided Fitch, in today's political parlance, with an extraordinary opportunity to "define" him and, for that matter, to define the entire Republican machine.

He issued a statement expressing no surprise that Davenport did not testify. He speculated that Davenport would not want to "submit to an examination in regard to what he did in 1888"[57] with money that he collected both from the government and from the Republican Party, and what he was doing in 1892. Davenport collected more than $98,000 during the four years of the Harrison administration, not a dollar during the Cleveland administration, and "it is generally believed that he received in one payment from the National Republican Committee in 1888 $50,000."[58] Said Fitch,

> He sets detectives upon Democratic voters in one capacity, arrests them as Chief Supervisor of Elections, and has them brought before himself as Commissioner[59] to be judged. He holds them until it is too late for them to vote. He prevents [them] from voting and [by] inspiring fear of arrest in others, deters them from attempting to vote. If his charges were sustained, his course would be justified, but his practice of holding alleged offenders twenty-four hours and discharging them shows that his purpose is intimidation. Davenport is interesting chiefly as an illustration of what federal control of elections means and the manner in which it might be exercised under such a law as was contemplated in the Lodge Force Bill.[60]

Some newspapers viewed the investigation differently, one calling it a "device of Tammany,"[61] to prevent an executive officer charged with important duties under the laws of the United States from due performance, by summoning him to appear before a congressional investigating committee. But the longer Davenport remained silent the more difficult it was to believe it.

While Fitch pursued Davenport, his reelection campaign rolled on. On October 18, 1892, he was nominated by acclamation for his fourth consecutive term in

AN IGNOMINIOUS PLIGHT FOR THE HERO OF THE IRON CAGE.

9. *New York World,* January 27, 1893.

Congress to represent the new Fifteenth District, the upper east side that included Harlem. While his nomination was no surprise, the seconding speech by Michael J. Mulqueen, Thomas Gilroy's son-in-law, was. Mulqueen said, "The name of Ashbel P. Fitch is known and revered in every home in this district." He referred to Fitch as "kindly," "brilliant," and "fearless."[62] Although Fitch's relationship with Richard Croker was problematic, he remained close to Gilroy, an influential Tammany sachem. The following night Fitch reciprocated by delivering a heartfelt nomination speech in favor of Thomas Gilroy for mayor, declaring that Gilroy was "close to the heart of every man who knew him. He has held every office in the Tammany Hall organization from the lowest to the highest. He has started with the humblest of us here, [and is now] the head of [the Department of Public Works,] the largest and most important department in the municipal government."[63]

The *Harlem Reporter* added to Fitch's acclaim by declaring that "The re-nomination of Ashbel P. Fitch for Congress . . . is an event of national importance and national benefit . . . his name has become a familiar one in every part of the United States and he is everywhere recognized as one of the very few members of Congress who have a share in shaping and controlling the work and policy of that body . . . as a defender of the interests of the city of New York he has no peer in the city's delegation."[64] Fitch's ability to integrate the interests of New York with the interests of America, and vice versa, was unusual for his time. Certainly Republicans who viewed New York with repugnance did not, nor did Tammany Democrats, who saw New York as a business opportunity.

The Fitch investigating committee began taking testimony nineteen days before the election. Failing again to persuade Davenport to appear, the committee heard testimony from Edward Mitchell, a Benjamin Harrison Republican appointee charged with approving Davenport's expense accounts. Mitchell admitted that he hadn't paid much attention to the accounts, asking a subordinate to review them, and hadn't realized that Davenport had submitted unpaid vouchers to cover all four years of the Cleveland presidency to Mitchell "as soon as Mitchell took office."[65]

Stephen Walker, Mitchell's predecessor as district attorney during the Democratic Cleveland administration, explained that Davenport had brought his expense accounts to him. While he was unable to approve them, he did offer "to go into court and cross-examine him" before a judge and that "if the cross-examination were satisfactory to me and to the judge I would approve them. Mr. Davenport then took his accounts away and never came to me again."[66]

A day or so later, Louis C. Ferrell appeared on the witness stand. Ferrell was a senior assistant to the first controller, a Republican in a Republican administration. "He did not appear to relish admitting that in the documents on which Davenport had been paid . . . there was nothing beyond the bare claim of Davenport to indicate that the work had been done. But he had to admit it when Chairman Fitch pinned him down."[67] Ferrell said that Davenport would be paid twice, once on an arrest and once on release, and that there was no proof that arrests claimed were made or that arrested citizens even existed. There was one warrant for $3,298.70 dated April 15, 1892, marked: "Approved, Benjamin Harrison, President," and another one endorsed to Cornelius N. Bliss, the treasurer of the National Republican Committee.[68]

Every day for the two weeks leading up to the election, headlines such as "Davenport's Queer Ways," "This Is Force-Bill Johnny" "Davenport Got Big Sums from Uncle Sam," "Davenport's Roll of Bills," and "Davenport Warrant Given To C. N. Bliss"[69] rained down on Republicans, who had no defense because Davenport remained silent.

As the election neared, serious matters began to take even more serious turns. The *New York Herald*'s reporting led off with "What a combat of keen wits it is

10. King, Moses, 1899. *Notable New Yorkers, 1896-1899*. New York: The Orr Press.

which is leading the way to Tuesday's great battle of the ballots, and perhaps a battle of the clubs and revolvers also!"[70] The Democratic Party had written a letter to both Davenport and United States Marshal John W. Jacobus, "request[ing] that you instruct the supervisors and marshals that they have no right to arrest voters before they have deposited their ballots," that view being based on explicit case law.[71] The letter was signed by a four-man committee, joined by several prominent attorneys who lent the weight of their position to it and who included such anti-Tammany Democrats as Frederick Coudert, E. Ellery Anderson, and Francis Lynde Stetson, Grover Cleveland's personal attorney, who probably signed with Cleveland's approval.

Davenport reportedly received the letter "with quiet contempt, making no reply to it."[72] Jacobus, however, responded quickly, "I know of no way of preventing a man from fraudulently voting except by arresting him when he attempts to so fraudulently vote."[73] Meanwhile, Sheriff Gorman was swearing in a huge force of deputies, rumored to be in the thousands, all sworn to keep the peace while Jacobus was swearing in deputy marshals sworn to uphold the election law.

Simultaneously, Fitch issued a public notice imploring "any registered voters who may have received threatening letters, or who may be arrested and charged with offenses against the election law on election day or who may be interfered with at the polls"[74] to send their addresses and statements of the facts to the committee. Further, it was well publicized that a subcommittee "will be in session on election day . . . to receive evidence."[75]

From across the country the *San Francisco Examiner,* under the headline "Fitch Foils the Republicans," put matters into perspective. On Fitch's public notice, the paper wrote, "This action of a regularly empowered committee of the House of Representatives places one wing of the National Government in open antagonism to the Department of Justice and lifts the Supervisors' dispute above the plane of a controversy with the laws and officers of a [single] state."[76]

The *Examiner*'s reasoning was that whereas the Republican National Committee had circulated a "manifesto" excoriating Fitch for inciting citizens to break the law, Fitch, with the full authority of the United States House of Representatives behind him, had instructed citizens who were arrested to get the name of the marshals who had arrested them and come to Room 135 at the Post Office, where his committee would be taking evidence. The *Examiner* said, "The effect [of Fitch's notice] was crushing on the Republican Committee," and, as a result, "There is now less fear of a clash at the polls."[77]

One well-known Civil War veteran[78] and "lifelong Republican, declare[d] that for the first time in his life he will vote the Democratic ticket and use all of his influence for the Democrat nominees. . . . He [said] he speaks for thousands of disgusted

Republicans in openly . . . resenting [Davenport's] unwarranted intrusion of federal power in the peaceful conduct of New York's municipal affairs. He believes the citizens will rebuke these Force Bill methods."[79] The *New York Times* opined, "Davenport . . . is instructive . . . as an illustration of what Federal control of elections means and the manner in which it might be exercised under such a law as . . . the Lodge Force bill."[80]

Election day brought another impressive Democratic victory and no violence at the polls. Fitch should have been feeling satisfied. His friend, for whom he had worked long, hard, and effectively was elected president of the United States. "Harrison came down to Harlem Bridge with about a sixty-five thousand [vote] plurality. Cleveland wiped that out [in New York City] and piled up a plurality of forty-one thousand in the state"[81] a far cry from his 13,000-vote loss four years before. Who can know how many of the 104,000-vote Cleveland plurality in the city resulted directly or indirectly from the Davenport investigation?

Another good friend, Thomas Gilroy, was elected mayor of New York City. Early returns showed Cleveland's New York City vote to be 168,920,[82] only a few hundred votes shy of Tammany's Gilroy. The Fifty-third Congress would continue to be solidly Democratic; in his own campaign, which consisted of stump speeches by night and well-publicized hearings by day, Fitch was victorious in his fourth consecutive run for a seat in Congress, this time by the largest plurality[83] of any congressman in the state. In four congressional elections, one running as a Republican and three as a Democrat, he had received 55, 59, 69, and 61 percent of the popular vote.

In an interview a few days after the election, Fitch said that Democrats won for several reasons, the first being the issues, primarily the tariff and the Force Bill. Of the Force Bill he said, "we were greatly helped by the attitude of John I. Davenport and Mr. Jacobus. [They] gave our people an idea of what we would have under the Force Bill in case of Republican success, and turned thousands of votes in our favor."[84]

To celebrate Grover Cleveland's election, Fitch and forty of Cleveland's closest and most loyal supporters—Carl Schurz, E. Ellery Anderson, Francis Lynde Stetson, Daniel Lamont, William Lloyd Garrison, William C. Whitney, William R. Grace, and William Steinway among them, gathered at Sherry's for a private dinner given by Henry Villard[85] to honor the president-elect. Interestingly, four newspapermen were in the party.[86] A grateful Cleveland warmly acknowledged his "stanch friends" and the "splendid campaign" they had so "masterfully arranged."[87] Then with considerable foresight, he warned his friends not to be "misled to our undoing by other lights of false Democracy which may be kindled in broken faith, and which, shining in hypocrisy will, if followed, lure us to the rocks of failure and disgrace."[88] Four years later, William Jennings Bryan engineered a populist revolution within his party, and Cleveland's worst fears were realized. Not to be outdone, Villard, in a prescient toast to Cleveland, said, "a splendid and unexpected triumph, indeed, has been secured for our cause, but while we have a right to be proud of it, do not let us forget that *it is sometimes more difficult to properly utilize a party victory than to achieve it*" (emphasis added).[89]

The celebration ended at midnight, and as the guests left they went singly to avoid attracting attention. Grover Cleveland, the twenty-second president and twenty-fourth president-elect of the United States, and his friend and attorney Francis Lynde Stetson left together, walking alone at night in midtown Manhattan. "They walked up Fifth Avenue to Fifty-first Street where Mr. Cleveland lives. They studied Orion, the Pleiades and the Great Bear."[90]

The president-elect may have pondered the potential danger of an economic wreck to the country. He was perched on the leading edge of a series of staggering convulsions that would rock the nation. They were many and they were far-reaching. One was the attendant, looming specter of silver, the accumulated damage that silver coinage inflicted on the nation's gold reserves as well as the public's confidence in the dollar and the divisiveness it wrought among Democrats. Past silver purchase laws would help plunge the country into what may have been its worst depression ever, and cracks in the economy were beginning to show. The Democratic Party would split in half, and Cleveland's personal popularity, at its zenith when he came to office, would plunge by the time he left.

His thoughts may also have strayed to the corruption he always saw in Tammany Hall. As he looked forward to his second presidency, a budding reform movement was gaining traction in New York City. Within two years Tammany and Croker would be routed, thus placing Fitch in an intriguing new position. But at this point, that was all in the future and as the excitement of the campaign wound down Fitch returned to his daily routine. He still spent more time than he wanted in Washington, living at a private house on B Street, between Seventeenth and Eighteenth Streets, spending days on Capitol Hill and evenings in "the corner in the Arlington lobby" telling stories with his friends "before adjourning to Chamberlin's for a nightcap."[91]

The second session of the Fifty-second Congress opened on December 5, 1892. The Davenport affair was moving beyond Davenport and toward election law repeal. Before it did, however, there were matters of Davenport's expenses and his testimony. As to expenses, Fitch wrote to Republican Treasury Secretary Foster protesting Foster's payment of $108,000 to Davenport.[92] Foster answered that Davenport's expenses had not been submitted but no doubt would be. While he had no authority to refuse payment, he said that District Attorney Mitchell was responsible for examining the accounts before their presentation to the Treasury, and there was provision within the law for public hearings before approval.[93] Fitch again wrote Foster, saying that the statutes Foster had alluded to were "not new to me" but that they were contradicted by Mitchell's sworn testimony.[94] With his eye on New York politics, he ended his letter to Foster with his original sort of irony, "I am not particular whether Mr. Mitchell is right in saying that it rests with you, or you are right in saying that it rests with Mr. Mitchell. It may be divided as you please among you. The transaction will be fully understood by everybody in New York."[95]

The *New York Times* observed, "When the first Foster-Davenport answer was made to Fitch's request . . . it was evidently assumed that [Mitchell] had done all that the law required him to do. . . . The second letter, in which Mr. Fitch made it plain that the secretary did not know the whole story, must have led to some correspondence with Mr. Mitchell, and perhaps to some remonstrance against perfunctory and careless observances of the law regarding the examination of accounts."[96]

Meanwhile, Davenport petitioned Speaker Crisp to allow him to testify. Crisp with evident sarcasm, referred Davenport's petition to Fitch who laughed when he read it saying, "Mr. Davenport is suffering from an exaggerated sense of his own importance."[97] The petition was ignored.

The investigating committee's report condemned the Federal Election Law and urged its immediate repeal. The Republican *New York Tribune* called the report of the Fitch Committee "a partisan document which abounds in misstatements and submits recommendations which are either wholly unsupported by the testimony taken or altogether unworthy of consideration" and described the minority report as a "crushing reply to the majority report."[98]

Agreeing with the minority, the *Albany Journal* accused Fitch and the Democrats of "resisting the enactment of the federal election laws" and "contesting their constitutionality until they were upheld by the Supreme Court." Warming to the subject, the newspaper continued, "It is hatred of the nation; hatred of national protection to national elections that inspires the average Democrat to denounce the federal election laws. It was the wholesale debauchery of the suffrage of the Tweed Democracy of the city of New York in 1868 which led to the enactment of these laws. In that year Grant was cheated out of the electoral vote of the state of New York . . . by the Tammany Democracy of the metropolis."[99]

Old wrongs died hard. But Pulitzer's *New York World,* plainly on the other side, proclaimed that the election law "is a law to interfere with the freedom of elections by the direct intimidation of voters with threats of federal vengeance. It vests arbitrary power in an irresponsible agent holding office without limit of tenure. It is a law obnoxious to the spirit of popular government and dangerous to free institutions. It is a law that ought to be swept out of existence, and the committee will bring in a bill for that purpose."[100]

Within a week Congress passed an amendment to the Sundry Civil Service Bill that eliminated Davenport's ability to collect from the federal government. While Congress was debating silver, Postmaster Dayton notified Davenport that he would need to vacate the premises. When Davenport refused, Dayton ordered a locksmith and sent his private secretary and a maintenance man to "take charge of the rooms."[101] Davenport was finished. No longer would United States marshals patrol New York's voting booths arresting American citizens before they could vote.

8

Repeal of the Election Law and Sherman Act

Fifty-third Congress, 1892–1894

> Every day it was becoming more and more evident that honest men cannot be in Tammany and remain honest. It may be done by Mr. Fitch, who I believe to be honest.
>
> —RICHARD WATSON GILDER, editor of *Century Magazine*, February 1894

The panic of 1893 and the tragic depression that followed began before Grover Cleveland took office.[1] One of several reasons for the disaster was the fifteen-year injection of silver into the nation's money supply, which ultimately led to a debilitating and catastrophic loss of confidence. Before Cleveland's inauguration, during the last months of the Fifty-second Congress, House members prepared for another silver fight to determine whether it was possible to repeal the Sherman Silver Purchase Act,[2] then less than three years old, before Cleveland took office. Fitch, strongly in favor of repeal, said, "with a little more work we could get such a measure through the House"[3] before Congress adjourns.

But within a week, a vote to consider repeal was lost, proving again that the fight would be difficult and that repeal was dead, presumably until the Fifty-third Congress convened in December of 1893. That schedule assumed that the president would not call Congress into a special session. The *New York Times* called the result "disastrous to the advocates of repeal."[4] Cleveland would not wait that long. Unlike the tariff, the Sherman Act could be repealed quickly, and it was urgent that it be done, even if it took a special session of Congress.

Fitch met with Cleveland in early May,[5] presumably to discuss an appointment for their mutual friend Dayton, but it seems likely that they discussed the silver question as well. According to the New York *Times*, Fitch's "estimate of the probabilities of silver legislation in Congress possesses peculiar value [to Cleveland] because his sympathies are on the right side and because his seven years in

Congress give him familiarity with that body."[6] The Republican *Mail and Express* said that Fitch's "interview with the president has worried [pro Cleveland] anti-snappers . . . because it was said that Mr. Fitch presented some 'opinions' from Tammany," and added, "Mr. Fitch has a very clever way of treating both factions with ease and grace."[7]

Shortly after Fitch returned to New York, Cleveland appointed Charles Dayton postmaster of New York City. Dayton had served in the New York Assembly a decade before and was one of five young men who worked for Cleveland in Albany, the others being Daniel Lamont, Charles Tracey, James Eckels,[8] and Eddie Apgar. It was generally agreed that Apgar first brought the Buffalo mayor to the attention of Democratic power brokers in 1882. During Cleveland's first term, it was thought that his five friends would have positions in Washington but only Lamont was so fortunate, an outcome that gave some credence to Croker's legendary ironic assessment of Cleveland to wit, "Cleveland does nothing for his friends. We're not his friends so maybe he'll do something for us."

Fitch continued to lobby for the repeal of the Sherman Act well into June when, in an interview with the *New York Times* he said he was "emphatically in favor of the immediate repeal of the Sherman law. Ever since its enactment it has seemed clear that sooner or later its operation would bring about the state of affairs we have now. . . . The gentlemen from the West and South who derided our predictions have now an opportunity to see in their closed banks and ruined business enterprises the proof that the New York position, based on the experience and wisdom of our city bankers, was correct." Continuing, he said, "One difficulty has been the deep-rooted dislike and distrust in some parts of the west, southwest and south of what is called 'Wall Street.' There is a very general belief through these sections that in some mysterious manner all the railroads and steamboat lines, telegraph lines, and the money loaning institutions are leagued together against the interests of the producers and farmers. . . . There has grown a strong belief that more money and cheap money was in the interests of the farmers and that our attempts to put the currency on a solid basis were really inspired in a spirit of enmity to the sections of the country where agriculture is the chief business."[9]

Three weeks later, Grover Cleveland, faced with a grave national emergency and unwilling to wait until December to act, called for a special session of the Fifty-third Congress to meet on August 7, 1893. Amid financial devastation of historic proportions, his purpose was to force Congress to consider "unwise laws which must be executed until repealed by Congress,"[10] which to him meant the Sherman Act.

On August 10, three days after Congress convened, leading anti-silver House Democrats met with Treasury Secretary Carlisle at his home to determine how best to put forward the president's silver repeal program in a way that would avoid dividing the party further. Fitch, according to different newspapers, seemed to have several ideas that carried the day. He was variously credited with limiting the time of debate to ten days commencing immediately ("the business interests of New York were such that immediate action was demanded")[11] and with suggesting that Congressman William L. Wilson of West Virginia introduce the bill ("the name of Mr. Wilson will make the bill acceptable to the House").[12]

The next day the silver spokesmen, among them William Jennings Bryan, pressed their case to lead off affirmatively with a free coinage bill, not a repeal bill that they would have to argue in the negative. Taking the opposing view, Fitch argued, and he prevailed, that it would be "disrespectful to the president and unwise in the Party"[13] to take up as an affirmative proposition a free coinage bill and ask the supporters of the president to argue in the negative. Until then, developments were moving in Fitch's favor. The *New York America* reported that "Congressman Fitch, who has suffered from rheumatism for several days, is much better. Mr. Fitch has worked very hard since he has been here. So far his judgment has been excellent, and both the president and Secretary Carlisle have had frequent consultations with Mr. Fitch."[14]

On August 23 Fitch delivered a plainspoken speech on the House floor aimed at undermining the arguments of the silver men who opposed repeal, and it was well received in New York. The *New York Telegram* said, "Several good speeches were made, notably that of Congressman Fitch."[15] The *New York Times* observed that he "addressed himself to his topic and to the House with more than his usual cleverness combining argument for the repeal with wit that was not galling and admonition that was suggested by an intimate knowledge of the stringent condition of business in his own city."[16]

Growing agony amid the burgeoning unemployment facing the country was having critical political consequences. Whereas Sherman Act repeal had lost narrowly in February during the waning days of the Fifty-second Congress, in a stunning reversal it carried by 130, with 240 for repeal to 110 against, only seven months later at the special session of the Fifty-third Congress that was only slightly less Democratic, as even the erstwhile silver men could see the economic devastation. "There was an air of jubilation on the faces of the anti-silver managers—Cockran, Tracey, Fitch and Rayner and the rest of the men who have taken such an active share in the great fight on the repeal side."[17] Referring to Fitch as "one of the most effective of the organizers" the *Times* reported several days later that Fitch credited the well-earned victory to the friends of repeal who "were businessmen and went about the work in business fashion . . . and . . . the press. From all the editorial pulpits of the great cities, our views were indorsed and our opponents attacked."[18]

The vote was followed by lopsided House rejection of free coinage at all exchange ratios[19] and of the Bland Allison Act.[20] From the time Bland Allison became law in 1878, the silver movement gained traction, always moving forward, gaining an aura of invincibility. The House of Representatives stopped it in the summer of 1893 but even then, no one believed it was dead. The repeal bill was then referred to the Senate for what would prove to be a lengthy debate.

In late August, after silver repeal had moved on to the Senate, Speaker Crisp gave Fitch's special investigating committee permanence and visibility. He continued him on Foreign Affairs and as chairman of Private Land Claims in the Fifty-third Congress, but in addition, he appointed him chairman of the Committee on Election of President and Vice President and Representatives in Congress. From there Fitch would be in the best position to continue the special committee's work on the repeal of the election statutes.

From the moment the Sherman Act was repealed in the House, Fitch's personal state of affairs began to deteriorate. He was presumably still fighting gout in New York and, in spite of telegrams from Crisp urging his return, he stayed away. Crisp wanted to move on election law repeal immediately, while the silver debate raged in the Senate. Fitch was in no hurry. Unlike Sherman Act repeal, which was a sectional issue, election law repeal was a highly partisan question. "'The President . . . was for unconditional repeal . . . he favored no compromise . . . he would not consider any.' . . . But some of his supporters were 'afraid that the projection [of election law repeal] into the House before the repeal of the Sherman Law . . . would cause embarrassment . . . and would destroy the close cohesion which has existed among the hard money members of both parties.'"[21]

No sooner did Fitch return to Washington from New York than he received a telegram summoning him to the bedside of his dying mother. Fanny Parmelee Fitch had been an invalid for years. She had pneumonia, and her condition was deteriorating. Fitch left Washington on September 10 to be with her. Before he left, perhaps too quickly or perhaps underestimating the second ranking member on his committee, Congressman Henry St. George Tucker,[22] Democrat of Virginia, he instructed Tucker to do what he could with the repeal bill in his absence.

With Fitch away, the two southerners, Tucker and Speaker Crisp of Georgia, saw a window of opportunity to reestablish state control of federal elections that had been threatened by the Force Bill three years before. Although the election law of 1871 had little or no direct impact in the South because it applied only to cities with a population of twenty thousand or more, its enforcement provisions, also part of Lodge's 1890 Force Bill, did. They knew that with the repeal of the Sherman Act still undecided by the Senate, their political leverage would never be greater. The sooner they introduced an election law repeal bill of their own, the more likely it was that it would pass.

Tucker, acting as committee chairman, began leading the committee well beyond the repeal of those sections of the election law that offended New York Democrats and that Fitch intended to have repealed. He claimed that the entire election law was unconstitutional. He wanted not only to repeal sections of the law that offended New Yorkers, such as marshals arresting voters at the polls, but also to dismantle the law's enforcement mechanism, including the ability of a plaintiff to bring suit in federal court on the basis of racial discrimination at the polls. It was the same enforcement mechanism that was inserted into the Force Bill, and Tucker knew that as long as it was part of the 1871 law, it could and probably would be part of future Force Bills.

Tucker's repeal bill "wipe[d] off the statute books everything relating to federal supervision of registration, to federal interference with the conduct of elections at the polls and to the prosecution of citizens of the states under federal statutes for alleged offenses against the elective franchise. The entire control of elections is left in the states and the [crucial] power to transfer election cases from the state to federal courts . . . was taken away."[23] As a practical matter, Tucker's bill rendered the Fifteenth Amendment to the United States Constitution inoperative.[24]

Tucker's aggressive timetable for election law repeal was "causing a great deal of uneasiness"[25] among those most concerned with repealing the Sherman Act. If Fitch were leading his committee, he would have accommodated the Sherman Act repeal forces led by Carlisle and instrumental to Cleveland that was his own effort too. In fact, several newspapers reported that Fitch had asked Crisp to slow Tucker down.[26] But Tucker, with Crisp's backing, had no intention of slowing down, and the *New York Morning Advertiser* reported that he "was still actively interested in wiping the reconstruction legislation from the statute books . . . instead of waiting a few days for Mr. Fitch."[27]

On September 13 the president called Crisp to the White House to tell him that the Election Bill "must not be brought forward at this time because it would endanger the Silver repeal law."[28] Crisp offered Cleveland no assurances, thus confirming Fitch's earlier observation in the *North American Review* that the Speaker of the House had become the "second person of importance in our government."

When Fitch returned to Washington on September 19, his first public comment was that "the businessmen of New York are impressed with the idea that to press [election law repeal] will prejudice the progress of the silver purchase repeal in the Senate." He said that an election law repeal bill could be reported out and a vote delayed but that he would "talk that over with gentlemen here tomorrow." At the same time he characteristically expressed no ill will toward Tucker, admitting that he had telegraphed him to "go ahead and do the best he could. It was for him to be judge of the best way."[29] Crisp and Tucker sensed correctly that if they timed the election law debate concurrently with the Sherman Act debate in the Senate, they would have an advantage. To Cleveland and the northern Democrats, Sherman Act repeal was paramount, and whatever price was needed to be paid would be reluctantly paid.

Fitch's return from New York enabled him to participate in the rules fight on the House floor that was brought about by Tucker's aggressive scheduling of the repeal debate. Over strenuous Republican resistance led by "Czar" Reed, who ironically objected to the dictatorial rule of Speaker Crisp, the election repeal bill went on the calendar to be taken up on September 26 and debated through October 9. But early on September 21, Fitch was again called to his mother's bedside. He arrived at his sister's home in Rye, New York, just before she died that day. Days later, Tracey, Dayton, Ehret, Ruppert, and a host of his German friends paid their respects, thereby closing another chapter in Fitch's life.

Fitch returned to Washington in time to rejoin the debate on October 2. He spoke cautiously while the Senate silver debate continued. Tucker, too, was judicious, arguing his case on the House floor with "a carefully prepared and well considered speech, devoting himself principally to the Constitutional points involved,"[30] cautiously avoiding any hint of southern bitterness. But having taken over the direction of Fitch's committee, with Cleveland and many others concerned about the success of Sherman Act repeal, and with a sympathetic Crisp as Speaker, Tucker was in a very advantageous position. The *New York Tribune* called it an "impudent attempt to override the Constitution."[31]

Fitch, by now concerned not only with Tucker's aggressive schedule but with the equally aggressive content of his bill, introduced amendments to Tucker's bill that left intact certain sections relating to enforcement. In the words of the *Indianapolis Journal* "Chairman Fitch's . . . substitute . . . above all, leaves in force the declaratory principals of the Fifteenth Amendment."[32] The differences between the Fitch and Tucker proposals were stark and precise:

> Mr. Tucker's bill repeals entirely sections 2002, 2005 and all sections on the Revised Statutes continuously from that number up to 2020. Mr. Fitch's bill began with section 2011 and repealed all continuously numbered up to 2020 leaving the earlier sections in full force. . . .
>
> Section 2005 simply provides that state registration officers shall extend like privileges to all citizens of the United States qualified to vote under the state law. *Section 2006 to 2010 enforce this privilege and provide that suits may be instituted in the federal courts if discrimination is made on account of color. . . . These*

> *sections were enacted to carry out the provisions of the Fourteenth and Fifteenth Amendments of the Constitution.* They do not in any way authorize interference with state or local officials at the polls. For these reasons a number of northern members are of the opinion that they ought not to be repealed by the Democratic House. (emphasis added)[33]

Tucker's intent was clear. He believed "that the state has the right to fix the qualifications of voters with the limitation as to color, and the sections of the revised statutes which my bill repeals, but which are left in force by Mr. Fitch's bill, deal with this question." Furthermore, said he, "Wherever the federal government attempts to control the right of suffrage or the right of registration, which is an incident of suffrage, we wipe it out. We also wipe out the penalties imposed in connection with registration, which are proposed to be enforced through the federal courts. We do not desire to give to those courts jurisdiction over the enforcement of state laws, nor to create federal laws interfering with state laws for them to enforce."[34]

Faced with the competing bills from Tucker and Fitch, and to avoid an open fight on the House floor, the Democrats caucused to decide on one. "Mr. Fitch . . . said the Northern democrats were in favor of the sections granting all classes the right to vote, and *if there was any wrongdoing for them to answer in the Federal courts*. . . . As far as he was concerned he wanted the Negro to vote, and, besides, the sections he desired left in protected his own vote" (emphasis added). But he added, "'No matter how the caucus decides, . . . I shall abide by its decision.'"[35]

By the time the caucus met it was preordained that the southerners would have their way on the election bill. Tucker's version of election law repeal was voted on by the House. The *Detroit Tribune* in a somber editorial said, "The democrat party has committed a great mistake in running counter to the strong sentiment among the American people. Mr. Fitch's amendment is a confession of partial error very significant. . . . It is a confession that the southern democrats are going too far in their attack on the election laws. . . . It is striking evidence that the democrat party has committed a another blunder in putting itself on record against honest elections of the southern democracy."[36]

The northern men had to be content with carrying the day on silver, and they no doubt were. But it was not a good day for America. If the enforcement provisions of the Election Law of 1871 had remained in place, it seems likely that there would have been cases brought in federal courts before 1965, when the Voting Rights Act was passed. And "Had Mr. Fitch been present it is believed that his would have been the bill reported from his committee."[37]

Ironically it was Sereno Payne who gave Fitch the idea of election law repeal more than a year before and who "closed the debate on the Republican side," predicting that in New York City, repeal would "fraudulently increase the Democratic majority ten or fifteen thousand."[38] Fitch made the concluding speech (see appendix C) opening with a descriptive account of the birth and life of the election laws. From there he passed to a lively and eloquent defense of New York City.

The saying quoted by Emerson, that "Countries are cultivated not as they are fertile, but as they are free," is as true of the city as of the country. The soul of New York's life, the spirit of which has made her what she is, was given her when the Constitution of the United States was adopted and the first Congress met in Wall Street. When Washington rode his horse down the Bowery at the head of his veterans, to take possession of the town from which the British had been driven, he brought with him the future greatness of New York. The history of the chief city of America is the history of American liberty.[39]

He aimed his final thrust at the impact of the election laws in New York and what his investigating committee had learned, and he finished with a plea for their repeal. The *Camden Courier* said Fitch's "eulogy of New York partakes of the nauseating," and then made reference to New York's "largely preponderating of foreign population and government by the same, and her great sewers of crime run wide open, the result of the lowest human civilization." The *Courier* concluded that "she is the smallest [city] in morals without exception, as would naturally be expected of a town built-up by the constant accretions from the slums of Europe,"[40] a not subtle but hardly exceptional American depiction of New York City.

The House repealed the election law by a vote of 200 to 101 on a strict party vote, and the Senate followed suit. Historians have pointed to the 1890 Republican attempt to pass the Force Bill as America's final effort to advance the civil rights movement that had gone back and forth from the Civil War, through Reconstruction, and up to that 1890 debacle. But the final episode was the 1894 repeal of the Election Law of 1871, which eliminated the last faint hope of voting rights for southern black citizens by effectively neutralizing the Fifteenth Amendment. Like so much of the saga of the American Republic, it was a story of unintended consequence.

It began with Davenport's failed effort to legislate Judge Shields from office. From that almost chance encounter, it occurred to Fitch that there was a real opportunity to legislate Davenport from office. The idea gained strength as he and Whitney realized that election law repeal, a civil rights effort to protect the voting rights of New Yorkers, might strengthen Cleveland's presidential campaign. Crisp and Tucker recognized that a northern effort to protect the voting rights of New Yorkers might be used to stop the future advancement of black voting rights in the South.

The Fifteenth Amendment remained "law" then, like a barren piece of marble offering no hope of life, warmth, or actuality for seventy-five years of Jim Crow, until the Voting Rights Act of 1965 breathed new hope into its lifeless words. The Sherman Silver Purchase Act was also repealed. The special session of Congress was adjourned on November 3, 1893. Following the vote on the election law on October 9, Fitch's work for the session was finished.

He may also have been preoccupied in the final days. Richard Croker had decided that Fitch should be the next controller of New York City. On October 17 Fitch gleefully telegraphed Lizzie in New York, "I seem to have been nominated tonight for the best office in New York City. Love to all. Ashbel P. Fitch." He was euphoric, anticipating his return to New York. The New York controller was well paid, and, as he would say, it was in his line of business. From the moment he took office, he would be working for his home city, the city that provided him with every opportunity that he ever had.

9

New York City's Watershed

Many people, I am well aware, imagine that things will go wrong in the office because a Tammany man is at the head of it. But I wish to say now to the businessmen of New York and to those who have dealings with the comptroller's office that they need have nothing to fear. My administration will be clean, fair and blameless. I am a Tammany man, but an honest one; I could not be anything else.

—ASHBEL P. FITCH, 1893

Fitch's nomination for city controller was a surprise to New Yorkers. It was a turning point in his career, from legislating and speech-making to the executive management of a large enterprise, and it came at a turning point in the city's history. The country was on the brink of financial ruin. Just as New York's sound money men had predicted, the nation's and the city's economies were in free-fall. There were no jobs. The panic of 1893 was a harrowing human tragedy, perhaps the very worst in America's history, but certainly on a scale with the Great Depression of the 1930s. In New York, unemployment soared, businesses shut down, and banks limited withdrawals.[1]

The *Philadelphia Inquirer,* under the headline "Feeding the Poor in New York City" reported, "Many stories of starvation and want are daily told in the papers. In the last two weeks ten deaths from starvation have been reported by the Health Department, a record that has never been made in the history of the city. There are, no doubt, hundreds of other deaths due indirectly to the want of proper food and nourishment."[2]

Compounding life's daily misery for thousands of New Yorkers was the escalating discontent with Tammany's corruption and Richard Croker's domination of New York. Reverend Charles H. Parkhurst of the Madison Square Presbyterian Church fueled the city's outrage. Two years before, Parkhurst had called New York "thoroughly rotten."[3] He leveled his oratorical thunder at Tammany mayor Hugh Grant and district attorney Delancey Nicoll. Parkhurst accused "the guardians of the public peace and virtue, vulgarly known as the police, with being a force of corrupt bribe takers."[4] In the autumn of 1893, anti-Tammany fury was nearing a climax.

Republican senator Thomas Platt saw the opportunity to investigate Parkhurst's accusations, and so the Lexow Committee took shape, led by Republican state senator Clarence Lexow of Rockland County. It was yet another probe of city Democrats by upstate Republicans. The committee's charge was to investigate the New York Police Department, and it would do that during 1894, through sensational hearings that shocked New York. The twin tragedies of economic disintegration and police corruption hovered over New York as election day 1893 drew near.

The history of the New York City controllership is remarkable. In 1894 it was a powerful office, more powerful in the financial realm than New York's mayor, a fact that often goes unnoticed. Twenty-five years before, in the midst of the Tweed scandal, there had been a convulsive shake-up in the office. Samuel J. Tilden, as part of his plan to topple Boss Tweed, convinced Tweed's controller, Richard B. Connolly, to transfer the responsibilities of his office voluntarily to a hand-picked-by-Tilden deputy controller, Andrew Haswell Green.[5] Connolly, hoping for leniency, remained in office to help the reformers unravel the rotten, tangled affair. In those days, the mayor appointed the controller. In the years following Tweed, the controller was endowed with a degree of independence from the mayor that was previously unknown. Ultimately the controller was elected by the people, another fact that has escaped the attention of some historians.[6]

Green was a prominent lawyer and civic leader, known as a lead sponsor of Central Park, who would later become known as the father of New York's consolidation. He might also be known as the father of New York's Finance Department. During the succeeding five years and with whatever help he could muster, he laid down a system of audit, budget, and other financial controls that served New York well and that was still followed twenty-five years later when Ashbel Fitch was elected controller. The impact of Green's Finance Department on the future of New York, often unrecognized by present-day historians, was immeasurable. It seems problematic, for instance, that New York's consolidation in 1898, wherein the tax bases of the separate boroughs were seamlessly meshed into one, could have been carried off were it not for the smooth, professional functioning of the Finance Department.

The Consolidation Act of 1882, a comprehensive piece of legislation incorporating all laws relating to New York City passed by the legislature and still in effect, provided for an appointed controller to serve a four-year term. In 1884 that was superseded by a new law that provided for an elected controller to serve a three-year term.[7] Three men were elected between 1884 and 1893, each of whom compiled outstanding records in their service of New York City. Edward V. Loew, the first of these, was elected in 1884 to serve a three-year term through 1887. Theodore Myers was elected twice, in 1887 and in 1890, to serve two three-year terms that ended on January 1, 1894. Ashbel Fitch in 1893 was elected to a three-year term that was scheduled to end on January 1, 1897, but was extended to December 31, 1897, by the provisions of New York's constitution of 1894.

Another reason for the preeminence of New York's Finance Department, also virtually lost to history, came in the person of Deputy Controller Richard A. Storrs. Storrs joined the department in 1857, rising to deputy controller under Controller Connolly. When the Tweed frauds were exposed in 1871, Storrs resigned in favor of Green. Green, however, recognizing Storrs's ability, asked Storrs to stay on as his assistant. Storrs became invaluable to him as together they unraveled the department's sordid affairs. Storrs was renamed deputy controller in 1877, a post that he held continuously under succeeding controllers to the time of Fitch's election in 1893. Storrs was a dignified, prototypical public servant who tied the Finance Department together and connected it to its notorious destruction and resurrection in 1871 and 1872. His dedication as well as his institutional memory served New York well and enabled a succession of controllers to excel in office.

In 1893 the mayor's term of office was two years. The controller's and the mayor's annual salaries were $10,000 each,[8] but with fees the controller's annual income might range to $50,000 or more.[9] The mayor and the controller managed New York in tandem, with the controller independently overseeing the city's financial affairs,[10] while the "executive power of the corporation" was "vested" in the mayor.[11] When the Lexow Committee appeared in 1894, whatever it determined was wrong with the Police Department was separate and apart from the Finance Department. Some Gilded Age historians, in their overviews of New York, tend to pass from the Tweed fiasco, a crime carried on within New York's Finance Department in the late 1860s and early 1870s, to the Lexow hearings that unearthed crimes occurring in the Police Department in the 1890s, thus linking them either by design or by omission. Both scandals were crimes against New York that were committed at different times and in different municipal departments by different people.

The controller's duties and responsibilities to the voters of New York covered every aspect of the city's finances. He was a member of the Board of Estimate and Apportionment, the Commissioners of the Sinking Fund, the Board of Street Opening and Improvement, the Gas Commission, the Aqueduct Commission, the Board of Trustees of the Brooklyn Bridge, and the Board for the Revision and Correction of Assessments, along with other lesser boards. His presence at Sinking Fund Commission meetings was necessary to provide a quorum. He was the auditing officer of the municipality. All claims against the city requiring the payment of money were presented to him for adjustment, and he had the power to settle or adjust them or both. He was the custodian of the funds accumulated in the sinking fund. And he borrowed in the open market during the course of each fiscal year some $30 million on revenue bonds in order to run the city government until taxes were collected in October.[12]

As Richard Croker contemplated the controller's election of 1893, he could easily have renominated Controller Theodore W. Myers, who was widely regarded as a forthright public servant. But Myers, his term expiring, was delaying several projects that Tammany wanted completed. It was widely assumed that a new Tammany controller would finish them. If Croker turned down Myers, however, in the midst of mounting calls for reform, his nominee would need to be highly regarded and clearly electable in order to preempt Republicans and independent Democrats from launching an independent candidacy, for Myers in particular or for anyone else. When Croker decided not to renominate Myers for a third term, he said that Myers had served two three-year terms and that was enough for the controller's office.

Richard "Dick" Croker was born in Ireland in 1843, his family having arrived there with Cromwell two hundred years before. Alfred Henry Lewis in *Richard Croker* refers to the Croker family's "inherited Presbyterianism."[13] Croker's parents came to America when he was three and, according to the *New York World,*[14] the family settled in a squatter's shanty near Ninety-ninth Street, an area that is now part of Central Park. The *World* also reported that Croker's father was a blacksmith and that Croker was a child of the 1850s New York City streets. Lewis attributed such reports to "critics of Richard Croker," writing that Croker's home instead was on Twenty-eighth Street near Fourth Avenue in a "reputable" area, that his first school was at Twenty-sixth Street and Madison Avenue, and that Croker's father "practiced the mystery of horse surgery," meaning that he was a veterinarian.[15] Both sources attribute inordinate skill with his fists to Croker, the *World* reporting that he beat "Reddy" Haskins in a neighborhood cellar, "Pat" Kelly in a saloon at the corner of Thirty-fifth Street and Third Avenue, and memorably "Dickie" Lynch one Sunday morning in Jones' Wood.

Croker had a series of city jobs. The last two were fire commissioner under Mayor Edson and city chamberlain under Mayor Grant. The rest of his career was spent leading Tammany Hall, and he accumulated considerable wealth along the way. Richard Croker was very tough and very smart. New Yorkers today can still see his name chiseled into a granite tablet high on the wall of the East Sixty-seventh Street fire station.[16]

The city's relentless march northward was fueled by an enormous influx of immigrants into southern Manhattan, and it provided Tammany with rich opportunities for self-dealing wholly outside of the stream of tax revenue that flowed into the city's coffers. "The Board of Street Opening and Improvement [for example, was] empowered to lay out, open, widen, straighten, extend, alter and close streets and avenues, and to order proceedings to acquire title to land for parks," all activities that "might increase or diminish the value of property. Tammany leaders do

11. Richard Croker, ca. 1900. Photographer unknown. Alfred Henry Lewis, *Richard Croker*. New York: Life Publishing, 1901, frontispiece.

not deny they have taken advantage of these opportunities . . . receiving tips on projected public improvements."[17]

The frantic pace of development overtook all of Manhattan. Friends of Tammany Hall who may have done well were not alone in that regard. Numerous other New Yorkers were also doing well. Cornelius Vanderbilt and William C. Whitney, for instance, may have used inside information as they put together their transportation empires. The *New York Post* noted later that "those men [who became rich through real estate tips] are Tammany men and all of them are under the influence of the Mayor [Gilroy]," then added, "excepting perhaps Comptroller Fitch who shows a disposition to act with some independence."[18] Members of a Board of Street Openings today would be precluded from real estate transactions in their jurisdictions, but not in 1894.

Exactly why Croker settled on Ashbel Fitch for controller remains unclear. There may have been a connection between Fitch's nomination for controller and his vote for Crisp for Speaker, but that was two years before. Fitch was just as well known as Myers, and he had an equally spotless reputation. Beyond that he was an experienced campaigner with influence in the impatient-with-Tammany German community. But there may have been other candidates. The *Mail and Express* said that ex-controller Edward V. Loew was expected to "get the place," but that Croker had raised Fitch's name "last week."[19] The *World* said J. Edward Simmons declined the nomination.[20] Perhaps Gilroy spoke up for Fitch. And how could anyone know whether Fitch, while effective in Congress, could administer the Finance Department? It is not possible to know. There was no comment in the press at the time as to any reason why Fitch was nominated, and Croker did not have to explain himself. There was considerable comment, however, both pro and con, after the nomination was put forward.

The *New York Times,* a long-standing Tammany adversary, said, "Ashbel P. Fitch is one of the best, brightest and soundest of Tammany's young men. Every voter in New York can vote for him with perfect confidence that he will perform the duties of controller with strict fidelity and in a businesslike way." The paper concluded that "while the character of Tammany's nominees is in the main excellent," Tammany had acted against the public interest by pulling Fitch out of Congress where he was "conspicuously useful."[21]

Other newspapers that consistently opposed Tammany did so in this instance, each for its own reasons. The *Philadelphia Bulletin* said "Mr. Fitch still retains some of the respectability, which he acquired while a member of the Republican Party, but his subserviency must be pretty well-established when the ring is willing to accept him as the auditor of its accounts."[22] The *Brooklyn Eagle* noted, "There can be no valid reason for taking Mr. Fitch out of Congress . . . he has given no proof of fitness to administer large financial concerns."[23] The *New York World* and the *New York Mail and Express* each reported that it was arranged prior to Fitch's nomination that he would be replaced in Congress by brewer Frank A. Ehret.[24]

While the newspapers were sorting out their reluctant respect for Fitch from their loathing of Tammany, Controller Myers spoke out. "Mr. Fitch is a good man," said he, "a man who has an unspotted reputation and, while not experienced in the kind of work required, he undoubtedly has the willingness to do his duties well."[25] The *Times* joined Myers, calling Fitch "a good man" and "among the ablest and soundest of the young men that this city has sent into political life in the last decade. . . . He is trusted, respected, and admired by his fellow congressmen of both parties. His character is without a blemish."[26] The *New York Uptown Visitor* observed, "Our metropolis has never had, either in Congress or elsewhere, a bolder or more eloquent champion of her good name, than Ashbel P. Fitch. His speech for the repeal of the federal election laws . . . has forever endeared his name to New Yorkers."[27] Even Henry Robinson, the Republican nominee for the office, whom Fitch had defeated for Congress the year before, said, "We have been friends for years, and I think [he] is a fine man, but he is on the wrong side of the political fence."[28]

To make matters more difficult for Myers's supporters, Fitch received more than fourteen hundred letters in support of his candidacy, one from an unbending enemy of Tammany Hall, former Mayor William R. Grace. Said Grace, "You are as good a man as could be selected to fulfill the duties of the office, and I hope to see you fill a greater office in the future. I am, as you know, opposed to the organization that has nominated you, but I feel that the city's best interests will be perfectly safe in your hands."[29]

In the end, Fitch's candidacy, while frequently criticized ("he belonged in Congress not in city hall," "had no experience in managing a financial enterprise," "was subservient to Tammany," or "was part of a deal to send Frank Ehret to Congress"), was salvaged by his untarnished reputation. That he was well liked and respected by his opponents preempted any vigorous opposition. Myers's "firefly" candidacy, engineered by the City Club,[30] burned brightly for five days. Efforts were made to persuade Robinson to withdraw from the race, which would have united Republicans and anti-Tammany Democrats behind a single candidate. When Robinson refused to withdraw, Myers realized that to be one of two candidates opposing the popular Tammany candidate, whom even he liked and respected, would never carry the day.

For his part, Fitch yearned to rejoin his family in New York. He said, "The nomination was an entire surprise to me. I had no idea of it until it was wired to me after the convention. Yes, I shall accept. . . . The place . . . is a most congenial one to me and just in the line of my business."[31] A few days later he added that he did not regret being called from Congress. "I have spent eight years in Congress. It has been virtually an exile for me. My family has been in New York. My children are growing up here, and I want to be with them. My business is all here. To sum it all up, New York is my home, and I'm proud of the big city and like to be here."[32]

Along with the fourteen hundred letters and telegrams was a special one that said, "My heartiest congratulations. With love, Lizzie A. Fitch."

The rumor that Frank Ehret was Tammany's candidate to replace Fitch was dispensed with quickly. By the first of the year it was announced that Isador Straus, who would perish on the *Titanic* nearly twenty years later, was Tammany's nominee. Straus, born in Bavaria, was raised in Georgia. Too young to fight for the "Lost Cause," he was sent to London to wait out the war. When he returned to America he joined his father's firm, L. Straus & Sons in New York, which took charge of the china and glassware department for R. H. Macy & Co. in 1874. After Macy's death, Isador and his brother Nathan gained control of Macy's in 1895. Straus was well-known, a businessman and philanthropist and a personal friend of Grover Cleveland.

Fitch, formally accepting his nomination for controller, said, "This is the fourth time that this organization has nominated me for office. It has sent me to Congress three times, and, if I have met with any degree of success there, it was because I was proud of New York City and proud of this organization," a sentiment that he would modify later. He continued, "If I am now transferred back to this city, where I can be among my own people, I will discharge the duties of controller with a full sense of the responsibility I will owe to the people and to this organization." And then with care and forethought he added, "I recognize that the better the duties are performed the better will be the credit reflected upon this organization and upon myself,"[33] his first line of defense against Croker's imminent patronage attempts.

Fitch chose his words carefully. At a dinner later in the month he said, "I know that it is a hard thing to follow Comptroller Myers at this time. He is my friend and I like him, but many people, I am well aware, imagine that things will go wrong in the office because a Tammany man is at the head of it. But I wish to say now to the businessmen of New York and to those who have dealings with the comptroller's office that they need have nothing to fear. My administration will be clean, fair and blameless. I am a Tammany man, but an honest one; I could not be anything else."[34]

From that point on, he moved energetically into his fifth campaign for office. Some newspapers, horrified by Tammany's apparent impending control of New York's finances, feared the worst. The *New York Commercial Advertiser,* entirely missing the point of Fitch's return to New York, moaned, "Mr. Fitch is not a typically 'bad man' of the Tammany school; but he is a weakling and his pitiable pliability, as made clear in his submission to orders in retiring from Congress, has increased contempt for him."[35] The *New York Evening Post* said, "No man doubts that Mr. Fitch will obey the orders of the mayor [Gilroy] and 'the organization' so no questions or other annoyance is expected from him. They [Tammany] are waiting for Mr. Fitch to replace Myers so that the business will run more smoothly."[36] The anti-Tammany hysteria that would seize New York and hold it firmly in its grip during the Lexow Committee hearings was demonstrably on the rise well before those hearings commenced. Nevertheless, when the returns were in, Fitch led the ticket with a nearly 70,000 vote plurality out of about 220,000 votes cast, a margin of nearly two to one over Robinson.

On Monday, January 1, 1894, Ashbel P. Fitch assumed his new duties as controller of New York City. "Mr. Fitch arrived just about noon. There was already a large crowd in the office growing larger. The controller's desk was almost covered with flowers, a basket of orchids and roses, another of calla lilies and chrysanthemums. Comptroller Myers and Comptroller-elect Fitch exchanged congratulations as they shook hands and wished each other a Happy New Year."[37] Mr. Fitch told Mr. Myers, "I thank you for your kind wishes my friend. I only hope if I live to leave this office I will have as many friends as you made and be as popular as you are."[38] The new controller had a statement for the *New York Recorder;* said he, "The comptroller's office is a business office, not a political office and no changes should be made in haste. I will not have the department used as a football for politicians."[39]

Ignoring the controller, the newspaper opined, "today the Tammany tiger breathes easier, for at last he has got his capacious paw on the city's strongbox, the only part of the municipal machinery which he has been unable to control for many a year."[40] The *Syracuse Journal* editorialized, "a new [Tammany] wigwam might as well be set up in the city hall for Tammany owns it all now, offices, officials, treasury, everything."[41] Each side had its say, but very few newspapers were undecided, and their analyses were often inaccurate.

Another of the early objections to Fitch's candidacy that evaporated after he took office was his lack of experience as a financial executive. The management of his law firm must have had administrative relevance. From the day Fitch took office he was comfortable amid a dizzying array of issues begging for his attention. The surging flood of immigration added to misery in the streets. There was the genesis of the city's rapid-transit system, schools, docks, street cleaning, garbage disposal, and a host of other particulars such as bond issues, tax collections, and budgets. He helped to dispense the mayor's new relief fund, donations by city employees,[42] and there was a wrangle about plans for a new city hall.[43] He proclaimed, after the Dock Department asked for an issue of $3 million of dock bonds, "I think this is too much," twenty-nine days into his term. "I do not think the department needs so much at present. It got along on $1.75 million last year and it now has $275,000 on hand. I think $1.5 million is enough at present."[44] In the midst of New York's cruelest economic catastrophe, he was committed to economy in government from his first day in office.

The dock board's plans were approved the previous September by the Sinking Fund Commission with the exception of then controller Myers, who asked for additional time to review them. When Fitch assumed office, he too asked for time. The deadlock prompted impatient letters from senior officers at both White Star Line and Cunard urging that the impasse be broken. The *New York Herald* referred to Fitch as the "treasury's watch dog."[45] The Board of Education also felt the Fitch treatment when he trimmed its budget from a requested $2.5 million to $1.35 million. The board said Fitch was playing to the galleries. The *New York Sun*[46] called him a "wise comptroller" for overhauling the board's request.

He refused to issue bonds for land takings and construction of Corlears Hook Park in spite of a court order directing him to do so unless the city was compensated for the land that was taken that it owned.[47] The matter was resolved after the property owners agreed to hold out money to pay the city. Similarly, he refused to issue bonds to build the Harlem River Drive because of technicalities[48] that threatened their legality. The matter was settled in the affirmative by an opinion of the city's legal counsel. He wrote letters opposing "a batch of bills that were before the assembly that affected New York's finances."[49] He watched every city expense. He was dedicated personally to be precisely correct in the face of doubters who associated him with Tammany Hall; and he was dedicated institutionally to uphold the sterling reputation of the Finance Department.

Fitch had more responsibilities than he could discharge. These included ex-officio seats on the boards of both the Rapid Transit Commission and the Brooklyn Bridge Commission. Just as he compiled a poor attendance record in Congress, his attendance at both commission meetings was equally unsatisfactory because he believed that both commissions were badly managed and their meetings were unproductive.

There was no press speculation as to what impact, if any, the new controller's seven years in Washington would have on his performance as controller. Nevertheless, whether his work on specific legislation ever carried over to his new position, it is undeniable that his experience and reputation in Congress lent him stature and credibility in his new office that he would not have had otherwise. As reformers attacked Tammany and attacked him, and as Republican newspapers joined in, other observers time and again gave him the benefit of the doubt and, based on his unimpeachable seven years in Congress, waited for the facts to emerge before reaching conclusions.

Perhaps adding imperceptibly to whatever anxiety went along with the controller's job was the apparently little-known fact, reported by the *New York Sun,* "that the comptroller [was] personally liable for the acts of his subordinates and is individually chargeable for any collection which they make and fail to account for, . . . and that very few Tammany men are on the bonds of the officers in his office."[50] His bondsmen included George Ehret, Jacob Ruppert, and William C. Whitney. He could ill-afford to have things go wrong.

The politics of Fitch's position were as extraordinary as the vexing issues that trailed him throughout the day. Stated simply, his presence as a "Tammany controller" was as inexplicable to Tammany's friends as it was to its enemies. Tammany "friends" insisted that Fitch cooperate, but he would not. Republican enemies, surprised and pleased with his independence, were at a loss to explain his Tammany connection. Try as they might, their dramatic, passionate, sometimes overwrought hand-wringing about Tammany often ended with a footnote that "tried to explain Fitch."

One month after Fitch took office, the New York State Senate unanimously adopted a resolution authorizing the appointment of the Lexow Committee. The day before, "Fitch had scarcely time to familiarize himself with the duties of his new office when the Tammany leaders flocked in upon him and demanded the places which had been held by members of the old County Democracy machine."[51]

The *New York World's* headline blurted out, "The [Tammany] Tiger Is After Fitch."[52] Five days later it read "Are Croker and Fitch Out?" The paper reported that "Boss Croker and Comptroller Fitch have quarreled because the latter has been too slow about turning the anti-snappers and other mugwumps out of his department and putting good Tammany men in." Remarked an unfazed Ashbel Fitch, "This is all news to me . . . efficiency in the service is the first consideration in this department. I expect to make some changes soon. But it will be only when I have found men at least as efficient as the men displaced, and if possible, more so."[53] Richard Croker's relationship with New York's new controller seemed to be off to a doubtful start, and it would not improve.

Meanwhile, the *Philadelphia Inquirer* also reported that "nearly 70,000 men [were] out of work. . . . In sections of the great East Side, the habitation of those who have come to this country from foreign shores with the hope of bettering their condition, the scenes are truly pathetic."[54] The grim statistics were catastrophic, giving an indication that New York was on the verge of collapse. There were no jobs, there was very little money to buy food, and New Yorkers, rich and poor, had to have been fearful. That in turn fed into the frenzy that was prompted by the Lexow Committee.

In the midst of the tragic collapse, Mayor Gilroy called a meeting in his office in early January to determine what might be done to "employ the city's unemployed."[55] Street Commissioner William S. Andrews said, "I can employ about 100 more men [in the Street Cleaning department] *without endangering my appropriation*" (emphasis added).[56] Public Works Commissioner Daly said, "I can put three hundred men to work three days in the week."[57] The Park Department chipped in with "thirty to forty men in the twenty-third and twenty-fourth wards this week and one hundred more men could get about sixty days work at $1.76 per day."[58] And on it went department by department. The mayor suggested that a bill be prepared for the governor's signature "to allow the Park Department to issue bonds to the amount of $1 million to be expended on the public parks under the joint supervision of the commissioner and the Board of Estimate,"[59] and, as in many such well-meaning efforts, this too would have unintended consequences.

The authors of *Gotham,* that widely respected magnus opus of all things New York, accuse Mayor Gilroy, in spite of his "call for a government jobs program," of doing little more than asking for donations from city employees, which he did. At the same time, they recount that "Governor Flower grudgingly signed a bill in February 1894 that authorized New York City's Park Department to spend up to one million dollars on public improvements,"[60] which was intended to create jobs. "Grudgingly" or not, Flower did sign the bill promptly, and there is evidence reported by at least a half-dozen New York newspapers[61] that the bill he signed was prepared by the mayor a month before Flower signed it. The *Gotham* reporting is instructive when measured against evidence that the Tammany mayor did more than ask for contributions because the reporting discourages further analysis of the frightened, panic-stricken response of the reformers to what the mayor really did. An indictment of the park commissioners a year later demonstrated what would later become evident, that the reformers' first objective was to pursue and destroy Tammany Hall.

By early June, the city warmed, hunger abated, and the icy winter's social emergency receded. By then it was apparent that with the best of intentions the city had erred in administering Mayor Gilroy's million-dollar employment program. The Park Department hired workers without knowing what they would do, hiring them directly so as to pay them directly and avoid paying contractors, thus circumventing the city's own fiduciary practices. Controller Fitch refused to pay a collection of small bills for asphalt. The *New York Mail and Express* wrote that under the law, the Park Board was required to advertise for jobs in excess of $1,000 and to require contracts. To get around the law, presumably to expedite job creation, the city bought asphalt in $990 lots and there were no contracts.[62] Fitch said that he was not sure whether it was against the law, and until he was sure he could not pay the bills.

Ten months later, in April 1895, with a reform administration in office, park commissioners George Clausen, Nathan Straus, and Abraham D. Tappen were arraigned upon indictments charging fifty-three separate violations of the law in connection with Mayor Gilroy's million-dollar employment program of the year before. "The illegality charged lay in the purchase in the open market of asphalt for resurfacing walks and driveways in Central Park instead of purchasing it in the usual manner of advertisement for proposals which the law says shall be the method of all amounts over $1,000."[63]

The district attorney, apparently imagining corruption everywhere, indicted three of New York's leading citizens. Born out of the Lexow investigation, a seventeenth-century Salem-like hysteria swept New York in 1894 during the Gilroy administration. The 1895 indictments by the reformers reflected a "too hasty conclusion that [police corruption] extended to every branch of municipal government"[64] including the Park Department. When Fitch was asked whether the Board of Estimate had stipulated the work not be done by contract, he said, "They certainly did desire the work done by day's labor and not by contract. But that did not apply to materials. That was the view I felt obliged to take when the asphalt bills came in, running through a number of days and all just under $1,000. The board claims that the laws gave them discretion, and there is a question, which I did not assume to decide. They may be right, but I could not pay where there was a doubt."[65]

When the indictments were handed down, park commissioner, Macy's co-owner, friend of Grover Cleveland, and indictee Nathan Straus released a statement that said in part, "the whole machinery of the District Attorney's office and the powers of the grand jury have been directed against three well-known citizens, and they have been subjected to the humiliation of an indictment because they made a harmless mistake—if it was a mistake—about the law! While this evidence of zeal in the cause of reform may be pleasing to some of our people, it may be worth inquiry whether such a position will not tend to drive from public service the very men whom it is part of our public policy to invite, not to repel."[66]

The unproductive zeal that characterized New York's reform movement was fundamental to Straus's statement. Far more poignant was the untimely death of former park commissioner Abraham D. Tappen a year later. The headline read "Heart Broken . . . Crime in Reform's Home." It was a lengthy article that examined and commented upon Tappen's death. The cost of Tappen's legal defense made "a serious inroad in a modest fortune." But more significantly, Tappen was a "type of public man of an earlier time who took these things seriously, and to whom no imputation could be more galling than that of lack of fidelity to a public trust. From one end of the country to the other the news was flashed that [the commissioners] were the latest batch of public thieves which the grand jury had branded with indictment. It was said that the indictment caused the old gentleman to fret his life away . . . that it so wounded his proud and sensitive nature that it fretted the strong man into a premature grave."[67] The burden of a public flogging of this man of conscience was profound, one of many consequences of reform.

The *New York Morning Advertiser* said,

> The public conscience of New York was profoundly stirred in the summer and fall of 1894 by revelations of corruption in the police administration of the city. It was perhaps, a natural, but undoubtedly a too hasty conclusion, that this extended to every branch of the municipal government. The startling evidence which had been brought out before a committee of the State Senate, not without a careful regard to theatrical effect, created an atmosphere of suspicion which enveloped everything relating to the city administration. Looked at through such a medium, acts themselves admirable became painfully distorted, and individuals wholly above suspicion were regarded as little better than rogues. There was a great public outcry for the punishment of the chief offenders, and the Extraordinary Grand Jury, which undertook to sift the testimony taken before the Senate Committee, came to its work full of the desire to make a record worthy of the occasion.[68]

Weeks after the indictments were handed down and the "New York press and the public recognized the absurdity of the proceeding," a bill legalizing the asphalt purchases was passed by both houses in Albany and signed by Governor Morton.[69] The indictments were dismissed one month later. The new law authorized such noncontractual purchases if they were made at "reasonable rates."[70] Lessons for the governance of a modern metropolis from conditions that had not been seen before were, yet again, first learned in New York.

Returning to early 1894, as the Lexow Committee geared up, the legislature authorized the appropriation of twenty-five thousand dollars for the committee's expenses. In May, Governor Flower vetoed the appropriation bill and filed a spirited memorandum with his veto. Flower accused the committee of a political motivation and wasting taxpayer money. He insisted that "no city in the state is so well governed as New York." He acknowledged that "bad men sometimes get in office, that frauds upon the city treasury sometimes occur" but said, "these things are as equally true of every city in the world," and, indulging in his own political gamesmanship, perhaps "truer of other cities of our state than of New York."[71]

To Flower, it was a matter of home rule, just as Fitch had written to state Republicans eight years before. Flower believed that New York's citizenry should fix whatever problems there were in the city, not the Republican minority party of the city that happened to hold a majority in the state. Without state funding, the Chamber of Commerce was forced to step into the breach with a $17,500 loan in order to save the Lexow Committee from an early demise.

Yet serious problems within the Police Department became readily apparent as Lexow testimony began. Some of it was appalling, and whether or not it should have been, it was all laid at Tammany's doorstep. Passion for reform was heating up, and it would reach its boiling point on the next election day. Politicians became nearly hysterical about corrupted government, and they would go to great lengths to root it out. Richard Croker saw it coming, and by the middle of May 1894 he had "retired" from Tammany, too shrewd to testify before Senator Lexow's committee, leaving John Sheehan at the helm of Tammany Hall.[72]

New York City was captivated by the Lexow testimony. The inimitable Joseph Choate,[73] who was asked to serve as counsel for the Lexow Committee and declined, in a chance moment of candor before an audience at Cooper Union laid bare his anti-Tammany xenophobia for all to hear. Said Choate, "We are tired of being submitted to the despotic control of a handful of foreigners who have no stake in the soil, and who are using the countless treasure of this city . . . for political aggrandizement." According to a *New York Daily News* reporter, he caught himself perhaps disingenuously, "and we would be just as tired of that if they were not foreigners, if they were Republicans, and governed by the same means and for the same purposes."[74]

The Lexow Committee laid bare deeply ingrained corruption within the Police Department, and sophisticated community leaders like Choate, in part because of their disdain for foreigners, were too willing to see foreigner-inspired corruption everywhere. When told of Choate's comment, Mayor Gilroy smiled and had no rejoinder. Fitch, as fond of eye-catching jewelry as he was of fashionable clothes, pointed to his Sons of the Revolution button and said, "Mr. Choate cannot mean me. My people immigrated in 1688 and they've been owning bad farms in Connecticut and vacant lots in New York ever since."[75] But cultures clash and so it was when the Republican *New York Press,* in a clumsy attempt to associate Fitch with Tammany and "foreign," observed,

> All the members of the Board seem to have in a marked degree the Tammany man's fondness for jewels. Comptroller Fitch likes variety and bright color in stones. His left hand is almost as profusely adorned with jewels as the hand of a society belle at a ball. On one finger he has two large rings from which flash four diamonds and several rubies and amethysts. Another ring is plainer, but is evidently a costly article. The scarf pin he usually wears is a thing of beauty. It is oval in shape; about as large as a silver quarter, and is studded with precious stones chiefly diamonds. The pin seems to have a dazzling effect on the other members of the Board when combined with the flashes from the rings. When the Comptroller turns the full blaze of the pin on his fellow money distributors and waves that jeweled hand in gesture, all argument subsides and the Comptroller's motion, whatever it may be, is carried unanimously.[76]

Other citizens, enraged and embarrassed by the scurrilous Lexow testimony, joined the anticorruption frenzy by speaking out against Tammany Hall. The *New*

York Herald, for example, reported remarks by Richard Watson Gilder,[77] editor of *The Century Magazine,* poet, critic, author, one of the more influential forces in late nineteenth century American literature, and friend of Grover Cleveland.[78] Gilder characterized Tammany Hall as "a homogeneous edifice with its foundations in false registration and illegal voting and its proper superstructure in blackmail. Every day it was becoming more and more evident," he said, "that honest men cannot be in Tammany and remain honest." And then that momentary awkward moment of conscience and qualifying back-pedaling just as Choate had done at Cooper Union: "It may be done by Mr. Fitch," said Mr. Gilder, "who I believe to be honest, but if he obeys Tammany he cannot help losing his character."[79]

In July of 1894, one and one-half years into Mayor Gilroy's administration, a snippet in a Rochester newspaper summed up New York City politics. Headed by "Result of a Bad Reputation," it noted, "Tammany Hall has such a bad reputation that any charge made in good faith against it . . . is likely to be believed. It is a rule of law that a man is to be considered innocent until he is proved to be guilty, but this rule has been reversed in the case of Tammany Hall."[80]

As Tammany members complained that Fitch was not cooperative, and friends tried to explain him, skeptics put him to the test. Under the headline "Piling Up a Big City Debt-Comptroller Fitch Tries to Explain Wigwam Extravagance" the *New York Mail and Express* reported "that the city debt has increased $3.6 million during the six months ending June 30, 1894 has caused the Tammany administration no end of uneasiness and has provoked from Comptroller Fitch four pages of typewritten explanation. This statement was, doubtless, prepared in accordance with instructions from [Tammany's] headquarters for the increase has furnished a convincing argument for those who contend that the next mayor should be a businessman."[81] Fitch quickly pointed out that "the increase is more apparent than real." He said that the amount of new bonds issued during the first six months exceeds the total of old bonds redeemed, because revenue from the redemption fund are mostly payable in the second six months.[82] The *New York Times* concluded that the increase "has no special significance and is no indication of a corresponding increase for the entire year."[83]

A week later headlines across the country reverberated, "Looks Like a Big Fraud," "Millions Stolen," "A Citizens Investigation-Not Within the Province of Lexow," "Alleged Rottenness," "Fraud May Be Unearthed, Fitch Is Uneasy," and "Proofs of Fraud—Comptroller's Office said to be Honeycombed." It was an old story about fraudulent bonds that had its roots in the Tweed scandal and was resurfacing under a new controller. Fitch admitted that he had heard it "before he took office, from a man who said he would be sorry if he did not dismiss certain employees."[84] Deputy Controller Storrs volunteered it was "an attack on me, not the first from the same source."[85] The *Bond Buyer* weighed in, "as far as we can see, the story now some twenty years old has been revived. . . . We can say to our subscribers that from very close and careful scrutiny for twenty years that the duplication of city bonds to any large or small amounts could not have been possible without early discovery of the fraud."[86]

Nevertheless, a citizens committee was appointed to investigate the new charges of the existence of duplicate, fraudulent bonds. Fitch, unruffled, said, "It tickles me that the committee should think it necessary to secure a peremptory order from the Supreme Court to examine the books . . . all you have to do is to come here and everything will be laid before you."[87] To another reporter he said, "They don't need thumbscrews to find out whatever is in this office. Everything is open and above board."[88]

As the police scandal played out, Fitch's mayoral stock soared. Weakened by public disapproval and Croker's escape to England, Tammany was eager for respectability. The *New York Herald*[89] released a sketch and profile under the heading "Mayoralty Gallery—Number Three" that sketched Fitch's career and was accompanied by his stern and decisive countenance. He must have considered the mayoralty and the obvious attractions the job would hold for any politician. But when he faced the facts he knew that as mayor he would come under unrelenting patronage pressure from Tammany and that the potential for conflict with his clients would increase. In Congress he could conduct his legal business and represent New York without conflict. As controller he could do the same. As mayor, the issues would be more complex and the income less, and he knew it would become more difficult. Every time his name came up for the job, as it did periodically, his answer was the same, "I would not accept a nomination for mayor if it were handed to me on a gold plate."[90]

Election day was approaching and the Lexow hearings were winding down when a *New York Sun* reporter called on mayor and Tammany sachem Gilroy to ask questions about the alleged mismanagement of the city. The mayor, no doubt advised by Fitch, told the reporter that not only had Tammany not mismanaged the city, but that "the taxpayers of New York had a better return for their money than they had in any similar period in the city's history."[91]

The reporter asked questions about the per capita cost of government, the size of the city's debt, growth in expenditures on docks, education, public health, and public works as well as the tax rate. His final question alluded to scandals in the Police Department. To each and every question the mayor had an answer that amounted to rigorous budgeting, either lower taxes or lower public debt or both, and a lighter tax burden than that of either London or Paris, most of which reflected the work of the Finance Department. Regarding the police scandal, the mayor showed the reporter a list of thirteen police commissioners dating back to 1880, consisting of five non-Tammany Democrats, five Republicans, and three Tammany Democrats. To Gilroy this was ample evidence that there were plenty of places to point fingers besides Tammany Hall for whatever was wrong with the Police Department.

Echoing his controller's oft-spoken theme of economy in government, Mayor Gilroy emphasized that "one fact should outweigh [all the others]. Capital," the mayor said,

> can safely be trusted to promptly discover conditions that would impair the credit of an individual or corporation. Nothing can be more sensitive to such influences than financial circles are. If the government of this municipality . . . was as extravagant, as inefficient, as corrupt, and as dishonest as its detractors seek to show, the financial credit of the city would be the first thing to be affected. On the sixteenth of this month, Comptroller Fitch advertised for bids of about $1.6 million worth of city bonds bearing interest at a rate of 3% and exempt from taxation. Bids were received at premiums ranging from 1–3 percent and the proposals were for amounts aggregating more than $10 million,[92]

a sure sign of investor confidence in New York.

Fitch's response to doubters and his most reliable connection to reality was the rate of interest that the city paid to borrow money. Throughout his term as controller, through panics, Lexow investigations, silver Democrats, and other major and minor distractions, New York City often financed at or below the cost that the United States government financed, and most of the city's bond offerings were oversubscribed. This to him was the test of the city's financial health and investor confidence. In the Gilded Age, New York relied, as it does today, on the sale of its bonds both at home and abroad to finance its day-to-day operations. Any interruption or slowdown in the city's access to credit would create a dramatic falloff in the city's economy. In the late nineteenth century, when credit analysis and communications were far more primitive than they are today, investors' confidence was just as important and more subjective. Rumors, unfounded or not, concerning the city's ability to meet its obligations, salaries, contracts, interest, and the like could be self-fulfilling. One of the controller's more important responsibilities was to maintain confidence in the city's ability to pay in the face of enormous prospective outlays for rapid transit and mischievous rumormongering by opponents of Tammany Hall.

The Lexow Committee's final report, filed in January of 1895, consisted of nine recommendations that would lead to weak local governance and seemed to provide ample future opportunities for upstate Republicans to criticize and investigate New York City Democrats. Chief among those were the recommendations of a four-person bipartisan Police Board to which an operating superintendent of police would report. Lost in the anti-Tammany hysteria was the lonely, unheard voice of the city's state senator, Jacob Cantor, the token Tammany Democrat on the committee, who filed a minority report. Cantor, a powerful figure in the assembly and senate for many years and a schoolmate of Fitch's at Thomas Hunter's Thirteenth Street School, filed his dissent "chiefly as a protest against the grossly partisan character of the majority." Cantor "emphatically dissent[ed] from the proposition [that] provides for the creation of a bipartisan Board of Police Commissioners. The principal is bad in theory. It is worse in practice. It is a divided responsibility, and there is no way in which the people can hold either individuals or a political party to a strict accountability for the actions of the board." Said Cantor, "I would provide first for a single-headed commission of the Police Department for the city of New York. I believe that the force, in the hands of a practical man, honest, faithful and conscientious, would be relieved of the abuses shown to have heretofore existed, and can be honestly relied upon to exercise true and efficient police duty."[93]

A scant four months later, Theodore Roosevelt, by then president of the four-man bipartisan Police Board that Cantor opposed, referred to the Platt-Lexow Bipartisan Police Act as either "foolish or vicious" as he tried to circumvent it.[94] Whether Roosevelt was aware of the act and of Cantor's dissent, the vesting of ultimate police power by Republicans in a bipartisan police commission resulted, as Cantor warned, in a hopelessly hobbled commission that frustrated Roosevelt, doomed his ambitions in New York, and helped return Tammany Hall to power.

Although Gilroy's interview with the *New York Sun* was serious and well-prepared regarding all matters relating to New York, events conspired against him, and by early November it was clear that the Lexow hearings had put him and Tammany Hall hopelessly out of step with New York voters. It is no wonder he decided against attending the grand opening ceremonies of the new north wing of the Metropolitan Museum of Art, opting to send Fitch in his place. The new wing, opened on November 5, 1894, election eve, "enabled the museum to exhibit treasures that have been sitting in cellars and storehouses for a long time." One of the prominent speakers contrasted "the first little museum on Fourteenth Street less than twenty-five years ago with the magnificent structure of the new wing."[95]

On the evening of the dedication "covers were laid for sixty guests at a banquet at the Hotel Waldorf" and none other than "Joseph Choate presided."[96] Seated on Choate's immediate left were Cornelius Vanderbilt, Chauncey Depew, J. P. Morgan, and Seth Low, in that order. Also seated around the table were Francis Lynde Stetson, Elihu Root, Stanford White,[97] and a blur of upper-crust, probably nativist New Yorkers that would have undoubtedly made the "foreign," Irish-accented, immigrant Mayor Gilroy uncomfortable the night before an election day that was sure to see his administration repudiated at the polls.

During the afternoon dedication ceremonies, it was the duty of the soon-to-be-indicted George Clausen, president of the Park Department, "under whose direction [the new wing] was erected,"[98] to present the new wing to the museum's board of trustees. As president of the board, it was Henry Marquand's job to accept it. Fitch's responsibility, substituting for the mayor, was to declare the new wing open to the public and to thank those who were responsible for the miraculous New York City asset. He seized the opportunity, as he had so many times before, to trumpet the miracle of New York to the audience before him:

> It is not enough in the view of those of us who love New York that our city should have the largest population in this country. It is not enough that our banks should control the money markets and our streets contain the commerce of a continent. It is not enough that the city should be the most delightful to live in this country and be chosen as a residence by people from the Pacific Coast and New England. What we desire is that in all which makes for the highest form of civilization, in the arts, in literature, in music, and in her schools of the professions, New York should lead the country of which she is the chief city. . . .
>
> . . . New York was the birthplace of American art and American literature. It is the town where Irving was born, where Cooper wrote, where Alexander Hamilton lived, the praises of which were sung by Halleck and Drake. Here it was that Bayard Taylor did his work, that William Cullen Bryant spent his beautiful life, and that George William Curtis, from the press and the platform, taught the doctrine of culture and patriotism. Here every man of talent in every profession comes, if he can, for study in our schools or for appreciation and reward for his work.[99]

Fitch may well have been wondering how his life was about to change. In his first year as controller, under scrutiny for his Tammany connection, he was among friends and associates, a Democratic controller in a Democratic administration. He must have wondered what his life would be like in a reform administration. Tammany, failing to find the respectability it sought in its candidate, nominated the former mayor and Tammany sachem Hugh Grant to replace Gilroy, while the reformers nominated businessman and neophyte politician William L. Strong.

Strong, a "warm personal friend of Governor and future president William McKinley,"[100] was raised in Ohio and came to New York in 1853 to seek his fortune. He began in the dry-goods business, first working for others and then for himself at Wm. Strong & Co., where he was said to have made a fortune. Strong had an interest in politics, running once unsuccessfully for Congress in 1882, but that was the extent of his political experience. He entered the race with high hopes for reform. Fitch, the pragmatist, was suspicious of "reformers." If Strong were to win, the *New York Commercial Advertiser* observed, "the Board of Estimate and

Appropriation which directs the expenditures of the people's money would not pass out of the hands of Tammany altogether. The comptroller has the veto power on all issues of bonds not specially authorized by law and he can be a great assistance to a reform mayor in this connection. Much will depend on Comptroller Fitch in carrying out the will of the people if they declare against Tammany."[101]

To that it might have added, "and much will depend on Mayor Strong's willingness to respect the established procedures of the Finance Department that were laid down twenty-five years before by Samuel J. Tilden and Andrew Haswell Green."

10

Reformers in Charge, 1895

New York is a stepchild whose existence would be gladly forgotten by the gentlemen in charge of legislation in this House.

—ASHBEL P. FITCH in Congress, 1890

Election day brought victory to the reformers. Strong's 60 percent of the popular vote[1] was a remarkable showing for a New York Republican, notwithstanding his reform candidacy. Jubilant headlines trumpeted, "Tammany Crushed," "Turn the Rascals Out," "Richard Croker Is Blamed," and "Tammany Men to Be Driven from Public Crib." Croker, ever the canny philosopher, said "One trip into any Tammany ward would have told you that Tammany voters were going to vote against us this year. Our people could not stand the rotten police corruption. They'll be back at the next election. They can't stand reform either."[2]

The election marked other significant New York City milestones. Voters approved two monumental referenda, consolidation[3] and rapid transit, as well as a new constitution that promised home rule for New York City.[4] Democrats nationwide and Tammany in New York were in full retreat. Cleveland's popularity, at its peak in 1892, plummeted with the economy two years later, and Croker, severely criticized, left the country. Straus won Fitch's seat in Congress by a third of Fitch's prior margin, while Fellows's seat was lost to a Republican, only the third Republican to win a seat in Congress from the city since 1878.[5]

Although Fitch must have been disappointed by the election, there was a silver lining. The new state constitution added a year to his term of office. While reformers awakened slowly to the fact that the "Tammany" controller's term would run as long as the reform mayor's, which was also extended, the controller was matter-of-fact as he described how the old law provided that his original term expired on January 1, 1897, and the new constitution provided that when such office expires in an odd-numbered year, the term shall be extended to the end of that year.[6]

The reformers toppled Tammany on the strength of Lexow testimony that uncovered deep-seated police corruption. While Strong's victory captured city hall, it remained to be seen what would come of it. Some thought it was the end of

Tammany and Tammanyism, but others, possibly anxious about the Tammany controller, were not so sure. The Republican *New York Commercial Advertiser* placed the burden on the controller to bend to reform, without mentioning the larger responsibilities of the reformers.

Fitch brought to his job the unconditional belief that New York's finances were exceptionally well managed by the Finance Department; that the auditing, bookkeeping, and budgeting systems that had been established twenty-five years before by Tilden and Green were the reason; that they were inviolate; and that their continuance served New York well. Whether he anticipated that those views would come under attack we cannot know, but in time it became clear that they did.

Pundits turned quickly to the uncertain impact of Strong's victory. Newspaper articles appeared, such as one headlined "What Strong Can Do."[7] Attention centered on the Board of Estimate, where "unless the legislature passes a Power of Removal Bill for his [Strong's] benefit, his party will be in the minority during his entire term of office."[8] The board was made up of the mayor and the president of the Department of Taxes and Assessments, a mayoral appointee, and the controller, corporation counsel, and president of the Board of Aldermen, all of whom were affiliated with Tammany. The same was true of the Sinking Fund Commission and the Board of Street Opening and Improvement. Several members of these commissions were beyond the mayor's power to remove. Even with their removal, however, the elected Tammany controller "would have the power alone to negative by his veto."[9]

There was intense citywide interest in the binding rapid transit referendum, which had passed easily, and in the nonbinding Greater New York referendum, which had passed handily in New York, gained a narrow victory in Brooklyn, but passed nevertheless. As the stunning impact of the comprehensive election results were sinking in, there began a brief period of adjustment, reflection, and waiting, a momentary calm before a storm, a cease-fire, before reformers took hold of the reins of city government at the turn of the year.

In mid-November, the city brought an issue of 3 percent bonds to market that sold at a small premium. Just one month later, in the midst of another duplicate bond scandal flurry, the *Bond Buyer* reassured its readers that "the bonds of New York City are a better investment today than those of the United States at present prices."[10] The *New York Mercury,* reaching its own conclusion said, "The *Bond Buyer* declares that the bonds of New York City are a better investment today than those of the United States government at prevailing prices. Of course they are. But what comment is this upon the cry of the 'reformers' that New York is the worst governed city in the country. The truth is that it is one of the best governed."[11] These were the unseen results of the policies laid down by Andrew Green twenty-five years before that had been carried forward by Richard Storrs under three capable, honest, popularly elected city controllers.

As the Christmas season drew near, one of the more entertaining and revealing holiday dinners was the annual St. Andrew's Society banquet for 260 friends of Scotland at Delmonico's. "The Earl of Aberdeen, Governor General of Canada, in the full national costume of Scotland and wearing the tartan of the Gordon clan, of which he was the hereditary chief, was guest of honor."[12] Other speakers were Chauncey Depew, Joseph Choate, Andrew Carnegie, General Horace Porter, and Ashbel Fitch.

Choate, an adept humorist, whose humor was often intolerant, at the expense of others, or both, was equal to the task that evening when with a nod to the governor general he said, "sitting here for the last four hours cheek by jowl with the Governor General of Canada, I take great shame to myself that I did not leave off my trousers before I came here. . . . The distinguished Governor General has said that from his early youth he has aspired to join the ladies. Well I think he has come very near doing it tonight."[13] Choate's biographer, recounting this night in late 1894 as well as Choate's earlier remarks at a St. Patrick's Society dinner in March of 1893, both of which were reminiscent of his "antiforeigner" Cooper Union comments of March of 1894,[14] concluded that Choate's comments were inoffensive and taken in stride.[15] Depew, a witness to both faux pas remembered them differently. He recalled that "Mr. Choate was never invited to an Irish banquet again," and "Choate lost invitations to future Scotch dinners."[16]

Antiforeign sentiment had held New York's elite in thrall for years. Kenneth Ackerman in *Boss Tweed* lays bare Thomas Nast's "anti-Irish, anti-Catholic slant"[17] and his "ugly stereotyping of immigrants,"[18] which had so powerfully affected New Yorkers twenty-five years before. And whether they "influenced" or "persuaded" New Yorkers or "reflected" already widely held opinions is a moot point. The contrasting views of aliens, on one hand by the immigrant Nast, whose antiforeign point of view was a prominent feature of his work, and on the other by the Pilgrim and Puritan Fitch, whose embrace of foreign cultures years later was well-known, is a remarkable contrast. Choate, while not part of the Strong administration, was a Republican insider, and his xenophobic words and deeds had meaning.

As the reform administration's time grew near it seemed that some of the new mayor's reform backers believed that they had a claim on Strong's victory. Tammany Hall was not the only political organization seeking patronage. Republicans wanted patronage, too. Some suggested that the Committee of Seventy would "investigate the characters of applicants and report to the mayor whether they were worthy of appointment."[19] The committee had appointed subcommittees to investigate every department of the city government that would need to be heard, and "the reports will be made to the mayor with the support and sanction of the Great Committee of Seventy, the body which made a union ticket possible and nominated William L. Strong for mayor."[20] That committee also began drafting the Power of Removal Bill that was brought to the legislature at its opening.[21] For Strong, there were political risks attached to either his acceptance or his rejection of the committee's advice.

The new mayor's first day in office began at noon on January 1, 1895. He was New York's first Republican mayor since the Civil War. During the forenoon, messengers laden with floral gifts paraded to city hall. "The Star Spangled Banner, worked out in red, white and blue flowers, was another offering of congratulations. The words 'We Serve' were inscribed on the piece. This design came from the Republican Club." Mayor Gilroy, who led Strong through a throng of applauding well-wishers, said, "Mayor Strong, the hour of twelve o'clock having arrived, my term of office has expired and it becomes my duty to turn over to you the keys of the office, desks and other contents. I will say that it is my sincere wish that your administration will be successful and prosperous. I wish you every success and a happy new year."[22]

Mayor Strong, holding Gilroy's hands in his, expressed his "warm appreciation" for the courtesy Gilroy had extended to him at the last meeting of the Board of Estimate and Apportionment. Said Strong, "During those deliberations I obtained valuable insight into the duties and details of the mayor's office, and I will say that you are the best presiding officer at a board that I have ever seen, and I am confident that if I display only one quarter of the talent and ability which you possess my administration will be successful."[23] With that surprising but apparently sincere endorsement, the Strong administration was in business—one more demonstration of the single most important element of the American democracy, the orderly transfer of power between fierce rivals.

The first few months of 1895 found Republicans and Democrats alike on unfamiliar ground, jockeying for position. Fitch was no exception. He was seen in city hall "in some what of a flurry. 'How are you Mr. Comptroller?' called out a friend, but the comptroller only replied: 'I can't stop. The mayor has sent for me and I must go right in and see him.'"[24] Fitch seemed intent on reinforcing his position on the Board of Estimate and, through that, his relationship with the new reform mayor. His year's experience in office should have given him an advantage. His dealings with the new mayor and his appointees, each with no experience in city government and differing agendas, experiences, and personalities, would keep him alert, but the reformers showed little respect for the Finance Department and each would resist it in his own way, directly, indirectly, or in the mayor's case by a surprise attack. It

12. King, Moses, *Notable New Yorkers, 1896-1899*. New York: The Orr Press, 1899.

would take only ten months, until election day in November 1895, for the world to learn what New Yorkers learned about reform.

The mayor too was in an equivocal new position. There was no end to the "advice" he received from machine Republicans like Senator Tom Platt, from real reformers on the Committee of Seventy, and from all those in between. The mayor would say only "I propose to have every department of the city government investigated from top to bottom, going back over the accounts as far as it may seem necessary."[25] Such sentiment gave rise to speculation as to what it might take to conduct an investigation of the Finance Department. While Fitch maintained an open door, welcoming friends or foes on legitimate business, he had no intention of relinquishing his authority over his department. Under the headline "Strong's Investigators—Do They Know Enough to Tell Fraud When They See It?" the *New York Sun* observed, "The Finance Department is the largest bank in the city. To investigate this great institution requires not only a theoretical, but a practical knowledge of bookkeeping and finance."[26] Nevertheless, the mayor confirmed an essential purpose of reform, which was to look backward to find reason to blame and ultimately to destroy Tammany Hall.

Republican governor Levi Morton, three days in office, told the legislature, "A Power of Removal Bill for the city of New York, placing in the hands of the mayor absolute and unquestionable authority to remove any of the appointive officers of the city government and to appoint their successors is an immediate requirement at your hands."[27] Behind the scenes Tammany officials waited, unsure whether the bill would become law. "Corporation Counsel [William H.] Clark is ready to go. He says he doesn't want to be kicked out but he is not going to resign until he is sure he will be removed. Commissioner of Public Works Daly went to city hall but did not call on the mayor. He said he would not go till he was asked."[28] Clark was an interesting case. While he seems not to have impressed Mayor Strong, historian Nelson in *Fighting for the City* credits Clark with "appointing lawyers of merit, not mere party hacks,"[29] and, in general, continuing the professional manner of the law department, during his term of office, in the Whitney tradition.

Strong was immobilized until the bill passed the assembly in late January and the senate two weeks later, but when it did he got rid of Clark, four police commissioners, the commissioner of public works, and several others. Fitch now stood alone in a Republican/reform administration, the only Democrat at the top of the New York City government.

As the mayor moved ahead, two appointments he considered before he took office, a street commissioner who declined the offer and another who accepted, were among the most colorful that he would make as mayor. New York streets in the late nineteenth century were havens of indescribable filth. “sewerage, running water, and trash removal were private, not municipal services. Garbage was a matter of social class, and conditions in the poor parts of New York were squalid. On the streets rotted piles of garbage and rubbish. Human and animal wastes mixed with ashes and street dirt. Flies were everywhere.”[30] And in those streets children played, citizens walked, and wagons rode.

Of all the problems facing New York, Strong fastened his immediate attention on the streets. He charged his Board of Health to see that there was a “thorough understanding of the primary health ordinances. He ordered the police to be particularly vigilant in making arrests for violations and Police justices to be more than usually severe in inflicting punishment on violators.”[31] In December 1894, Strong invited Theodore Roosevelt to become street-cleaning commissioner for the city of New York. “Roosevelt declined the invitation although exactly how he expressed the decision to Strong is not known. He said in his autobiography, ‘I did not feel that I had any special fitness.’”[32] Strong denied making the offer,[33] but he kept Roosevelt in mind for other work.

As his second choice for the street cleaning post, Strong tapped George E. Waring of Rhode Island. “[Commissioner William S.] Andrews had expected Mayor Strong would need him for some time, perhaps for months but the decision in regard to Col. Waring”[34] was made quickly. Waring, age sixty-two, an author, inventor, and engineer who specialized in municipal sanitation, appeared to be well suited for the job. He was part engineer, part actor, part martinet, and part snob. Among other of his interesting personal characteristics, Waring “wore a Kaiser Wilhelm mustache, thin and straight, two pencils of hair strained toward his ears, then turned at right angles to stand at attention. That mustache was the very epitome of manly will triumphant over natural disorder.”[35]

An intriguing character, Waring achieved what no man had ever achieved before, at the same time spending more money achieving it than any man had ever spent before, thus rendering somewhat unclear the net value of his accomplishments. Nevertheless, he turned out to be arguably as successful a symbol of reform as there was in the Strong administration. What he accomplished and how he did it cost money, and his tilts with the controller who was charged with overseeing New York’s finances would entertain New Yorkers for the ensuing three years. The mayor’s laissez-faire approach to the street-cleaning budget, which ran counter to the city’s rigorous budgetary practices, was that whatever funds were needed would be available whenever they were needed,[36] although even he sided occasionally with the “Tammany” controller against his own appointee.

Fitch leaned forward in his pursuit of a relationship with the mayor, and he left nothing to chance. The *New York Commercial Advertiser,* a Republican newspaper, said, "Comptroller Fitch has constituted himself the instructor of Mayor Strong and President of the Board of Aldermen Jeroloman. . . . All the resolutions contained full and complete information but Mr. Fitch stopped every time to explain to 'His Honor' and to 'Mr. President.' The impression was created that the controller thought that the mayor and Mr. Jeroloman are totally ignorant of city affairs and must be taught by the kindergarten method of instruction."[37] The newspaper's condescension raised doubts as to whether the mayor listened to the controller, but the mayor's subsequent actions left no room for doubt.

Later, and apart from Strong's assuming office, the *New York Times*[38] ran an editorial essay that went to the heart of the reform administration's future conflicts with the controller. The *Times* attacked the use of the mistaken word "comptroller" in place of the correct word "controller." While the subject may have been of passing interest to etymologists, it could have been of interest to reform politicians. The point of the article was that the controller's function was to "control" or oversee the city's financial affairs, not to count them. The *Times* "propose[d] an amendment to the revised statutes of the United States, of the state of New York, and of every state in the Union where the need of it exists . . . that . . . controller . . . be spelled controller that being . . . the true and right spelling . . . and that 'comptroller,' born of ignorance and continued in darkness, be discarded."

The *Times* explained that the word controller "came into the English language . . . from the medieval Latin *contrarotulator,* the keeper of a duplicate roll, register, or check list. It is not derived from the Latin word *computare,* or the French *compter,* and it has nothing to do with 'counting.'" The *Times* further pointed to the Consolidation Act of 1882, which stated under the duties of the controller, "The Finance Department shall have control . . . of the fiscal concerns of the corporation. *All accounts rendered to or kept in the other departments shall be subject to the inspection and revision of the officers of this department*" (emphasis added). The act also obligated the controller to "furnish each head of department, weekly, a statement of the unexpended balances of the appropriation for his department."[39] When the reform administration seized the reins of city government, whether it was because of Fitch's nomination by Tammany Hall, because he was a Democrat, or for some other reason, the reformers failed, time and again, either to understand or to accept the controller's oversight responsibility, or that it was created by a reform administration a generation before.

Returning again to early February 1895, Fitch brought a small issue of 3 percent city bonds to market and was startled at their cool reception. After some inquiry, he learned that he was likely facing a 3 percent market for United States bonds that would effectively eliminate demand for 3 percent city bonds. It so happened that at the time President Cleveland and his Treasury secretary, Carlisle, were negotiating a government loan with bankers to stem the outflow of the nation's gold supply. So

Fitch asked for and "received authorization from the Board of Estimate to offer city bonds at 3½%."[40]

Within days, he changed his mind, telling the Board of Estimate that he "had decided to issue only gold bonds, unless there was objection by the board."[41] He explained "that he was fully empowered . . . to make bonds payable in gold at his option."[42] Meanwhile the Treasury had issued $62 million of 4 percent "coin bonds," redeemable in either silver or gold, at 104½. The silver interests in Congress blocked the issuance of gold bonds that would have carried a 3 percent rate of interest. On February 18, 1895, J. P. Morgan met with the mayor and Fitch at city hall to discuss the city's impending gold-bond issue.[43] Two days later, the United States coin bonds that were sold to underwriters at 104½ were resold to the public at 112¼ and within days went to 119.

On the twenty-second, Fitch again announced the sale, this time of $3.2 million of 3 percent city gold bonds, and less than a week later he sold them at a small premium over par, approximately two-thirds of them going to the Morgan-led syndicate. In comparing the two issues, the city's 3 percent bonds, even at par (100), would have traded at a 12 percent premium over the 4 percent United States bonds at 119.[44]

New York City had financed at a significantly lower cost than the United States because of the premium that investors were willing to pay for a bond that was redeemable in gold. It was not an insignificant innovation. The city's credit rating, always important, took on added meaning at a time when the economy was trying to recover. It would be tested further by the uncertainties surrounding consolidation and $50 million of prospective new borrowing for rapid transit, roughly half of the city's total debt outstanding.[45] "Mr. Fitch, of course, felt very happy this morning as he passed through Wall Street and received the congratulations of financiers and he said that the operation showed that the credit of the city of New York was now even better than that of the Government under the administration of Mr. Cleveland."[46]

The following week the newly appointed corporation counsel, Francis M. Scott, "charged" at a Board of Estimate meeting "that the tax rate of 1894 was notoriously fictitious." The *New York Evening Post* said that "the tax rate of recent years has been 'juggled' for political purposes in order to make it appear that the Tammany administration was economical" and that "Mr. Fitch . . . admitted . . . the truth of his [Scott's] assertion about the fictitious tax rate."[47] The *New York Morning Advertiser*'s headline read, "Tax Rate Fictitious—The Fraud Is Exposed." "The truth of the charge," it said, "was admitted by Comptroller Fitch who is one of the few Tammany Hall heads of departments remaining in office."[48] Fitch replied to the *Evening Post,* "allow me to say in the paper which many of my friends read that I never made the idiotic statements which you attribute to me."[49]

According to historian Nelson, "when the reformers . . . obtained legislation [to remove] Clark . . . the Law Department of William Whitney was still, to a significant degree, in place. But under Scott it largely disappeared. . . . Scott brought politics back to the Law Department." Nelson asserts further,

> We should hesitate about taking at face value the claim of the turn-of-the-century reformers that they hired all "the best men." Admissions standards for the elite schools from which reformers hired entry-level attorneys were not based on merit but on lineage and wealth. Many able youths, who were excluded from the Ivy League and comparable schools, had to claw their way up through institutions like Tammany Hall. While graduates of the elite schools probably had superior educational experiences, many of the young men whom Tammany brought into the Law Department possessed real talent and were fully capable of performing the city's legal work despite their lack of the elite educational credentials,[50]

conclusions not dissimilar to those put forth in this volume with respect to the Finance Department.

The mayor had little to say either about the city's first gold-backed bonds or about Scott's charges. But he was off to a good start. Assisted by the much-needed Power of Removal Bill from Albany, he remained above the usual daily discord. His relationship with his "Tammany" controller, however, was still taking shape. Fitch, on the other hand was surely annoyed by the assessment imbroglio, and to make matters worse, he was sick with the grippe and his attacks of gout were becoming more frequent. He sent word to the mayor that he would be taking a long weekend in Virginia Beach at the end of March to try to recuperate. By the first of April the mayor, with Fitch absent and still determined to investigate every municipal department, decided to test the Finance Department.

In his annual message to the aldermen, the mayor charged that the city's debt was inflated to cover wasteful Tammany spending and that the size of the debt as well as the spending was hidden by a system of "financial jugglery." The mayor said that "every technical subterfuge was availed of"[51] to defer issuing bonds that had been committed to, so that new debt would fall into 1895, the first year of the reform administration, rather than 1894. The mayor's message included such phrases as "the comptroller furnished a statement," "the comptroller furnished a further statement," "Bonds previously authorized as shown by the comptroller's statement," and "an examination of the statements as submitted by the comptroller."[52] Strong words in more ways than one, all aimed directly at the "Tammany" controller.

Republican newspapers spread the charges of New York "jugglery" and "subterfuge," and they received widespread attention, especially among bondholders in America and in Europe: "The message bristles with facts and figures that speak for themselves."[53] "Tammany's Financial Jugglery Exposed in Strong's Message."[54] "Message Shows Up Financial Jugglery of the Former Administration."[55]

The *New York Tribune* tried to rationalize their respect for Fitch with what they thought they knew about the Finance Department, reporting, "In recent years well-informed citizens have known that the Tammany rulers had added to these methods of obscuring facts and averting judgment the device of an essentially fraudulent tax rate. We deem it not improper to express our amazement and indignation that Comptroller Fitch, a man whose personal honesty has never been smirched, should have prevailed upon himself to consent, at least by silence, to the practices which his books reveal. He knew well what financial jugglery and subterfuges were being employed to deceive and virtually to swindle the people, long before Mayor Strong extracted from him the facts which are now matters of universal knowledge."[56] The *Springfield Republican,* echoing the *Tribune,* said, "This state of things is eminently characteristic of Tammany methods, and would be repeated should a gang of politicians get hold of the city again."[57]

That the *Tribune* and other newspapers would print unsupportable claims as fact about what "well-informed citizens have known" and what Controller Fitch "knew well" was illustrative of the reformers' war on Tammany. But the controller's credibility shows through the reporting, too. The *Tribune*'s only faint restraint grew out of its respect for Fitch. Even so, the newspaper was wrong, and when that became known, the truth would take its toll both on the city and on the reform administration. Rather than directing his energies toward the needs of New York, the mayor manufactured a scandal out of whole cloth and blamed Ashbel Fitch, the "Tammany" controller, for his own delusion. Three months into the new administration, it remained unclear whether the reformers would ever be able to be anything but anti-Tammany when the nation's metropolis needed leadership.

Fitch, ailing at home, sent word that he would come to the office to draft a reply.[58] He took the city's credit seriously and personally. The Finance Department was responsible for New York's finances and credit rating, and he was well aware of the damage the mayor's loose talk could do. For months he had patiently tried to explain the details of New York finance to a reform administration that refused to listen. The irony of the episode was that reformers, elected only five months before to put a stop to Tammany "extravagances," were themselves becoming "extravagant."

Fitch's statement, issued the next day, referred to "statements prepared for [the mayor] with great care by the Finance Department which are correct [and] two or three statements of [the mayor's] opinions which so far as they relate to the Finance Department and its work that are curiously incorrect."[59] The mayor charged that Fitch was purposefully understating the true amount of the city's debt: "he takes my statement of the forty-nine items amounting to $7,020,616.88 of bonds and stocks authorized by the Commissioners of the Sinking Fund and the Board of Estimate and Apportionment which remained unissued December 31, 1894 and announces that these stocks and bonds remained unissued because every technical subterfuge was availed of to prevent their issue, in order to have some moral or political effect."

The bonds, Fitch said pointedly, were not issued because the work was not done. "When the action of the Board of Estimate is required to enable the controller to issue bonds, a resolution authorizing the issue is adopted before the contract is entered into. . . . The bonds are actually issued by the controller only when payments have to be made on account of progress in the work." Explaining further, he said, "There has not been a year when the issues of bonds and stock authorized but unissued did not amount to millions of dollars," that the practice "was well known to the corporation counsel and to everybody who is at all familiar with these matters," and that "any controller who would issue bonds regardless of the time when the money would be needed would subject the city to enormous sums of interest unnecessarily and would deserve indictment or punishment."

The chastened mayor's immediate response was unconvincing. Said he, "I shall make no reply to Mr. Fitch's statement. I am satisfied that he is quite correct. I sent that message to the aldermen to draw out the controller, so that people would know the city's exact financial situation. I'm glad Mr. Fitch saw fit to reply as he did."[60] The *New York Times,* under the headline "Pleased with Mr. Fitch's Reply," gave the mayor the benefit of the doubt, explaining that the amount of the authorized but unissued bonds could obviously not be a part of the "annual statement of the city's debt,"[61] but it might be useful to know.

The Democratic *New York Daily News* saw more to it. "The mayor," it said, "knowing the extravagant tendencies of his Republican associates tried to shield them from the wrath that he sees coming by calling out that they were not responsible, but the wicked Tammany men . . . were. Now comes the comptroller who tells him that he sees only a bogeyman."[62]

Other newspapers, some less kind, ran headlines such as "Wisdom for Strong, Mr. Fitch Gives Him a Lesson in Finances," "Strong's Costly Nonsense," and "Strong's Queer Message." The *New York Sun* concluded, "Mayor Strong has long been making a very poor record for himself, and this last ridiculous attack upon Comptroller Fitch completes it."[63]

In the days that followed, Fitch refused to let the matter die, insisting that the mayor had committed a financial blunder of consequence. "Comptroller Fitch said yesterday that two of the largest bond buying houses on Wall Street that had prepared bids for an upcoming bond issue, had decided, after reading the mayor's

WISDOM FOR STRONG.

Mr. Fitch Gives Him a Lesson in Finances.

13. *New York Mercury,* April 5, 1895.

message, not to bid."[64] The issue was sold, but for 83 basis points (.83 percent) less than similar bonds brought a month before.

The *Bond Buyer,* possibly at Fitch's urging, weighed in a week later with regard to its own earlier bland commentary, saying, "we were not as emphatic as we might have been in condemnation of [the mayor's] inconsiderate use of information which the chief financial officer of the city had given him." Continuing, it said, "The system of auditing and bookkeeping established by Green has been approved by and continued under several of the ablest of the city's financiers; and during all the several administrations of the Controllers of various factions and parties that system had been under the personal direction of one man, Deputy Controller Richard A. Storrs, recognized by bankers and politicians and editors as one of the ablest and

HE DREW HIM OUT.
THE MAYOR: It's all right. I did it just to draw him out.

14. *New York Mercury,* April 6, 1895.

most faithful public officials. To lightly or hastily attack that carefully compiled report of the Finance Department . . . was a very injudicious act for the mayor to commit." Further, the *Bond Buyer* observed that "Mayor Strong is the first mayor . . . who has attacked the Finance Department on political grounds in twenty-five years and the mayor was wholly without warrant as he has practically admitted."[65] While the mayor was obviously lost, he was not the only reformer to be blinded by the frenzied pursuit of Tammany.

Fitch's upstate Republican hometown paper, Malone's *Franklin Gazette,* noted, "The credit of New York City is a matter in which every citizen of the state is interested and it becomes the duty of all men, no matter what their political faith may be, to see that no false statement affecting that credit is allowed to go unexposed or

APPEARANCES ARE DECEITFUL.

Mayor Strong Says He Is Glad that Comptroller Fitch Answered Him the Way He Did, but His Face Doesn't Show It.

15. *New York Daily News*, April 6, 1895.

uncorrected." Continuing, it said, "The *Bond Buyer* pointed out that of the six largest cities of the nation, New York's tax rate is the lowest of all except Boston and that the percentage of bonded debt to the assessed valuation is the smallest of the six cities named. The more the matter is publicly discussed the greater the service recently performed by Comptroller Ashbel P. Fitch to the city of New York becomes."[66]

The day before Labor Day, several newspapers carried a story that the mayor was not pleased. The *New York Times* asked, "Is Mayor Strong Dissatisfied?" The article reported, "After the legislature had authorized an additional appropriation of $100,000, the commissioners of accounts hired a force of expert accountants and a number of detectives. If anything has been discovered in the way of corruption under the Tammany administration the commissioners of accounts have kept it carefully concealed."[67] *The New York Journal* reported, "as yet they have failed to find what they expected. This seems to worry His Honor. Nearly $50,000 of the appropriation has been expended with no results."[68] The *New York Press* said the commissioners "had found nothing wrong in the Tammany accounts."[69]

The mayor was not the only reformer to resent the controller. Strong's Street Commissioner was a case in point, and he, like the mayor, had his own obstacles to overcome. The *New York Times* outlined the challenges facing George Waring: "The chief problems to be solved are the efficacy of the present patrol 'system,' the wisdom of the prohibitory enactment in favor of 'American citizens,' the doubt which exists in regard to the application and validity of the veteran [preference] statutes, the removal of snow and ice, the collection of ashes and garbage, and the question of separate receptacles for them and their disposition, as well as the disposal of other collections in street cleaning. Another question is how far the malign influence of politics affects the operation of the Street Cleaning Department."[70]

The "malign influence" meant Tammany Hall. Waring's predecessor, William S. Andrews, a Tammany incumbent to the office who was under unrelenting pressure to improve street conditions, blamed the snow-covered streets on the "new law, which requires that only citizens of the United States shall be employed on city work."[71] Said Andrews to a reporter, "I would have had two thousand Italians at work last night, and all the principal streets would have been cleaned today. The trouble is that native born citizens don't take to this sort of work."[72] A grand jury convened for the purpose of investigating the Street Cleaning Department, said "The Department of Street Cleaning has an immense appropriation for this purpose, and the utter failure to keep the streets in a decent condition shows that the management of the Department cannot be conducted with foresight or efficiency."[73] Six months later, with little or no change in the dollar amount, the Grand Jury's "*immense appropriation,*" shrank to the size of an "*insufficient appropriation*" (emphasis added)[74] under George Waring's administration.

As the new commissioner gathered his forces, New Yorkers received their first few inches of snow. Waring was ready. At 5:30 A.M. on the twenty-ninth of January 1895, the day began "and in less than three hours 1,955 extra men were distributed through the city, sweeping crossings and piling up the snow in the streets ready to be carted away. The force of extras grew to 2,600 men late in the day. The total force was nearly 3,800."[75] The full year's budget for snow removal was $40,000. "Of this amount Andrews [had already] spent $31,000 [and other bills and snowfall absorbed the rest]. Waring . . . obtained an $18,000 transfer from his sweeping account to his account for removal of snow and ice."[76] The Board of Estimate made no objection.

The Republican *New York Tribune* reported, "The work of the Street Cleaning Department surprised and delighted many New Yorkers on account of its contrast with the slow and slovenly methods during the administration of Andrews and other Tammany commissioners. There was a general feeling of gratification"[77] notwithstanding the fact that the year's budget for snow removal was spent removing a few inches of snow in January. A Tammany commissioner could not have done that without being reproached.

Two days later a disappointed job seeker[78] told a reporter that Waring acquired a new and quite elegant Hansom cab[79] for his personal use at the city's expense. The *Herald* headline read, "Waring Buys a Cab, Got a Beauty, Cost $828."[80] Fitch, when asked, "seemed amused. . . . Commissioner Waring consulted me about it. Since he wanted a cab and that one pleased him I don't see how I could have withheld my consent." Waring was quoted by the *New York Sun,* "That cab is a reality, and I'm very glad I have it. It's a pretty good cab, the best I could find. It suits me perfectly. I paid $828 for it and the city footed the bill. I propose to use the cab and [my] horse for public business and for my own business. It has been said that the cab is a luxurious one. It is. I'm going to get all the comfort and luxury out of this office that I can." Controller Fitch added, "Yes it was bought and that was the price. I'd be willing to buy a Roman chariot, a Trojan horse or a circus wagon for the use of a man who will keep the streets clean."[81]

By the first week of February the first results of Waring's extravagance came to light. "I have an embarrassing statement to make" he told the Board of Estimate, a $50,000 deficit that he couldn't explain. "When he launched this warning shot everyone looked at him but nobody spoke for a moment"[82] The upshot was a request for an additional $55,000 for the snow removal fund as well as a new request for a $33,000 self-propelling dumping boat. Both requests were referred to the controller. Said Waring later, "I shall go ahead and create more deficiency if necessity demands it. . . . I am aware that I'm spending more money than any of my predecessors, but the city is much cleaner than it was."[83] At the next board meeting the appropriation was approved.[84]

Fitch's relationship with Waring was deteriorating. He knew what it might cost the city if the bond market believed that no one was mindful of city expenses. Waring wandered into a Sinking Fund meeting the next day and began to explain the $50,000 item of the previous day. "'Wrong board, Mr. Waring' interrupted Comptroller Fitch. 'The Board of Estimate is the one you want to talk to about that.'"[85] The *New York Daily News,* musing about Fitch's willingness to buy a Roman chariot et al. for a man who cleans the streets, not knowing the price of the merchandise, asked whether "it would have been cheaper for the comptroller to have purchased these classic articles for the new Napoleon rather than give him carte blanche to spend what he does not have."[86]

In succeeding days, workmen began to protest that they were not being paid, and a war of words began. When some were paid several days later, the money came from a second transfer of $75,000.[87]

Soon there was a third transfer request for $50,000 on the Board of Estimate's agenda. This time Waring "got a red-hot scoring from Mayor Strong who told him in so many words that he had not cleaned up the streets and not done the work he should have done with the money expended."[88] The *New York Herald*'s headline read, "He Scolded Waring—Mayor Strong Sharply Calls the Commissioner of Street Cleaning to Account." The mayor was especially anxious about snow removal from tenement streets. "I think it ought to be removed from those streets first," said the mayor. "If I were in your place I'd remove the snow from the tenement districts, where it affects the health of the city before Broadway is touched.[89] The boys on Broadway can look out for themselves a little."[90] "Then businessmen would howl," said Col. Waring. "Let them howl," replied the mayor with emphasis "The people in the tenements have no one to howl for them and it is our duty to protect them. The public health is of more importance than anything else."[91]

Waring continued to generate headlines, his modus operandi being neatly summarized by a *Daily News* article headed, "The Gentle Art of Making Enemies."[92] The newspaper said "the gallant colonel has been up to his neck in a dozen schemes all bearing on everything except the cleaning of the city's streets"[93] and concluded that "Waring is the most notable vote-winner that the Democratic party ever had." Another newspaper reported that one of his insults was directed toward the Grand Army of the Republic, which he referred to as a "d——d lot of drunken bums."[94] That drew retaliatory remarks from all directions. The article dealt with Waring's antagonism of his workers, expenses charged to the city before he took office that were rejected by Fitch, and his new war with the GAR.

Interrupted only by a week's spring fishing at Ragged Lake, Fitch returned to New York to find that Waring's deficit was continuing to climb. The *New York Mail and Express*[95] reported a figure of $600,000. The mayor, under mounting pressure to control expenses, appointed an ad hoc committee of himself, Fitch, and a few others to investigate the deficit's causes and amount. Throughout the coming weeks newspaper estimates ran between half a million dollars and $1.5 million, and it seemed that Waring could not survive. The *New York Journal* reminded its readers of Richard Croker's comment, uttered as he left for Europe, "If a Tammany Hall man had made such a showing as this, he would be in prison or on his way to it."[96] The headlines broadcast the news that Waring was finished, "Waring May Have to Go," "No Hope," and "Waring's Doom Near."[97]

Waring solved his budgetary problem by cutting wages and laying off workers, and for the first time he unveiled his storied white uniforms for street cleaners, who became known as "white wings." The workers were not accustomed to

HE IS ALL RIGHT WHEN HE CONFINES HIMSELF TO STREET CLEANING.

16. *New York Evening World,* April 25, 1895.

attracting attention, and they were discomfited by the absurdity of "men clothed in spotless white digging and raking in mud piles."[98] More to the point, the men bought their suits themselves, "paying $2.86 for the suit, trousers and jackets each at $1.25 apiece, cap $.25, belt $.60, buttons @ $.05 and $.01 for each of the rings that held the buttons in place."[99] One worker said, "That is a pretty good outlay for a man who gets as little as we do. Then we are compelled to keep the clothing clean. Look at me now. I have been at work for two hours. The suit is disgracefully dirty now. I'll have to have it washed tonight or I'll not be allowed at work tomorrow."[100]

While speculation spread as to the actual size of Waring's deficit, it was clear that New Yorkers liked clean streets. Whatever Waring's shortcomings, New York had never had clean streets before his arrival. Within weeks the Board of Estimate came to Waring's rescue by clearing him of any dishonesty or extravagance, and by determining that the amount of the deficit was $600,000, which might equate

FOR THE SAKE OF COL. WARING'S HEALTH.

17. *New York Daily News,* June 21, 1895.

to as much as $10–15 million in today's dollars and would need to be financed by a bond issue.

Fitch signed the board's report, but at the same time he filed a vigorous formal letter of "protest against the precedent established of allowing departments to exceed their appropriations"[101] in violation of the Consolidation Act, a core issue that separated him from the reform administration. He pointed out that "the duty of the heads of all departments [was] not to, in any one year, exceed" their budgets. He added, "Under the law it is the duty of the Finance Department every week to notify each department . . . exactly how its appropriation stands. These provisions of law are parts of the admirable system of safeguards for the city treasury devised by such men as Samuel J. Tilden and Andrew H. Green." Continuing, he said, "Since the enactment of these laws no city Department has until now undertaken to exceed its legal annual appropriation. If one department can do this another can spend its entire appropriation in six months or ten days."[102]

HAS TO TAKE HIS MEDICINE.

Fitch Administers a Bitter Dose to Waring.

18. *New York Mercury,* March 3, 1895.

But then with considerable flexibility and a bow to the exigencies of the situation he added that he was "ready to protect the city in any legal way. In this case it is most important for the health and comfort of our people that the work of cleaning the streets should not break down for want of money and I shall join willingly in any legal arrangement to have it continue through the balance of the year."[103] Reflecting the spirit of Goethe, he was unwilling to sanction Waring's spending money first and only then trying to account for it, even though he was willing to do what he thought best for New York. As he became accustomed to the reluctance of reformers to obey the law if the law interfered with reform, he became more insistent that technicalities be observed.

The *New York Times,* siding with the reformers, and giving short shrift to the long-established policies and procedures of the Finance Department, concluded that

THE LAST WORD.

19. *New York Evening Telegram,* June 29, 1895.

the controller need not be troubled about the precedent if the money is spent "with honesty and judgment."[104] The Democratic-leaning *New York Daily News* had a decidedly different view, to wit, New Yorkers should be thankful that an honest and intelligent Democratic controller was left in office after the last election. The newspaper charged a cover-up of "Waring's breaches of law and municipal honesty" that would never be ignored or tolerated from a Tammany administration.[105]

During the first week in July, Fitch opened bids for $2.7 million of 3 percent gold bonds and found bids for only $2.2 million.[106] The *Bond Buyer* said, "The mischief which Mayor Strong in his ignorance of the financial condition and debt of the city of New York did at the time of the previous offer of city bonds, continued to work damage."[107] Another journal, referring to the lack of investor interest in the city's bonds said, "The daily papers take little notice of this failure to place the gold bonds of New York. They say casually that it is 'unusual,' but they do not realize that it is unprecedented. The enormous increase in the expenditures of certain departments and the consequent increase in the rate of taxation for the next financial year have alarmed investors."[108]

In early October, Fitch spoke again to the press about the city's need for economy. He listed proposed budget increases of more than $3.7 million in five major city departments. He warned that the tax rate might increase to $2.17 from $1.91 in 1895 (13.6 percent), between two and three times the rate of increase of the year before, and that the added tax burden would fall heavily on small holders, renters, merchants, and storekeepers.[109]

Six months before, Theodore Roosevelt joined the mayor and the street cleaning commissioner on Fitch's roster of reformers who provided a daily test of wills for the Finance Department. Roosevelt entered office with a long-standing disdain for the controller, in part because Fitch had left the Republican Party seven years before and in part because Fitch was nominated for controller by Tammany Hall. In April 1895, published reports declared that no one knew of "any offer being made to United States Civil Service Commissioner Theodore Roosevelt."[110] In the wake of that pro forma denial, negotiations were held behind a veil of secrecy, while the mayor awaited the passing of the Power of Removal Bill that enabled him to create openings on the Police Board. On May 1, 1895, "Mayor Strong revealed that he had chosen Roosevelt and Frederick Dent Grant, oldest son of Ulysses S. Grant"[111] to be police commissioners. Five days later at ten o'clock in the morning "Theodore Roosevelt strode into the mayor's office, shook hands with Mayor Strong and took the oath of office. His term of office was six years at $5,000 per year," half the controller's salary.[112]

Roosevelt brought with him a rigid anti-Tammany assessment of New York's governance and what would prove to be a serious lack of due diligence with respect to the limits on the authority of the commissioner's role he was about to fill. He had convinced himself that New York needed him, but he moved quickly because the opportunity presented itself and he needed New York. His political career as Civil Service Commissioner in Washington was stalled.[113]

It took Roosevelt a mere thirty days to identify a *cause célèbre* to propel him into the limelight. Summoning the commanders of the police force to his office in June, he ordered them to enforce rigorously the Sunday excise statute banning the sale of liquor and beer on Sundays.[114] Roosevelt said that as long as the law was on the books, it offered opportunities for police corruption, that is, certain saloonkeepers paid the police and they were allowed to stay open while others did not and they were closed. He thought that enforcement of the Sunday closings law would go a long way toward eliminating the police corruption identified by the Lexow Commission.

It is hard to comprehend how Roosevelt, after a scant one month as police commissioner, determined that highly visible saloon closings would be a more effective corruption deterrent than some other, such as clamping down on policemen who were caught taking bribes. It would have been clear to him, however, that the course he chose would attract more headlines than any other course available. His pioneering political strategy was followed a century later by Rudolph Giuliani and Eliot Spitzer, like Roosevelt minor New York politicians with lofty ambitions. The ploy was to find an obscure issue, moralize it, criminalize it, and prosecute the violators. In Giuliani's case it was insider trading and for Spitzer it was arcane instances of white-collar crime. In all three cases it was hard to find a victim, but the prosecutor vaulted onto the national political stage using unshakable morality and the magnificent platform that has always been New York.

To Fitch, the Sunday closing law was a question of personal liberty. To him, the law was an obsolete statute passed nearly forty years before by upstate, small-town, nativist Republican legislators with an expressed purpose of managing the lives of urban, often immigrant, Democratic voters. Beyond that he surely believed that the strict enforcement of the Sunday closing law was not the best way to eliminate police corruption, and he was influenced by the thousands of German workers he knew who worked from Monday through Saturday and enjoyed their beer at a beer garden on Sunday. He also knew that Sunday closings cost jobs and hurt the local economy. But the law was on Roosevelt's side, and Fitch knew that, too. Fitch would take some time before he found his political footing regarding Roosevelt's new, austere policy.

He was first quoted as counsel to the Lion Brewery, "I know of no solution to this question. But the outcome will be that the present attempt to enforce the law will break down ridiculously. I would hail with great delight an extra session [of the legislature] which would repeal the law."[115] While that was his best solution to the problem, it never gained traction, nor could it in the face of upstate temperance Republican opposition.

Several days later he reentered the discussion with an even less effective line of reasoning, that is, that the reformers had gained office saying they would not enforce the Sunday closing law. "The gentlemen who are enforcing the law got the power which they are exercising by means of distinct promises not to do this very thing."[116] While he struggled to find his voice, the public and those most interested in the outcome were also sidling up to the issue, hoping both not to make it worse and that it would go away.

The *New York Recorder* said, "It is a fact that it was more difficult to get a drink on Sunday last than it ever was before but no one will pretend in private conversation that the saloons were closed."[117] Most papers reported, "Saloons All Closed." The *Recorder* announced, "Slightly Wet. Not So Dry as It Might Have Been. Side Doors Open."[118]

Fitch, still trying to gain traction on the question, wrote Roosevelt a letter in which he made note of a city ordinance that required owners of vacant lots to fence them in. If the owners refused, the city built the fences and billed the property owners for them. According to Fitch, owners were complaining that too often they received the city's bill after the fence had been built and then stolen. He told a reporter, "It seems to me that if the Police Department spent a little more time watching people's property rather than trying to find out who drinks a glass of beer on Sunday it would better serve the public interest."[119]

Roosevelt replied, "Mr. Fitch would do better to attend to the interests of the public rather than those of the liquor dealers and not to confound the position of comptroller for the city with that of counsel for the Liquor Dealers Association."[120] The reporter, correcting the police commissioner, added that Fitch was not counsel for the *liquor dealers* but for the *brewers*. After Roosevelt rose to the bait, Fitch noted, "I think Mr. Roosevelt is getting rattled,"[121] and "I regret that Theodore seems to be losing his temper."[122] He wondered aloud "what his [Fitch's] connection to the brewers had to do with the failure of the police to detect thieves who were walking off with property belonging to others."[123]

He recited the damage that Roosevelt inflicted on New York's economy; for example, two thousand men would soon be out of work on account of the reduced consumption of beer, "a minor consideration in these reform times." "On Sunday," he said, "George Ehret's sales dropped six thousand barrels below the average," and he could have added, "in a city that was still recovering from tragic unemployment of two years before." He concluded, "the fight against Mr. Roosevelt is a fight for personal liberty and against class distinction."[124]

Fitch's strategy for dealing with reform had finally evolved, no doubt spurred on by the imminent election, less than four months away, and by his daily confrontations with Strong, Waring, and Roosevelt. As the popularly elected overseer of the city's finances, at the start of the reform administration's first budgeting season he would insist on holding reformers to the "higher standards" that they promised the public. If the reformers told him that it had not been done that way before, he would ask them to act in the spirit of reform, or "to do better." He would insist that the reformers follow the letter of the law. For those who disagreed with him, there was always the court. A few days later he was at Ragged Lake for the month of August with his family.

Scarcely one week after Fitch left the city for his Adirondack vacation, Mayor Strong invited Roosevelt to lunch and they "disappeared into the inner room [and] remained nearly an hour." The subject was the enforcement of the excise issue. "The mayor wants all laws enforced but it is said he would like to have the excise law enforced with a little less austerity. . . . The mayor had no sooner got through with President Roosevelt then Street Cleaning Commissioner Waring called on the mayor and bitterly complained of the efforts of Comptroller Fitch to cripple his department."[125]

The election season began in earnest after Labor Day. Although 1895 was an off year, with no mayoral, gubernatorial or presidential race in the offing, in New York City municipal elections would test the staying power of reform. And it was Roosevelt more than Strong, Waring, or anyone else who held the key to the election. In spite of Strong's efforts to restrain him, Roosevelt persisted in his Sunday enforcement, and New Yorkers were offended. German immigrants came to America to be free. The mayor and other Republicans, notably Senator Platt, were alarmed by Roosevelt's intransigence. The United Societies for Liberal Sunday Laws,[126] an alliance of German social clubs and societies each with the common goal of Sunday entertainment, planned a protest parade for the last week of September.

The Societies invited Roosevelt, not thinking he would accept, but he responded typically, "If possible I shall be present. Will you kindly tell me where I am to go and at what time?"[127] When the day arrived, "the good Germans who had invited him as a joke were stunned when with smiling face he climbed into the place on the reviewing stand reserved for those who want their beer on Sundays."[128] Fitch

"WHY NOT DROWN HIM, WILLIE, BEFORE HE BITES?"

20. Circa 1895. Source unknown.

was one of many onlookers standing with him, sometimes vouching for him to his German friends who didn't recognize him.

F. A. Ringler slipped a "Liberal Excise Laws" button in Roosevelt's lapel, but he quickly removed it.[129] "There were bands and drum and fife corps sprinkled throughout the line and every parader carried an American flag."[130] There could have been no better opportunity for Roosevelt to answer his critics. "Hisses from the mighty throng that were intended for the head of the Police Board were quickly drowned out by tremendous applause."[131] He was all good humor, good cheer and spontaneity in the face of placards that read "No Police Yokes for German Necks," "Sunday Was Made for Man," "American Citizens Are Their Own Masters," "We Are Free Citizens of a Free Country" and "No 16th Century Bigotry for Us."[132]

To Roosevelt, it must have felt good to be alive. But to the protesters, adding to their basic appeal for personal freedom, there was an aura of class resentment hovering over the parade. One of the floats portrayed "a rich man in his club made up to represent Mr. Roosevelt sipping his wine on Sunday unmolested, while in the rear a poor seller of beer is being held up by a wicked copper."[133]

The morality of the Police Board's methods, their liberal use of informers that was soon to become another *cause célèbre,* had not yet surfaced. But no amount of the Roosevelt charisma could alter the essential fact that New Yorkers despised the laws that had been enacted forty years before by upstate lawmakers who supported the national temperance movement, and they had no use for the old-country traditions of German-American citizens in New York.

Roosevelt in another milieu said, "there is not a city on earth that deserves an honest government more than New York, and no city in the Union lacks that kind of government more than our city."[134] Whether those debatable sentiments stemmed from what he knew, from a human but utterly xenophobic reaction to the immigrants or children of immigrants who governed New York City before reform, or from somewhere else is unclear. Whatever the facts, he insisted he was right, and in spite of across-the-board Republican entreaties to relax his enforcement of the Sunday law, he worked hard to convince New Yorkers to support him until the day the polls opened. When they did, the people spoke, and they had very little good to say about Roosevelt or reform. "Although Republicans carried upstate, Tammany Hall swept the city."[135] The Hall "saw its full slate of municipal candidates elected by landslide margins."[136] Richard Croker had told them that his people didn't like reform.

And Croker was only half right. Democrats, it seemed, also benefited from Republican defections. Croker himself, after the election said, "Roosevelt helped to a great extent and Tammany received large support from the Germans."[137] Roosevelt biographer Edmund Morris wrote, "Republicans won overwhelmingly elsewhere in the state. . . . There could hardly have been a more crushing indictment of reform in general and Police reform in particular. The contrast between local and state returns only emphasized Roosevelt's unpopularity in his native city."[138] One Republican leader said, "Another year of Roosevelt and nothing would be left for us in this city."[139]

Even Elizabeth Cady Stanton credited the inactivity of women's suffragists as well as the "stringent enforcement of the excise law"[140] for the demise of reform. But another Republican worker said "if Waring had deliberately started out to assure Tammany supremacy forever he could not have done worse."[141] Roosevelt, Waring, and the German vote were all factors, and the Democratic controller affected them all.

Fitch's view of the election results was, not surprisingly, thoroughly original. While he did make note of "Mr. Roosevelt's tyrannies and absurdities," he added, "The economical and saving German taxpayers were also much stirred up by the extravagances in city expenditures." Continuing, he said,

> In the month of October there was paid into the city treasury for taxes, $22.5 million. These taxes were paid by many thousand taxpayers most of whom stood on a line for hours waiting their turn. . . . The reason $22.5 million was paid in October was that they could obtain a deduction [that was not available in November] from their taxes of interest at the rate of 6 percent per annum from the date of payment to the first day of December. The savings to many of these people was only a few dollars yet to get it they came from all parts of the city and spent hours waiting on the line to make their payment. It is very easy for gentleman accustomed to handling large sums of money to say that the amount of the tax rate is a matter of indifference so long as the money is honestly spent [referring to a *New York Times* editorial]. No one, however, who has seen these people pay their taxes, will believe that [they] are at all indifferent to the amount of their tax bill.[142]

The shining light of reform that burned so brightly during the first few months of 1895 flickered during the summer months of Sunday saloon closings and was effectively snuffed out in the off-year election of 1895. During the year, reform was badly served by an inexperienced, indecisive mayor who showed poor judgment, an erratic street commissioner, and a self-absorbed police commissioner. They, in turn, were challenged by a city controller who, after being unfairly attacked by the mayor, decided to call into question every excess or bad judgment he found. Waring did clean the streets, and Roosevelt did improve police morale, but it was not enough, and the net effect was an inexorable, steep decline in New York's confidence in reform.

11

A Crash and a Bang

> We have had a long personal acquaintance with Ashbel P. Fitch and while having been opposed to him for several years politically we know . . . that he is one of the best, brightest and most fearless of city officials and political leaders. He is a Democratic leader and has a large and devoted following in the party and at the same time has many friends and admirers among Republicans. While a typical American he has a remarkably strong influence among the Germans.
>
> —*North Adams Transcript,* July 23, 1896

The first budgeting season for the Democratic controller and the Republican-reform administration of Mayor Strong began before the election. Accompanying press reporting of the Board of Estimate meetings were headlines[1] such as "High Price of Reform," "Want Six Millions," "1896 Budget Grows," "Millions For Schools," "Waring Wants More," and "Vast Sums Apportioned," all of which dampened the spirit of reform.

The *New York Times* tried again to set a positive tone with an editorial headed "Give Them What They Need." The *Times* argued that "what the people of this city want is not cheap government but good government at an honest cost,"[2] an idea that may have misjudged New York's high regard for well-established budgetary laws and practices. Neither Strong nor the *Times* seemed to understand how or why the city's finances had been stabilized twenty-five years before.

Fitch was undeterred. At the Board of Estimate, he "scrutinized the Police Department figures remorselessly."[3] At the next week's meeting, Fitch complained "that the [Department of Public Works] estimates were not accompanied with an itemized statement so as to enable the board to make comparisons. He therefore refused to vote for an increase from $214,837 to $231,735 for the care and maintenance of the aqueduct. The other members overruled him on a vote." The comptroller, smiling grimly, "remarked that they could not put anything in his budget without his vote."[4]

Just as he appeared to be predictably negative, the Board of Education arrived in the mayor's office. Fitch declared, "I have been supplied with a detailed statement of the Board of Education's estimate for 1896. I have gone through it carefully.

Nothing could have been more business-like than the way in which the estimate has been drawn up, and I am free to say that I shall vote for every item on the estimate. Mayor Strong leaned back in his chair in astonishment,"[5] again failing to grasp the Finance Department's reliance upon consistency and process. When the estimate was presented, corporation counsel Scott moved that it be adopted as the provisional estimate. Fitch said he would vote for it. Strong responded, "Well I am not prepared to vote that way. I have had no chance to go over it except in a cursory way."[6] So just before the election of 1895, the reform mayor was publicly resisting expenditures on education while the "Tammany" controller was promoting consistency, sound budgeting, and money for education.

While the election proved the unpopularity of reform, for the men who managed New York, Strong, Fitch, Roosevelt and Waring, for example, it was difficult to see any change. Fitch was "holding up some bills for work authorized by the heads of some departments on the ground that they violated either the spirit or the letter of the law that provides that work which will amount to $1,000 or over must be let by bids."[7] He refused to pay certain rapid transit workers because they "didn't pass a civil service examination,"[8] and he withheld payment of printing bills for a lack of documentation.

Not all budget hearings were contentious. Fitch gave Waring an increase he asked for, going out of his way to note that he was making an exception to his own rule opposing increases. "I am as anxious for clean streets as anybody" he said. "I have been reading [old] newspapers. . . . All the Democratic [Tammany] commissioners during my memory have insisted that the money given them was insufficient and they have asked for more. . . . Every one of these people was denounced, attacked in the sharpest language for their failure to keep the streets clean. . . . I am very glad to vote for every dollar that the other gentlemen of the Board conclude is the proper amount of money to give Mr. Waring."[9]

Waring admitted that "for more than six months I have been given more money than I could use and even Comptroller Fitch is now my friend and ally and that's most fortunate because the comptroller of New York City is very powerful."[10] When the mayor, impatient with Waring's lack of progress toward ending the city's practice of dumping garbage at sea, publicly criticized Waring, essentially telling him to solve the problem, and quickly, Waring shot back, "Mr. Mayor, my family motto is 'He who goes slow, goes safely, and he who goes safely, goes far.'"[11] Unable to resist, Fitch observed that he too had a motto, "'pay as you go, and if you can't pay, don't go.'"[12]

But Waring persisted in his petulance, and a few months later he called a strike of his street cleaners against the city because the controller would not pay a contractor's bill. Fitch "called Waring absurd" for calling a strike, explaining that he

A HARD BLOW IN THE CITY DEPARTMENTS.

21. *New York Evening World,* October 24, 1896.

delayed payment of the bills "on account of legal questions connected with the civil service law and the street cleaning law and the desire of the Finance Department to perform the duties for which it was created."[13] Waring, apparently ignorant of the controller's responsibilities, found Fitch's delay to be a matter of principle, that is, his department's relationships with its contractors. Fitch pointed out that even the Police Department "did not withdraw the patrolmen from the streets" because of an unpaid invoice.[14] Waring's "white wings" returned to work. It was another of the trifling farces by reformers that helped sink reform.

At the dawn of the New Year, the budget was finally in place, a $6.5 million, 12–13 percent increase well in excess of the prior year's increase that in the end Fitch did not oppose. The *New York World,* no doubt hoping for a row, seemed disappointed to note, "Comptroller Fitch did not stick to his expressed determination to oppose any increase in the budget over the last year." But Deputy Comptroller Storrs said, "Comptroller Fitch's work this year and the work of this department generally speaks for itself. I think that Mr. Fitch has made it pretty evident that he will guard

WHITE WINGS.

There's a quiet in the city,
There's a sombre air to-day,
And the streets seem dark and dingy,
For the White Wings—where are they?
With their spotless coats of linen,
Like little birds they flit
About the town—but not to-day.
Their boss won't hear of it.

Within the coop he's locked them,
And he will not let them out,
For he fears a fate impending—
There's a bold, bad man about.
Mr. Fitch is out a-gunning,
And the White Wings won't be free
Till he squares it up with Waring,
Let us hope it soon will be.

22. *New York Journal*, October 24, 1896.

the public purse from all encroachment. The Finance Department was never in finer working order or more efficient than it is now." And then, said Storrs, "*We are not professing reformers but we do our work all the same*"[15] (emphasis added).

While the divide between the controller and the reform administration was widening, the *New York Evening Advertiser,* in an editorial under the heading

"Mayor and Comptroller," tried to set the proper tone. The Republican newspaper said, "Comptroller Fitch has a legal right to scrutinize. . . . Mr. Fitch is a Democrat but he is a good Democrat. He was not appointed to office by Mayor Strong. He was chosen by the vote of the people."[16] Even at that, it was more than Fitch's "right" to scrutinize; it was his duty.

The election energized Tammany and cast a long shadow over reform, but the same people who ran the city before the election ran it afterward. Probably no one was more disturbed by this state of affairs than Senator Platt. The upstate Republican power broker now saw Roosevelt, whom he had long considered a nuisance, as a dire threat to New York's Republicanism. After the election, the *Syracuse Herald* reported, "all of the local and state machinery will be used at Albany next winter to legislate Theodore Roosevelt and his fellow Police Commissioners out of office. It will be argued that Roosevelt has now arisen from a municipal sensationalist, into a national mischief maker and that another year of his puritanical administration will increase the Tammany majority so that New York State will be lost to Republicans."[17]

Shortly after that article appeared, a cautious exchange took place during a December Board of Estimate meeting that months later led to "one of the most extraordinary scenes that ever occurred in the mayor's office."[18] It was mid-December of 1895, and the 1896 budget was under discussion when police commissioner and treasurer of the Police Board Avery D. Andrews and Controller Fitch traded views on how the Police Department should spend its money. Andrews "asked for a contingent fund [for 1896] of $20,000. The Comptroller said he would be willing to give $11,000, the amount given for 1895."

Andrews argued that without the added funds, policemen would need to spend money from their own pockets, to which Fitch replied, "'I wish in some cases they had to.' 'What do you mean?' asked Andrews. 'I refer' said Fitch, 'to the pernicious practice of spending money for the purpose of finding out whether a policeman can get a drink of brandy and then arrest the man who was duped. You use this money for that purpose don't you?' 'Yes' said Andrews, 'and to get evidence against disorderly houses too.'"[19] Mayor Strong interrupted the fractious debate before it went further. The contingency fund, at $11,000, left the Police Department without the funds it needed.

Earlier discussions of the Sunday law had centered on the rights and wrongs of Sunday beer and saloon closings, police corruption, obeying the law, and personal freedom. In his brush with Andrews, however, Fitch raised a more subtle—he used the term "pernicious," meaning evil, insidious, or corrupting—aspect of the police routine, to wit, the use of paid informers to commit crimes in order to obtain evidence of criminality. Fitch did not approve of it. He believed it was intrusive and wrong, and he would not approve the use of taxpayer money to pay for it. Roosevelt believed it was the best way to enforce the law and that strict enforcement would reduce police corruption.

Three weeks after the Andrews—Fitch exchange, the mayor displayed a schizophrenic appraisal of the Police Department in his annual message to the aldermen, the same occasion he had used to attack Fitch the year before. This year Strong applauded the police commissioners' efforts "to restore discipline in the force" and "to enforce the laws . . . upon the statute book." Then he added, "I do not believe that the most healthful enforcement of the law can be had . . . by the employment of a system of espionage that creates suspicion either as to its fairness or the manner in which it is exercised."[20] While the mayor tried to satisfy both sides, his reference to "espionage" endorsed Fitch's argument and it couldn't have pleased Roosevelt.

Coincidentally, Fitch received an unsolicited letter from the controller of the United States Treasury requesting his "opinion of claims arising under statutes which the comptroller deems unconstitutional."[21] The inquiry from Washington publicly reinforced the New York City Finance Department's professional standing. Fitch lost no time in offering the department's advice. "It has been the uniform practice of the Finance Department," Fitch wrote the Treasury, "to refuse to audit and pay claims against the city of New York arising under statutes which the comptroller deems unconstitutional . . . the presumption existing in favor of the Constitutionality is never allowed to outweigh the deliberate judgment of the comptroller."[22] The question from the Treasury was not the issue at hand, but it gave New Yorkers an unusual perspective on the national reputation of the city's Finance Department. Unlike today, no officials anywhere were asking the New York Police Department for its professional opinion.

Nothing more was said about police practices, and the matter lay dormant through February before it resurfaced. By then Fitch had submitted his written report to the Board of Estimate outlining his opinion of the illegality of a subsequent transfer Andrews had asked for after he was denied his December appeal for an increase in the contingency fund.[23] At a board meeting in the mayor's office Fitch recounted the history of the transfer request, summarizing his opinion, "I do not think that it requires any extended argument to show the impropriety of using money levied [in 1892] for the erection of a station house in the ninth precinct, for contingent expenses . . . incurred in 1895."[24]

He contended that the police commissioners had exceeded their appropriation and that they were trying to make up the shortfall with a transfer that amounted to an illegal appropriation. No doubt recalling Roosevelt's accusation that he was furthering the interests of the criminal class, Fitch accused the Police Commission of breaking the law, for which they might be indicted. Andrews, reeling from Fitch's verbal onslaught, said that Tammany Boards had made such transfers before and Fitch had not objected, to which Fitch answered, "No matter what the old boards did, this [reform] board is expected to do better than the old one isn't it?"[25]

The meeting ended with a motion from Counsel Scott that Andrews amend his resolution and resubmit his request with a "detailed statement of what [the expenses were] to the comptroller's office. . . . Mr. Andrews tried hard to avert [disclosing the itemized expenses] but the board would not listen."[26] Some historians have failed to grasp the controller's election apart from the mayor and that the controller's responsibilities differed from the mayor's. The controller's duty was to oversee city expenditures. In the matter of closing saloons on Sunday, Roosevelt was enforcing the law. In the matter of overseeing the expenditure of city funds, Fitch was following the law. Earlier reformers had intended it that way.

Within weeks the Senator Platt–backed Raines Bill to further regulate New York City saloons on Sundays became the Raines Law, another transparent effort on the part of Albany lawmakers to legislate the big city's social behavior. In this instance it appeared that it was intended to raise the cost of saloon licenses to placate temperance advocates and to "close" the loophole in the Sunday law that allowed drinks to be served with meals. In fact, the Raines Law "closed" the loophole only by providing that drinks could be served in hotels having ten rooms or more if they were served in rooms or with a meal. It also "creates an entirely new and magnificent political machine," including a "state commissioner of excise with a salary of $5,000 a year" with an "army of subordinates."[27] Platt's hand was out for more city patronage. A cottage industry of "Raines Law hotels" appeared above saloons or adjacent to them, and prostitution became a new supplemental line of business.

Meanwhile the Police commissioners needed to fund their Sunday enforcement operation, which was made more expensive by the Raines Law. The *New York Recorder* disclosed, "Police Commissioner Andrews is expected to ridicule the charges of Comptroller Fitch . . . the document of Commissioner Andrews, it is whispered, will be a hair-raising affair for the comptroller."[28] True to expectations, "Commissioner Andrews answered [Fitch] with a statement at great length,"[29] the gist of which was that many transfers had been made many times before and that unpredictable transfers were required by the unpredictable nature of police business.

When Andrews was finished, Fitch "suavely said that the author of the document was full of misinformation, and added that the figures given were erroneous." He did admit that he might have voted for past transfers, "but that is no reason why I should do so now. Now . . . I oppose it. . . . I may have reformed. Nobody has a patent on reform and there are as many ways of reforming as there are cures for rheumatism. . . . The controller was smiling and looking toward the mayor. . . .

Proceeding with his argument, Mr. Fitch said that because former Police Boards had done similar things that did not justify the present incumbents." After Fitch made one more unsuccessful effort to reach an agreement, he declared that a unanimous vote was needed to make the transfer.[30] The others mistakenly said they believed a majority would do, but nothing more happened.

In the meantime, the consolidation of New York into one great city had held the metropolis in a state of nervous anticipation since the passage of the referendum in the fall of 1894. Talk of consolidating the boroughs had circulated in New York for years. New Yorkers complained as far back as 1833, when "the village of Brooklyn . . . applied for a municipal charter"[31] apart from New York. But it was not until 1890, after a commission was formed to study the matter, that the movement gained momentum.

In November, 1894, consolidation was put before the voters, who voted for it by a wide margin in New York but were almost evenly divided in Brooklyn. The referendum, while adding enormously to the drive for consolidation, had the countereffect of attracting attention to details and sharpening the opposition, especially in New York. After eighteen months, through commissions, proposed bills, and shifting positions, consolidation narrowly passed the state legislature in April 1896.

Senator Platt, an original opponent of consolidation, came to view it as an enormous patronage opportunity, a possible restoration of "the legislative commission system in Greater New York with Republicans in the key positions."[32] Then, too, it might also provide him with an opportunity to rid New York of Theodore Roosevelt, an added incentive if any were needed.[33]

Tammany, sensing its own local opportunities, first sided with Platt but then opposed him. Other opponents of consolidation worried about its details and urged that a charter be drafted only after the details were agreed to.[34] Some New Yorkers saw the threat of a reversal in their steady advance toward home rule. As Fitch contemplated consolidation, he naturally focused on its financing and the differences presented by combining the high and low real estate evaluations of Brooklyn and New York respectively.[35] The probability that increased taxes were in store for New York began to be understood and that, along with Senator Platt's unpopularity in Brooklyn, strengthened the anti-consolidation movement.[36]

The Consolidation Bill passed the legislature in Albany, was vetoed by both Mayor Strong and Brooklyn's Mayor Schieren and then repassed on April 22 over their vetoes.[37] The final vote was 78–69 and "Seventy of the seventy-eight votes by which it was passed came from Republicans."[38] There were those who hoped Governor Morton would veto the measure, but under pressure from Platt, he signed it.

New York's consolidation of the five boroughs into Greater New York was a matter of law, decided by upstate Republican politicians over the objections of both the mayors of New York and Brooklyn and by many others whom it would most affect, and it was set to occur on January 1, 1898. The *New York World* proclaimed, "Now for the Charter."[39]

As 1896 unfolded, the reform administration, in office for more than a year, still lacked direction. Roosevelt's aggressive intransigence with respect to the blue laws, Strong's Tammany investigation yielding nothing, uncertainties surrounding rapid transit and consolidation, and, in spite of the fact of cleaner streets, Waring's indiscretions, all contributed to the disarray.

It fell to Fitch to oversee reform expenditures and to float the bonds that funded the reformers' ambitions. In late March the *Bond Buyer* paid notice to his offering advertisement of $4 million of city bonds to be offered at 3 percent, the journal having heard a rumor that the rate would be 3½ percent. While quashing the rumor, the paper credited Fitch for consistently placing bonds at a premium in the face of rising debt and Mayor Strong's accusations. "Controller Fitch, who is a Democrat holding office by popular election at a time when the City Administration is overwhelmingly Republican . . . sold the City bonds . . . at a fair premium." Continuing,

THE CITY'S HAPPY FAMILY.

23. *At left,* Police Commissioners Theodore Roosevelt and Andrew D. Parker, with Controller Fitch's picture on the wall appearing to be looking on. *At right,* Mayor William Strong and Street Cleaning Commissioner George Waring. *New York Daily News,* April 18, 1896.

the paper pointed out that city debt was now the responsibility of Republicans and "the administration now labors as Mr. Fitch has labored all along, to secure premiums in the face of pending legislation threatening many millions more of bonds to be issued in the near future."[40]

The warning was prescient. Opening the envelopes for the next bond offering, Fitch found bids for only $175,000 of the total of $4.3 million of bonds to be sold. The breakdown of the bond market gave opponents of consolidation a boost, and more gloomy headlines rained down on the reformers.[41] Fitch explained the situation with considerable clarity, stating, "Any business house which is known to have within a year greatly increased its yearly expenditure, added very largely to its outstanding obligations, and is known to contemplate immense additional expenditures uncertain in amount, and to have in view consolidation with other business houses whose credit and assets are doubtful, would find difficulty in borrowing money at the same rates at which it had before been able to borrow. The city of New York is in precisely this situation."[42]

Within a few days Fitch announced that the bonds would be reoffered, probably at 3½ percent.[43] A month later the issue came with a 3½ percent coupon and drew fifty-five bids for an aggregate of $41 million of bonds that sold at a 4 percent premium. Always optimistic about New York, Fitch opined that the Greater New York proposal had not damaged New York's credit and that there were plenty of investors willing to invest in New York. But he warned, "We are obliged to borrow money constantly, and will be for years to come, and our rate of interest will go down again to 3% or below our go up to 4% or more, depending on how we increase or decrease our yearly expenses and our permanent debt."[44]

After the Board of Estimate meeting in early March, the Police Department's transfer request remained unresolved. Roosevelt and Andrews were silent. Fitch's position was straightforward, that is, the money will be paid if the court rules that it should be paid. The headlines, aside from the considerable influence of party politics, seemed to show that the newspapers understood. The Democrat *New York Daily News* for example, led with "No Money for Police Spies" with a subheading "Comptroller Will Not Yield."[45] The Republican *New York Evening Advertiser* led with "Police Upheld" and "Money for Detectives." But its subheadlines read, "Illegal Says the Comptroller," and "He Will Probably Refuse to Pay and Courts Will Have to Act."[46] Only the Police Board seemed to believe that the money would be forthcoming without disclosure of the lurid details of their expenses and without a court ruling.

Several newspapers[47] speculated that the Police Board would go to court and that the controller hoped they would. All reports contained the Police Board's condemnation of the controller, but it took no action. Rather typically, "Roosevelt said he supposed the controller was simply doing his small share in hampering the Police Department in their contest with the criminal classes."[48] Fitch replied, "Mr. Roosevelt exhibits his usual good sense and temperance in the use of language. He is constantly saying that everybody in journalism, in office or in politics who disagrees with him on any subject is 'aiding the criminal classes.' He probably honestly believes that it is criminal to oppose him in anything."[49] Years later, Fitch's ironic observation of Roosevelt's lack of "good sense" was almost fatally born out by his (Roosevelt's) calamitous decision to explore an unknown river in the interior jungle of Brazil. Candice Millard, in her riveting volume *River of Doubt,* observed, "No one who knew Roosevelt would have been surprised to learn that . . . he quickly chose the [alternative] that . . . offered the greatest unforeseen difficulties."[50]

Another ten days went by. Two small articles[51] appeared carrying news that the Police Board was seeking to have a grand jury indict Fitch. At the same time both papers reported a "possibility" that the Police Board itself would be indicted, "for incurring expenses without having a fund to meet them." Days later, amidst more speculation about what the Police Board should do, and how the police were "still suffering from the decision of the comptroller,"[52] an impatient Fitch said, "I shall be pleased to have legal proceedings instituted at once. I am anxious to have the matter brought up in court and if there was any way by which I could mandamus myself I would do so."[53] The *New York World,* reporting under the headline "Come On, Says Fitch," wrote, "legal proceedings couldn't begin too soon to please him."[54] Still, five months after the matter first surfaced, the Police Commission had done nothing.

On May 5, an agitated Theodore Roosevlt finally reached his wits' end. The Board of Estimate met at eleven o'clock to discuss garbage contracts with Commissioner Waring. The *New York Sun* described the scene: "a look of anxiety was discernible on the mayor's ordinarily calm visage. In another part of the room was Commissioner Theodore Roosevelt. He evidently had something on his mind. Sometimes he sat on a chair. Occasionally he jumped up and paced the room, carrying on an earnest conversation with himself. Occasionally he glanced toward the comptroller. It was not a look of love. . . . There was a storm in the air, inside and out, but the one on the inside came first and with a crash and a bang."[55]

The *World* said, "For a long time President Roosevelt's presence was scarcely noticed. Mr. Roosevelt was left entirely to his own devices and the sad sweet harmony of a highly checkered scotch tweed suit, which was distinctly audible at twenty paces. It was an essentially new suit, evidently donned for this particular occasion. He could see himself in the mayor's private looking glass on the far side of the executive chamber. At stated intervals he snapped his teeth and smiled gleefully. He was plainly content with himself."[56]

When Waring finished, Roosevelt came to the table and pulled up a chair at the mayor's left hand, "glowering fiercely" at the controller as he got settled. Mayor Strong stated Roosevelt's case. His "enunciation was clear and perfect." When he was through, Fitch spoke up. "What's that?" The mayor, his rhythm broken, regrouped, restating the case in a louder voice that was followed by an awkward, stone-dead silence in the room. "In the far corner, clerk Hedges, who had been surreptitiously reading *The Quick or the Dead,* shot the volume into a pigeonhole of his desk and peered around nervously."

Fitch broke the silence. "This matter has gone far enough, I think," he said. "We have had this proposed transfer of funds up for consideration before and I have opposed it. I doubt if we can do it legally." With that the mayor sank into his chair while Roosevelt came out of his, "shaking his finger" and accusing the controller, who was listening complacently. "Yes," Fitch said monotonously, "Pay them for spy work. Pay them for going into a saloon Monday, Tuesday, Wednesday, Thursday, Friday and Saturday so that they can sneak past the lookout like old customers on Sunday and arrest the bartender. Pay them for employing children to get evidence. Nay, nay, not if I know it."

Roosevelt erupted and shook his clenched fist at Fitch while the controller "simply chuckled derisively. His eyes twinkled, and the corners of his mouth twitched as if he would laugh outright at any moment. His amusement was visibly huge and he could scarcely refrain from bubbling over. 'Yes, yes,' he said, 'the same old story; we've heard it before.'"

Roosevelt shouted blame at the controller for shutting down the Police Department, so Fitch asked him, "Why did you not do as I advised a month ago and go to court? When your board met, you declared that my action was in the interest of the criminal classes. Then you shut up, and we heard no more until the next meeting. I guess I wasn't hard to find, was I? I'm at my office every day and it wouldn't have been difficult to serve me with a mandamus if you could have procured one. But you didn't. You . . . forgot all about this matter. Your poor, starving prisoners were not considered, were they? If anyone is to blame, you are the man."

Roosevelt denied it, and Fitch said he didn't want to discuss the matter "in this fashion" and that Roosevelt was "not satisfied unless [he was] fighting." "'I fight when I'm attacked,' said Mr. Roosevelt hotly. 'Oh! Go on, I don't want to fight with you,' said the controller, toying idly with a pencil on the table. 'I know you won't fight. You will run away,' said Mr. Roosevelt, snapping his teeth more vigorously than ever. 'Perhaps, but never from you,' drawled Mr. Fitch. 'You dare not fight,' the Police President shouted, like a boy with a chip on his shoulder. 'Oh, I don't, hey?' said the Comptroller. 'Just name your weapons. What do you want? Pistols?' 'Pistols or anything else you see fit,' Mr. Roosevelt snapped out."

COMMISSIONER ROOSEVELT AND COMPTROLLER FITCH HAVE HOT WORDS

24. *New York Herald,* May 6, 1896.

The mayor, slamming the table, threatened to have them both arrested. Fitch's final words to Roosevelt were to stop scolding and take the matter to the courts where it would be decided. "You have been guilty of a flagrant violation of the law and I believe you can be proceeded against criminally. I think you should be indicted for spending money not appropriated for your department." Roosevelt's retort was to remind Fitch again that he had approved such transfers in the past.

The newspapers recounted the row in every detail. The *New York Herald, New York Journal,* and *New York Morning Advertiser* ran large drawings re-creating the drama of the preceding day. Both men received multiple offers for seconds. The *Sun* proposed "a meeting in the city hall plaza with fire department hoses at thirty paces, each combatant advancing as he fired the Croton[57] at the other side."[58] Mayor Strong received a toy pistol to help him maintain order at Board of Estimate meetings. Fitch "was reported to have collected a small arsenal of gift weapons."[59] There was considerable attention drawn to Roosevelt's heroic western exploits and Fitch's sword work as a German student. The implication was that while no one should encourage violence, it would have been quite a fight.

ROOSEVELT THREATENING COMPTROLLER FITCH IN THE MAYOR'S OFFICE

25. *New York Journal,* May 6, 1896.

The *New York Recorder* opined, "Knowing both gentlemen as we do we are quite sure that the encounter could not have been bloodless. Mr. Fitch and Mr. Roosevelt are both thoroughbreds. And if the mayor had not taken the bull by the horns there would have been no other interference to apprehend. The police of this city would never take it into their heads to arrest Theodore Roosevelt; and of course he would not permit them to arrest his antagonist. So the affair might have been pulled off in Madison Square Garden to the immense entertainment of a waiting and wondering world."[60]

More sober editorial reaction cast neither man in a favorable light, but Roosevelt received the worst of it, not only because he started it but because so much was expected of him. The following were examples of the commentary:

> Nor can it be denied that of the two, Mr. Roosevelt was the principal offender. Mr. Fitch appears to have been moved more by a characteristic spirit of devilment. But we cannot understand why it is that the young Police commissioner loses his temper at such inopportune and frequent intervals. He is in danger of degenerating into a public scold. (*New Haven Register,* May 6, 1896)

> Police Commissioner Roosevelt is a good man with no judgment, bad temper and very bad manners. His conduct was that of a vulgar blusterer. . . . It is not in

> keeping with the reputation of a man from whom better things might be very properly expected. (*Brooklyn Eagle,* May 6, 1896)

> As between Comptroller Fitch and Commissioner Roosevelt the public much prefers the temperate attitude of the comptroller. He has been tried in the public service and never found wanting. Roosevelt, I regret to say, is always wanting something; among other things, discretion, self-control and desirable dignity. (*New York Recorder,* May 7, 1896)

> Comptroller Fitch had notified him a month ago that he was not authorized to make such transfers unless ordered to do so by the courts and had advised Roosevelt to apply for a mandamus to that end. Roosevelt had no time for the peaceful but effective expedients of law. (*Washington Post,* May 7, 1896)

The *New York Evening Sun* captured the irony of the affair, optimistically concluding that the verbal exchange that sounded menacing was not. "This is comforting, because the controversialists are both public spirited and mettlesome men whom the city could ill spare. Personally they are amiable and very human."[61]

An unrepentant, angry Roosevelt wrote to his friend Cabot Lodge, "I have continued a somewhat stormy career here. Yesterday I lost my temper with Fitch, which I should not have done, but he is so contemptible and does so much mischief that I found it difficult to pardon him."[62]

What followed in the succeeding few weeks were lowered voices, lightly resisted efforts to secure the transfer,[63] and finally a mandamus. But the details of the mandamus made clear why Roosevelt was anxious to avoid public disclosure of the detectives' expenses. Among the items asked to be paid for by the taxpayers were, "cab hire, $6; paid May Williams for exposure of person, $5; 6 pints of wine, $15. And again, woman, $7.50; drinks, $4; and cigars, $1."[64] And on it went, hundreds of dollars for dress suits, cabs, wine, women, and cigars to reimburse Roosevelt's detectives.

The perplexed judge termed the bills "monstrous and illegal" but nevertheless approved them "so that the case could be immediately taken to the appellate division." The Republican *New York Tribune* said, "Many persons who had been inclined to believe the comptroller was at fault said that revelations of the most shameful and abominable methods in the work of obtaining evidence against disorderly houses were so shocking as to deserve even stronger censure than that expressed by Justice Pryor[65] . . . the comptroller could not be blamed for holding back the money."[66] The judge observed that the expenses claimed were "not for getting evidence but for manufacturing the very crime itself."[67]

26. *New York World,* May 13, 1896.

Six months later, in October 1896 the appellate court ruled unanimously that Fitch was to transfer the funds. The court ruled that, "It is [the comptroller's] duty to scrutinize the legality of expenditures of the various departments. But where an appropriation has been made and a department is entitled to its appropriations so as to make its expenditures itself, we do not see but that the comptroller is bound to deliver the appropriation into the appropriate hands holding the recipient to the accountability which the law imposes."[68] The court's conclusion, as Fitch himself might have said was "clear as a pike staff." If he believed that funds had been misappropriated his recourse was "to cause the bonds of the treasurer of the Police board to be prosecuted for the indemnification of the city."[69] He chose not to pursue that course.

MAYOR STRONG: I'll see if I can't find a gimlet.

27. *New York News,* May 14, 1896.

Within days of New York City's $4 million bond sale and Theodore Roosevelt's public display of temper, Deputy Controller Richard A. Storrs died.[70] Storrs was a model municipal servant, and his passing was mourned by all those who knew him. He labored in the Finance Department for nearly forty years and was deputy controller for nineteen years. His knowledge of New York City was unsurpassed.

28. *New York World,* May 21, 1896.

Storrs had been ill, and the day before he died the *New York Times* printed its interview with Andrew Haswell Green, which, considering the source, merits recounting verbatim. Green's own words tell a compelling story of his relationship with Storrs during the aftermath of the Tweed scandal, and the reconstitution of the New York City Finance Department:

> Mr. Storrs had been in the controller's office a number of years . . . when I took charge of affairs there in 1871, and he was with me during my entire administration which lasted about five years and a half as Assistant Controller. It was in 1871 that, owing to the exposures made in the *New York Times* of the Tweed Ring frauds and the resultant strong pressure of public opinion, Richard B. Connolly who was controller at the urgent solicitation of Samuel J. Tilden and William F. Havemeyer appointed me Deputy Controller, Storrs having resigned his office to make room for my occupation of it. I virtually had control of the administration

> of the Finance Department and I retained Mr. Storrs to assist me in my labors. It was a memorable epoch in the affairs of this city. Nothing had occurred before that was comparable to it and Storrs had been for so many years in the office that he was a very encyclopedia of information, which, backed by his experience was invaluable during those trying times. I had the utmost confidence in him, and he placed all his experience, his native ability and his best efforts at my service. When I was appointed by Mayor Hall I naturally continued him in his position, which was essentially confidential. He was a very important and potent aid in exposing the doings of the fraudulent combination of city officials.
>
> I have always regarded him as a very able and upright gentleman. He is polite and winning in his manner. He is a man well calculated to deal with the complicated affairs of the Finance Department. He is quick of apprehension and has a remarkable memory. Altogether he is a very faithful and serviceable public officer. Few persons now remember or have any conception of the extreme difficulties which hampered the administration of the city's finances during the time that Storrs was with me in the controller's office. A state of affairs existed which had never been equaled before or since, and during that time Mr. Storrs rendered me most viable and loyal assistance.[71]

Fitch was visibly affected by the news of Storrs' death. "He was a splendid man. . . . The more I knew him the more I admired him. Without exception he was the most valuable man in the employ of the city government. His death will be a heavy loss to this department and heavy loss to the entire city."[72] Storrs's pall bearers included Andrew Haswell Green, Edward V. Loew, Theodore W. Myers, and Ashbel P. Fitch.

Spring of 1896 was an intriguing time for New Yorkers, as it was for Fitch as he searched for Storrs's replacement. Consolidation and rapid transit were effectively background noise for him, but Roosevelt's annoyances, the bond market's snub of the city's debt, and Storrs's death held his attention. His moves to replace Storrs recalled an interview that Richard Croker had given to the press before he embarked on another of his "escapes" to London.

In early February 1896, in New York on a visit, Croker had words to say about the failure of reform and the Strong administration. "It is very well-known," said the boss, "that conservative people and all others acquainted with the science of municipal government are ready to admit that the so-called reform administration of Mayor Strong and his associates has proved to be a failure." Croker pointed first to the administration's spending and its negative impact on the tax rate. Along the way he ridiculed the mayor's $100,000 fund appropriated to "ferret out the corruption of Tammany officeholders," saying that for fourteen months, all they had come up with was "a clerk guilty of an error involving the stupendous sum of

$1.88." He said that the administration provided the street cleaning commissioner with a budget of $3,250,000 "to do the work we had $1,800,000 for. If Tammany had run the appropriation for cleaning the streets up to $3,250,000, the Chamber of Commerce would have had a dozen meetings a month to denounce us." Croker echoed what many others had said, "if such a state of things had existed under Tammany the Committee of Seventy would have been after us with sharp sticks. Now no responsible voice is uplifted in protestation."[73]

Fitch absorbed many of the attacks on Tammany for those fourteen months, drawing attention, almost on a daily basis, to the errors and absurdities of reform to which Croker referred. He was commonly referred to as the "Tammany comptroller," sometimes "backed by Tammany," but at the very least Tammany nominated him to fill the office, and he was believed by Roosevelt and many other Republicans to be under Tammany's influence. It was curious, then, that when Croker attacked the reform administration, he omitted any mention of Fitch's name, let alone crediting him for his alert opposition to the "extravagances" of reform. With Gilroy retired, Fitch's well-worn relationship with Croker and Tammany appeared to be ended.

After the Croker interview and immediately following Storrs's passing, Fitch "called upon the presidents of various banks and insurance and trust companies to help him select a deputy controller. Tammany Hall was not among the institutions to whom he appealed."[74] His letter said, "I do not propose to be governed by personal or party preferences." Following a meeting with more than a half dozen bank presidents and within two weeks of Storrs's death, Fitch named his choice. It was not a process that Croker would have used to fill the office.

So much of the foundation of present day New York was laid in the 1890s. Curiously, Mayor Strong's reform administration played a disappointingly small part in that transforming work, far less than might have been expected. It consistently failed to come to grips with the fine points of governance, the cost of government, or the reality of the people's will, spending far too much time and effort chasing Tammany's shadow.

The two most visible stars of reform were Waring and Roosevelt. Waring's public work was based on the straightforward idea of clean streets. Other street commissioners might also have cleaned the streets if they had the benefit of Waring's budget, but Waring accomplished it, whereas others did not. Roosevelt's work, on the other hand, was too closely linked to the strict enforcement of a wildly unpopular law, a flawed model that provided a precarious foundation for police reform.

Both Waring and Roosevelt, in spite of their records, too often made the bright ideals of reform and their genuine accomplishments look like a circus rather than like serious work. Strong, a bungling politician, hampered by Platt and others with separate New York agendas, was unable to control them. Roosevelt in particular made Strong's hard job harder, and the resulting tumult was enervating and costly on election day. Roosevelt resigned within a year to begin his meteoric ascendance to the presidency. Strong chose not to run for reelection and was dead within three years of his leaving office.

Too little attention has been paid to the moderating efforts of the independent controller. He was determined that New Yorkers would know how their tax dollars were spent. Far from crippling reform, he was the conscience of reform, although no reformer, because of the frequent and public means by which Fitch highlighted their shortcomings, would make such a concession. Estranged from both Tammany and Reform, it is no wonder that the straightforward work of the controller would be lost to history.

After the bright promise of reform was gone, what remained was a feeling that the disappointments were self-inflicted. The controller, however, seemed to be where he wanted to be. He must have looked forward confidently to the prospect of a new century and the probability that he would be the first controller of the giant Greater New York. But he was not on solid ground. Disappointments were in store for him, and they would provide some further measure of the man.

12

Silver and the New York Elections of 1896 and 1897

> Fitch is the best man named for controller. He has held the office one term and has by good conduct earned a second. There is not a stain on his management, not a speck on his past, not a flaw in his record. The city money is all there; count it; and the city credit is safe with Fitch.
>
> —ALFRED HENRY LEWIS, *New York Journal,* October 21, 1897

In June 1896, Governor Levi Morton released the names of nine men[1] that he selected to join six others[2] already named who would frame a charter for Greater New York. Included were General Benjamin F. Tracy, former secretary of the navy in the Harrison administration; Seth Low, president of Columbia College and former mayor of Brooklyn; and Ashbel Fitch.

The *New York World* referred to Fitch as comptroller and "a possible Democratic candidate for mayor of Greater New York."[3] The *New York Morning Advertiser* said, "while not a Tammany man [he] is acceptable to the organization as he is to Democrats who are not within the wigwam."[4] The *New York Recorder* said, "though selected to his [present] position by Tammany, he has commended himself to citizens generally by an honest and a careful administration of the office."[5]

As a whole, the nominations were well received. Headlines such as "Representative Men," "Wise Men All" and "Remarkable" adorned the newsstands.[6] Fitch said he was "honored" and that he had "not yet determined whether [he could] act." He added, "How the funding of the indebtedness of the various municipalities can be most satisfactorily effected will be the greatest financial problem with which any municipality was ever troubled."[7]

Within days of his nomination, questions arose as to whether he could hold two offices at once. No one seemed sure, but some doubted he could serve without resigning as controller.[8] Fitch had no doubts,[9] but the following week he wrote Morton a long letter reluctantly declining the position, citing two reasons, neither being that he was not eligible to serve. The first of these was that future questions as to his eligibility might compromise the city's future financing and even a small risk was unacceptable.[10]

The second reason was the potential conflict inherent in the position. As the financial officer of the city, he believed that he should be free to act only as New York's advocate. He ought to present the city's case to the commission instead of sitting in judgment upon it, free from duties to other communities. [11] One would have thought that Morton could have determined this himself before he made the appointment, but Fitch was honored to be asked to serve and may even have been disappointed. His friend Mayor Gilroy was appointed in his place.

Several weeks before, Fitch "hobbled into the meeting of the Sinking Fund commissioners suffering from a bad attack of gout. Seeing the discomfiture on Mr. Fitch's face, the mayor smiled broadly, for Mr. Fitch had often twitted him because of his foot. The mayor said 'Have you tried . . . ?' 'Yes, yes, I've tried them all' roared the comptroller, explaining that in his short walk across City Hall Park he met a dozen people each of whom had a remedy. 'Mine was the best though,' said the mayor, 'I was going to prescribe a mandamus.'"[12] Their relationship was improving.

In early June, the *New York World* carried a long article on the silver question, quoting a number of New York's leading businessmen and financiers, including Fitch, Everett P. Wheeler, Henry Beekman, John DeWitt Warner, and Gustave Schwab. Fitch opined that eastern Democrats would not be dragged into a campaign for free silver. He said it was impossible for Illinois governor Altgeld[13] and "Bryan[14] who is merely a clever stump speaker and declaimer to carry the businessmen and intelligent working men who make up the mass of the Democratic Party, into their absurd schemes."[15] He would be proven wrong.

Silver coinage was the ubiquitous political and economic question that divided and bewildered America during the late nineteenth century. Through the carnage of economic collapse and still in the shadow of Sherman Act repeal, it emerged stronger than ever and was on the verge of engulfing the country. Republicans, rather than settling for indecisive language in the 1896 party platform that was "anti-silver" or stood for "maintaining our present standard," substituted forcefully and directly the words "the existing gold standard should be preserved."[16] McKinley, however, was not nearly as forthright as was the platform he ran on. For some years he had been bimetallic.[17] Once nominated for the presidency he continued to emphasize the tariff and only reluctantly referred to "good money" and "full dollars" as though "the gold standard had never been written into the Republican platform."[18] He was reluctant to lead without being sure that the country would follow.

The party of the people was more easily tempted by silver and the prospect of easy money. Cleveland had heroically protected the nation's gold supply more than two years before. At the first of the year he issued more bonds to further fortify the nation's gold reserves.[19] But as the Democratic convention approached, Cleveland felt the gold standard slipping away. Too little and too late, he issued a statement warning of the potential ruinous effects of free silver on the party and on the nation, but it fell on deaf ears. His only reward was William C. Whitney's cancellation of his trip to Europe and his (Whitney's) recommitment to fighting his last battle for hard currency at the Democratic convention in Chicago.

As late as July 4, Fitch planned to serve as a delegate from his old Fifteenth Congressional District.[20] But the *New York World* and the *New York News* both reported on July 7 that Whitney would be taking his seat.[21] The *News* said that the silver men, to keep Whitney off the floor, were insisting that in the event of Fitch's absence his elected alternate, not Whitney, was to take his seat. However that was resolved, Whitney took Fitch's seat in what turned out to be Whitney's only convention victory.

The convention's first order of business was the selection of a temporary chairman, who would in turn "permit control over committee appointments, the seating of gold delegations from contested states, and the recognition of sound money speakers."[22] This was lost, and when it was, all was lost. "The silver-controlled committee on credentials . . . increased the delegations from all the Territories, unseated four Michigan gold men, thereby giving that state to silver under the unit rule, and expelled the entire Nebraska gold delegation of sixteen, seating instead the silverites headed by William Jennings Bryan!"[23]

The convention framed a platform that was virulently anti-Cleveland and distinctly pro-silver. Bryan was afforded the opportunity of his life before a packed convention. To his wildly enthusiastic, cheering supporters he proclaimed, "*You shall not press down upon the brow of labor this crown of thorns—you shall not crucify mankind upon a cross of gold*" (emphasis added), spoken to the Democratic convention in the truest spirit of demagoguery. His words made his mark and secured his legend forever. The Cleveland hard money men were out. The Democratic Party stood for silver. The impact would be far-reaching and long-lasting, especially in New York, where Cleveland Democrats bolted their party, leaving Tammany Democrats as the only New York Democrats standing in the presidential race.

Ashbel Fitch quickly issued a public statement that he could not support the ticket. He said, "The platform is not a Democratic platform and the candidate is not a Democrat. I served with Mr. Bryan four years in Congress and know him well. I listened for seven years to the arguments of all these gentlemen, Democrats and Republicans who were supporting the views which he advocates. The one thing on which they are all united is hatred of the city in which I live and abuse of the men in both parties for whom I have had a lifelong respect. The result of a careful personal study of them and their theories and their methods is the sincere belief on my part that no more serious calamity could befall the country than their elevation to power."[24]

He sensed that his warning of four years before might be realized. He had told the *New York Evening Post* then, "This silver foolishness will hurt us–it will practically wipe us out–if carried far enough; and the Republicans will have the House and the Senate and the Presidency, and everything else. Then I hope the men who have done the damage will enjoy a view of the wreck they have made."[25]

Fitch was not alone in repudiating the Democratic candidate and his silver platform. The *New York Tribune* compiled a list of more than one hundred "prominent [New York] Democrats who will not endorse the Chicago nominee."[26] The list included Charles Dayton, William R. Grace, Oswald Ottendorfer, Thomas Fortune Ryan, Isador Straus, William Steinway, Jacob Ruppert, and other well-known German and Irish Democrats both inside and outside of Tammany Hall. Tammany, ordinarily coldly proficient in differentiating its interests from the nation's, although hesitant at first, ultimately backed Bryan. Days later Fitch added, "no fears need be entertained regarding the attitude of our German-American fellow citizens. They will present a practically solid front in opposition to the plot to destroy the financial honor of the country."[27]

The Democratic Party was in a historic state of agony never before or since encountered by a major American political party. New York newspapers of every political stripe revealed their eastern persuasion in support of Fitch's position. "Fitch's Firm Stand," "Congratulate the Comptroller," and "Mr. Fitch's Stand Approved" were examples.[28] Republican newspapers quickly recognized the potential power of the Democratic schism to fuel the campaigns of their own candidates. The Republican *North Adams Transcript,*[29] for example, said this about Fitch: "We have had a long personal acquaintance with Ashbel P. Fitch and while having been opposed to him for several years politically we know, as is almost universally recognized by New Yorkers regardless of party affiliations, that he is one of the best, brightest and most fearless of city officials and political leaders. He is a Democratic leader and has a large and devoted following in the party and at the same time has many friends and admirers among Republicans. While a typical American he has a remarkably strong influence among the Germans. . . . It strikes us that Mr. Fitch in this frank statement has given conclusive reasons enough why no Democrat need feel under the slightest obligation to support or endorse the work of the Chicago convention."

McKinley's road to the presidency was not as straightforward as the Democratic disarray might indicate. When it came to silver, Republicans were as divided as Democrats. Cautious by nature, McKinley carefully measured the nation's pulse. Historian Leech observed, "McKinley was obliged to discuss the financial question every day, but he dexterously kept the tariff to the fore by means of lightning transitions, which at first were seriously disquieting to his critics. He slipped smoothly from sound money to high wages, from good dollars to good times, from free silver to free trade, from open mints to open mills."[30] In his search for a winning position, he found it difficult to find a stance that he and the American people could support together. Needing to learn the depth and breadth of eastern opposition to silver, he sent Mark Hanna[31] to New York in late July to sound out Republicans and Gold Democrats alike.

Hanna was McKinley's confidant, his most trusted advisor, and his financial backer. The respect was mutual. Hanna's "admiration of McKinley was profuse. He appreciated men who stuck to a losing bargain,"[32] and that was the quality he most admired in McKinley. After reaching New York, Hanna "arrived at the Lawyers Club in the Equitable Building at about 12:45 [on July 30, 1896. After a ten minute conversation with a member of the club] a score or more members of the club, who had come in for lunch shook hands with Mr. Hanna. A few moments after 1:00 ex-Mayor Grace arrived, closely followed by Comptroller Fitch. Mr. Hanna retired to another room with the ex-Mayor and the comptroller. The three were in consultation for some time, but nothing could be learned of the nature of the matters discussed."[33]

29. Mark Hanna, *center left foreground*. Across the table, *from right,* Ashbel P. Fitch, Charles W. Dayton, Charles S. Fairchild, William R. Grace, and Smith M. Weed. *New York Morning Advertiser,* July 31, 1896.

The *New York Press* said, "The most significant feature of Mr. Hanna's activity yesterday was a conference which he held with ex-Mayor Grace, Comptroller Fitch and Smith M. Weed, three prominent sound money Democrats in the Lawyers Club."[34] After dinner with Ogden Mills and J. P. Morgan at Whitelaw Reid's Ophir Hall in White Plains, and a good night's rest, Hanna was back in New York the next day raising money for McKinley at the Union League Club.

Before the Chicago convention, the *New York Evening Post* reported, "Comptroller Fitch redeemed bonds to the amount of nearly $3 million which were issued in war times when money bore a high rate of interest. . . . The bonds have been bearing interest at the rate of 6% and money can now be obtained for 3½%."[35] But the paper savings began to erode when Fitch opened bids for $400,000 city gold bonds at 3½ percent and found bids for only $100,000 at par. His brief return to the city from his Adirondack vacation in mid–August to open bids for $3.5 million of city bonds confirmed the market's earlier judgment. While sufficient bids were received, they were lower than he expected. Fitch, with the mayor, City Chamberlain McCook, and Alderman Olcott, argued briefly to accept the bids so that the city could pay its bills. Fitch told them that he had been mandamused to pay the insane tax to the state and that unless he did so he was liable to go to prison. "I'll go with you," said McCook. "Me too," added the mayor. Looking at Olcott, Fitch said, "If we had a fourth we could have a little game."[36] And with that they rejected the bids.

A month later Fitch "announced that there would be no bond sale until after election day."[37] Less subtle, the story's headline read, "Will Sell When Bryan's Beaten." Fitch planned a $10 to $12 million bond sale, "the largest amount ever offered by the city at one time." By publicly identifying New York's Finance Department with the forces for hard currency that opposed Bryan, Fitch made a courageous stand for New York. And then he backed it up with an extraordinary sales effort to redeem his promise.

As election day drew near, he "issued a long statement calling public attention to the now-proposed $16 million bond sale to be made by the city."[38] Whether it was Fitch's inspiration, and it may have been, it was his decision to delay the sale until after the election. And until the election had passed, he was hard at work selling New York City bonds. "No matter what the result of the election may be," he said, "the intrinsic value of these bonds cannot be affected, for they are payable, principal and interest in gold coin of the United States of America of the present standard of weight and fineness. Moreover they are non-taxable."[39] He added, "that in 1889 [the city] sold at a premium millions of dollars of bonds bearing 2½% interest and they were not gold bonds either. If the bond market should revert to the conditions of that year, these 3½% bonds, in order to sell on a 2½% basis, would have to be quoted at over 117. With the exception of a few bonds sold last summer, no tax exempt bonds bearing so high a rate of interest as 3½% have been sold since February 26, 1885."[40] The largest single bond sale in the city's history would take place about one week after an election that would decide the result of the sale. Fitch expected McKinley, to win and he scheduled the city's financing accordingly.

On November 3, 1896, William McKinley defeated William Jennings Bryan to become the country's twenty-fifth president. "The Nebraskan failed to carry sufficient mid-western states, and received 6,467,946 votes to McKinley's 7,035,638. Bryan's electoral vote was 176, [McKinley's] 271. Palmer,[41] [the candidate of the National Democratic Party], polled only 131,529 votes and no electoral votes, but his strength was so strategically divided among critical [southern] states that they were tipped into McKinley's column."[42] "In state after state in the South,—Alabama, Georgia, Louisiana—Bryan's vote ran behind that of Cleveland in 1892."[43] McKinley also carried New York City 54 percent to 46 percent, the first time that a Republican had ever carried the city.[44] Cleveland was gratified by the many voices that credited the victory to him rather than to Hanna or McKinley.[45]

Several days after the election, an article in the *New York Times* that led with "Great City Bond Sale" reverberated throughout the city's newspapers. "More than $16 million worth of New York City bonds will be offered for sale by Controller Fitch today," it reported, and it described the upcoming event as "the largest in the history of the city."[46] The Republican *New York Mail and Express* said that the sale would be "one of the most striking evidences of the real meaning of the recent election."[47]

After the offering, the *New York Tribune* exulted,

> The heaviest bond sale the city ever had resulted yesterday in the largest premiums ever bid. Everybody said it was one of the magnificent results of the election of William McKinley and a wonderful triumph for the present municipal administration . . . the mayor's telephone began to jingle and congratulations poured in upon him . . . the comptroller was likewise showered with congratulations on the amazing success of the sale . . . the entire amount of the bonds offered was bid for nearly five times over at premiums that will reach an average of nearly 5 percent. Comptroller Fitch [credited the success of the offering in part to] the value of advertising. I advertised the bonds on both sides of the Atlantic and the money was well spent.[48]

It was a dramatic change from the lukewarm reception that had been accorded New York bonds just three months before. The nation's good news about its leading city was widely reported from Boston to Chicago, Pittsburgh, Detroit, Baltimore, Albany, and Hartford, all eager triumphantly to declare the defeat of silver.

30. Ashbel Fitch opening bids for New York City's then largest bond offering ever. Mayor Strong seated at right. *New York World,* November 10, 1896.

As the year drew to a close, Fitch persisted in his rigorous oversight of city expenses. As another budgetary season approached, he "complained of the failure to correct rents at Essex Market";[49] he told Police Commissioner Andrews that "you gentlemen are running up the estimates at a great rate";[50] he "assailed the charity board for extravagance";[51] and he complained to the mayor, "Mr. Mayor, I think you had better send the commissioners of accounts to the correction office. The books there need looking after."[52]

And he "caused something of a sensation at [a] budget meeting by telling the board that the amount required for the redemption of the city debt was more than $2.4 million as compared with his provisional estimate of $260,000."[53] "Thus at one stroke the tax rate for next year will be increased more than twenty points over what had been estimated."[54] The mayor, who may have hoped for a small decrease, was annoyed. "I have no criticism to make," he said. "I don't pretend to account for this way of doing business, and I have only sympathy for any man who makes such mistakes."[55]

Refusing to offer a detailed explanation before the budget was completed, Fitch was, nevertheless, prepared. "I cannot help it," he said, "if anyone was taken by surprise. It stands to reason that if you go on increasing debts month by month that at the end of the year when the day of reckoning comes you will have a large account on your hands to settle and you must settle it."[56]

The mayor thought Fitch had misled him. After the budget was finalized he said, "It is, of course impossible to accuse the comptroller of willfully and intentionally misleading the Board of Estimate for the express purpose of increasing the budget . . . but it is unfortunate that the comptroller should have been so careless and inexact in his preliminary estimates, and leads to the reflection that perhaps the good management of the finances of the city in the past may have been due to the caution and accuracy of . . . Mr. Storrs. . . . During his lifetime, errors and oversights such as I have pointed out were not permitted to occur."[57]

Fitch retorted, "Last year [when Storrs was alive] the comptroller's final [budget] estimate exceeded the provisional estimate by $642,000 and the mayor expressed no surprise. This year [it was] $612,000 and the mayor deems it extraordinary."[58] It was at times like this that the mayor must have rejoiced that his term of office had but one year to go.

As the new year began, Fitch, vocal in his opposition to the Democracy's populist turn, and against a leader, Bryan, whom he considered unworthy and dangerous, had placed his political future at risk by refusing to support him. Tammany Hall's nominees always endorsed Democratic nominees. With the budget fixed, Fitch began the final year of his term, and notwithstanding his public opposition to Bryan, he no doubt anticipated becoming the first controller of the new metropolis.

As the consolidation of the boroughs approached, the New York municipal election of 1897 began sooner than usual for local elections, and it remains today the most momentous and convoluted municipal election in the nation's history. At the stroke of midnight on January 1, 1898, Brooklyn, New York, America's third-largest city, disappeared. It became a part, not the largest part, of the world's second-largest city behind London. The city's governance and its taxation changed overnight.

In their anticipation of consolidation, the city's political parties were disoriented, speculating on what consolidation would mean to them and how to enhance their standing. Brooklyn's political establishment, to avoid being taken over, searched for safety. Senator Platt sought opportunities for upstate Republicans to reestablish control of the city. Reformers had their own ideas. Tammany, without Croker, and wracked by dissension that came from electoral defeats by reform in 1894 and McKinley in 1896, was unusually uncertain as to where its interest lay. The *New York Post* said, "Since the election the Tammany leaders appear to have lost interest in Bryan and free silver. In fact Sheehan is very anxious to make the people of this city forget that there was a candidate named Bryan and that Tammany supported him. They have turned their attention from [Bryan] to the coming contest for the control of Greater New York. Further evidence of Tammany's desire to drop Bryan is the fact that the deserters will be allowed to retain their old positions. There will be no punishing."[59] The situation was chaotic. The traditional idea of two major parties each nominating a slate of candidates to oppose each other bore no resemblance to New York's municipal election of 1897.

A letter to the editor[60] appeared in the *New York Commercial Advertiser* in November 1896, nearly a year before the election, that reflected a reader's early concern for the future of the city's financing:

> No more important issue will be before the citizens next year than the readjustment of the great financial interests involved in consolidation. The question is one of such gravity that it would be worse than folly to run any risk of having the great work in inferior or inexperienced hands. We want a man who knows all about the debt of New York, about the sinking fund and its sources of income, and who will absolutely and steadfastly uphold the financial honor and credit of the city against every encroaching influence. We want a man who stands by the gold standard, and who has at once the business capacity, ability, knowledge and experience to do the work of readjustment thoroughly and at the same time the proven integrity necessary in an official with such a great trust in his care. The year of a Greater New York election will be no year for changing horses, as to the Finance Department, while crossing the stream. Mr. Fitch has been suggested for Mayor, but it seems to me that he is just the man for us all to unite on for comptroller.[61]

Whether or not Fitch wrote the letter, which seems doubtful, it was as accurate a statement of his claim to the controllership as there was even though circumstances stood in his way. He had bent over backwards to assert the independence of the Finance Department from political influence and by so doing had made enemies in Tammany. His position in the Strong administration, notwithstanding his opposition to undisciplined spending, connected him to reform, now wildly unpopular in New York. Brooklyn's absorption into Greater New York was politically awkward. There was large opposition to consolidation in Brooklyn that would resist its assimilation and that argued for one of the leading municipal candidates to be from Brooklyn.

The weakness of the contenders added to the confusion. Tammany was out of power, beaten first by reformers in 1894 and then by McKinley in 1896. Democrats were riven by silver. John Sheehan, appointed Croker's heir by Croker himself, was no Richard Croker.[62] The reformers were splintered and weakened by their lackluster performance in office. Republicans had been losing strength in New York City for years, although they remained viable in Brooklyn,[63] and this too argued for a top-of-the-ticket candidate from Brooklyn. If either the mayor or controller were to be from Brooklyn, it would surely be the controller, but none of it was clear at the time.

In his annual message to the aldermen, the mayor rationalized the steady increase in the city's debt, averring that "the people demanded the outlay" and that the money was used for "permanent improvements." He referred only briefly to the unexpected late addition to the budgeted expenses and blamed the August failure of the bond sale on the "exigencies of a national campaign." Regarding the massively successful November bond sale, the *New York Journal* reminded its readers that "Not a scintilla of credit is given to the comptroller for the extraordinary efforts he made. . . . Fitch, for the first time in the city's history, advertised in Europe and personally wrote to many German bankers urging the advantages of the loan."[64] He was given no credit by reformers for selling New York's bonds, or by Tammany Hall for resisting the "extravagances" of reform.

Nonetheless, Fitch's record in office, his proven ability to win New York City elections, and his influence within the German-American community made him an obvious choice of many for mayor. The *New York Commercial Advertiser* said, "In Democratic circles the name most frequently heard for mayor of Greater New York is that of Ashbel P. Fitch."[65] The *New York Times* said, "Many German-Americans are speaking of Comptroller Ashbel P. Fitch [for mayor]".[66]

But as he had so many times in the past, Fitch quickly made his intentions clear: "I am not a candidate for mayor. I would not take a nomination if it were offered to me on a salver of gold. I would like to be comptroller again, and that is the only office I do want."[67] The Democratic *New York Daily News* eagerly belittled Mayor Strong while it appraised Fitch's denial. "It may be that the comptroller's intimate association with the mayor has taught him the knack of saying what he does not mean, but the open confession of Mr. Fitch that he only desires a re-nomination for comptroller must be regarded as sincere."[68]

The mayor, lending credence to the opinion the *Daily News* held of him, suddenly and gratuitously created another uproar. At a Board of Estimate meeting, the

31. *New York World,* March 26, 1897.

question at hand was the cost of a new Hall of Records. Fitch cautioned the mayor on the size and trajectory of the city's debt. The mayor, pushing back against what he saw as false economy, decided to make a small speech. As reported in the *New York Times,* he said, "Take the case of Tweed. [He] did more in the way of public improvements for this city than has been done since his day. If he had been content to take $100,000 or $200,000 a year as salary for what he did I for one would have gladly voted him that amount for the good he did. I am in favor of public improvements."[69]

The *New York News,* adding its own mischievous nuance, reported the same conversation as, "What if he did take $100,000 or $200,000 a year? He was worth it and if he were alive today I would vote to give him an annual pension."[70] The mayor, still seeking renomination, saw headlines the next day that read "Admires Tweed," "Strong Praises Boss Tweed," and then "Praise of Tweed Arouses Critics."[71] Fitch, seeking renomination as well as separation from Strong, said, "I don't think a single commendatory word ought to be said about Mr. Tweed, and I don't believe that, in point of fact, the great public improvements which the city enjoys were in any large degree started or encouraged by Mr. Tweed at all. The whole of Mr. Tweed's career in the city government was a disgrace to the city and to American civilization and I do not think his name ever ought to be mentioned with any degree of praise or compliment."[72] The mayor blindly continued explaining, to no avail. The *New York Times,* disgusted, said, "Tweed was a vulgar, coarse-grained and brazen public plunderer to whose memory this city owes nothing but detestation."[73]

By late spring, Fitch appeared to be in a strong position to gain Tammany Hall's nomination for controller. The *New York World* said, "Mr. Fitch and his friends are making a vigorous campaign for the place."[74] A few weeks later, the same newspaper said, "Tammany Hall will demand at the Greater New York Democratic convention the nomination for both mayor and comptroller . . . the movement to re-nominate Comptroller Fitch backed as it is by the powerful brewers' organization and favorably regarded by the German-American citizens will in all probability be successful."[75] And still later, "Discussion of candidates at the Tammany Society meeting last evening revealed the fact that Comptroller Ashbel P. Fitch will be strongly backed for re-nomination."[76] The Republican *New York Commercial Advertiser*'s campaign to have Republicans nominate Fitch was gaining strength. But it was all speculation. Nothing was sure. Word from Tammany was carefully qualified.

The recently resigned police commissioner of New York City, always pleased to see his name in print, gave an interview to the "September *Atlantic.* [Roosevelt told] the magazine what he accomplished during the two years he spent as a practical head of the Police Department . . . and [he] condemns all who did not approve of his method."[77] Roosevelt's delusional view of New York politics and Fitch's relationship to Tammany Hall was apparent. Continuing, he said, "The Tammany officials still in power, headed by Mr. Fitch, the comptroller, did everything in their power to prevent the new administration from giving the city an efficient government. The Tammany officials, headed by the comptroller, made a systematic effort to excite public hostility against the police for their warfare on vice."[78] Roosevelt's problems were of his own making. Fitch had no position at Tammany, and at that very moment he was having a difficult time securing Tammany's renomination for controller.

Meanwhile, Richard Croker was planning his return to New York. Alfred Henry Lewis, author, columnist, and an authority on Richard Croker, related the story of Croker's departure from New York several years before. According to Lewis, Croker said, "There is but one thing which will bring me back to any active part in politics, and that is the safety of my friends."[79] Whether Croker said that or any other such noble sentiment, Tammany's declining fortunes since Croker's departure might have prompted his friends to wish his return. It is also possible that the potential spoils of a Greater New York might have turned the boss's head from his London racing stable, probably a cash drain. For whatever reason, Lewis reported, "Richard Croker returned to power in 1897," and "in February he had already reassumed in fact the post of leader of the organization."[80] Nonetheless, Croker remained in England until he sailed for New York on the last day of August,[81] arriving on September 6,[82] just as Fitch returned from the Adirondacks. When asked, Fitch "said that he had been away out in the woods, hadn't read the papers and didn't know that any person had been nominated for mayor or had come back from Europe,"[83] evidence that he knew Croker had returned.

Croker's return was bound to obstruct Fitch's candidacy. Croker would not have forgotten the controller's independence. He was incisive, not easily slowed by shades of gray. New York's greater interests would also not be a factor. Croker was determined to restore Tammany to power, and he would know what he needed to do. He would know that Tammany's candidate for any office could not be opposed to the Democratic nominee for president. He would know that no Tammany nominee could have voted for McKinley. And he would know that the Tammany nominee for controller would be from Brooklyn.

Meanwhile, Fitch's responsibilities were unrelenting, magnified by the looming New York City consolidation. In January, he tried unsuccessfully to reestablish the 3 percent rate for city bonds. The one–million-dollar auction yielded no qualifying bids, thereby showing clearly that a new, higher rate market threshold had been reached.[84] The controller also needed to maintain his vigilance over city spending, which he did, and manage his nascent political campaign, such as it was. Moreover, "a bill was introduced in the Senate in Albany authorizing Comptroller Fitch to ascertain what bonds of the communities consolidated under the Greater New York charter are to fall due on January 1, 1898 and to sign warrants in advance of that date."[85]

Of even greater import, the *New York Financial News* reported that "the legislature of the state paid a great compliment to our city comptroller when it passed the bill placing the matter of arranging for Greater New York's accounts entirely in his hands. It provides for a financial survey and authorized the employment of expert accountants to investigate and report upon the finances of the several cities, departments and bureaus comprehended in the new charter."[86] The *Albany Argus* said, "On Comptroller Fitch . . . rests the chief responsibility of evolving order out of confusion in the financial arrangements and he is at present sending out notices to the heads of all city departments requesting . . . their estimates of funds required for 1898."[87] Such were the signs of public confidence in Fitch and in the Finance Department.

Fitch returned from the Adirondacks to a city engulfed by politics. The press reports of his term in office were mostly generous and occasionally glowing. One, the Republican *New York Tribune,* credited Fitch with originating the city's use of gold bonds and the resulting interest rate savings and added to his list of achievements thusly: "Controller Fitch is known as extremely resolute in the enforcement of the Civil Service Laws, and he has consistently refused to pay the salaries of employees appointed in disregard of [them]. The present excellent regulations requiring the payrolls of all departments of the city government to be certified by the Civil Service Board before they are transmitted to the Finance Department for payment is due to Mr. Fitch's efforts to prevent evasions of the law."[88]

Away from his duties and to recognize the twenty-fifth anniversary of his Arion Society membership, Fitch was awarded a Tiffany sterling silver presentation urn by the Society, upon which was written the following inscription:

> Presented to the Honorable Ashbel P. Fitch by friends in the Arion Society on his twenty-fifth Anniversary as a member of the Arion, with our thanks for his illustration in Congress and in charge of the Finance Department of New York City of the courage and independence of the German student. September 1897.[89]

It is striking that the Arion, defining the real meaning of Fitch's service to New York, chose the phrase "in charge of the Finance Department" rather than "as controller." Fitch's leadership of the Finance Department in Tammany-dominated, reform-governed New York was the highest and best depiction of his service, exceeding his personal title or office.

But regardless of the favorable press coverage of Fitch's record in office, he was unable to separate himself from the other candidates. The names of those who would be running for which offices and with whose backing remained a tangle. At least three types of Democrats (Tammany, Jefferson Democracy, and United Democracy) were nominating candidates. Two types of Republicans (Republicans and Citizens Union) and assorted Prohibition, Socialist-labor, and a few others completed the list.[90]

The larger of these had separate organizations in several of the boroughs. The strongest candidates for mayor and controller were Seth Low and Fitch respectively even though neither was elected. J. P. Morgan, fearful of the silver sentiment in New York, made a good faith attempt to join Low and Fitch into a sensible, powerful ticket. Had he been successful there is ample evidence that the ticket would have won. Instead, Morgan learned a lesson about politics. Low was unacceptable to Senator Platt, who ran the Republican machine. Fitch was unacceptable to the Brooklyn Republican arm of the Citizens Union, and probably to Low, because he was a Democrat. A frustrated Morgan retired from the field.[91] For his part, Croker believed that "Tammany Hall can win with almost anybody on the ticket."[92]

Before Tammany chose its nominees, and to no one's great surprise, the Republicans nominated Fitch for controller of Greater New York. His name was put forward by none other than Chauncey Depew, who said, "Whatever may have been the difference of public expression as to who was the best man to be the first mayor of Greater New York there never has been any question in the Republican newspapers or Democratic newspapers or financial newspapers but that the best man for controller was Ashbel P. Fitch. Mr. Fitch having demonstrated his fitness for public office by his services to our city and to the country in Congress has five times submitted himself as a candidate to the suffrages of this community and has never been beaten."[93]

His relationship with Depew is instructive of Fitch's ability (and Depew's) to build and hold personal relationships. Throughout the preceding dozen years, Fitch both supported and opposed Depew on a variety of questions, but he must have done it skillfully and cheerfully. No one else could have been nominated to the same office in 1893 by the wily Irish immigrant Democrat Richard Croker and in 1897 by the patrician Republican presidential hopeful and business tycoon Chauncey Depew. Fitch's acceptance letter stipulated that he "learned from the remarks of Mr. Depew [that his nomination] was based on the record of the Finance Department and on the position taken by me against free silver. The record of the Finance Department speaks for itself. The position which I took against the election of Mr. Bryan I adhere to most firmly. I would rather be defeated on that position than elected by any compromise of it. I therefore accept your nomination with thanks."[94]

The Republican ticket was headed by the reluctant General Benjamin Tracy, a sixty-seven-year-old uninspiring attorney and ex-secretary of the navy under Benjamin Harrison. Fitch's acceptance, brief and to the point, was narrowly constructed by design to avoid any hint of Republicanism that Tammany might use against him. Undeterred even for a moment by that, Croker alertly jumped at the opening that Fitch's Republican nomination presented. "What do you think of Mr. Fitch's nomination?" a *New York Herald* reporter asked Mr. Croker. "'Mr. Fitch now is back with his old love the Republican Party where he belongs,' he [Croker] replied."[95] Not to be outdone, Fitch rejoined, "Might it not be just as well for the city of New-York and the Democratic party if Mr. Croker were back where he belongs,"[96] a not so subtle attack that indicated that Fitch knew then what Croker would do.

The Citizen Union's candidate for controller turned out to be banker and ex-secretary of the Treasury Charles Fairchild, with Seth Low for mayor heading the ticket.

Croker, delaying until he knew all of the contending nominees, put forward Bird S. Coler, a thirty-year-old Brooklynite who had supported Bryan and free silver, for controller on a Tammany ticket headed by city judge Robert A. Van Wyck. The press generally dismissed Coler, who had been successfully engaged in his father's brokerage business and in Brooklyn politics. He was called "a mere boy [who] never represented anything or anybody in his life but the silver heresy. Against Fitch he falls into remote insignificance as a political antagonist."[97]

Many New Yorkers, certainly Cleveland Democrats, were stupefied by the news. William C. Whitney, for one, "had no intention of going across the water until spring. Of a sudden" he changed his plans and sailed for Europe after an interview he had with Mr. Croker. An "amazed Whitney learned that Croker intended to nominate Judge Van Wyck for Mayor and an obscure Brooklyn broker who had been urgent in the support of the free silver doctrine for comptroller of the Greater New York." When he found that out, he changed all his plans for the winter and deserted for Europe.[98]

The election, a second and final referendum on reform, was a Tammany landslide. Tracy drew only 20 percent of the vote and ran well behind Low. Van Wyck garnered 47 percent. Fitch, with nearly a quarter of the vote, ran ahead of Tracy and ahead of Fairchild, whose mayoral candidate was far stronger than Fitch's. But the consistency of the Tammany machine was demonstrated by the fact that Brooklyn native Coler defeated Fitch in thirty-two of thirty-five assembly districts in Manhattan. How could it have happened?

As were so many other New York City elections, 1897 was a Tammany versus anti-Tammany affair, and in this instance Tammany's road to victory was paved by its opponents' failure to unite. There were at least nine opposing slates of candidates, although the Republicans, Citizen's Union, and Tammany Democrats stood to attract most of the votes. Press coverage on one hand painted the anti-Tammany forces in disarray but nevertheless likely to win, and on the other Tammany also in disarray, with inferior candidates who were sure to lose. Fitch's advantage was that his record in office and his commitment to the gold standard made him the possible nominee of all the major parties. "Fitch May Run on Three Tickets" blared the *New York Herald*'s[99] headline, supported by "Friends Think Democrats, Republicans and Citizen's Union Will Name Him For Comptroller—Demand for New Yorker."

When Croker had left for London three years before, he had left John Sheehan in charge of Tammany Hall. Upon Croker's return, and without fanfare, Tammany changed direction. Sheehan had told the *Brooklyn Citizen* that Tammany would nominate Fitch. "The businessmen seem to want him."[100] The *Brooklyn Times* added, "The whole situation really turns on Mr. Fitch. . . . Owing to his social position and his popularity with the Germans it would be inadvisable to turn him down."[101] Tammany crosscurrents were many and they ran deep, but Croker cut though them, and the newspapers were slow to grasp the meaning of his return. The *Chicago Inter-Ocean*, for example, reported "Tammany in a quandary—It is flirting with both gold and silver elements."[102] "The sword of Bryanism dangles over Tammany"[103] said the *Herald*, a supposed sign that Tammany was in trouble.

The *New York World* said, "Richard Croker has offended Hugh McLaughlin. The breach between the former chieftain of Tammany Hall and the veteran leader of the Brooklyn Democracy has widened within the last few days."[104] "Croker Deceived Him," the headline declared. After Croker told McLaughlin that the next controller would be from Brooklyn, it was Sheehan, not Croker, who told McLaughlin's lieutenant Bernard York "that the nomination for controller had been nailed to a table in the Fourteenth Street wigwam."[105] "It was settled that Ashbel P. Fitch would be the candidate for comptroller."[106] McLaughlin thought he had been lied to. But three days later, another article appeared that led with "Croker is not with Sheehan." Croker said, "There will be a conference and the question of the controllership will be talked over."[107]

When Croker returned he reversed Sheehan's policies. According to Lewis, "Croker was gone from the command of Tammany Hall four years. His absence, however, in its true effect might best be understood. There was not, during those years, a moment when the throttle and the levers of complete leadership were not within his reach. He had but to stretch his hands to have them,"[108] which he did in early 1897.

A reporter asked Croker the probability of Fitch's renomination, to which Croker responded, "I couldn't say." Persisting, the reporter asked, "Is he not regarded favorably in the organization and is it not your intention to nominate him? Fitch is a good man" he said, "but there are plenty of good Democrats around."[109] Croker, guarded, and hardly transparent, nevertheless deceived no one other than those willing to be deceived.

Sheehan had lost his position at Tammany Hall. Two weeks later, "Richard Croker stopped at Tammany Hall for five minutes today to leave his orders with John C. Sheehan for the work of the day. Richard Croker has taken personal charge of the Tammany campaign."[110] Croker had completed his return to power within six weeks of his arrival in New York from London.

While Croker resumed control of Tammany Hall, the Citizens Union and the Republican parties operated on his political right. The Citizens Union executive committee began its consideration of candidates deliberately and narrowed their list to three for controller, only two of whom were "seriously considered," Fitch and Fairchild.[111] On September 28, the *New York Tribune* said, "it is more than probable that during the next day or two Mr. Fitch will be formally announced as the choice of the Citizens Union for controller."[112] Two days later, the *New York Sun* reported that the Citizen's Union nomination for controller was "first offered to Fairchild and he refused it."[113] Just then, the Republicans nominated Fitch. The

Sun also reported that "an intimation from Mr. Fairchild that he would accept and the nomination of Mr. Fitch by the hated Republicans has probably put the present comptroller out of the race."[114]

During October the "Cits," as they were called, and Republicans engaged in feelers, proposals, and counterproposals. The negotiations centered on whether Tracy or Low should withdraw in favor of the other or someone else, or whether Fairchild should withdraw in favor of Fitch. Later, under some pressure to remove himself, Fairchild said, "You bothered me to death to get me to accept when you could have got such good men as Mr. Fitch and Mr. Rhoades. I refused you twice, but you gave me no peace and I accepted. Now I'm going to stick."[115]

After the election, The *New York Commercial Advertiser* reported that a Citizens Union committee had sought Mayor Strong's advice regarding the party's nominee for controller. Strong recommended Fitch. The committee agreed and reported it to Seth Low. Low, unwilling to forge a genuine union, rejected the advice in favor of "new men in office with him if elected. The result," said the paper, "was that Mr. Fairchild was nominated by a majority of one, fourteen for Fairchild and thirteen for Fitch."[116]

With Platt in charge, the Republicans arrived at their slate more expeditiously. Both Platt and the Citizens Union said they wanted fusion, but Platt's price was too high. Platt demanded Low's withdrawal even in exchange for Tracy's withdrawal, if that would do it. Platt turned down Low because Low's independence and popularity made him anathema.[117] The *New York Tribune* in an editorial said, "General Tracy in his address made no concealment of the fact that he reluctantly took the nomination with the intention of relieving himself of the burden if he should find it possible to do so."[118]

On the surface, Fitch was every bit as independent as Low, which caused the *Brooklyn Eagle* to comment,

> [Mr. Platt] is a firm believer in [Republican] partisanship. A year ago Fitch voted for William McKinley, which shows that he will not permit his partisanship to run away with his patriotism. Nothing could have made clearer the fact that Fitch is disposed to be independent. Now if there is one thing which more than another is calculated to provoke the implacable hostility of Thomas C. Platt it is independence in politics. The platform adopted yesterday rakes Democracy fore and aft . . . Upon that platform only the most independent kind of a Democrat can possibly stand. It is fair to assume that Mr. Fitch was consulted about yesterday's proceedings and that he has committed himself. If he has done that, he has made it evident that he is even more independent then Seth Low himself. As an independent, the president of Columbia [Seth Low] was turned down by Republicans and as neither one thing nor the other, Fitch has been taken up by Platt. This is slightly confusing.[119]

Independence in the controller's office, however, as opposed to the mayor's office, was a political plus for Platt, and Fitch, unlike Low, had no higher political ambition. Platt knew Tracy was a weak candidate and Fitch, with his German backing, was not. "Many citizens who are friendly to Mr. Fitch asked that the Republicans should not let pass this chance to wrest some votes from the wigwam. Mr. Fitch's nomination by the Republicans might bring many votes to the entire ticket from Democrats who hold Mr. Fitch in high esteem,"[120] especially Gold Democrats who might reject Tammany's embrace of Bryan and silver.

Among the latter were many of the men who were supporting Fitch's candidacy and working for his reelection. Fitch prepared and circulated as his primary campaign document what Depew in his nominating speech referred to as "an unsolicited tribute never before paid to the financial officer of a municipal corporation."[121] This was the endorsement that showed Fitch "had won the confidence of the bankers of the city and that almost to a man, the managers of the big financial institutions favored his reelection to office."[122] The *Philadelphia Press* made note that

> Mr. Fitch was nominated for comptroller by Tammany in 1893, although not a member of that organization. But it was presumed when he was nominated that he would be subservient to the Tammany organization and that he has not been. He has been absolutely faithful to the ideal civil service administration, and in his negotiations of the bonds representing millions for the funding of the debt of New York he has known neither friend nor foe, although at times very powerful influences were brought to bear upon him for the disposition of favors. For these reasons Tammany was disposed to drop Mr. Fitch and to name a Brooklyn man as the Democratic candidate for comptroller. He has been criticized for subserviency to technical points . . . but the financiers of the city have realized that Mr. Fitch, even though at times he may lean backward, has always done that in the interest of the city.[123]

The written endorsement included a statement from twenty-seven bank, trust company, and life insurance presidents, among them James Stillman of the National City Bank and J. Edward Simmons of the Fourth National Bank, asking for his reelection. Another statement was from twenty-eight downtown businessmen urging his "joint and unanimous re-nomination." Theodore Myers was in that group. Simmons, also president of the New York Clearing House, wrote a separate letter. And five private bankers led by J. P. Morgan wrote in support of his reelection.

Nevertheless, the Republican convention was lukewarm toward Fitch. Notwithstanding the glowing tributes to his time in office, his personal popularity, and his rock-ribbed devotion to the gold standard, "several leaders protested against the nomination of a Controller whose political affiliations were with Tammany

Hall and whose sympathies were Democratic,"[124] and, it might be added, against a "turn-coat" who had jilted the Republican Party nine years before. When the iconic Republican Depew finished his nominating speech, "There was little hand clapping, but it was subdued and died away when [after there were no more nominations] the motion was made to [nominate] by acclamation."[125] In the world of politics, Fitch looked like a Democrat to Republicans and like a Republican to Democrats. At one time his broad-based appeal had helped launch his political career. Twelve years later it helped defeat him.

Operating on Croker's political left was the socialist Henry George, against whom Croker had been forced to nominate Abram Hewitt in order to carry the mayoralty in 1884. But socialism had lost its appeal in New York by 1897. George was again a candidate for mayor, representing a group of free-silver Democrats who called themselves the United Democracy. Searching for political relevance in New York, George held conversations with the Citizens Union and the Democratic Alliance, among others.[126] From out of nowhere Charles Dayton, perhaps Fitch's closest friend, agreed to join George's mayoralty bid as the United Democracy's candidate for controller, even though his views contradicted George's on every question.

For months Dayton had been a leading candidate for mayor. He undoubtedly believed that if it were not for Croker's interference he would have been Sheehan's and Tammany's mayoral nominee and that he and Fitch would have led the Democratic ticket, a marvelous contemplation for them both. "The tremendous demonstration made in that [Tammany] convention when the name of Mr. Dayton was read lingered in the minds of every person who witnessed it. Under ordinary circumstances it would have carried a convention off its feet and would have resulted in a stampede and the nomination of the convention's choice, instead of Mr. Croker's."[127]

Just as Dayton had been bitter about Grover Cleveland's slight of Eddie Apgar, he was furious at Croker. "All the [Tammany] leaders knew that [Dayton] was the most popular candidate before the convention and that he would have been nominated [for mayor] if Croker had not intervened."[128] His answer to Croker was to "fight bossism."[129] His chosen way of doing that was to run with Henry George for controller, even though Dayton and George were poles apart on every issue that mattered. As Alfred Henry Lewis wrote in his column, "The naming of Dayton to the [George] ticket, the begging of Dayton to accept, and at the same time Dayton standing for gold, for anti-Bryan, for anti-Chicago platform,"[130] the opposite in every way of what George's friends believed he stood for, had opened their eyes. Nevertheless, "Mr. Dayton's friends are convinced that a city ticket composed of George and Dayton would divide the Democratic vote, and they figure that the Republicans will split even between Tracy and Low."[131] Dayton shared his miscalculation with Low and Platt and all the other characters who somehow believed that more anti-Tammany candidates were better, when in fact the opposite was true.

In the same column, Lewis foresaw a Fitch victory, predicting that "As affairs shape, however, it seems likely that Fitch will be elected. . . . He will be the one brand plucked from the Republican burning. Fitch will be saved, while the rest of the Tracy ticket perishes."[132]

Within days of Dayton's strange announcement and weeks of Fitch's rejection by Tammany, Fitch, Dayton, and De Lancey Nicoll[133] ate lunch at a Pine Street restaurant where Croker was seated alone. Nicoll went to chat with him. Croker, seeing Fitch and Dayton, said, "I see a couple of my old friends over there. I guess I will go over and congratulate them." Nicoll tried to dissuade him. Croker stepped over to their table and extended his hand which they, surprised, accepted. Croker told them, "You have both been my friends, and I hope that although we differ politically you will not permit it to interfere with our personal relations. I know you must rap me a little, but then, that is politics."[134] However corrupt, Croker was clear eyed. Fitch owed his office to him. Croker had given him the "best job in New York."

Many Republican newspapers agreed with columnist Lewis that Fitch's candidacy was bound to succeed. "One [story circulating] was that Bird S. Coler would withdraw and that Fitch would be nominated [by Tammany]."[135] Another said "Dayton is simply putting up a big bluff for Fitch. He has long been a partner of Fitch and has had fully his share of the legal practice connected with the comptroller's office. He hopes by taking the nomination to compel Tammany to withdraw its candidate and endorse Fitch."[136]

The *Brooklyn Standard Union* trumpeted "Coler's Fate—Dayton's Acceptance Makes Him a Dead Bird in the Pit. Leaders Plunged In Gloom."[137] "A member of the Tammany Executive Committee admitted today that Mr. Dayton's nomination assures the reelection of Mr. Fitch."[138] "The Germans and the sound money Democrats are going to vote for Fitch."[139] "Tracy Will Sweep All."[140] "Tracy Is Ahead."[141] Other papers wrote "Tammany is all at sea"[142] and about "a break" between Croker and Sheehan.[143]

With less than two weeks to go, Lewis had more to say to his readers.

> It would seem that Tammany Hall has found unpleasant certain slight words of commendation spoken by me of Ashbel Fitch. Tammany objects to my approval of Fitch. And so I say again to those who have the city money at heart in its safety, vote for Fitch. He is the best man named for the place. He has held the office one term and has by good conduct earned a second. There is not a stain on his management, not a speck on his past, not a flaw in his record. The city money is all there; count it; and the city credit is safe with Fitch. . . .

> . . . Be slow to dismiss an honest purse-bearer. I can find you orators and writers and thinkers and men who will state you a code of morals in the abstract—I can bring such to you by herds and droves; but that officer who can carry your treasure for four years, missing none of it, is as rare as rubies, priceless as a star. And I say—stick to Fitch, vote for and elect Fitch.[144]

Amid the anti-Tammany hubbub, Croker, whom Lewis described as "utterly and blackly bad"[145] emerges as the one and possibly only politician who understood from the minute he arrived from London how to win. He knew what Republicans had done under the banner of reform, and he knew that New Yorkers wanted the reformers out. He knew all about Tammany's discipline. It was his own. He paid little attention to the difference between silver and gold. He knew that Tammany was the home of Democrats and that Tammany did not reject Democrats. To Croker it was elementary, and he was brilliant, while at the same time he was aided considerably by his adversaries' miscalculations.

Croker's discipline stands out from that of his opponents, who were conflicted or delusional. Three weeks before the election, following Charles Dayton's announcement, Croker said, "I do not see any reason because of recent developments to change my opinion about the certainty of the success of the Democratic tickets. I believe Tammany is gaining every day. You cannot destroy a well-disciplined army . . . as easily as some people suppose. . . . I do not care to further discuss the action of Mr. Dayton. . . . He is a disappointed man and his actions show his disappointment. I do not think he will hurt Tammany very much."[146] A week later he said, "Van Wyck would positively win by seventy-five thousand votes."[147]

The perceptive observer Lewis surveyed the scene immediately before the election. On Tracy, "Tracy is Platt's mask." On George, "one doesn't want George for mayor just as one doesn't want to smoke a cigar in a powder house. There's nothing sinful per se in smoking in a powder house . . . yet there are explosive risks." And on Low, "Born rich, Low is still rich. The lessons of life are the struggles of life, and Low who never struggled, never learned. I know of no one on the list save George so imperfectly made up to govern a great city as Low." Concluding, he wrote, "Tammany might better be thanking its stars for a trio of opponents such as Tracy, George and Low. It will go further on their weakness than on its own strength."[148]

Leslie's Weekly explained the controller's race this way:

> The anomalous thing in this mixed condition is that Mr. Fitch, the present comptroller, should not have been nominated on all of the tickets. As controller he has been a model officer, and he fills every requirement as to efficiency desired by the adherents of Mr. Low; he has always been a Democrat—serving in Congress as such and elected to his present office as such—and might have been put up by

> Tammany, as he was before; he is just as much of a George man as Mr. Dayton is, and therefore he might have been selected with quite as much propriety as Mr. Dayton to run on that ticket; he is selected, however, by the Republicans alone, and he is running on the ticket of a party to which he has long been opposed and with which he never acted till the campaign against Bryan and the free silver heresy. In a sense, perhaps, it may be said that his nomination by the Republicans is recognition of the services of the gold Democracy. But however this may be, it is surely a very mixed condition of affairs.[149]

On the day before election day, the *Boston Traveler* carried a penetrating analysis of the New York election, on a par with Croker's. The paper's observations came in two parts. The first was "The Citizens Union campaign made up largely of men who claim to be reformers made a great mistake in not placing Ashbel P. Fitch upon their ticket. . . . The result of the diversity of [anti-Tammany] candidates may be the election of Coler." Then,

> There is one thing that strikes the close observer very forcibly and that is the utter unreliability of the great [New York] newspapers in representing the news of the campaign. Facts are wholly ignored except as they suit the policy or predilections of the editors. The news columns are absolutely colored and twisted and distorted to fit the editorial page. The reporters only find in the mélange of rumors, statements and claims what their employers' want them to find. All else is ignored. The *Tribune,* the *Herald,* the *Times* and the *World,* four of the historic papers of New York, and metropolitan in the widest sense of the term, lead the lesser papers in this base prostitution of the proper and legitimate functions of journalism to partisan ends. The *Evening Post* and the *Mail and Express* follow the lead of the big morning papers. The result is that a perusal of these great journals confuses the reader, and leaves him in a state of total obfuscation.
>
> The only organization and the only organs that base their claims of success upon actual figures are those representing Tammany. The Tammany leaders and presses have constantly given out the results of their canvass.[150]

As Fitch stood in line to vote, he made sure he held ballot number thirteen and then told a reporter that he was not superstitious.[151]

13

Passage

> Controller Fitch is known as extremely resolute in the enforcement of the civil service laws. . . . The present excellent regulations requiring the payrolls of all departments of the city government to be certified by the Civil Service Board before they are transmitted to the Finance Department for payment is due to Mr. Fitch's efforts to prevent evasions of the law.
>
> —*New York Tribune,* September 24, 1897

Fitch was surely disappointed, probably annoyed, perhaps puzzled, but not surprised by his defeat. He had wanted to be Greater New York's first controller and he knew he deserved it, but again Goethe's philosophical influence showed through. He was beaten by events that were beyond his control. He was sadly disappointed, but rather than suffer in defeat as Viele had done eleven years before, he faced facts and moved on.

At police headquarters on Mulberry Street, where the official returns were tallied, the mayor and the controller, who despite their daily jousting had become warm friends, arrived at about 8:15 P.M. "The mayor looked the reverse of pleasant." A *New York Telegraph* reporter asked him what he thought of the election. "'I'll not concede the election to Van Wyck till every ballot is counted,' growled his honor and he passed on. . . . 'Want to ask me the same question?' said the controller with a benign smile. 'Yes.' 'Well,' announced Mr. Fitch, still smiling, 'give my love to the people of New York.'"[1] This undoubted ironic expression was as close as he came to revealing his enormous disappointment.

The following day he was back on an even keel, "bright and smiling and nobody would have imagined"[2] that he had lost. He said, "I feel very grateful to the many friends who stood by me so nobly when success seemed more than doubtful." And then, "certainly I have no complaints to make as to the action of either friend or foe."

Further postmortems were left to others. The *New York Times* said Fitch "was a good deal put out over his defeat."[3] The *Philadelphia Inquirer* noted that the combined vote for Fitch, Fairchild, and Dayton would have defeated Coler handily.[4] A few days after the election Fitch hosted a breakfast at the Manhattan Club for the candidates for controller, to follow up on an earlier dinner in which they had placed their predicted vote totals in sealed envelopes. At breakfast they opened the envelopes "amid much laughter."[5]

The complex work of consolidation proceeded apace as Coler visited the controller's office to begin learning the duties of his office. "Combining the Finance Departments of all the parts of the new city," Fitch said, "will be much harder than combining other departments,"[6] and he volunteered his assistance. A month later he budgeted an additional thirty thousand dollars for clerks' salaries in the coming year, and Coler announced that he would "retain nearly all of the present employees."[7]

In December, Fitch advertised for bids for over $6 million of 3½ percent gold bonds for the final time.[8] One week later he opened nine bids for the bonds, totaling $21.5 million, which came in at substantial premiums ranging between 103 and 108.47.[9] It was old New York's final bond sale. The *Bond Buyer,* ever generous to Fitch said, "We may congratulate the city on the administration of Comptroller Fitch. He goes out in a blaze of glory and leaves to his successor an unimpaired credit for the new metropolis."[10]

Fitch owed his life's opportunity to New York, and it was never far from his mind. When in March of 1898 he spoke to the Sons of Oneida County, he told them, "New York always was the place for the man from somewhere else. It attracts to itself the brightest men in our state and from all the states, in every calling and profession, because here is the fairest chance for recognition, and the greatest reward for success. There is always ready here a gold box and the freedom of the city for any man from anywhere who can earn them. The question the city asks of the latest comer is not 'where do you come from?' but 'where are you going?' If you are going ahead in your profession or in your business or in the arts, and can lead the way, the city will welcome and reward you, as will no other place in America."[11]

The Board of Estimate's final meeting came on Thursday, December 30, 1897, and his last official act was to endorse a twenty-five-thousand-dollar check for Dock Department improvements on the Harlem River.[12] Through the *New York Herald* Fitch sent his "best New Year's wishes to the gentleman who will succeed me and the faithful and efficient men in the office who, through many administrations have taken care of the city's money and credit."[13]

Old New York passed into history at midnight on December 31, 1897. With the city's demise went the Street Opening Board. Its work went to the Board of Public Improvements of the new city. Fitch did not attend that board's final meeting, nor was he there when Coler occupied the office. The new controller said, "Mr. Fitch has done all that was possible to make me at home in this office. I have been here frequently since election day and Mr. Fitch and I left the office together last evening.

I did not expect him here today as he had an engagement that took him out of the city. He knew from me that I desired to enter upon the duties of my office quietly, and to avoid anything suggestive of a formal reception."[14] Unfortunately, Fitch's relationship with Coler would worsen before it improved, and the source of the problem was, not surprisingly, Richard Croker.

Rumors persisted that Croker was standing in the way of rapid transit because of his own and Tammany's interests in the street railway companies. As the new administration was settling in there was talk that the city was operating closer to its legal debt limit than was supposed.[15] If that were so, it would be difficult for the city to finance the construction of a new rapid transit system or even to make improvements. One newspaper said, "The former comptroller, Mr. Fitch, one of the most careful and faithful of all our finance ministers insists that the objection raised by the mayor is without foundation. Those who drafted the charter and who have examined the figures representing the city's financial condition do not agree with the mayor."[16]

Nevertheless a crisis appeared when the mayor's corporation counsel reported that the city's 10 percent debt limit was exceeded by $30 to $50 million.[17] Coler was critical of the prior administration in ways that irritated Fitch. "Quote me as saying that $30 million is a conservative estimate of the amount by which the debt limit has been exceeded,"[18] Coler said. Fitch was content to observe that "the debt limit was not exceeded by Mayor Strong's administration."[19]

Ever alert, Richard Croker, no doubt with a vengeful twinkle in his eye, opined, "If New York has exceeded already her legal debt limit. . . . I do not think we have a right to enter into any more contracts or current additional obligations."[20] Echoing Mayor Strong's hunt for "jugglery" in the Tammany administration, Croker needled, "And you can say that the last city administration has made itself liable to indictment for making appropriations after the constitutional debt limit was reached."[21] Fitch rejoined, "I have no desire to get into a controversy with Mr. Croker. This is his inning and he can say what he pleases."[22] "Mayor Strong's administration did not exceed that limit. When the indictments come we shall be well prepared."[23]

By way of explanation the *New York Post* offered, "behind the oblique hints and innuendoes of Mr. Croker is a desire on the part of Tammany somehow to nullify the contracts for public improvements that have been let in order to relet them to Tammany contractors."[24] Two large contracts "were let to the firm of which John C. Sheehan is a member. . . . Croker, it appears, does not think that Sheehan has been sufficiently punished yet."[25]

Coler's official report, claiming that New York exceeded its debt limit by more than $50 million, brought the matter to a head.[26] The *New York Post,* quoting an unnamed source, claimed Croker had two things that he wanted "taken in hand" by the new administration, the first being "the Rapid Transit Commission and its scheme" and the other "contracts let by the Strong administration in its last days."[27]

Coler's report declared that "all contracts entered into by the former city of New York subsequent to the date when that city exceeded its constitutional limit of indebtedness must be absolutely void."[28] The immediate result was that thousands of workers were thrown off jobs that were connected to ongoing work on the "void" contracts. Implausibly, work was halted on millions of dollars of city contracts and up to forty thousand workmen who drew a payroll estimated at more than $700,000 per week were either sidelined or on their way out of work[29] even though most newspapers doubted Coler's report.[30]

The *Philadelphia Press* noted that on one hand the city had recently sold 3½ percent gold bonds at a good premium, and on the other "the controller makes out a case of bankruptcy. It shows that New York's obligations exceed its legal capacity to pay its debt by more than $50 million. If there were any faith in the controller's statement it would probably cause something like a panic, for a great city like New York could not acknowledge its insolvency without serious financial disturbances."[31] In fact it was the city's faith in their former controller that helped hold emotions in check.

Within days Fitch released a long, detailed statement, his final public service to the city of New York. The *New York Tribune* said he "riddled" Coler's report.[32] The *New York World* said he "demolished" it.[33] The *New York Mail and Express* said that Fitch's "able manner is very suggestive in its effect of a healthy western tornado applied to a house of cards."[34] He began his statement somewhat flabbergasted that he had to say anything at all because in his view the controller's statement was "so obvious and its reasoning so strained that it seemed to answer itself." "But," he went on, "the consequences of the step taken by the controller are so serious in their effect on public and private interests that it appears now that a few words of explanation may be valuable."[35]

There were two items that pertained to the controller's conclusion. First, there was the value of contracts to be paid for by the city in future years that were subject to an array of uncertainties. Coler recorded those at $25 million. The second item was an amount needed to acquire land that would be paid for by assessments on private property and by the "Fund for Street and Park Openings" that was in turn replenished annually from the tax levy. Coler calculated that at nearly $38 million. By adding the two items together he appended $63 million to the city's outstanding debt.

"The contention of the comptroller [Coler] is absolutely new," said Fitch. "None of his predecessors in the Finance Department, none of the distinguished lawyers who have been counsel to the corporation, no mayor in considering the affairs of the city in his messages, has ever tried before" to prove this method of calculating the city's debt. "If this new method is left out," as it had been by "every other comptroller," the old city on December 31, 1897, was "inside the debt limit by $39.8 million."[36]

Fitch's letter began Coler's reversal. "The contractors to whom the city owes some $60 million of work done had an interview with Comptroller Coler. They had with them the opinion of former Comptroller Fitch."[37] Within two weeks Coler admitted that his report was based on definitions of city debt supplied by Corporation Counsel Whalen. Under mounting pressure, Whalen then issued a series of three more opinions, each one concluding that the overage was lower than previously calculated, until his final report concluded that there was indeed surplus debt capacity.

Two newspapers, the *New York Post* and the *New York Tribune,* each gave their readers their biting analysis of events. Croker, meanwhile, had returned again to England. The *Post* said,

> So long as it appeared that our ability to incur debt had been exhausted and such hateful improvements as a new public Library, new school buildings, and an underground rapid transit system could be prevented every Tammany heart beat with joy. It was for the purpose of putting an end to such uses of the public money that Tammany had been restored to power.
>
> Mr. Croker realized this as soon as the election was over and he at once bent his mind to the task of finding a sure way by which the proposed expenditures could be stopped. The result was his discovery that the abominable reform administration of Mayor Strong had exceeded the constitutional debt limit and bankrupted the city. He sent for his Corporation Counsel, John Whalen, and told him to "get up the law" in support of that view and in due time the learned Whalen got it up. When he had got it up, he handed it to Mr. Croker's comptroller. . . . When the [Coler] report was published it was soon made clear that if Coler had understood it he never would have presented it.[38]

The *Tribune* recounted its fictional reconstruction of a conversation between a wise man and Counsel Whalen as follows:

> Look here Whalen, you have made just about the stupidest mistake in the history of Tammany politics. You haven't a legal leg to stand on in this debt-limit business. Fitch, who has forgotten more about municipal finance than you're ever likely to learn, . . . has riddled the statement which Coler based largely on your assumptions, and, in fact, has made monkeys of both of you. . . . We could stand legal opinions

> and financial calculations which were merely ridiculous, but what do you suppose we are going to say to contractors who have been held up, with about six thousand laboring men behind them? The quicker you ascertain that their contracts are valid and their men can be paid the better.[39]

Three years earlier, Mayor Strong had attacked Tammany and Fitch. This time, the situation reversed, Croker attacked Strong and Fitch. In both instances, Fitch's fitting public explanations were grounded on the consistent, expert work of the Finance Department, carried on between the warring forces of Tammany and reform.

Two months later, the *New York Tribune* noted that "Comptroller Coler has submitted to the municipal assembly a statement setting forth the amounts to be raised by taxes by the old city of New York for the current year. The comptroller finds that the estimate of former Comptroller Fitch was correct."[40] After eight months of the Coler controllership the *Bond Buyer* admitted that "Controller Coler has maintained the city credit which the mere political officials were fast frittering away . . . he restores the city's credit to the basis on which Mr. Fitch left the credit of the old city."[41]

Fitch's life after leaving office was hectic, even though he remained out of the public eye. A spate of newspaper headlines announced the founding of the Trust Company of America. Its business was to function as a nationwide clearinghouse. Its initial capital, oversubscribed by about three to one, was expected to be $5 million drawn from different cities across the nation, and he would be its first president. There were twenty-four board members that included the heads of the New York Telephone Company, Metropolitan Life, American Sugar, Society Savings of Cleveland, Consolidated Gas, Hanover National Bank, International Paper, and Lehman Brothers. The company's offices were at 149 Broadway, and it opened for business on June 26, 1899.[42]

Later announcements described the new firm as "the 'financier' and clearinghouse for all the funding and capitalizing efforts of a host of minor trust companies and banks."[43] "Hanover National Bank was to be the Trust Company's registrar and had $5 million deposited to its credit."[44] The list of the new company's 350 original stockholders and directors included Henry Havemeyer, Levi Morton, John Jacob Astor, John F. Flagler, Murray Crane of Dalton, Massachusetts, Bird Coler's firm of W. N. Coler, Daniel Lamont, Grover Cleveland, George Crocker of San Francisco, Henry Frick, Mark Hanna, and Frank Rockefeller.[45] The Sunday, July 16, 1899, *New York Times* carried an account of Fitch's life and career in the *Illustrated Magazine Supplement,* with his picture displayed prominently on the cover.

By 1900 Fitch's early warning concerning the "silver foolishness" and what would happen if it were carried far enough[46] had come true. Republicans controlled both houses of the Fifty-sixth Congress as well as the White House. The Democrats nominated Bryan again in 1900 to run against the incumbent McKinley. Perhaps weighing a third ticket, Fitch declared, "I am going to do everything I can to defeat Bryan. And I am a Democrat. . . . I do not say that I will vote for McKinley, but I will certainly do all I can to defeat Mr. Bryan."[47] Three weeks later, having rejected the idea of a third ticket, he added, "A third ticket could have served no good purpose. I consider it my personal duty to support Mr. McKinley. I would not support Mr. Bryan on the best platform that was ever framed, and I would not vote for the best candidate ever nominated on the platform on which Mr. Bryan is running."[48] Carlisle, Fairchild, and Hewitt were among many other Democrats committed to McKinley, and he won in a landslide. Bryanism, which Fitch believed was dead in 1896, died again in the election of 1900. Fitch and other Cleveland Democrats were left standing amid the wreckage of the Cleveland Democracy that was Bryan's legacy.

In the summer of 1901, Fitch wrote to Lizzie, who was traveling in Europe with their three daughters, "We are very busy getting ready for the close of the second year & our report to the banking department on July 1. I feel well about the business which seems to grow in a healthy way & failing something now unforeseen, to promise good results in the future." In the Trust Company's second year it showed "$16.7 million of deposits and a good addition to the undivided profits after paying dividends etc. Now I can take things a little easier," unless two banks that had failed recently "make some mischief in the market." To keep her fully informed he wrote, "there has been more or less talk about my being nominated for mayor but I don't want the place." He wrote, "Your trip [to Europe] will soon be over & I think will have been enjoyed from all I can see from your letters. Then we will have a nice vacation at the camp for which I long very much."

He wrote her next at Ragged Lake in early September, "I got my train all right at Owls Head but could not get any supper as the buffet car was on the other section. On the way down I learned of the shooting of Mr. McKinley and as the story was that he was dead I expected much trouble in the market here. The train was an hour late so I headed straight down to the Trust Co. in order to be there by ten o'clock [Friday, September 6]. Nothing serious occurred although stocks fell five or six points. How it will be tomorrow [Monday, September 9] no one can tell but the banks and trust companies will act together and try to avoid any panic and if Mr. McKinley seems likely to recover everything will quiet down." And then, "The mayoralty business is boiling & I must send a card or interview or something to stop the use of my name tomorrow. I would have done so yesterday but the town is thinking of nothing but the president's illness and it would have been out of place. It looks as if I can have the nomination but it would be a calamity to me."

In fact, his eager supporters had even produced lapel pins to stoke the fires of a Fitch campaign for mayor and increase the pressure on him to run. But Fitch wrote an open letter to the *New York Times* that ended any idea of his return to elective politics. It also contained a stern warning to candidates who would try to "make the habits of all our vast population conform to [their] own or to experiment with fanciful schemes," thinly veiled reminders of reform. He challenged Richard Croker to do "what he did when he named Mr. Hewitt for mayor and what he has often done as to the judgeships and name a candidate of high character and standing in the community." And once again he used the opportunity to describe his beloved New York City as "a place to which people come from everywhere . . . and from which nobody ever moves away."[49] McKinley was dead within the week

A few months before, the *New Yorker* wrote,

> Ashbel P. Fitch, ex-comptroller and ex-congressman, now an executive of the Trust Company of America and legal adviser of the New York brewers, is one of the busiest men in New York, but his work does not depress him for he is always in cheerful spirits. Perhaps that may be due to the fact that he takes a great deal of exercise, chiefly walking. He and his friend, ex-Postmaster Charles W. Dayton, may be seen these bright days walking up Broadway after their day's work is done. They turn in at the Manhattan Club in Madison Square for a "duster" before dinner. . . . Mr. Fitch goes to Washington occasionally . . . he made a record in Congress. He is a

32. Fitch for mayor laminated campaign button, ca. 1901.

> New Yorker who serves the city well by dwelling within it. He is a good citizen in every respect.[50]

Life was pleasant for prosperous New Yorkers at the turn of century, and it was for Fitch. He was active, successful, and no doubt pleased that he had made his own way in New York. He devoted his time to his work, to his Ragged Lake property, and to his children, who were now young adults. Ella was married the year before, and Fitch made a small sensation by giving her a house at the corner of West End Avenue and Ninety-seventh Street as a wedding gift. Ashbel Junior was married that fall. Bessie's wedding would be in April. Morton, at twenty-two, was just graduated from college, and Littleton, twenty, was still at Yale. All three boys attended Yale and were or would become attorneys. Doris was in her teens and living at home. These were the contours of Fitch's life after politics. He was hampered only by an array of health issues, some of which had been with him for years. But above it all he remained grateful to his friends, his family, and to the city of New York.

Two years later, returning to New York from Ragged Lake in September 1903, Fitch wrote Lizzie, "I am still uncomfortable at times but manage to do my work & may be able to work out of it. I don't dare go to the doctor for fear he will say something to make it worse." In fact, he had suffered a heart attack, but he believed he had recovered.

On May 4, 1904, two weeks after his daughter Bessie's wedding and shortly after the birth of his first grandchild, following a routine day at his office, Fitch returned home for dinner with Lizzie and four of the children. While preparing for bed he collapsed and died.[51] He was fifty-six years old. When news of his death reached the mayor's office, "He at once ordered that the flag on the city hall be set at half-mast,"[52] a singular honor for a past city official. Dayton wrote Lizzie immediately. "It seems as if a brightness has gone out of my life, leaving a shadow which cannot be lifted."[53] Fitch was buried with his sisters and parents at Woodlawn Cemetery. Old friends, Dayton, Cantor, Lamont, Ehret, and Ruppert among many others, said their final farewells.

Fitch was described variously in the press, in one instance as "a great exponent of personal liberty,"[54] a stark reminder of his dueling days at Jena, his pursuit of John I. Davenport, and his well-publicized row with Roosevelt. Also "Mr. Fitch had the unique distinction of being a sitting member of one Congress as a Republican while he was Representative-elect to the next Congress as a Democrat."[55] The *Harlem Reporter* said, "He stood like a stone wall between the city treasury and the extravagance of the Strong administration, the only Democrat with Tammany affiliations on the Board of Estimate."[56] He occasionally occupied himself with "literary work"; the *New York Sun* said, "he was of a scholarly habit. He had one of the finest German libraries in the city. He had considerable literary ability which was shown in [his] frequent contributions to the pages of the *Sun*."[57]

In spite of the fact that he "had some sharp encounters with Mayor Strong they never failed to fight it out in the open."[58] "He got along famously with Mayor Strong. He was genial, and at all times courteous and obliging."[59] "Genial" seems to be a word often associated with recollections of Ashbel Fitch. It may be for that reason that the following little story was so widely circulated three weeks after his death: "The late Ashbel P. Fitch of New York once described in Congress an encounter he had with a Washington newsboy. 'I was on my first visit to Washington,' Mr. Fitch said, 'and naturally I had some little difficulty in finding my way about. There was an alert looking newsboy in a corner and I accosted him.' 'My lad,' I said, 'I want to go to the White House.' 'Very well,' said the boy, 'you may go; but don't stay more than half an hour.'"[60]

The *Malone Palladium* observed that his

> actual residence in Malone was that of a young boyhood only. . . . But [as he was] descended from the ablest and probably the best-known divine ever having a charge here, and who was remembered for a generation with reverence and awe, . . . there have been few men of intelligence in Franklin County who have not watched Mr. Fitch's career with an interest and pride that were almost personal. . . .
>
> His partiality in later years for the woods and waters has made him so often a visitor that his local acquaintance had become considerably extended. . . . Mr. Fitch had in an eminent degree the quality of making and holding friends. There was a depth and sincerity of good fellowship, cordiality, interest and eagerness to serve, manifested alike in his conversation and in his conduct that won men to him quickly, and held them surely. As to few men in New York City did the personal equation, both in business and in politics, go farther in building success. . . . In public and in private life alike, Mr. Fitch's work and record were honorable to himself and useful to his city and to the country at large.[61]

Such very personal endorsements would have pleased him. But none would have pleased him more than a letter to Lizzie from Lewis Burchard, vice president of the Thomas Hunter Association, written three years after his death. Burchard recalled Fitch's last appearance at the association's annual meeting:

> I remember the occasion well. Mr. Fitch was sitting at ease with his friends and was called on without a minute's warning and stood up and made the best speech that I ever heard made to Dr. Hunter's "old boys," full of good fellowship and comradeship, joy in the recollections of boyhood, and pride that he was "a citizen," not by adoption merely but by heritage and birth, "of no mean city."

He glowed and made us glow with the same home patriotism that a Bostonian feels for his Boston, an Athenian felt for his Athens, a Scotsman of "old Reckie" for his Edinborough. "How many of us," said he, "stood in line all night to see Lincoln as he lay in state in the city hall!"

He was indeed a man—by far the best president the "Hunter boys" ever sat under, and it is a pleasure to send you this hearty tribute from one who knew him only a little and from afar, one who to him was only one of the school's "old boys," but nonetheless sure of a warm handgrip and a friendly greeting.[62]

Conclusion

Our metropolis has never had, either in Congress or elsewhere, a bolder or more eloquent champion of her good name, than Ashbel P. Fitch.

—*New York Uptown Visitor,* November 11, 1893

It is a responsibility to write a life's story. What should be said or not said? Ashbel Fitch was smart, honest, loyal, pragmatic, loving, serious, hard-working, progressive, independent, outspoken, courageous, cheerful, and fun-loving. Where should it end? Goethe said, "One ought, every day at least, to hear a little song, read a good poem, see a fine picture and, if it were possible, to speak a few reasonable words." Whether Ashbel Fitch did just that seems unlikely, but Goethe was his beacon. It is sad and unfortunate that his life was cut short. He adored his wife and children, and they loved him in return, and their lives, especially his children's, were greatly changed without him. Lizzie lived on for another nine years, until her death in 1913. She lived quietly in and around New York and spent "part of each summer"[1] at Ragged Lake, which remains today in the hands of Fitch's descendants.

Fitch's early German education and his devotion to Goethe, solidly built upon Thomas Hunter's school, his natural attributes, and the sturdy foundation of his parents' affection, prepared him to meet life's joys and disappointments with equanimity, poise, and good humor. He was tolerant for his time, warmly embracing New York's surging immigrant tide and celebrating the diversity it spawned.

He made friends for life. His brewing clients Ehret, Ruppert, the Schaefers, and others were with him always. So were Dayton, Lamont, Cantor, and his cousin Morton. There are very few letters from the pen of Grover Cleveland that exuded such warmth as he displayed for Fitch.

Fitch was a popular politician. While his Tammany endorsement no doubt enabled him to win elections, he always ran ahead of his ticket, and he won by wide margins. He triumphed in 1886 without Tammany's endorsement, although Tammany tolerated, rather than supported, his opponent, and the German community was solidly behind him. He enjoyed continuous German support throughout his political career, but in 1897 he was unable to overcome Tammany's active opposition, especially with two other well-known anti-Tammany candidates in the race. Although his 1897 loss was his biggest political disappointment, New York's shabby treatment by Congress during the World's Fair debate was a singular disappointment too.

In business he built a thriving law firm and successfully founded a trust company. He led the anti-silver forces in the House in 1892, and he was influential in the great tariff debate of 1888. His drive to remove John I. Davenport from office contributed to Cleveland's New York victory in 1892.

His zealous protection of New York City's budget and credit during one of the nation's worst economic debacles was heroic. His harshest words were reserved for Bryan and Davenport, two men who he believed were out to hurt his country and his city. His vote for Speaker in 1890, while puzzling, may have been made to appease Croker, but that is not clear.

Fitch was unique, perhaps, in the annals of New York history, to the extent that he was in effect a German politician who was not of German descent. He was independent and dedicated to principles, principles that determined the course of his political career and provided the best measure of his character.

33. Ashbel P. Fitch at the Trust Company of America, ca. 1900. Photographer unknown. Photograph from the Ashbel P. Fitch archives.

He advocated tariff reform that Republicans promised in their platforms of 1880 and 1884, years in which Fitch was becoming engaged with politics. His commitment to tariff reform was a promise he made to Charles Dayton; it differentiated him from Veile in his first try for office, and it was the first major national issue he encountered as a freshman congressman in the Fiftieth Congress. In 1888, Republicans, casting principle aside, moved away from tariff reform, but Fitch stood his ground.

He was committed to a gold-backed currency. Hard currency was a sectional issue, and New York Democrats and Republicans were by and large of one mind in that regard. So his conversion from Republican to Democrat in 1888 occasioned no change in his support of a gold-backed currency. But in 1896, when Democrats transformed their party from the gold-backed conservatism of Grover Cleveland to the silver-backed or bimetallic opportunism of William Jennings Bryan, Fitch stood his ground again.

While controller, he was criticized at times for his strict enforcement of civil service laws, and his was a principled voice for personal liberty in his consistent opposition to temperance laws. He was singularly committed to upholding New York City's budget discipline, first promulgated by Andrew Haswell Green in the wake of the Tweed scandal in 1872. Each city department was to set its budget annually and, as a matter of law, live within it. Mayor Strong's administration believed that voters had authorized reform spending without regard to the law. In defense of New York, Fitch stood his ground a third time.

The *New York Press,* with the good cheer that was reminiscent of the subject of their commentary, wrote:

> When Controller Fitch retires from office the city will take leave of one of the most capable officials it has known. He fought thirty-two duels or something like that number at Heidelberg, and Great Scott only knows how many battles he has had on his hands since he took office. He has been the fighter of the Strong administration. He has been the watchdog of the city's treasury. His is the eye that has never been closed. He has withheld so many salaries that even the Mayor himself was afraid he would not get his $10,000 a year without an argument and proof that he had earned it. He had Teddy Roosevelt in a fine frenzy and laughed at him for weeks while the police department hungered and thirsted for funds. There was talk of a duel at which the Controller smiled and did his duty.[2]

Fitch's principled positions throughout a twelve-year political career created a narrative that in its making inevitably created a list of political opponents. His career retells the oft-told story of profiles in courage that have dotted the American political landscape since the founding of the Republic.

His life, which began on the Canada border and ended fifty-six years later on the Upper East Side of Manhattan, was remarkable. He accumulated a small fortune, and he had a loving wife and family, far more friends than enemies, and an untainted political record. Throughout, he remained eternally grateful for the enormous opportunity that was New York, and he would tell anyone who would listen. On platform after platform, in speech after speech, in letter after letter, he offered only praise for the excellence, opportunity, and diversity that to him was New York.

Following the death of Samuel Cox in 1889, Fitch was the acknowledged leader of the New York City congressional delegation (1889–93), and he was the chief officer of New York City's Finance Department (1894–97) during a period of dreadful economic turmoil. He won five New York City elections. He was devoted not only to promoting the best interest of the citizens of New York, but to repeatedly proclaiming the city's liberal, multicultural virtues from his public pulpit. It was Fitch's hero Goethe who said "One must be something in order to do something," fitting words to describe Ashbel Parmelee Fitch.

Appendix A

Appendix B

Appendix C

Notes

Bibliography

Index

APPENDIX A

NEW YORK, November 29, 1887.

DEAR SIR:

The Republican party, with a good State ticket, after a thorough and eloquent canvass of the whole State by its recognized leaders, has again been defeated.

This defeat was plainly caused by the adverse majority in this city, where the Republican vote for the State ticket fell to 60,000. On the basis of such a vote in this city, there does not seem to be any reasonable probability of success for the party at the future elections in this State.

I ask you to allow me, as one of the city Republicans, to mention to you as one of the newly-elected Republican members of the Legislature, the causes which many of us here believe to have brought about this shrinkage of our vote.

The city of New York is the largest city in the country, but it is not great in population or in wealth alone. Its professions and business circles are filled with the brightest and most successful men from all parts of the United States, among them doubtless many whom you know from your own section. With them are associated citizens of different nationalities, who are not the less loyal or the less valuable to the city of their adoption because they keep the language and some of the customs which were taught them in childhood. All the world has been freely invited to come here, just as our ancestors came, and people from almost everywhere have accepted the invitation. The German, the Irishman, the Frenchman, Swiss, and Italian have each been gladly received, and each has earned his right to a cordial welcome and a fair chance with the rest of us. The mutual and united efforts of all have caused the city to grow and prosper beyond all precedent. There is no story of modern development more striking than that which has taken place, in the last quarter of a century, on the island of Manhattan, and there is nothing in that story so interesting as the manner in which the different elements of this curiously constituted population have grown to respect and like each other and to live and work together. Any one who may claim that there is in this great population any larger percentage of vice or ignorance than exists anywhere else in the country, is misinformed or is prejudiced.

In this city there is as much local patriotism as exists anywhere else in the State. Aside from the vast pecuniary interests centred in the city, which makes its development important to its citizens, there exists among them a growing interest and pride in the history and the future of the metropolis.

They are of the opinion that the welfare of their city and its development ought to be a matter of interest to every citizen of the State which contains it, whether his political party happens to hold the municipal offices and has a majority of its votes or not.

It has, however, come to be believed here that the Republican party cares nothing for the interest or sentiments of the city. Among many of the native- and almost all the foreign-born voters who formerly acted with the Republicans this belief is universal. The large German vote which former candidates of the party received, and to which many of its successes in the State are due, has been turned entirely against us.

It is said by these voters that a large part of the city is virtually denied representation by the Republican party ; that taxation has been arranged so as to unfairly benefit other districts of the State ; that laws designed to take for the use of the State excise moneys which belong to the city are adopted by the party caucus, and that much of the time of each legislative session is devoted by the party representatives to arranging schemes for improving by force of statute the morals of the city, which are, however, carefully worded so as not to apply to the districts which these gentlemen themselves represent. It is even said that while the Legislature will pass the most enthusiastic endorsement of Home Rule in Ireland, it cannot be induced to give to the chief city of this country as much control over its own affairs as is allowed to the smallest village in the State.

These beliefs are much more widely held and more discussed than they were three years ago, owing, perhaps, to recent legislation, and they will have much more effect at the next Presidential election than they had at the last one.

How far these allegations are true, you can judge as well as I can. It is easy enough for any one who may choose to do so, to deny that they have any basis of truth at all. The trouble is that such denials carry no weight at all with the voters.

For instance, in this Assembly District, the 23d, we have 21,000 voters, and have been entitled, by any fair computation, for some years to have three Assemblymen instead of one. During these years there has been a Republican majority at Albany. Do you think it possible for the Republicans here to persuade our neighbors that the Democratic party, which would gain these Assemblymen if they were allowed, is responsible for this state of affairs? And how do you fancy that the citizens of any interior county would vote if they believed that any political party, having the power to do so, refused to give them their undeniable right of representation?

The question then is not whether you will deny these allegations, but how you will meet the fixed and settled belief of your former political friends that they are true.

It seems to many of us here that this can only be done by the Republican majority at Albany, of which you are a member.

If the Republican party in the coming session shall choose to legislate for New York City much as if it were a foreign colony or a conquered province; if the wishes of the people here are overruled to satisfy the fancied sentiment or the interest of the country districts, it will be necessary for the party to arrange to get such votes as it may need to elect its candidates in those portions of the State which its legislation favors, and it may expect even less help than it had this year from the city.

If, on the other hand, the members of the Legislature belonging to the Republican party will lay aside all questions of so-called party advantage and party patronage, and in legislation for this city will aim to give the people who live in it and have built it up the control of their own affairs, and if they will take steps to give the city its rightful representation in the Legislature, they will, as we believe, take the natural and proper course to strengthen their party among the voters of the city.

More votes can be got in this city by common fairness than can be got by any combination or by the nomination of any particular candidate.

Many gentlemen in the party will disagree very emphatically with the views expressed in this letter. Some of them apparently have no consideration for the views of any one whose birth, education, or ideas differ in any degree from their own. Some of them will even urge you to go farther than before in special legislation for this city.

This letter is not written in ignorance of their wishes or plans, but because of them.

Which of us is right cannot be very hard to ascertain.

Yours very sincerely,

APPENDIX B

Congressional Record

FIFTIETH CONGRESS, FIRST SESSION

WASHINGTON

Tariff Reform

SPEECH

OF

HON. ASHBEL P. FITCH

OF New York

IN THE HOUSE OF REPRESENTATIVES,

Monday, May 16, 1888

Unless the tariff men take heed, unless they consent to a rational and considerate adjustment of the tariff such as only can be made by the full light that a careful statistical study of the subject will bring, I fear from them, more than any other source, a reaction which will bring us by and by into free trade and all its consequences of evil to the manufacturing interests of the country.

I desire to say that, in my judgement, it is not the best mode of defending a tariff to denounce every man who does not pronounce the shibboleth after our fashion as an enemy of the tariff – *James A. Garfield*, July 13, 1868.

The house being in Committee of the Whole on the State of the Union, and having under consideration the bill (H. R. 9051) to reduce taxation and simplify the laws in relation to the collection of the revenue –

Mr. FITCH said:

Mr. CHAIRMAN: In the brief remarks which I desire to make on the bill under consideration, in the spirit of the words which I have just read, I do not propose to discuss at length the arguments which gentlemen on both sides of the house have already presented, nor shall I attempt to review or to put a new meaning into the great mass of customs figures which have been so carefully prepared and explained by the gentlemen who have preceded me. I do not intend to debate the question whether or not we shall have a tariff, or whether that tariff shall be one for protection or not.

I assume that, whether this bill passes or not, we shall continue to have in this country a protective tariff, and that protective tariff, if it be fairly adjusted, if its burdens be distributed with justice so far as interests of my constituents are concerned, I expect to defend and advocate as long as I live. And as long as I live, whenever I find in the tariff laws or in any other of the laws which affect the people whom I represent anything which seems to me in any degree unfair or unjust, I shall not hesitate to advocate their revision and amendment. [Applause.] I propose here to discuss at this time only what seems to me to be the question before the House, whether or not the present tariff and the free-list which accompanies it should remain unchanged during the existence of the Fiftieth Congress.

In the discussion of this question I shall not attempt to imitate the gentlemen who have with such wonderful patience and industry examined the views of the earlier Presidents and the construction of the tariff of 1789, and who have so carefully reviewed the whole course of legislation on the subject since the foundation of the Republic. They have analyzed for you every fluctuation in the prices of our manufactures, and they have accounted satisfactorily for each financial crisis in history of the country. Every statesman who has in any way identified himself with this question has been quoted by them, and every textbook and essay on the subject has been examined. Each gentleman has found in the same material the most convincing proof that his particular theory was correct and that of his opponent mistaken.

For my part, and with the utmost deference to the learning and ability of gentlemen who have spoken, I am forced to believe that, owing to the changes in transportation, invention of new machinery, the growth and development of the country, and improvements which have accomplished modern civilization here and all over the world, the problem presented to us is entirely different from that considered by the earlier contestants over these questions. It seems to me that no two countries in Europe are today more strikingly different in the manner in which their inhabitants live, their means of communication, and their business customs than are the United States of fifty years ago and the country and people whose interests we are considering here.

I desire therefore to leave to other gentlemen who have done it so well the consideration of all the earlier precedents, and to speak only of what the Republican party in our day and generation has promised to do, and to consider what duties are incumbent on us here and now in connection with that promise. I propose also to speak of what I consider to be the interest of the people in my own district, whose condition and whose wants are naturally better known to me than those of others. It can hardly be denied that the present tariff was largely made up in this way: Different interests in special districts send information and delegations to Washington, urging the enactment of duties specially favorable to them, and sometimes elected Congressmen especially with a view to obtaining a protection which they deemed necessary for their district. It is not probable that the views of the persons represented in this way were always unselfish, and it is possible that the advocates of these particular interest were not unwilling to profit by taxes which bore unequally upon other sections of the country.

It is easy to say, and everybody says in the abstract, that we should legislate for our whole country and not for sections of it, and that this bill should be considered as to its effect on the people at large and not on particular classes. But how has it in fact been considered in this debate? One eloquent gentleman after another has told of the special needs of his district, and has protested solemnly against some proposed interference with the vested rights of his constituents in the present tariff. First of all, and above all, the gentlemen representing the farming interests have been heard. I have read, for instance, with profit, and almost with conviction, the argument of the gentleman from Michigan [Mr. BURROWS] for the continuance of the present tariff in all its parts for the protection of the farmers, who, it seems to him, are now insufficiently protected, and with equal interest have studied the seconding appeal of his colleague and my friend, Mr. BREWER, to the same effect. Nothing could have pleased me more than the touching tribute from the gentleman from Maryland [Mr. MCCOMAS] to the virtues of the farming constituency, among which he is fortunate to live, unless it were the kindly offer of my genial and eloquent friend from Wisconsin [Mr. GUENTHER], the guardian of the American infant, to put a duty of 4 cents per dozen on the fourteen million dozens of eggs which are now imported free of duty, and which we in New York eat and are obliged to pay for in order to protect the American hen and her rural owner against the combined poultry of Europe.

I concede willingly the truth of all that the gentlemen say in the praise of their country constituents. We in New York City have an intimate acquaintance with and a real liking for the New York State farmers, and will never willingly suffer them to be injured by any form of legislation if they will only be fair with us. It seems to us often that they hardly appreciate our friendship. It seems to us that they allow their representatives in the State Legislature to treat us unfairly at Albany. From there, in their wisdom, these representatives regulate our docks, and control our street openings; they fix the height of our buildings and the depth of our sewers; they manage the quarantine in our harbor and they arrange the rate of fare on our elevated roads. We are relieved by their kindness from any particular responsibility or trouble about our local tax levy, and they improve, as seems to them necessary from time to time, the charter of our city. Above all, our morals and personal habits and the manner of our observance of the Sabbath are their especial care. [Laughter.]

They study with great personal attention the errors of our metropolis, and they prepare yearly new and elaborate schemes for our reformation. They vote enthusiastic indorsements of home rule in Ireland and explain to us at the same time that New York is hardly fitted to govern itself. We recognize the truth of all the praises which have been bestowed on the farmers in this debate by almost every gentleman who has spoken, but we will never let pass any opportunity to ask them to treat their city neighbors and friends more kindly. And while their interests in this bill are so carefully watched and protected, it is perhaps not unfair that one of us from the city should glance over his district and see if there are no people of whom we can say, as my eloquent friend from Iowa [Mr. HENDERSON] said of the farmers, that they are "hard-working, earnest, intelligent, frugal, and moral," and whose interests may deserve some degree of consideration in connection with this bill.

The upper part of the city of New York is mainly a residence district. The majority of the people who live there live on fixed incomes paid them as salaries or wages every month, or by the proceeds of professional employment in which their incomes are limited. Some of them are architects, artists, clergymen, clerks in banks, insurance and law offices, journalists, musicians, lawyers, physicians, teachers, bookkeepers, railroad employees, drivers, conductors, policemen, firemen, telegraph and telephone operators, salesmen, mechanical engineers, civil engineers, stenographers, printers and skilled mechanics of all sorts not employed in industries which have protection under the present tariff.

In that district lives, too, an army of deserving women who earn their living by unprotected labor, and often that of others dependent upon them. There is perhaps a necessity within the course of this long debate that somebody should say a word for these people. The farmer has his eloquent advocates trained in the county and State fairs, who is in arms to defend every product of his ground. The workmen in factories and the manufacturers have their special advocates, who lie awake at night to study their interests and whose voices have been heard here every day since the beginning of this session, asking for one measure or another for their protection. Almost every class has had its advocates here, except perhaps the millionaires, whom nobody will own to represent, and who have no friends in this House.

Suppose as examples of the class of people to whom I refer in the city of New York, we take the policeman, who guards our houses; the fireman, who will risk his life for our children; the reporter and the printer, who spend the night in preparing our morning papers; the carrier, who brings it through all kinds of weather, and the locomotive engineers on the elevated railroad, who takes us up and down town. These classes of workmen have no direct protection. They are not overpaid, nor is their life more luxurious than it ought to be. The money which they draw at the end of every month is not more than they need, and they are often sorely pinched to buy even the taxed doll to fill the taxed Christmas stocking or to pay for the taxed medicine necessary for any member of the family.

Perhaps an impartial examination may show that these people are as intelligent, as patriotic, and as deserving of consideration in the matter now before the House as are the Rhode Island mill operators or the Kansas farmers. Their wishes and views may be even as important to the Republican Party. If you are to get any Republican votes in New York City you must get them from these people. These classes gave you under the wise management of Arthur votes enough to keep down the Democratic majority in the city so that a Republican President was elected by the vote of the State of New York. They gave in my district a Republican an election to Congress, largely because his Democratic opponent refused to support any measure of tariff reform, and voted against the consideration of the Morrison bill.

You can hardly afford to pass these voters over in your desire to conciliate the factory operatives and the farmers, unless, indeed, you have decided to elect your candidate without the vote of New York State. I have had it explained to me that this can easily be done. It is a favorite theory apparently of the same gentlemen who have decided that the city workingmen who gave the most outspoken and determined free-trader in this country, Mr. Henry George, 68,000 votes at an election when we could only get 60,000 for so good a candidate as Theodore Roosevelt, are wild with enthusiasm for the absolute maintenance of the present tariff; and of those other wise leaders of the party whose declared policy is to alienate the German voters who are still true to the Republican Party, in order to please the Prohibitionists, who laugh at their concessions and have always sought and always will seek the downfall of that party.

I for one am not willing to accept such theories or acknowledge such leadership. In the interest of the Republican Party, and in the interest of common fairness, I propose to ask gentlemen on this side of the House to consider for a moment how the present tariff, which we have promised to revise, now affects the people whom I have described, and to consider what they pay taxes on in the general distribution of the customs taxes now in force.

They pay upon everything. Look for a moment at what they eat. There is a tariff duty on beef, on pork, hams and bacon, butter and lard, cheese, molasses, grapes, wheat flour, oats, corn meal, rye, barley, potatoes, raisins, vinegar, honey, rice and rice meal, sugar, extract of meat, pickles, currants, apples, salt, and condensed milk. The list is substantially an inventory of the stock of the grocery store at which they buy. There is a duty on the coal which warms them, on their cooking and household utensils, on their entire clothing from their hats to their stockings, on the medicine given them when they are sick, and on the roofs over their heads. What the professional men object to pay is shown by a letter which I will ask to have printed as a part of my remarks:

NEW YORK, *May* 15, 1888

To Hon. Ashbel P. Fitch, M.C. :

I beg to address you as a member interested in the revision of the tariff. My plea is in behalf of instruments used in scientific medicine, which is the same as saying that they contribute to the exact information of the profession at large and are without money profit to the possessor.

I can make you understand me by citing my own case.

For six years I have been pathologist to the New York Foundling Asylum, making *post mortem* examinations for purposes of study upon the children that die, and recording the findings in detail. I have contributed to the professional stock of exact records nearly 1,500 cases. These are available for all time to the profession for reference.

A complete case for purposes of study consists in a carefully recorded clinical history with *post mortem* findings and microscope examination of the structural charges in the tissues of the organs.

Now, it is the expert work of the pathologist to make the examinations, both gross and microscopic, of the ravages of disease, and it is upon this kind of work that medicine is to advance to the dignity of an exact science.

For my microscope I sent to Jena, where are made the best instruments for my work. At the factory it cost $94; to get out of the custom-house 40 percent more.

Later I sent for an oil immersion lens, and paid $80 at the factory, 40 percent more at the custom-house.

Hermann Katsch, of Berlin, makes an instrument called microtome, for cutting infinitely thin sections or shavings from the surface of a piece of an organ of the body, hardened in alcohol. Herr Katsch is the only man in the world who makes this particular variety of the instrument. To prepare a section thin enough for careful study under the high powers of the microscope this mechanism is necessary. To get this microtome from the custom-house I had to wait two weeks and pay a duty of 40 percent on its factory price.

The celebrated Dr. Koch, of Berlin, published a report of the cholera commission, conducted under the auspices of the Government. At most, twenty men in this country could require this work, and they must needs pay 25 percent duty to get from the custom-house after paying its publisher's price and freight. What use could this report be to these scientists? To aid them in maturing methods of recognizing the disease when it appeared on ship-board in our harbors; to devise means to suppress it; to protect the country.

It was to the expert work of one such scientist that the city of New York must give its gratitude, that a certain steamship just developing cholera among its steerage passengers was detained at quarantine and the city escaped overwhelming infection.

For Koch's report he paid 25 percent duty and never received anything from the city or Government.

When we look up from our laboratory tables, microscopes, microtomes, and alcohol–taxed to suffocation–and read in the papers of the United States Treasury filled to suffocation, we reflect that our scientific work takes much time, brings no money return, increases our outgoes, and has not even the encouragement of the Government or laity.

Respectfully yours,

DR. WILLIAM PERRY NORTHRUP

Is it unfair to ask for these people a little consideration? Grant that we are to have a protective tariff; must we have this particular one forever?

The gentleman from Indiana [Mr. BROWNE], whose argument against this bill has interested me greatly, said the other day, "Human wisdom has never devised statutes of taxation or methods of industrial development which are not subject to just criticism." I cannot put in any better words my conviction that this tariff is a fair subject of discussion. We had lately a Republican President, under whose able and skillful management the Republican party was an important factor in political affairs in New York City, and who gained for us the last victory which our party has had in the city of New York. Few men knew the people of that city of all classes as well as he did. He had been collector at the port of New York and knew well the practical effect of the tariff, and he said in his message:

I recommend an enlargement of the free list so as to include within it the new numerous articles which yield inconsiderable revenue, a simplification of the complex and inconsistent schedule of duties upon certain manufactures, particularly those of cotton, iron, and steel, and a substantial reduction of the duties upon those articles, and upon sugar, molasses, wool, and woolen goods.

On such Republican doctrines as that I am satisfied to rest. On such Republican doctrines as that we can ask for votes in the city of New York from the classes I have spoken of, and we will not then be forced to stand and defend, before people whose monthly wages hardly suffice for their necessary expenses, a tariff which imposes 25 percent on the India-rubber boots and shoes and 10 percent on precious stones. [Applause.]

The commerce of New York where most of the customs are collected, while it asks in vain for the money which is necessary to improve the waterways where $147,000,000 of our revenue is collected every year, pays cheerfully taxes which are used to keep up custom houses where nothing is ever collected, and to carry the mails on routes which use up the profits of the city offices, to build harbors in Texas, where a sailor who happened to be stranded there would be lost and lonesome, to improve rapids in Tennessee which no one but the lumberman ever sees, and to dredge out creeks in Georgia which the Government engineers who are given charge of the work spend a month in trying to find. Just so the people of the city of New York, sooner than object in any way to the protective tariff, which they believe to be, if properly laid and fairly administered, for the good of the whole country, have paid without objection and cheerfully, on everything they use or touch or handle, from the beginning these custom duties for the benefit of the manufacturer and his employee and the long-suffering farmer. The time has now come when a revision of the tariff has been promised by both parties, and when the present duties yield so large a revenue that its further accumulation has become admittedly dangerous. Is it strange that at this time and under these circumstances they ask that a readjustment, partially at least, in their interest, may take place? And is it unreasonable to ask that a tariff which puts jewelry at 25 percent and oil cloth for tenement-house floors at 40 percent ad valorem; which brings in silver-plated harness at 35 percent and children's cotton stockings at 40 percent; under which India shawls of the finest quality pay 40 percent and common woolen shawls 86 percent should be modified? On the theory of protecting or pleasing the manufacturing laborer and the farmer the mass of people in my district in the city of New York have paid for many years, each of them, out of money which they can ill spare, more for their meals, their shelter, their clothes, and their medicines than these things ought to cost them.

The appreciation and kindly feelings which exist towards us in return from the most highly protected manufacturers is shown by the remark in this debate of the gentleman from Pennsylvania, Mr. O'NEILL speaking in opposition to this bill, that " New York is in a large measure a foreign city." It is true, of course, that New York has many foreign-born citizens, and among them are a large number who bear the name of the gentlemen from Pennsylvania. [Laughter and Applause.] All of us in this country are foreign-born or are descendants of European immigrants. Whoever speaks deprecatingly of the patriotism of the citizens who came to this country by choice and not by accident throws thereby a doubt on the integrity of that ancestor of his who first took the oath of allegiance to the United States.

I have little regard for the man who contrasts his own patriotism with that of his grandfather, to the disadvantage of the latter. It is true, too, that a visitor from Philadelphia, when he first steps into the busy streets of New York and sees the movement of the commerce of a continent, when he enters first into the life and amusement of a city as interesting as London and as charming as Paris, may easily feel that he has passed a boundary line, and is in another country than his own. [Laughter.] But if the gentleman meant, as he probably did, that New York was a foreign city in the sense of being un-American, he was simply as much mistaken as he would have been if he had said that William Penn was a native American, or that the German settlers in Pennsylvania and their children were not as good and patriotic citizens of this country as we are.

Now when we ask of the manufacturers who are represented by our kindly critic, Mr. O'NEILL, a fulfillment of the Republican promise to remedy the admitted irregularities of the tariff, they say that if we touch one article in the present dutiable list, if we add one article to the present free-list the whole protection scheme is in danger. Let me answer them by a quotation again from General Garfield, in the debate on the duty on coal, on March 10,1871, in this House:

> I was surprised at a remark of the distinguished gentleman from Michigan. He asserted that there is no identity in the whole tariff that can stand alone on its own merits, but that all must be taken in a lump in order to stand. That coal must take salt by the hand, and they, too, must take something else by the hand; and thus all interests unite with all forces before they can make a stand before the country. If this remark be true it strikes a blow at the whole tariff system, a blow I am not willing to strike. I am unwilling to admit that bad taxes must be tied to good ones and thus be kept afloat. I think it unwise to continue this duty on coal, and I am therefore in favor of its repeal.

That, gentlemen, was the view of the last Republican President when a member of this House. I quote him always with peculiar pleasure, for he was one of the Republican candidates who could not only excite great enthusiasm in his own party and among his personal friends, but who could get votes enough from the business people, who care little for politics, to be elected to office. It seems to me that General Garfield fully answered that objection, but the highly protected manufacturers have endless objections. They seem to think that they are to have a monopoly of objections. We must not ask for cheaper vegetables in the city; the farmer objects. We must not want cheaper clothes; the wool-grower objects. We must not ask for cheaper carpets or household utensils; the manufacturer objects. We must not ask for cheaper coal; the mine owner objects. We must not claim cheaper sugar or rice; the planter objects.

Well, for one, I, for my district of consumers, object to this chorus of objection. We do not own sheep; we can not raise rice or vegetables or sugar; we mine no coal in the Thirteenth district of New York. If every interest in this country which is protected is to come here and cry out at any proposed addition to the free-list or reduction of the tariff taxes, in the interest of the great principle of protection, we, in our turn, shall ask that our monthly wages and the limited incomes on which many of us must live shall have the protection promised us by both political platforms, and that not by and by, but now in the Fiftieth Congress.

We shall ask this courteously and modestly now. If we are met only by selfish and determined refusals the request will have to be made more emphatically. Certainly we are willing to have a protective tariff, but we do not want an unreasonable and unchangeable tariff. We want a tariff which shall protect where protection is needed, and a free-list which shall give us the necessaries of life on terms that are at least fair to all.

Gentlemen say that the tariff builds up a home market. Very good. In the residence district of New York City we are the home market; we use our monthly pay the whole year around to buy your goods. Now that you have an opportunity, now that you can afford it, now that you have promised it, be fair to your home market. Show us by timely and reasonable concessions that you are not entirely selfish, and we will, as we have heretofore, go on cheerfully paying more for everything which we use than we think the goods ought to cost us.

The answer to this seemingly reasonable demand on our side of the House seems to be this in substance: It is true that the tariff ought to be revised. The party platform promised it; the last Republican President and his Secretaries advised it; the party conventions in many States have agreed to; but it must be done only by the Republican party in a House of which that party shall have a majority.

There are two objections to this answer:

First. It is a postponement, an indefinite postponement of something which was promised four years ago, and ought to have been done before now. Whatever hopes gentlemen may have of the future, no one can say when we shall be strong enough to make and carry through by Republican votes alone a revision of the tariff. If you are to read out of the party everybody who reminds you of your promises, or who has any of the old Republican habits of free speech and candid criticism, perhaps you may never be strong enough to control the House. [Applause.] Even if the fall elections should return a majority of Republicans, nearly a year and a half must elapse before the Fifty-first Congress can even meet, and if a tariff debate like this should then ensue, certainly two years must pass before the present tariff can be changed. And it is more improbable that even then the highly protected industries would still find some new reason why action should be postponed for another indefinite period, and that their representatives would vote again as many gems of poetry and prosaic tables of figures as we have heard for the last two weeks to demonstrate that the slightest alteration of the sacred tariff for the relief of the people, on whom some portions of it weigh heavily, would end forever the prosperity of the country.

And it is still more likely that gentlemen who are interested in the preservation intact of the present tariff would claim that the election of a Republican House was a verdict of the people against any revision whatsoever. [Laughter.]

For my part I desire to consider this question now, in the Congress to which I was elected partly for the purpose of considering it. Whether the Fifty-first or Fifty-second or Fifty-third Congresses are to be Republican or Democratic, what their action may be in the changed circumstances under which they may meet, is something which concerns me at present very little. I propose to do what I can–recognizing how very little it is–toward filling the promises of the party on this subject now, when I have an opportunity. [Applause.]

Second. It is an unpatriotic answer to the reasonable demand that our promises to reform the tariff be fulfilled to say that as a condition-precedent we must first have a success of our own party. If the revision is right, if it is in the interest of the business and development of the country, as our conventions and our leading statesmen have said it was, I for one am willing to make it, whether there is any political capital in it or not.

It is a business question more than a political question, and it is a business question on which we are committed.

If a revision of the tariff is necessary, it seems to me to be as absurd to vote against it on party grounds as it would be to oppose the admittedly necessary appropriations for the Government because they are prepared in a Democratic committee and proposed to a Democratic House.

I am one of those who were disappointed that we have as yet before us no Republican bill to reform the tariff. I do not forget the excellent bill putting coal, sugar, molasses, rice, wool, and some raw materials on the free-list, introduced by my Republican friend from Minnesota [Mr. NELSON], whose 43,000 votes at the last election demonstrate what a hold on his people his fidelity to their interests has given him. I admired his speech and I would gladly vote for his bill. But I mean that I had hoped that before this we would have had submitted to us a bill put forward by authority, framed by gentlemen whose length of service and great ability fitted them for such a task, a bill in regard to which all of us would have been consulted, in which our varying views could have been compromised, a bill in which all of us would have yielded something to reach a common agreement.

For such a bill, framed by such high authority, perfected by such consultation, and giving to the people of our city some of the benefits to which we think they are entitled, even if it did not give us all which we could desire, I would have given my support most heartily. Instead of such a bill, those of us who think that the reform of the tariff is a business question, and who are committed to its support, are given so far only an eloquent denunciation of the manner in which this bill under consideration was made. For myself, I do not know that I care particularly how it was made or who made it. If the gentlemen who denounce its authors and the place where it was constructed will prepare, in a manner in their judgment more suitable for the purpose, a better bill than this one, I shall certainly be glad to give my support to their measure in preference to any other. But if I am asked to oppose this bill, not so much on account of its contents as on account of its history, I must decline to do so, even if I stand alone on this side of the House.

The history of the bill before it came before us is as immaterial to me as was the political history of the voters who sent me here before their appearance at the polls. I did not decline their suffrages on account of their antecedents, and if 6,500 of them could afford to forget their Democracy and give that district to a Republican, I can in my turn forget the origin of this bill in the consideration of the question whether it is in the interest of my district and in the line of what I claimed in the canvass to be the belief of my party and my own belief. There is something better than Republicanism or Democracy, and that is common honesty. I have insisted, over and over for years in my district, that the Republican party was committed to tariff reform. I have attacked, in the canvass, my Democratic opponent for doing exactly that which gentlemen here propose that the Republican party should do. If the gentlemen in charge of the party interests on this floor propose to abandon the position which I and others have defended and insisted upon, it is not for me to criticize their wisdom; but I cannot recognize their authority to make me give up the convictions which were good Republican doctrine when I adopted them and to break promises which I feel bound in honor to fulfill.

I cannot as yet know in what shape this bill will come before us for final action. I believe that it should be amended in many particulars before it is passed, and I have submitted and shall submit some amendments which seem to me necessary. I cannot as yet know whether or not a Republican substitute will be offered, or if there be one what it will cover. This much, however, I know now, that whenever I have an opportunity to vote for any measure which seems to offer the relief which I believe my people are entitled to have, and which I have myself for years insisted should be given them, I shall not fail to vote in their interest and for my own convictions, without regard to the consequences of my vote to myself. [Applause.]

APPENDIX C

Congressional Record

FIFTY – THIRD CONGRESS, FIRST SESSION

WASHINGTON, MONDAY, OCTOBER 9, 1893

REPEAL OF THE FEDERAL ELECTION LAWS.

SPEECH

OF

HON. ASHBEL P. FITCH,

OF NEW YORK,

IN THE

HOUSE OF REPRESENTATIVES,

MONDAY, OCTOBER 9, 1893.

The House having under consideration the bill (H. R. 2331) to repeal all statutes relating to supervisors of elections and special deputy marshals, and for other purposes—

Mr. FITCH said:

Mr. SPEAKER: It seems to me particularly fitting that at the end of this long debate the last argument to be made in favor of the repeal of the Federal laws relating to the supervision of elections should be made by a Representative from the city of New York.

It was in the city of New York that the scheme of these laws had its origin. In that city their enforcement and operation was most conspicuous, and it is on account mainly of the public indignation over the results of these laws in that city that they are about to be repealed. In presenting to the House the request of the most important city of the Union for the repeal of these laws, I propose to relate briefly what we know in that city of their origin, their operation, and their results.

These laws had their inception in the fertile brain of a political adventurer, who twenty-three or twenty-four years ago sought to find a foothold and a position for himself in New York politics. He was entirely destitute of all the resources which are ordinarily necessary for success in political life. He had nothing of the eloquence in public discussion which sometimes compels public attention and admiration. He had nothing of the personal qualities which sometimes fix friendship and attract a following and influence. He was utterly destitute of the high character and conscience which sometimes command public respect and confidence. He had, however, been educated in a school in which he had learned that political success may sometimes be achieved without eloquence or personal attractiveness, or character, or conscience. He had for years been the personal companion and an apt and devoted scholar of Benjamin F. Butler. He saw two prejudices then largely prevalent in the public mind, of which he believed he could make use, and with peculiar adroitness he conceived a scheme by which he might take advantage of them for his personal profit. He used them so successfully as to intrench himself in a position where, under cover of law on one side, and under cover of party loyalty on the other, he has looted for nearly a quarter of a century alternately the Treasury of the United States and the treasury of the Republican national committee. [Applause.]

The first of these prejudices was that of the Republicans in the rural communities against the Democratic city of New York. Because the city gave great Democratic majorities they had been taught and they came to believe that the great mass of the population of that city was made up of wicked and designing persons, without principle or patriotism, who, in their corrupt desire to overrule the wishes of the respectable voters in the country, habitually committed frauds at elections which resulted in enormous Democratic majorities. The second of these prejudices carried with it the belief that somewhere in the South there were great numbers of white and colored Republicans who, if they could be allowed to vote without fear or restraint, would carry for the Republican party a number of States then solidly Democratic.

When, therefore, the author of this scheme presented to the leaders of the Republican party in Congress a plan by which he proposed to reduce or perhaps wipe out altogether the Democratic majority in the city, the vote of which controlled the most important doubtful State in the Union, and to bring out in the South a Republican vote which should carry many Democratic States into the Republican party, his proposal was hailed with delight; the scheme was framed into legislation and he was promptly put in charge of the machinery which he had conceived. His plan was an excellent one for the only object for which it was designed, namely, for his own personal profit. Part of what it has done for him may be easily seen in the Treasury records which are printed in the report of the investigating committee of the Fifty-second Congres, over which I had the honor to preside. And if the record of the hundreds of thousands of dollars which he had obtained in five national campaigns from the Republican national committee were obtainable all the rascals in Christendom would view his performances with the sincerest envy. [Laughter and applause.] What his plan did for the Republican party may be best seen in the result of the election last fall, while his system was in full force, of a Democratic President, a Democratic Senate, and a Democratic House of Representatives, elected by immense majorities in the city and the States which he had contracted to control. [Applause.]

So far as the city of New York was concerned the enactment of these laws was part of the methods adopted by the short-sighted, unreasoning, and incapable men who of late years have controlled the policy of the Republican party in relation to the affairs of the city of New York. Because the city was Democratic it was attempted to rule the island of Manhattan as if it were a conquered province. At Washington and at Albany Republican legislation was invariably hostile to the city of New York, and it is largely because of this hostility, manifested in every possible spirit and in every possible form, that the intelligent voting population of that city has gone by a vast majority into the Democratic party, whose ranks are filled now to overflowing with men who came to them from the Republicans, driven out by Republican hostility to the city in which they lived.

For twenty years the Republican party, more violent against the city from year to year, when it had power at Albany, by its legislation and by all the power of the State government, inflicted every injury which could be conceived upon the Democratic metropolis. The city was made to bear a greatly disproportionate share of the State taxes; it was denied its just and proper representation in the State senate and Legislature. The rights and habits of its citizens were attacked by arbitrary and unjust laws, such as were not made to apply to any other section of the State, and the aspiration of its people for the right to manage their own affairs and to have some kind of home rule, such as existed in the Republican cities of the State, was steadfastly denied them. And in hand with this legislation at Albany went the enactment of these Federal election laws, the very design of which was to control by force and influence by bribery the conduct of elections in the city. [Applause.]

Because New York was a Democratic city all of the dearest interests of its inhabitants were attacked by legislation hostile to the whole town. There never was a more short-sighted policy displayed in politics. The result was the inevitable result. Thousands of men of intelligence, influential in the Republican party, resented these attacks upon their city and upon their own financial and personal and political interests, and joined the Democracy in its fight for home rule and fair play for their own town. These men, driven out of the Republican party under these circumstances, have made the city and the State in which they live more strongly Democratic in sentiment from year to year, until now the Republican party has as much power and influence in the city of New York as it has in the State of Texas. [Applause.]

When Davenport was given these powers, which he has abused; when Mr. Platt and Mr. Hiscock, and the other Republican leaders from the interior of the State, commenced their absurd attempt to legislate New York into a Republican city the Republican party had three or four members of Congress from the city at Washington, numerous members of assembly and the senate in the Legislature at Albany, a dozen distinguished Republican lawyers in high judicial places on the bench of the different courts, and a strong minority representation in the local government, and the board of alderman. As a result of the policy which I have described, and the performances of Davenport under these Federal election laws there are at this time no Republican members of Congress from the city; nor are there any in the adjacent communities of the three States of New York, Connecticut and New Jersey close to the metropolis and where the influence of New York is felt. [Applause.] The thirty members of the Legislature and all the senators who represent the city are Democrats.

The Republican party has no representation whatever in the local government and has lost every place on the bench but one, which is filled by a distinguished jurist in whose reëlection the Democrats cordially and willingly joined. [Applause.] One may well say to the Republican leaders who have wrought this ruin of their party in the State and city of New York, as the distinguished gentleman from Maine says to the Democratic party in his regular monthly lectures to us on our conduct, "What a spectacle you present." [Laughter and applause on the Democratic side.]

In fact, the attachment of the people of the city of New York, formerly much divided on political issues, to the cause of Democracy became so evident and awakened such feelings of hatred and resentment against the city, that the last State campaign was waged by the Republicans solely on the lines of an attack upon the city of New York, its local government, the intelligence and the morality of its people, and its right to local self-government. Headed by Mr. Fassett, the candidate for governor and one of the very men who in the State Legislature had attacked and injured in every possible way the chief city of his State, a campaign was made in which the prejudices of the country against the city were sought to be aroused and the rural voter entreated to rally to the defense of the State against the city.

The spirit of that campaign is best shown by the remarks of Mr. Owen, of Indiana, formerly a member of this House and afterward appointed to office by Mr. Harrison, which were often quoted in that campaign, and are to be found on page 1610 of the RECORD of the Fifty-second Congress:

> New York is a foreign city on American shores. The foreigner who comes to New York is flung into a tenement house. He has no opportunity to catch the genius of American institutions. His children do not learn the English language; employers pay him pauper wages; and with his hopes in America blasted, he lives on the dangerous line of disappointment and poverty. He can not make a good citizen. [Laughter on the Democratic side.]

Mr. Speaker, I know something of the foreign-born residents of the city of New York and of their thrift, prosperity, and success. No one is more willing than I am to exclude all undesirable elements of immigration, but for one I resent the attack upon our naturalized citizens of which these laws are a part and the attacks upon our city, which are exemplified by the remarks of Mr. Owen. [Applause.]

If no foreigners had ever arrived in this country no one would be here now, except the Indians and the ancestors of Mr. Owen, of Indiana. [Laughter.] We are all the descendents of men who were "foreigners" when they came here. They cleared the forest, they established the town meeting, they laid the foundation of our Republic—

> She that lifts up the manhood of the poor,
> She of the open soul and open door,
> With room about her hearth for all mankind!

[Applause.]

When did New York become a "foreign city?" Was it when the first Congress met there at the corner of Wall and Nassau streets, and when Washington lived in Pearl street? Was it when her seamen fought the battles of the war of 1812, or when her soldiers led the triumphant advance into the City of Mexico? Was it when her militia saved Washington in 1861, or when the long procession of her regiments answered every call of the nation in the civil war? Was it when her women organized and maintained with hundreds of thousands of dollars the sanitary commission to care for the sick and wounded, and her bankers gave the Government the loans needed to carry on the war? Or was it when, in 1889, with the flag on every house, with the school boys in line, with patriotic music, and with a pomp and circumstance never seen before in this country, she celebrated the inauguration of the first President? [Applause.]

These appeals to the Tioga County farmer to rise in his might and save the State from city misrule and corruption, this assumption that the people in Chemung County are more patriotic and more honest than we are, and know better than we do how we should live and be governed, and how much money we should spend on our own city, are so many insults to each of us. When the Republican party had purposes beyond personal profit and principles instead of a price-list for a platform, these absurdities were unknown. [Applause.]

It is absurd to describe the people in New York as unintelligent. They have built up the best common-school system in the State, and have the best schools of medicine, of law, of theology, of science, of painting, and of music in the United States. They have the best newspapers and magazines in the world. New York is the market for intelligence in this country. If a citizen of Tioga County writes a book, where does he take it for criticism or recognition?

It is absurd to call them dishonest. They borrow money on their bonds cheaper than any county or village in the State can get it, and there is no Republican city in the country whose credit is so good. The New York merchants and bankers carry the finances of all the country counties, and are everywhere trusted and looked to for help.

It is absurd to say that they have no civic self-respect. They have chosen for themselves a judiciary, for instance, by popular election, which is celebrated all over the United States for its learning and its integrity. No city in the civilized world has judges whose decisions are more widely respected and more frequently followed than those chosen in the city which the Republicans say is so corruptly governed. [Great applause.]

If our city government were what the Republicans in this debate say it is, the people would leave Manhattan Island. Instead of that they leave the Republican country districts to come to us. Mr. Platt's county of Tioga, where he reigns supreme, lost in population over 2,000 between 1880 and 1890. In those ten years more than a quarter of a million people came to New York to live, and made their homes under this city government which the Republicans here pretend to be so frightened about. These people came to us from all over the United States, as well as from Europe. They and their children love this country, honor its flag, and would fight in its defense as readily as would any countryman in the State. And they will teach Mr. Davenport and his allies on this floor that no one can interfere with their interests and insult their good name without punishment. [Applause.]

Mr. Speaker, we who live in that city know well that the most valuable possessions of the city of New York are not in her municipal wealth, her noble parks, her well-managed charities and schools. They are not in the treasures of art in her Metropolitan Museum. They are not in her wonderful position, situate between the most beautiful of rivers and the most delightful of inland seas, at the head of a bay more charming than that of Naples, in which the Statue of Liberty looks down on the commerce of the world. [Applause.] They are not in the riches which her citizens have gathered together within the sound of the chimes of Trinity Church, nor the graceful luxury and magnificence of social life over which shine the lights of Madison Square. They are not in that avenue of palaces which stretches from the Memorial Arch to the Plaza, nor in the treasures of her gold and silver smiths which fill the square where Washington and LaFayette watch, immovable, the tide of travel and of pleasure in the city which they fought together to deliver from its enemies. [Applause.]

New York is rich indeed in all these and in everything which is the type or the result of the highest human civilization, but her greatest possessions are in the inheritance which she got from the Revolution, her share in the memories and in the hopes of the Republic of which she is the metropolis. Her material wealth and her achievements and possessions in architecture, music, sculpture, painting, and in literature are all fruit on the tree of national prosperity whose roots lie deep in our institutions and whose growth has been made possible by the free air and sunshine of national liberty. [Applause.]

She is the city of which we are proud because she is the chief city, not of a colony, but of a nation. She has the commerce of a continent to enrich her because that continent has been conquered and is ruled by her own countrymen, because the flag which flies over her bay floats over the Golden Gate on the Pacific, and the laws which she obeys are in force from the St. Lawrence to the Rio Grande. She is in command of the finances of a continent because a National Government has given to the whole country one system of currency and of banking. She holds her place as the home of literature because a national impulse has driven out all other languages and given to the English tongue the mastery in all our great territory. [Applause.]

No inheritance which New York's wealth can give to the children born in the richest homes on Manhattan Island is worth as much to them as is their birthright of citizenship in our great commonwealth of States, their share in the opportunities of the Republic.

The saying quoted by Emerson, that "Countries are cultivated not as they are fertile, but as they are free," is as true of the city as of the country. The soul of New York's life, the spirit which has made her what she is, was given her when the Constitution of the United States was adopted and the first Congress met in Wall street.

When Washington rode his horse down the Bowery at the head of his veterans, to take possession of the town from which the British had been driven, he brought with him the future greatness of New York. [Applause.]

The history of the chief city of America is the history of American liberty.

She made the first written protest against taxation without representation when her merchants, under Livingston and Bayard, a month before Boston acted, called upon Governor Colden to "join in an endeavor to secure that great badge of English liberty of being taxed only with our own consent." She took the first step toward a union of the colonies when her committee "to seek united action with the other colonies" was appointed October 18, 1764. Her committee of freeholders was the first to suggest, in 1774, the idea of holding the first Continental Congress. She gave to the earliest service of the Republic three of its most valued leaders, Alexander Hamilton, John Jay, and Gouverneur Morris. It would be hard to name, after Washington, three others who contributed more to the establishment of the United States than these three young men from the city of New York.

It is not necessary, Mr. Speaker, for me to discuss the prejudices against the South which, in addition to the hatred of the city of New York, furnished the ground and pretext for this legislation. Gentlemen from that section of the country have given that full and satisfactory extension. I pass, therefore, to the discussion of the operation of the law in the city of New York, merely stopping to quote, as a matter of interest in connection with the result of these laws in the South, and as showing that they had the same result there as with us, the interesting statement of my distinguished friend from Tennessee [Mr. PATTERSON], in this debate:

> When these laws were passed every Representative in both Houses of Congress from the eleven Southern States that were in the Confederacy was a Republican except five. Now, mark that, I repeat it. At the time these laws were passed, in 1870 and 1871, every Representative in Congress from the Southern States was a Republican except five. To-day every Representative from these eleven States in Congress, Senate and House, is a Democrat except four. [Applause on Democratic side.]

Having thus, Mr. Speaker, spoken of the origin of these laws and of the connection between that origin and the city on behalf of which I speak to-day, I desire next to describe their operation in that city. The workings of these laws under the management of their author had steadily grown more and more unpopular with us until the meeting of the last Congress, during the existence of which this system of Federal supervision was to be again exercised in the fall of 1892 in the Presidential election. As we in New York had determined, whenever the two Houses of Congress passed into the hands of the Democratic party, to apply to the National Legislaiure for the repeal of these laws, it seemed necessary for us to get into definite shape and form the legal evidence as to the injustice, the expense, and the partisan use of election machinery which resulted from their operation in our city.

We desired also to put in proper form for presentation to Congress such evidence as might be obtainable as to the frauds alleged to have been committed on the National Treasury by the chief supervisor of elections, together with any denial which he might desire to make of the charges which were made against him in the public press and any evidence which he might produce to substantiate such a denial. We desired, if possible, to take a photograph of the workings of these Federal election laws when in actual operation. We wished to lay before Congress, when we came here for the repeal, a picture as accurate as could be made on the spot and at the time of exactly what happened in our city under these laws.

In other words, Mr. Speaker, we wanted to come here, not with loose allegations or wild denunciations such as our Republican friends have used in this debate against us, but with sworn evidence taken as the court takes it of the facts in the case. [Applause.] Acting on behalf of the city, we desired to prepare her case against these laws and against their author as we would prepare for trial any case to be tried before a jury.

Accordingly, Mr. Speaker, in the first session of the Fifty-second Congress I introduced the following resolution:

CONGRESS OF THE UNITED STATES,
In the House of Representatives, July 19, 1892.

> Whereas it is alleged that gross abuses have existed in the administration and supervision of the election laws by Federal officers within the city and county of New York; and
>
> Whereas it is expedient that all such laws should be administered so as to preserve and not to violate the right of suffrage: Therefore, be it
>
> *Resolved*, That a select committee of five members of the House of Representatives be appointed by the Speaker to inquire into the supervision and administration of the election laws by officers of the United States within the city, county, and State of New York, so far as the same relate to the election of members of Congress, said committee to sit during the recess of Congress and to report to this House at the session thereof beginning on the first Monday of December next; and be it further
>
> *Resolved*, That the said committee be empowered to administer oaths to witnesses and to send for such persons and papers as may be necessary to properly complete the inquiry hereby committed to it, and it is hereby authorized to issue the mandate of the House to compel the attendance of such witnesses and the production of such papers; and be it further
>
> *Resolved*, That the expenses of the investigation above directed shall be paid out of the contingent fund of the House, and the Clerk of the House is hereby directed to advance to the chairman of such committee such amount of money as such chairman may request in sums of $1,000 at a time, said committee to account for and report upon their expenditures thereof.

This resolution was passed by the House on July 19, 1892, and under its terms the Speaker appointed a committee of five members of the House to make the investigation.

Now, Mr. Speaker, our Republican friends in this debate have had a great deal to say about the desire of the South to abolish these laws, and about the Southern sentiment on this floor against their operation. I desire, therefore, to call attention to the fact that I have shown, as I believe conclusively, not only that these laws were originated in the city of New York, but that the movement for their repeal had its origin also in the same place.

What sort of a committee was it, Mr. Speaker, which undertook this investigation? They were not the former slave-owners, the ex-Confederate brigadier-generals, the Southern State rights advocates, who disturb the dreams and fill the waking fancies of my belligerent friend from Maine [Mr. BOUTELLE]. [Laughter and applause on the Democratic side.]

The three Democrats on that committee were all Northern members of Congress; one of them from Connecticut, one of the foremost lawyers of a State which has been the nursery of law and learning in this country for two hundred years [applause]; one of them a lawyer from the State of New Jersey, of an old New York family, highly respected at the bar of both States for his learning and his character. [Applause.] The two Republican members of the committee were an alert, vigilant, and well-equipped lawyer from the central part of New York State, and a distinguished member of Congress from Philadelphia, whose long experience in public affairs makes him a most valuable member of every committee of the House on which he serves. Now, in common fairness, my Republican friends, was not that a committee fairly representative of Northern sentiment? [Applause.]

Now, Mr. Speaker, we started out in New York with a fair proposition to ask for the repeal of these laws only on evidence, openly and fairly taken, and on all the evidence that anybody chose to present. We started out with a fair-minded committee, and in an equally fair and open manner we made the investigation. Sitting in the Federal building in the city of New York, we began naturally and properly by asking the United States officials, whose offices were in that building and who were charged with the execution of the law, to come before us and to testify regarding the acts which they were committing from day to day. The Republican United States district attorney for the southern district of New York came at once before the committee, and in the most straightforward and satisfactory way put at our disposal all the records of his office, his accounts with the Government, the papers in connection with all proceedings in his charge under the law, and sent promptly before us such of his clerks and assistants as we desired to examine.

The Republican United States marshal for the southern district of New York, a well-known and very active political manager whose hostility to the Democratic party is well understood, answered at once the subpœna of the committee in person and gave us from his office, without question, all of the evidence and records which the committee desired to examine. The Republican Secretary of the Treasury, without waiting for a formal subpœna, on the written request of the committee sent to New York the bureau chief in charge of the accounts relating to these matters, with all the original vouchers and documents on file in the Treasury Department. These three high officials had no reason to try to conceal anything from the committee.

The chief supervisor of elections for the southern district of New York, on receiving the same subpœna which the other officials obeyed, took precisely an opposite course. He did what a guilty man always does, if he can, when called into court to face the charges against him. He got out of the way. He refused to come. He kept himself in hiding. He disobeyed the subpœna of the House, and he did it because, if he can help it, he will never consent to be cross-examined by a lawyer as to the money which has been paid him by his party and by the Treasury, and his disposition of that money. He loves to pose as a political martyr, and it would have delighted him to appear before the committee in that rôle were it not for the questions which would have been asked him as to what money he had received and what he did with it.

Mr. RAY. Will the gentleman allow me to ask him a question?

Mr. PAYNE. Will the gentleman allow me to ask him a question?

Mr. FITCH. No, not now. I did not interrupt you. Now, as to what happened in that committee——

Mr. RAY. I would like to ask the gentleman a question.

Mr. FITCH. My friend has stated his views very fully, and I desire now to state mine without interruption.

Mr. PAYNE addressed Mr. FITCH.

Mr. FITCH. I am speaking to my friend [Mr. RAY].

Mr. RAY. I want to know whether you will allow me to ask you a question?

Mr. FITCH. I prefer to proceed without interruption.

Mr. HALL of Minnesota. He should not allow an interruption.

Mr. FITCH. I know what my friend's question is, and can not yield. I consider Mr. DAVENPORT in the light of a fugitive from investigation and you consider him a much abused Christian statesman. I maintain that he did not dare to state the truth before that committee.

Mr. RAY. Do you know what the truth was?

Mr. FITCH. I decline to yield to my friend. He has had all his time and I have not had mine until to-day.

Mr. RAY. You should not be afraid of the truth.

Mr. FITCH. The truth is to be found in the evidence which was submitted to that committee under oath, and which no doubt has been fully read by members of the House, and which has been fully commented upon in this House. [Applause.]

Why, Mr. Speaker, an innocent man charged with what this man was charged with, if he had any touch of personal honor, would have crossed a continent to face his accusers. This committee sat across the hallway from Davenport's office, within a few feet from where from day to day they took the evidence, were the records of the chief supervisor's office, which the committee demanded and he refused to produce.

I do not propose, Mr. Speaker, at the end of this long debate to review all of the evidence which our committee took; but I desire to call the attention of the House to that portion of the report of the majority of the committee which explains the reasons why the committee recommended to the Fifty-second Congress the repeal of these laws. I quote from the report of the committee as follows:

The evidence taken before the committee and submitted with this report to the House relates entirely to the administration and supervision of the election laws by Federal officers within the city and county of New York.

It is assumed by the committee that the administration and results of such laws would nowhere appear more clearly or in a better light than in the city of New York.

It is believed that in the largest city in the country, where every class of our voting population is fully represented and where the respective parties have for years made their principal headquarters at important elections, and under the constant publicity given by the best organized and most effective newspaper press of the world, the actual workings of these laws and their good or evil results can be more clearly seen and appreciated and more intelligently judged than is possible anywhere else.

Your committee, after a very careful study of the operations of the Federal election laws before election and on election day in the city of New York, are of the opinion that all of these laws have entirely failed to produce any good results in the direction of the purity of elections or the protection of the ballot box, and have been productive of such serious and dangerous results that they ought at once to be repealed.

The reasons for our recommendation for the repeal of these laws, based on our study of their operation and results in New York, may be classed under four heads. They ought to be repealed—

First. Because they result in no convictions of offenders, and are therefore useless to prevent or punish crime.

Second. Because they cause great expense and are fruitful of constant and continuing frauds upon the Treasury.

Third. Because they are designed to be used and are used only as part of the machinery of a party to compensate voters who are friendly to it, and to frighten from the polls the voters of the opposing party.

Fourth. Because under and by virtue of these laws the gravest interference with the personal rights and liberty of citizens occur, and voters are punished by arrest and imprisonment for their political opinions.

In considering the first point above mentioned, it may be remarked in the first place that these laws are believed to have been, in the main, drafted and their enactment brought about by the present chief supervisor of elections in the southern district of New York. If anyone in the country was able to administer them in such a manner as to get good results from them the author of the system certainly ought to have been. Through most of the time during which he has held his position the National Government has been fully in accord with him and willing to aid him with all its power and resources. He has drawn from the public purse vast sums of money for his compensation in the administration of these laws and for the employment of thousands of deputies and assistants. He holds his office by a tenure which makes him practically independent of any criticism or danger of removal. He not only holds this office of chief supervisor of elections, but he has also had himself appointed a United States commissioner, so that he can sit as an examining magistrate.

With the power of the Government behind him and with the money of the Government to use, he has managed for years a detective bureau, by means of which he has sought to get proof of the crimes which he has claimed existed in the city of New York. When in his first capacity, as a detective, he had obtained such proof as he wished to use, he then in his second capacity, as a public prosecutor, issued the warrants for the arrest of the alleged criminals. Sometimes he gave these warrants to the United States marshal to be executed, and sometimes in a third capacity, as a sheriff, he seems to have made the arrest of the accused parties through his own deputies Then in his fourth capacity, as a United States commissioner, sitting as a magistrate, he has heard his own charges against the prisoner which he presented to himself as judge by himself as prosecuting attorney, and has decided himself upon their guilt or innocence.

In this way he has arrested many hundred persons at each election. This is not at all difficult under these laws. He has merely to decide on the names of the parties whom he desires to arrest or to keep from voting and issue his warrants for their arrest. But in order to have any of these persons indicted or convicted it is necessary for him to take his alleged evidence before the grand jury, and to try his case before a judge and jury in open court, and without the special advantages which up to this point the Federal election law has given him. He must then have a case. At this point he has invariably failed. With all this machinery in the hands of its inventor and the use of unlimited money the law has resulted in nothing so far as the conviction of offenders is concerned.

During the entire time covered by the examination of the committee there has not been one conviction for illegal voting in the southern district of New York in the United States courts, and under these laws. It is therefore clear that these laws do not result in the punishment of any crime, and they ought therefore to be repealed.

The second reason why, in the opinion of the committee, the law should be repealed is that it causes immense expense, and is purposely so arranged that there is no supervision over the cost, no limit to the amount expended, and no proper responsibility for the payment of the bills.

It is impossible to report upon the exact cost of the system, for the reason that the Treasury Department is unable at this time to state it. The witness Ferrell, sent by the Department before the committee, estimated the expense for this year at $1,000,000, but it is clear from his evidence that he had no accurate knowledge of the amount, which will doubtless be much more. When it is seen that the payments for the personal compensation of the chief supervisor in the southern district in New York for his services as supervisor and commissioner, entirely aside from the payment of his deputies and aside from the fees and disbursements, and the compensation of deputies of the United States marshal, have amounted during the present Administration to a sum exceeding $107,000, the abuses under these laws to which your committee desire to call attention will be plain. This amount will doubtless be increased by a further very large payment, the amount of which your committee is unable to ascertain, which has been demanded and is expected by the chief supervisor from the Treasury Department before the close of the present Administration.

In connection with these payments, attention is called to the fact that from March, 1885, till May 17, 1889, during which time a district attorney was in office who desired to examine these bills, the chief supervisor never presented a bill, preferring to go without the money sooner than submit to examination. As soon as the present district attorney came in the bills were presented and approved and promptly paid.

The third reason why the law should be repealed is that, in the judgment of the committee, it is used mainly for partisan purposes. It is believed that this will be admitted to be true in the city of New York by everyone who has any knowledge of the facts, and that an examination of the evidence taken before this committee will convince any impartial person that under these laws the power and the funds of the Government are freely used with the direct intention of affecting the result of elections.

It is not deemed necessary to enter into an extended argument to show that this should not be allowed.

The establishment for election purposes in the interest of one party of an army of political workers as large in number in the United States as the regular Army of the United States, and the giving to them the badge and authority of the National Government, is an act of arbitrary power without a precedent in the history of our country. No political party temporarily in power ought to have any such advantage over its opponents, and the majority of this committee would be as unwilling to see any member of their own party in the city of New York clothed with the power now given to the chief supervisor and marshal as they are to allow the present incumbents to remain in the possession of these unfair advantages.

The law was designed for partisan advantage. It is perhaps fortunate that its execution in the city of New York has been mainly intrusted to one of a common class of political adventurers whose only real object has been to get money out of politics. In the hands of a man of ability who cared little for personal profit, but who was devoted simply and without scruple to the success of his party, it might have been the source of much more serious trouble. The powers which it confers should not under our system of government be intrusted to anybody. In the interest of the people, whose right it is to act with any of the parties or in opposition to any of them, it ought to be repealed.

The fourth and final reason why these laws ought at once to be repealed is that under them great numbers of innocent persons have been and are at every election deprived of their liberty and interfered within the exercise of their undoubted right to vote. These facts are not to be disputed. They are known to all men in New York, and were brought to the personal knowledge of the committee and proven beyond question. The fact that all of the great number of citizens who were arrested during all these years were, with the exception of two, discharged as innocent after judicial investigation, is conclusive legal proof of the falsity of the charges. That most of them were discharged by the very magistrate who had caused their arrest shows the charges to have been not only false, but malicious.

Any system of laws under which, for any reason, citizens entitled to vote can be systematically arrested, held until their opportunity to vote is gone, and then discharged without redress, should have no place in the statutes of the United States.

Perhaps, Mr. Speaker, it will be of interest to the House to have some of the exact evidence in regard to two matters mentioned in the last paragraphs of the report which I have cited. Our opponents in this debate have insisted that these marshals were worthy and respectable officers of the law engaged in preventing from voting, by arrest, great numbers of unnaturalized foreigners in the city who endeavored to vote. I propose to show by the sworn evidence of the people whom they arrested that the persons thus deprived of the right to vote at the last election were almost all native citizens, born on the island of Manhattan.

And I propose, further, to show by a statement, giving names and addresses and police-court records, that many of these Davenport marshals, whom the Republicans pretend were appointed to defend the purity of the ballot box, were notorious criminals. As to the first point I read portions of the evidence, as follows:

William Weir, called by the committee, being duly sworn, testified as follows:

By Mr. FITCH:

Q. What is your name?
A. William Weir.
Q. Where do you live?
A. West Fifty-second street, No. 649.
Q. How long have you lived in that house?
A. About nine years in that house; seven months in the one room I am in now.
Q. But nine years in that house?
A. Yes, sir.
Q. Are you well known in that neighborhood?
A. I have been seventeen years in the same block; never lived out of it a day in my life—between Eleventh and Twelfth avenues.
Q. Your case was heard before Commissioner Shields this morning?
A. Yes, sir.
Q. What decision did the commissioner render?
A. Just asked me the same questions that you have asked me and discharged me.
Q. Are you a native-born citizen?
A. Born right here in New York.
Q. You brought him personally down before Commissioner Deuel, did you not?
A. Yes, sir; this gentleman took me over there and he came down to take him.
Q. Do you know the name of the commissioner before whom you went?
A. No, sir; he told me to bring him down to the United States court.
Q. Who gave you this paper on which you made the arrest?
A. This man inside of the poll.
Q. You don't know his name?
A. No, sir.
Q. Do you know where the polling place is?
A. Yes, sir.
Q. Where is it?
A. The twenty-ninth election district.

Next take John W. Powers:

By Mr. FITCH:

Q. Where do you live?
A. 25 Bowery.
Q. Are you a naturalized or native citizen?
A. Native citizen.
Q. Where were you born?
A. Madison street, this city.
Q. Lived here all your life?
A. Yes, sir.
Q. When you were arrested to-day what was done with you?
A. I was brought down here before the commissioner and discharged.

Take now the case of Patrick McKenna. Bear in mind what my friend [Mr. PAYNE] has said about the class of vagrant people without home or occupation that we want to have vote in New York but who are prevented by these laws:

Patrick McKenna, called by the committee, being duly sworn, testified as follows:

By Mr. FITCH:

Q. Where do you live?
A. 261 West One hundred and twenty-third street, city.
Q. How long have you lived there?
A. In that number about twelve years.
Q. How long have you lived in that vicinity?
A. Thirty-five years.
Q. What is your business?
A. Horseshoer.
Q. Are you well known in the vicinity?
A. Yes, sir; everybody in my neighborhood knows me.
Q. How long have you been in business in that vicinity?
A. About thirty-five years for myself.

And, Mr. Speaker, let me say that I have known him personally for many years and that he is well known and respected in Harlem.

Q. Did you register at this election?
A. Yes, sir.
Q. Where?
A. In Seventh avenue, between One hundred and twenty-third and One hundred and twenty-fourth.
Q. You registered before in that election district?
A. Yes, sir; very, very often—frequently.
Q. And voted?
A. Yes, sir; for the last thirty years.
Q. So that your name was on the register's polling list of that district for several years?
A. Yes, sir; I have had charge of that district for thirty years.
Q. What do you mean by having charge of that district?
A. In a political sense; I am captain of that district now.
Q. You mean for Tammany Hall?
A. Yes, sir.
Q. Were you arrested to-day?
A. Yes, sir.
Q. What were you charged with?
A. For false registration. I own the house which I registered from.
Q. Had you voted when you were arrested?
A. No, sir.
Q. Have you voted yet?
A. No, sir; I am going to, though.
Q. After your arrest you were brought before a United States commissioner?
A. I was fetched up to One hundred and forty-fifth street first, and from there down here.
Q. Before what commissioner were you taken?
A. Before Commissioner Shields downstairs.
Q. And you were examined?
A. Yes, sir; and he discharged me.

Daniel McCarty, called by the committee, being duly sworn, testified as follows:

By Mr. FITCH:

Q. Where do you live?
A. 354 East Tenth street, rear house, top floor.
Q. How long have you lived there?
A. Ten or eleven years.
Q. Are you a naturalized or native-born citizen?
A. Born here in the United States.
Q. Did you register at this election?
A. Yes, sir.
Q. Did you give your address at the number you have mentioned above?
A. Yes, sir.
Q. Were you arrested?
A. Yes, sir.
Q. When?
A. This morning.
Q. Before you had voted?
A. Yes, sir; I was going to vote and they challenged me and I cast my vote.
Q. And then you were arrested?
A. Yes, sir.
Q. What were you charged with?
A. For not living in the directions I gave.
Q. Charged with illegal registration?
A. Yes, sir.
Q. You were brought down here before Commissioner Shields?
A. Yes, sir.
Q. Did he hear the case?
A. Yes, sir; I guess he did.
Q. He heard the case and discharged you, did he not?
A. Yes, sir.
Q. Had you any knowledge that you were to be arrested to-day?
A. No, sir; not a bit of it.
Q. Did you register on the first, second, or third day of registration?
A. It was the second, I think.
Q. You think you registered on the second day of registration?
A. I can't tell that for sure.
Q. You never heard until to-day that you were charged with false registration?
A. No, sir; not until I went in there?

Now, the value of all this talk about the persons arrested being criminals or disreputable people is, perhaps, as well illustrated by the next case that I am going to cite as by any in the list:

TESTIMONY OF RAFFAEL A. JOSEPHSON

Raffael A. Josephson, called by the committee, being duly sworn, testified as follows:

By Mr. FITCH:

Q. Where do you live?
A. 287 Madison street.
Q. Are you a naturalized or native citizen?
A. Naturalized.
Q. When were you naturalized?
A. Five years ago.
Q. How long have you lived in the State of New York?
A. All the time; I have lived here eleven years.
Q. How long have you lived in the city of New York?
A. Over six months.
Q. How long have you lived from where you registered?
A. About two months; I moved there the 26th of September.
Q. What is your business?
A. Well, my business; I am a minister.
Q. You are a rabbi?
A. Yes, sir.
Q. Were you registered at this election?
A. Yes, sir.
Q. Where did you register?
A. In my district, on the corner of Madison and Montgomery streets.
Q. Did you register on the first day, or the second, or the third day of registration?
A. On the second day, I guess.
Q. If you don't know—it was the second or third day, perhaps?
A. Yes, sir.
Q. Before to-day, did anybody tell you that you were going to be arrested for false registration?
A. No, sir.
Q. You were arrested to-day, were you?
A. Yes, sir.
Q. When you came to vote?
A. When I came to vote I was led away and a man told me "I want to arrest you."
Q. Did you vote?
A. Yes, sir.
Q. And you were arrested then?
A. Yes, sir; I was.
Q. You were brought before Commissioner Shields?
A. Yes, sir.
Q. And your case was heard?
A. Yes, sir.
Q. And what was the result?
A. I am discharged.

Mr. WARNER. I should like to know whether this commissioner, who appears to have connived at all these "Tammany outrages" by discharging these men, is a Republican or a depraved Democrat?

Mr. FITCH. He is a Republican and has been one all his life.

A MEMBER. A "depraved" Republican?

Mr. FITCH. He is not a depraved Republican, because he is one who knows the law and who endeavors to administer it justly.

Mr. WARNER. And was he immediately deprived of his place by the Republican judicial officers after he had perpetrated these outrages in letting those men go whom Davenport had arrested?

Mr. FITCH. He was not. On the contrary he has been promoted by the judges of the United States courts, who, I hope, have seen that his conduct in these matters has been that of an upright magistrate. [Applause.]

Now, here is the testimony of John S. Leach:

Q. Where do you live?
A. 34 East Twelfth street.
Q. How long have you lived there?
A. The three past years I have registered from there and voted from there.
Q. You registered from there last year?
A. Yes, sir; and voted.
Q. So that your name was on the registry list or the polling list from that place?
A. Yes, sir.
Q. What is your business?
A. Upholsterer, and I work for Mr. Brown, and have done work for him for the last three years.
Q. Are you a naturalized or a native citizen?
A. Native.
Q. How long have you lived in the city of New York?
A. Fifty-one or fifty-two years.

Mr. McCALL. May I inquire of the gentleman from New York——

Mr. FITCH. I think I must decline to yield. Gentlemen on the other side were not interrupted to-day; and I prefer to proceed in my own way.

Mr. McCALL. I simply desire——

Mr. FITCH. I decline to yield to my friend.

I wish also to call attention to the testimony of Edward Flieger:

Q. Where do you live?
A. 53 Attorney street.
Q. How long have you lived there?
A. Between four and five months; I should iudge about five months.
Q. Are you a native or naturalized citizen?
A. Native; born here.
Q. How long have you lived in the city of New York?
A. Twenty-two years.
Q. What is your business?
A. I work for the fifth district court marshal.

He is a court officer of the city of New York, entrusted with the service of papers and the collection of money. He was arrested and was immediately discharged.

Now I turn to the testimony of John Barry:

Q. Where do you live?
A. 15 James Slip.
Q. Are you a married man?
A. Yes, sir.
Q. Live there with your wife?
A. Yes. sir.
Q. How long have you lived there?
A. Five months.
Q. Are you a naturalized or native citizen?
A. I was born here.

This man was arrested in the same way, and immediately discharged by the magistrate on an investigation of the facts.

Here also is the testimony of Alfred Newell Fuller. And if I ever saw a cultured gentleman and recognized him on sight, it was this man. I read his examination:

TESTIMONY OF ALFRED NEWELL FULLER.

Alfred Newell Fuller, called by the committee, being duly sworn, testified as follows:

By Mr. FITCH:

Q. Where do you live?
A. 17 Lafayette Place.
Q. How long have you lived there?
A. Since the 14th day of October, 1891.
Q. Have you ever registered from there before?
A. No, sir; but I have been a citizen of New York since 1885.
Q. What is your business?
A. A private tutor preparing boys for college.
Q. Did you register at this election?
A. Yes, sir; the 29th day of October.
Q. Before to-day did you have any intimation that you were to be arrested for any crime against the election laws?
A. No, sir; not until I presented myself to cast my vote.
Q. Have you voted?
A. No, sir; I have been over to Jefferson Market since half-past 1.
Q. You presented yourself to vote to-day?
A. Yes, sir; twice.
Q. Were you arrested?
A. Yes, sir; twice.
Q. Please restrict yourself to the arrest by the United States marshal; you were arrested by a United States marshal?
A. Yes, sir.
Q. Did he show you any warrant?
A. Yes, sir.
Q. What was the charge against you?
A. False registration.
Q. And you were brought before Commissioner Shields?
A. Yes, sir.
Q. And your case was heard?
A. Yes, sir.
Q. What was the result?
A. Discharged, with laughter, by the commissioner.
Q. Was there any foundation for any such charge against you?
A. No, sir; I can not see any. I left town on the 1st of July, and have been in Newport and Long Island, and I returned on the 30th of September; and I have been in the city ever since; although I am out of the city a great deal that is my residence.

Gentlemen talk about the "slums;" they talk about the degraded class of people who undertake to vote in the city of city of New York and whom Davenport arrests. I have cited the case of a minister of the Hebrew gospel; I have cited the cases of these other men, reputable citizens, born in the city of New York. Here is the case of a scholar, a gentleman who is engaged in the business of preparing boys for college, a man whose appearance was as significant of the character of a gentleman as that of anybody whom I have ever seen; he is dragged from the polling place and taken before a magistrate, who immediately upon investigation discharges him as entirely innocent.

Again, here is the testimony of Joseph Higgins:

Q. Where do you live?
A. 69 West Twenty-ninth street.

* * * * * * *

Q. Are you a native or naturalized citizen?
A. I was born in New York City.

Now, it is to be borne in mind that the great majority of the people whom we happened to have before us were people whom we caught "on the fly," because we could not tell whom Davenport would arrest. When arrested, they were brought before the commissioner. We caught them, as it were, by accident; we photographed this thing on the spot, as it happened. We found that about two-thirds of all the people whom Mr. Davenport arrested were native citizens, born in the city where they were trying to vote.

Now, Mr. Speaker, these are matters of public record in the city of New York. I am speaking of facts that took place in the broad light of day, not somewhere down in the South, where there is perhaps some question about what happens, but right under the blaze of the calcium light of the New York press, the strongest and the best and most independent press in the world; right at the center of the great business heart of this country, the center of its intelligence, in the greatest of Northern cities. [Applause.] These things have happened for years. We have brought you the proof of it. Therefore we come to you and ask you in our behalf and for our aid to repeal these laws. They were aimed at us. They have been tried on us.

Now we ask you to help us to get rid of them. We ask to have the laws repealed, not to oblige somebody in the South, not in the interest of the late Confederacy, as my Republican friends suggest, but on behalf of the greatest manufacturing and commercial town on this continent; on behalf of the metropolis of the country, where they have been tried a quarter of a century. We now ask you, now when we have a Democratic President, a Democratic Senate, and a Democratic House of Representatives, to relieve us from these laws forever.

Mr. BROOKSHIRE. Will the gentleman allow me a moment?

Mr. FITCH. Certainly.

Mr. BROOKSHIRE. The table prepared by the Secretary of the Treasury and printed by the gentleman from Illinois [Mr. BLACK] says that there were $1,100,000 expended from July 1, 1876, to June 30 of last year, and of that amount $610,000, or over one-half of it, was expended in the city of New York.

Mr. FITCH. That is true. There is no doubt of it, and if I were permitted by my time and the game was worth the candle it would be easy to show it even more fully.

I have tried, Mr. Speaker, to show the character of the people who were arrested. I desire now to speak of the character of the marshals who made these arrests. I desire to say, first, that of all the disreputable people, of all the ignorant and debased people, whom since my boyhood in the city of New York I have ever seen, these deputy marshals who appeared before our investigating committee were the worst. If they could be ranged up now in front of the Speaker's desk, their appearance alone would pass this bill. There is but one description of them in literature and that is the description of Sir John Falstaff's recruits. [Laughter and applause on the Democratic side.]

Now, to show to the House that it has always been so under this system, I send to the Clerk's desk to be read a statement which appeared in the New York World. That paper, in 1879, when a similar debate was up before in Congress, made some investigations as to these "conservators of the peace and purity," as these men were called, and a statement of the result of that investigation was printed in the CONGRESSIONAL RECORD. It was quoted by the Senator from Connecticut, Mr. Eaton, in a speech, and subsequently by the Senator from Tennessee, Mr. HARRIS, and has never been denied.

Who and what are these conservators of peace and purity?

Theodore alias Mike Anthony, alias Snuffey, of 24 Cherry street, a laborer, 35 years of age, married, and can not read or write. Anthony was arrested by Detective James Finn, of the Fourth precinct, on July 24, 1870, for larceny from the person, and was held in $2,000 bail for trial by Justice Hogan. He was indicted by the grand jury on the charge on the 23d of August last.

Joseph Frazier, of 279 Water street, is a thief and confederate of thieves.

James Miller is the keeper of a disorderly house in the basement of 339 Water street.

James Tinnigan keeps a similar den in the basement of 337 Water street.

James Sullivan, alias Slocum, keeps a disorderly house at 330 Water street, which is a resort for desperate thieves.

Frank Winkle keeps a disorderly house at 337½ Water street. The police are frequently called in to quell fights in Winkle's place, and it bears a hard reputation.

The authorities have appointed one John, alias "Buckey," McCabe a supervisor of the eighth district, Fifteenth ward. He is now under indictment for shooting a man with intent to kill. This precious "supervisor" originated here, and was first known to the police for his dexterity in robbing emigrants. His picture is in the "rogues' gallery" at police headquarters in this city, No. 225. He was known as "Pat Maddon," alias "Old Sow," alias Honsey Nichols, alias Dennis McCabe. His real name is Andrew Andrews. His wife resides in North Pearl street, and the "supervisor" of the eighth district, Fifteenth ward, New York, is down in the directory as a citizen of Albany.

Thomas McIntire, marshal Eighth ward; has been frequently arrested for beating his aged mother; sent several times to Blackwell's Island.

Timothy Lynch, marshal sixth district, Fifth ward; a Washington Market lounger.

Peter Mose, marshal Sixth ward; an habitual drunkard.

John Connor, supervisor first district, First ward; keeps a disorderly gin-mill, resort of lowest characters.

Francis Jordan, supervisor sixth district, First ward; lives in New Jersey; was turned out of the post-office by Postmaster James for bad conduct.

Bernard Dugan, supervisor eighth district, First ward; habitual drunkard. His wife left him on account of his drunkenness, and procured a divorce on that ground.

John Tobin, supervisor ninth district, First ward; arrested about six months ago for grand larceny.

Patrick Murphy, supervisor fourth district, Sixth ward; two years ago distributed fraudulent naturalization papers, and would furnish them to anybody that would promise to vote for Grant.

Edward Slevin, jr., supervisor second district, Fourth ward; has an indictment now pending against him in court of general sessions for cutting a boy named Kilkenny.

Michael Foley, supervisor fourth district, Fourth ward; well-known repeater, voting for anybody that will pay.

James F. Day, supervisor seventh district, Fourth ward; shot at a man in a fight between the Walsh Association and a gang from Water street.

John Connors, alias "Jockey," supervisor third district, Fourth ward; a well-known desperate character.

Michael Costello, marshal Sixth ward; bounty-jumper during the war.

Harry Rice; supervisor thirteenth district, Sixth ward; was connected with the Chatham-street concert-saloon murder, and fled to Nebraska to escape punishment.

Thomas Lane, supervisor seventeenth district, Sixth ward: formerly keeper of a notorious den at Five Points; headquarters of thieves and robbers.

John Lane, supervisor twenty-second district, same ward; was indicted for receiving stolen goods; has served a term in Sing Sing.

Edward Foley, supervisor sixth district, Ninth ward; arrested last year for stealing a watch.

Humphrey Ayers, supervisor eighteenth district, Ninth ward; arrested six years ago for robbing the United States mail.

John Dowling, supervisor nineteenth district, Ninth ward; arrested August 20, 1869, for till-tapping.

James Fitzsimmons, supervisor twentieth district, Ninth ward: arrested August 1, 1868, for robbery.

John Martin, supervisor fifth district, Twelfth ward; arrested a few years ago under an indictment for arson.

Samuel Rich, supervisor fourth district, Thirteenth ward; served a term of two years at Sing Sing for felonious assault.

John, alias "Buckey" McCabe, supervisor eighth district, Fifteenth ward; charged with shooting a man with intent to kill about a year ago.

William P. Burke, supervisor twentieth district, Eighth ward; served his term in the State prison of Massachusetts for burglary; also two years in the New York State prison.

James McCabe, supervisor fourth district, Eighth ward; now confined in the Tombs under indictment for highway robbery.

William Irving, supervisor fourteenth district, Eighth ward; has served a term in Sing Sing prison for burglary committed in the Eighth ward, and has never been pardoned.

Patrick Henry Kily, *alias* Fred Williams, supervisor twenty-second district, Eighth ward; keeper of a house of ill-fame, resort of the lowest and vilest characters.

Patrick Hefferman, supervisor of the tenth district, Sixth ward; arrested some time since for attempted murder.

Frederick Sterringer, supervisor Eighth ward; has been arrested several times for keeping disorderly house.

J. F. Baderhop, supervisor Tenth ward; arrested for murder a few years since.

Ed. Weaver, marshal in Eighth ward; has been but a short time out of State's prison, where he has been serving out his sentence.

Walter Prince (colored), marshal Eighth ward; now in prison awaiting trial for highway robbery.

Andrew Andrews, *alias* Hans Nichols, marshal; panel thief; been sentenced two or three times to State's prison, and has just returned from Blackwells Island.

Mr. VAN VOORHIS of New York. I would like to ask the gentleman what paper that is.

Mr. FITCH. That was published in the New York World, a tolerably well known newspaper, and was repeated in this House, or in the other House, in two separate speeches, and has been published before.

Mr. VAN VOORHIS of New York. Do you concede that all these bad people live in New York.

Mr. FITCH. I am sorry to say that they did live there, and were evidently well known there. Our court records are excellent. I do not know whether or not any of them came there from somewhere else to do this work, but they were the people who were selected by John I. Davenport to arrest our clergymen, college professors, and people in business in order to preserve the purity of the ballot. [Applause on the Democratic side.]

Mr. RAY. Will the gentleman allow me to ask him one question?

Mr. FITCH. I must decline to yield. My time is short.

Having considered, Mr. Speaker, the origin of these laws and our experience with them in operation, I desire briefly in conclusion to touch upon our reasons for their repeal. These reasons are those already quoted from the report of the committee. Let me repeat them, because I desire to emphasize the statement that we in New York do not wish these laws repealed because of any theories in regard to the Constitution or the rights of the States. We want them repealed because of the facts connected with the workings of these laws on our interests and our personal liberty. They ought to be repealed, as the report says:

First. Because they result in no convictions of offenders, and are therefore useless to prevent or punish crime.

Second. Because they cause great expense and are fruitful of constant and continuing frauds upon the Treasury.

Third. Because they are designed to be used and are used only as part of the machinery of a party to compensate voters who are friendly to it, and to frighten from the polls the voters of the opposing party.

Fourth. Because under and by virtue of these laws the gravest interference with the personal rights and liberty of citizens occur, and voters are punished by arrest and imprisonment for their political opinions.

In the course of this debate arguments of great length have been made in regard to the constitutionality of these laws or of any similar legislation. The gentleman from Virginia [Mr. TUCKER], of the committee of which I have the honor to be chairman, in particular, has argued very fully, and as if it were necessary to the repeal, that these laws are unconstitutional, and that the decisions of the Supreme Court of the United States in which their constitutionality is upheld are all wrong. He has been answered very fully by my Republican colleague, Judge DANIELS, whose distinguished career on the highest bench of New York for over a quarter of a century has reflected as much honor upon his State as it has upon him, with whose conclusions my two Democratic colleagues, Dr. EVERETT, of Massachusetts, and Dr. ENGLISH, of New Jersey, perhaps the two men in the House best read in the constitutional history of the country, agree.

Mr. Speaker, I practice law at a bar where any decision of the final courts of appeal in the State and in the nation is held in the highest respect and where it is not the custom to argue the law after the court has announced it or to denounce the court for its failure to follow the views of counsel. I submit that the question of the constitutionality of these laws is not before us. I do not feel, in voting on this question, that I must vote to overrule the Supreme Court in favor of the gentleman from Virginia. If it were constitutional for Congress to enact these laws it is constitutional for Congress to repeal them. I hope to vote in this Congress to repeal many laws about the constitutionality of which there is no kind of question. I am very happy to believe that, in order to understand why a bad law, made for a bad purpose, should be repealed, it is not a condition precedent that anybody should educate himself into the belief that he is a great constitutional lawyer.

In order, Mr. Speaker, to show that we are right in asking for this repeal on the grounds which I have stated and without adopting any particular theory about the Constitution, I call attention to the language of the platform adopted by the national Democracy at its convention at Chicago in 1892 on this subject. There is nothing about the constitutionality of these laws in the platform, although in the next sentence following the mention of them there is a statement in regard to the unconstitutionality of the tariff. The national Democracy did not ask for the repeal of these laws because of anything in the Constitution or on any theory of the rights of the States.

The national convention attacked the system on grounds precisely similar to those which I have stated, grounds on which we can all safely stand, and grounds which are more than sufficient to the justification of the repeal. The wording of the platform is as follows:

[Extract from the Democratic platform adopted at Chicago, June 22, 1892.]

FEDERAL CONTROL OF ELECTIONS.

We warn the people of our common country, jealous for the preservation of their free institutions, that the policy of Federal control of elections to which the Republican party has committed itself is fraught with the greatest dangers, scarcely less momentous than would result from a revolution practically establishing monarchy on the ruin of the Republic. It strikes at the North as well as the South, and injures the colored citizen even more than the white; it means a horde of deputy marshals at every polling place armed with Federal power, returning boards appointed and controlled by Federal authority, the outrage of the electoral rights of the people in the several States, the subjugation of the colored people to the control of the party in power, and the reviving of race antagonism, now happily abated, of the utmost peril to the safety and happiness of all.

On that platform, Mr. Speaker, on the evidence and the report of the committee of investigation in the last Congress, and for the reasons which I have mentioned, the city of New York comes to this House to-day with a request for the repeal of these laws. We ask this repeal in the interest of justice, in the interest of good government, and in the interest of pure and honest elections. The city has earned the right to be heard in a Democratic House. I am sure that her request will not be refused. [Prolonged applause on the Democratic side.]

621

o

Notes

INTRODUCTION

1. In a letter to his sister Anna ("Bye";), June 28, 1896. Roosevelt referred to Fitch as "a contemptible unscrupulous scoundrel, quite shameless if he can only hamper us." Elting E. Morison, ed., *Letters of Theodore Roosevelt* (Cambridge, MA: Harvard Univ. Press, 1951), 545.

2. Edmund Morris, *The Rise of Theodore Roosevelt* (New York: Coward, McCann and Geoghegan, 1979), 83.

3. William M. Tweed headed Tammany Hall and, with others, stole millions of dollars from New York City's Finance Department during the late 1860s and early 1870s.

4. Morris, *Rise of Theodore Roosevelt,* 236–37.

5. Roosevelt spent considerable time ranching and hunting in the Dakota Territory.

6. John Armstrong, *Love, Life, Goethe* (New York: Farrar, Straus and Giroux, 2007), 461.

7. "Police Board and Mr. Fitch," *New York Tribune,* Apr. 15, 1896.

8. The word "Democracy" was commonly used in the nineteenth century as a synonym for "Democratic Party."

9. "Swallow-tail" refers to the tailcoats of men in full evening dress. The term was used to identify anti-Tammany Democrats.

10. Robert McElroy, *Grover Cleveland, the Man and the Statesman,* intro. Elihu Root (New York: Harper and Brothers, 1923), viii–ix.

11. "Ashbel P. Fitch," *New York Times Illustrated Magazine Supplement,* July 16, 1899, 1–2.

12. Albert Bernhardt Faust, *The German Element in the United States* (Boston: Houghton Mifflin, 1909), 2:124.

13. Samuel J. Tilden was a prominent New York attorney, a Democratic power, and the party's 1876 presidential nominee.

14. Kenneth D. Ackerman, *Boss Tweed* (New York: Carroll and Graf, 2005), 236–40.

15. Thomas Carlyle, *Essay on Goethe's Faust,* intro. Dr. Richard Schroeder, trans. Ashbel P. Fitch (New Rochelle, NY: Knickerbocker Press, 1900).

16. Depew was president of the New York Central Railroad, a Republican presidential hopeful, and a noted raconteur.

17. "Hon. Ashbel P. Fitch, the Champion of New York City's Good Name," *New York Uptown Visitor,* Nov. 11, 1893.

1. FOREBEARS AND EARLY YEARS, 1848–1885

1. Frances Manwaring Caulkins, *History of Norwich, Connecticut 1866* (Chester, CT: Pequot Press, 1976), 148–55.

2. Louis B. Mason, *The Life and Times of Major John Mason* (New York: G. P. Putnam's Sons, 1935), 333.

3. John T. Fitch, 1993, *Puritan in the Wilderness: A Biography of the Reverend James Fitch, 1622–1702* (Camden, ME: Picton Press, 1993), 247–50.

4. Roscoe Conkling Fitch, comp., *History of the Fitch Family,* A.D. *1400–1930, A Record of the Fitches in England and America, including "pedigree of Fitch" certified by the College of Arms, London, England* (published privately by the Fitch family, compiled 1930), 2:4, 25.

5. Ashbel B. Parmelee, *Biography of Rev. Ashbel Parmelee D.D.* (Philadelphia: J. W. Lewis and Co., 1880), 5.

6. Parmelee preached on the death of Dewitt Clinton in 1828 and on the death of President William Henry Harrison in 1841, among many other current events. Ibid., 16–17.

7. Ibid., 17.

8. Wheeler added, "Mr. Parmelee was born under the dark shadow of Calvinism and his life and teachings were pervaded by its peculiar tenets. While he was always a cheerful Christian, and on occasion exhibited a refined tenderness, he was intensely and solemnly earnest in squaring away every thought and action by his severe religious standard. . . . In summer's heat and winter's cold, in storm and sunshine, he carried the gospel to the remotest cabin in the hamlet. His aggressive nature and intense convictions of duty impelled him to ferret out evil of every nature, and once found, gave it no quarter. He never avoided but courted discussion of his views upon whatever question. Not over tolerant, he always left upon the mind of his opponent a firm conviction of his entire honesty and sincerity, which his daily life never failed to confer. . . . Mr. Parmelee was no less earnest as a citizen than as a Christian. With him, religion and politics were convertible terms. . . . He prayed for good government and did his best to secure it by voting for it. . . . He was intensely American in his nature. He wrote me a letter in Washington during our late war, a few days before his death that bristled with loyalty and patriotism." "Reminiscences of William A. Wheeler," *Malone Palladium,* 1885.

9. "And the sons of Benjamin were Belsh, and Becher and Ashbel, Gera and Naaman, Ehi and Rosh, Muppim and Huppim and Ard." Gen. 46:21. Also, "the sons of Benjamin after their families: of Bels, the family of the Belaites; of Ashbel, the family of the Ashbelites; of Ahiram, the family of the Ahiramites." Num. 26:30. Fitch, Morton Cross, *The Weekly Budget after Thirty Years* (privately printed, 1920), 233–34.

10. In 1821 "claims were presented for $2,040 against Mooers for the town bounty on wolves of twenty dollars. Jabez Fitch opposed the allowance of the claims against his town." His efforts failed and the bounties were paid, but Jabez's objections have gone into recorded history as one early American citizen's protest against bureaucratic waste and fraud. Duane Hamilton Hurd, *History of Clinton and Franklin Counties, New York, with illustrations and biographical sketches of its prominent men and pioneers* (Philadelphia: J. W. Lewis and Co., 1880), 45.

11. Jabez Fitch, Jr. was examined, approved, and duly licensed to practice physic and surgery in January, 1816. He practiced in the Town of Mooers for many years prior to removing to Dannemora, where he became physician to the state prison. He was deacon of the Presbyterian Church in Mooers from 1838 to 1876. Hurd, *History of Clinton and Franklin Counties,* 330, 133; Morton Cross Fitch, *The Fitch Family at Mooers, New York,* monograph, 1932.

12. Tait came to America from England in the early 1850s. He quickly began frequenting and painting the Adirondacks and did so for years. Tait visited the village of Chateaugay, and he entered into a dispute with his landlord that required the services of an attorney. He found the lawyer, Edward Fitch, and he painted portraits of Fitch's family in lieu of legal fees and obviously had fond recollections of the enthusiastic seven-year-old Ashbel Fitch. Arthur Fitzwilliam Fitch to Ashbel Fitch, Oct. 26, 1900, Ashbel P. Fitch archives.

13. William Seward was New York governor (1839–43), United States senator (1848–61), and secretary of state (1861–69). In late 1856, Fitch wrote Seward on Parmelee's behalf. His blunt letter outlined the birth of the Republican Party in Northern New York, a historic event that was multiplied across the country and led to Abraham Lincoln's nomination for president.

14. Clark was elected New York governor in 1854. He ran on a Republican prohibition ticket.

15. Edward Fitch wrote Seward, "Dear Sir, The first of January, when our newly elected state officers will enter upon the discharge of their official duties, is fast approaching. There will then doubtless be the usual amount of scheming and 'strife' for appointments under the incoming administration. My friend Mr. A. B. Parmelee now holds the office of Canal Appraiser to which he was appointed in March 1855 . . . as the place is one desired and sought by many it is impossible to foresee what influences may be brought to bear. . . . I write you therefore to request as a personal favor to me that you will address the Governor elect on the subject and solicit Mr. Parmelee's re-nomination. Mr. Parmelee and others in this county including myself labored incessantly for the success of the Republican cause in the last campaign and by untiring diligence and labor we brought our vote in the county up from 177 in 1855 to 1470 in 1856 outnumbering our adversaries about 300 . . . considering Mr. Parmelee's devotion to the Republican cause, his ability and integrity and his faithful and able discharge of the duties of the office I think the interests of the cause as well as the state require that he should be re-appointed. His rejection under the circumstances would be equivalent to sending him home in disgrace and would be especially mortifying to me and his numerous friends in this county and gratifying to our opponents who have labored so long and ardently to accomplish his and my overthrow. I hope you will find it consistent with your views of right and duty to comply with my request. Edward Fitch." Parmelee was reappointed, and he remained canal appraiser until 1865. Edward Fitch to William Seward, Dec. 11, 1856, *Papers of William H. Seward,* ed. Janice L. Budeit (Woodbridge, CT; Reading, UK: Research Publications, 1983).

16. United States senators were elected by state legislatures before 1913.

17. Lewis S. Burchard to Lizzie Fitch, Feb. 11, 1907, Ashbel P. Fitch archives.

18. "Dr. Hunter's School Boys," *New York Times,* Aug. 22, 1897.

19. "Will Honor Dr. Hunter," *New York World,* Aug. 22, 1897.

20. "It was about a week ago, when Comptroller Fitch, Corporate Counsel Scott and Charles Putzel were eating luncheon that Dr. Hunter chanced to go into the restaurant in which they were. All three had been pupils of his . . . talk drifted to the old times and to a canvass of what had become of 'the boys' . . . reunion." "School Chums' Reunion," *New York Press,* Aug. 23, 1897.

21. Morton Cross Fitch, *The Weekly Budget after Thirty Years* (privately printed, 1920), 248.

22. Eric Homberger, *Historical Atlas of New York City* (New York: Henry Holt and Company, 1994), 98.

23. Jabez Fitch, Jr. to Ashbel Fitch, date unknown, Ashbel P. Fitch archives.

24. Circa 1900, Ashbel Fitch endowed a stained glass window in the Mooers Presbyterian Church in memory of Jabez Fitch, inscribed: "Jabez Fitch M.D. Deacon of the Church 1838–1876," Ashbel P. Fitch archives.

25. *Encyclopedia Britannica,* 15th ed., s.v. "Jena, city."

26. Ashbel P. Fitch, *Goethe in Youth and Old Age, March, 1891.* Ashbel P. Fitch archives.

27. "In 1815 students at Jena established a *Burschenschaft,* a fraternity that carried on the themes of the nationalist opposition to Napoleon. The three basic principles were national unity, individual freedom and constitutional reform." Armstrong, *Love, Life, Goethe,* 435.

28. "Fitch Had Thirty Duels in Heidelberg," *New York Journal,* May 7, 1896.

29. Frederick M. Binder and David M. Reimers, *All the Nations Under Heaven* (New York: Columbia Univ. Press, 1995), 88.

30. Johann Most was an 1882 immigrant whose favorite panacea was dynamite. Edwin C. Burrows, and Mike Wallace, *Gotham* (New York: Oxford Univ. Press, 1999), 1097.

31. "George in His Carriage," *New York World,* Nov. 3, 1886.

32. "A New Building for the Arion," *New York Times,* Dec. 31, 1885.

33. "Festival of the Arions," *New York Star,* June 17, 1888.

34. "A Liederkranz Festival," *New York Times,* June 24, 1888.

35. This quotation, and others contained herein are drawn from a collection of more than three hundred letters in the Ashbel P. Fitch Archives, written by Ashbel P. Fitch to his wife, Elizabeth Cross Fitch, between the early 1870s and 1900s and are not cited individually.

36. George Ehret, *Twenty-Five Years of Brewing with an illustrated history of American beer, dedicated to the friends of George Ehret* (New York: Gast Lithograph and Engraving Company, 1891), 50.

37. Ibid., 56.

38. "The Qualms of Brewers," *New York Herald,* June 30, 1889.

39. "Honoring Goethe's Memory," *New York Mail and Express,* Apr. 27, 1893.

40. In the Battle of Jena, Oct. 14, 1806, Prussia was vanquished by the armies of Napoleon.

41. The Franco-Prussian war (July 1870–May 1871) was a lopsided affair engineered by Count Otto von Bismarck, the Prussian chancellor. Prussian domination of all Germany was ensured when in January 1871 King William I of Prussia was proclaimed German emperor at Versailles, the former palace of the kings of France. French influence in German states was ended as Germany annexed Alsace, and most of Lorraine and France agreed to pay heavy war claims.

42. "Disciples of Wagner Feasted," *New York Herald,* Apr. 3, 1891.

43. "Stanton-Seidl," *The Musical Courier* 22, no. 14 (Apr. 8, 1891): 338.

44. Faust, *The German Element in the United States,* 2:126.

45. "New York in Congress: One Able Representative in the Delegation." *New York Advertiser,* Aug. 5, 1890.

46. Elizabeth Fitch Ostby, "This I Remember Hearing as a Child," Ashbel P. Fitch archives, Dec., 1951.

47. Lizzie to Fitch, Apr. 8, 1870, Ashbel P. Fitch archives.

48. Elizabeth Fitch Ostby to her sister Ella Fitch Remington. Oct. 10, 1953, Ashbel P. Fitch archives.

49. Elizabeth Cook Fitch (Ostby), born Aug. 17, 1875.

50. Homberger, *Historical Atlas of New York City,* 90.

51. Ibid., 99.

52. Ehret, *Twenty-five Years of Brewing,* 46.

53. "Mill Rock's Inhabitants," *New York Sun,* Sept. 29, 1883.

54. "Crushed Under a Shed," *New York Times,* Nov. 2, 1883.

55. Ackerman, *Boss Tweed,* 358.

56. M. C. Fitch, *Weekly Budget,* 294–99.

57. Matthew Josephson, *The Robber Barons* (New York: Harcourt Brace, 1934), 272.

58. Joanne Reitano, *Restless City* (New York: Routledge, 2006), 98.

2. POLITICS AND THE ROAD TO WASHINGTON

1. "Crushed by a Brewer's Wagon," *New York Sun,* Mar. 25, 1884.

2. "$750 for a Child's Life," *Brooklyn Eagle,* Jan. 10, 1885.

3. "$6,000 for a Child's Arm," *New York World,* Jan. 15 1892.

4. "Auction Sale of Valuable Unimproved Real Estate," *New York World,* June 29, 1883.

5. "Trustees Elected," *Brooklyn Daily Paper,* Feb. 1884.

6. "A Generous Settlement," *Brewers' Journal,* Nov. 1884.

7. "The Congressional Ticket," *New York Times,* Oct. 21, 1884.

8. "The delegates to the convention . . . ," *New York Tribune,* Oct. 21, 1884.

9. "In the Thirteenth Congressional District, another excellent chance for electing a Republican congressman exists. General Egbert L. Viele is the candidate of that faction of Tammany Hall which is led by Charles Welde. Sheriff Hugh Grant, of the Nineteenth Assembly District bitterly opposed General Viele's re-nomination and a violent scene occurred, when, to his astonishment . . . Welde came into the convention from the Twenty-third District and having the most delegates at command re-nominated the congressman. Though the sheriff endorsed him it was a disgusting pill to swallow and his friends won't forget this breach of etiquette." "In the Thirteenth Congressional District . . . ," *New York Times,* Oct. 24, 1886.

10. In 1857 Frederick Law Olmstead became superintendent of Central Park New York, while Viele was chief engineer. In that capacity, Viele proposed a straightforward, functional design for the park that was accepted by Mayor Fernando Wood. When state legislators in Albany stripped Wood of his powers, Olmstead and Calvert Vaux persuaded new commissioners to set aside Viele's plan and to hold a public competition. After the Olmstead and Vaux entry, "Greensward," won the competition, Viele's position was abolished and he was dismissed. "Two years later Viele sued the City of New York and received compensatory damages for unjust dismissal. However, his claim that his first plan for Central Park had been copied . . . was not upheld. Still the embittered Viele always described himself as the true designer of Central Park." Witold Rybczynski, *A Clearing in the Distance: Frederick Law Olmstead and America in the Nineteenth Century* (New York: Scribner, 1999), 155–73.

11. "The distance to High Bridge from the North River at a point where Spuyten Duyvil Creek joins it . . . is twenty-three miles. The Improvement would reduce that to 3½ miles . . . two million tons of merchandise through the cut annually could lead to cost savings of 22 percent to 70 percent according to distance and type of goods shipped. . . . The Improvement would [also] add about ten miles of wharves to New York City's waterfront." "The Harlem River Improvement," *New York Union,* Oct. 1889.

12. "Cutting Itself on Two," *Poughkeepsie Eagle,* Mar. 17, 1890.

13. "River and Sound Wedded," *Troy Telegram,* June 18, 1895.

14. "Gen. Viele Explains," *New York Morning Advertiser,* June 17, 1895.

15. "Ashbel P. Fitch Declines," *New York Tribune,* Aug. 28, 1884.

16. Morris, *Rise of Theodore Roosevelt,* 344.

17. Ibid.

18. Peter Cooper (1791–1883) was an inventor, philanthropist, and civic leader.

19. Faust, *The German Element in the United States,* 1:579–80.

20. Homberger, *Historical Atlas of New York City,* 98.

21. "Brewer Ehret's Boycott," *New York World,* July 14, 1886.

22. Reitano, *Restless City,* 98.

23. "The Boycotted Bakers," *New York World,* Apr. 23, 1886.

24. Burrows and Wallace, *Gotham,* 1098.

25. "Brewer Ehret's Boycott," *New York World,* July 14, 1886.

26. "Tricks of Boycotters," *New York Times,* July 14. 1886.

27. "Unions Turn to Politics," *New York Sun,* July 12, 1886.

28. Ibid.

29. "The brewers of this city . . . ," *New York Times,* July 10, 1886.

30. "A Protest from the Brewers of New York and Vicinity," *New York Herald,* July 10, 1886.

31. "Phases of the Beer Boycott," *New York Sun,* July 15, 1886.

32. "The Boycotted Bakers," *New York World,* Apr. 23, 1886.

33. There was no tariff levied on goods that were "free listed."

34. Allan Nevins, *Grover Cleveland: A Study in Courage* (New York, Dodd, Mead, 1932; repr., Norwalk, CT: Easton Press, 1989), 1:288.

35. "Unexpectedly—There expired . . . ," unknown newspaper, unknown date.

36. Ashbel P. Fitch archives.

37. "A Notable Speech," *Harlem Reporter,* Dec. 31, 1990.

38. "Ashbel P. Fitch for Congress," *New York Uptown Visitor,* Oct. 30, 1886.

39. Ibid.

40. "An Excellent Nomination," *New York Commercial News,* Oct. 1886.

41. Ibid.

42. "In the Thirteenth Congressional District . . . ," *New York Times,* Oct. 24, 1886.

43. "The Young Man's Independent Club . . . ," *New York Tribune,* Oct. 28, 1886.

44. "Mr. Fitch Rapidly Gaining," unknown newspaper, Ashbel P. Fitch archives.

45. "To the Voters of the Thirteenth Congressional District from the Young Men's Independent Club of New York . . . ," letter, Oct. 14, 1886.

46. "Mr. Fitch's Chances in the Thirteenth," *New York Commercial Advertiser,* date unknown, Ashbel P. Fitch archives.

47. Cummings had the singular distinction of being the chief proofreader at the *New York Tribune* when at midnight on February 27, 1860, the day of Abraham Lincoln's memorable speech at Cooper Union, Lincoln appeared in the composing room wanting to proofread the account of his speech. "Drawing a chair up to the table," Cummings remembered, Lincoln "sat down beside" the proofreader, "adjusted his glasses, and in the glare of the gas light read each galley with scrupulous care. When these words were read and corrected, he waited until the revised proof was prepared and brought in, and these he read and made the corrections himself." His "manner," Cummings remembered, "was that of a man accustomed or indifferent" to the "midnight sights and sounds" of a newspaper office. Harold Holzer, *Lincoln at Cooper Union* (New York: Simon and Schuster, 2004), 154.

48. Gabor Boritt, *The Gettysburg Gospel: The Lincoln Speech That Nobody Knows* (New York: Simon and Schuster, 2006), 119.

49. Lincoln was assassinated in 1865, Garfield in 1881, and McKinley in 1901.

50. "First District Troubles," *New York Times,* Mar. 26, 1887.

51. Reitano, *Restless City,* 66.

52. "By far the worst feature . . . ," *Brewers Journal,* date unknown, Ashbel P. Fitch archives.

53. "Citizens Arouse! Citizens Protest!" Unidentified newspaper advertisement, Ashbel P. Fitch archives.

54. "By far the worst feature . . . ," *Brewers Journal,* date unknown, Ashbel P. Fitch archives.

55. "For Music and Beer," *New York Herald,* May 8, 1887.

56. "Beer and Music," *New York Star,* May 8, 1887.

57. Ibid.

58. "Against the Blue Laws," *New York World,* May 5, 1887.

59. "For Music and Beer," *New York Herald,* May 8, 1887.

60. "I attended the Anti-Blue Law convention at Cooper Institute . . . ," *Brewers Journal,* date unknown, Ashbel P. Fitch archives.

61. George received 68,110 votes. Hewitt won with 90,552 and Roosevelt trailed with 60,435. Morris, *Rise of Theodore Roosevelt,* 356–57.

62. "Against the Blue Laws," *New York World,* May 5, 1887.

63. Burrows and Wallace, *Gotham,* 1097.

64. "Power of the Socialists in New York," *Kansas City Times,* July 24, 1887.

65. "Fred Grant at the Head," *New York World,* Sept. 15, 1887.

66. William M. Evarts, Joseph Choate's senior law partner, was chief counsel for President Andrew Johnson during Johnson's impeachment trial, and from July 1868 until March 1869 he was United States attorney general. Evarts served as counsel for President-elect Rutherford B. Hayes, on behalf of the Republican Party, before the Electoral Commission in the disputed United States presidential election of 1876, and he was secretary of state in the Hayes administration. From 1885 to 1891 he was a United States senator from New York. He led the American fund-raising effort for the pedestal for the Statue of Liberty and spoke at its unveiling on October 28, 1886.

67. Levi Morton was former minister to France, future vice president, and future New York governor.

68. "Referring to the delegates elected . . . ," *New York World,* Sept. 11, 1887.

69. Seth Low was mayor of Brooklyn, an independent Republican, and later president of Columbia College and mayor of New York.

70. "Fred Grant at the Head," *New York World,* Sept. 15, 1887.

71. "Liquor Men in Politics," *New York Sun,* Aug. 8, 1889.

72. At the Cooper Institute Fitch declared that if home rule were gained for Ireland, a little of it would do no harm to the city of New York. "Against the Blue Laws," *New York World,* May 8, 1887. At the state Republican convention, "Mr. Ashbel P. Fitch rose amid excitement that had stirred the whole body to support the proposition offered by Mr. Brodsky to demand home rule for the city of New York." "Mr. John E. Brodsky offered . . . ," *New York Times,* Sept. 15, 1887.

73. "Taking Note of It," *Kingston (NY) Leader,* Jan. 4, 1888.

74. "Fitch to State Senator Cornelius Van Cott," Nov. 29, 1887, Ashbel P. Fitch archives.

75. In 1895, the Republican legislature passed a power-of-removal bill that immediately gave Republican reform mayor Strong the power to remove Tammany appointees.

76. "Taking Note of It," *Kingston (NY) Leader,* Jan. 4, 1888.

77. "New York City Republicans," *New York Times,* Jan. 2, 1888.

3. NATIONAL PROMINENCE, TARIFF SPEECH: FIFTIETH CONGRESS, 1886–1888

1. Joanne Reitano, *The Tariff Question in the Gilded Age: The Great Debate of 1888* (University Park: Pennsylvania State Univ. Press, 1994), 1.

2. Nevins, *Grover Cleveland,* 1:379.

3. David S. Barry, *Forty Years in Washington* (Boston: Little, Brown, 1924), 193.

4. Gordon S. Wood, *Empire of Liberty* (Oxford; New York: Oxford Univ. Press, 2009), 102–3.

5. There was an income tax during the Civil War that was rescinded after the war, and another in 1894 that was struck down by the Supreme Court. The income tax was enacted again in 1913 and has been on the books since then. Steven R. Weisman, *The Great Tax Wars* (New York: Simon and Schuster, 2002), 4–5.

6. "The Customs Department," *New York World,* date unknown, Ashbel P. Fitch archives.

7., Six months later Cleveland removed Hedden, his own appointee, amid charges, publicized by the *New York Times* but with which Cleveland concurred, of Hedden's incompetence. Nevins, *Grover Cleveland,* 1:240–41.

8. "Silk Men Excited," *New York Morning Journal,* Nov. 7, 1885.

9. West Virginia Congressman William L. Wilson said the average tariff in 1888 was 47.1 percent. Nevins, *Grover Cleveland,* 1:392.

10. Ibid., 1:377.

11. Ibid., 1:378.

12. Ibid., 1:383. James G. Blaine of Maine served in Congress, was Speaker of the House of Representatives, senator, two-time United States secretary of state, and the 1884 Republican presidential nominee.

13. "Their Maiden Efforts," *Boston Globe,* Jan. 28, 1888.

14. "New-York City Republicans," *New York Times,* Jan. 2, 1888.

15. Watervliet is the site of America's oldest arsenal, founded by Congress in 1813. "Messrs. Ford and Cutcheon of Michigan and Fitch of New-York . . . ," *New York Times,* Mar. 3, 1888.

16. "A Democratic Republican," *Albany Express,* Apr. 20, 1888.

17. Tariff rates on several Southern products were left untouched, while northern products bore a heavier brunt of tariff reduction. Nevins, *Grover Cleveland,* 1:389.

18. Charles S. Baker of New York. *Congressional Record,* 50th Cong., 1st sess., 1888, vol. 19, 5:4328.

19. "1½% on net incomes" plus additional tax rates of 1 percent on incomes of $20,000 to $50,000 escalating up to 6 percent on incomes over $500,000, a maximum rate of 7 percent. Weisman, *Great Tax Wars,* 281.

20. "Good Democratic Doctrine," *New York World,* date unknown, Ashbel P. Fitch archives.

21. *Congressional Record,* 50th Cong., 1st sess., 1888, vol. 19, 4:3690, app. 47.

22. *Congressional Record,* 50th Cong., 1st sess., 1888, vol. 19, 5:4277.

23. "Live Washington Topics," *New York Telegram,* May 17, 1888.

24. "Mr. Fitch Makes a Sensation," *New York Herald,* May 17, 1888.

25. "Tariff Entanglements," *New York Times,* May 17, 1888.

26. "True to His Party's Doctrine," *New York Evening Telegram,* date unknown, Ashbel P. Fitch archives.

27. "Mr. Fitch on the Tariff," *New York Mail and Express,* May 17, 1888.

28. "Mr. Scott in a New Role," *New York Tribune,* May 17, 1888.

29. "Sensible Mr. Fitch," *Lancaster (PA) Intelligencer,* May 18, 1888.

30. "Mr. Fitch and His Party," *Jacksonville (FL) Times-Mirror,* May 18, 1888.

31. "No Protection for the Working and Burgher Classes," *Galveston (TX) News,* May 26, 1888.

32. "Plain Talk from Mr. Fitch," *Washington Post,* May 17, 1888.

33. "Mr. Fitch Congratulated," *New York Herald,* May 25, 1888.

34. Western Union telegram to Honorable Ashbel P. Fitch, June 1, 1888. Ashbel P. Fitch archives.

35. "The Week," *New York Nation,* May 31, 1888.

36. "A Blow Vigorously Dealt," *Albany Argus,* May 18, 1888.

37. "New York in Congress," *New York Advertiser,* Aug. 5, 1890.

38. "Ashbel P. Fitch," *New York Times Illustrated Magazine Supplement,* July 16, 1899, 1–2.

39. "Political Points," *Brooklyn Eagle,* May 29, 1888.

40. "A Renegade Republican," *Chicago Journal,* June 4, 1888.

41. "Representative Fitch of New York . . . ," *Burlington (VT) Free Press,* June 20, 1888.

42. "Mr. Fitch and the Republicans," *New York Tribune,* June 19, 1888.

43. "At length he goes to his own," *Troy Times,* June 20, 1888.

44. "A Radically Divided Party," *Troy Press,* May 17, 1888.

45. "Congressman Ashbel P. Fitch of New York . . . ," *Omaha Herald,* Aug. 16, 1888.

46. "Congressman Fitch Scored," *New York World,* May 30, 1888.

47. "Honest Politics," *Philadelphia Times,* July 12, 1888.

48. "Congressman Fitch Defended," *Albany Evening Journal,* June 6, 1888.

49. Terrace Garden was "the most prominent German gathering place, . . . Terrace Garden was demolished in 1927." Nathan Silver, *Lost New York* (New York: Schocken Books, 1967), 49.

50. "Congressman Fitch Scored," *New York World,* May 30, 1888.

51. "Congressman Fitch's Speech Bombarded," *New York Uptown Visitor,* June 9, 1888.

52. "New York City will choose eight members . . . ," *New York Sun,* June 8, 1888.

53. Chamberlin's was the mecca of Washington political dining. Visitors from New York often stayed at the Arlington Hotel and attended dinners at Chamberlin's.

54. "How the President of a Democratic Club was received in Washington," *New York Sun,* July 16, 1888.

55. Fitch to Andrew B. Humphrey, July 15, 1888, Ashbel P. Fitch archives.

56. "A Victory for Free Trade," *New York Tribune,* July 22, 1888.

57. "The roll call on the passage of the bill . . . ," *Chicago Tribune,* July 22, 1888.

58. "The Reform Club's Work," *New York Times,* July 28, 1888.

59. Faust, *The German Element in the United States,* 2:153.

60. "In Council at Midnight," *New York Press,* July 30, 1888.

61. "Cleveland's Fishing Over," *New York Sun,* July 31, 1888.

62. "After Their Scalps," *New York Press,* Aug. 1, 1888.

63. "Mr. Mills, of Texas, in Harlem," *New York Herald,* Aug. 5, 1888.

64. "A Gloom at Democratic Headquarters," *New York Tribune,* Aug. 10, 1888.

65. "Mr. Fitch and His Party," *New York World,* June 23, 1888.

66. "Congressman Fitch and the Republicans," *New York Evening Post,* Aug. 15, 1888.

67. "No man in the country . . . ," *Kingston (NY) Daily Freeman,* Aug. 18, 1888.

68. Ironically Roosevelt abandoned the Republican Party in 1916 to form his own "Progressive" Party. "Give Us a Fair Count," *Minneapolis Pioneer Press,* Oct. 2, 1888.

69. "Congressman Fitch of New York, who voted for the Mills Bill . . . ," *Savannah News,* Aug. 20, 1888.

70. "Congressman Ashbel P. Fitch of New York . . . ," *Omaha Herald,* Aug. 16, 1888.

71. "Mr. Fitch Resigns," *Utica Observer,* Aug. 16, 1888.

72. "Throwing Off Party Bonds," *New York Times,* Aug. 15, 1888.

73. The term "have to stay at home" meant "defeated." "The Political Campaign," *New York Times,* Sept. 16, 1888.

74. "Four hundred thousand documents were sent out yesterday . . . ," *Chicago Times,* Aug. 15, 1888.

75. "Welcoming Thurman," *Brooklyn Citizen,* Aug. 20, 1888.

76. "On the Horns of a Dilemma," *New York Times,* Oct. 8, 1888.

77. "Both," referred to as "fusion" or "union," meant the nomination by both Tammany and the County Democracy and was tantamount to election. Republicans' main chance of winning in New

York City arose if the County Democracy and Tammany Hall each nominated their own candidate and divided the Democratic vote.

78. William E. Nelson, *Fighting for the City* (New York: New York Law Journal, 2008), 65.

79. Gilroy was an Irish-born grand sachem of Tammany Hall, head of the Department of Public Works, and mayor of New York City. He was named to the Greater New York Commission to replace Ashbel Fitch.

80. "The Political Campaign," *New York Times,* Oct. 14, 1888.

81. "'Sunset' Cox and Ashbel P. Fitch Re-nominated to Congress," *New York Journal,* Oct. 13, 1888.

82. Jerome Mushkat, *Tammany: The Evolution of a Political Machine, 1789–1865* (Syracuse: Syracuse Univ. Press, 1971), 8.

83. William L. Riordon, *Plunkitt of Tammany Hall* (New York: E. P. Dutton, 1963; repr., New York: Meridian, a division of Penguin Books, 1991), 3–6.

84. Alfred Henry Lewis, *Richard Croker* (New York: Life Publishing, 1901), 149–51.

85. "Tammany's Day of Joy," *Baltimore Sun,* July 4, 1891.

86. From the Statue of Liberty, New York Harbor, by Emma Lazarus (1883).

87. "Will Tammany Destroy the Slender Democratic Majority Now Existing in the House of Representatives?" *New York Sun,* Oct. 16, 1888.

88. "Another Plea for Union," *New York Sun,* Oct. 19, 1888.

89. "Harlem's Democratic Barbecue," *New York Star,* Oct. 25, 1888.

90. "Tim's Thorny Footpath," *New York Journal,* Sept. 17, 1888.

91. "James Otis Hoyt Named for Congress," *New York Tribune,* Oct. 20, 1888.

92. "Ex-Republican and Free Trader Ashbel P. Fitch . . . ," *New York Press,* Oct. 24, 1888.

93. "Will Tammany Destroy the Slender Democratic Majority Now Existing in the House of Representatives?" *New York Sun,* Oct. 16, 1888.

94. "Fitch's Canvass Going to Pieces," *New York Tribune,* Nov. 15, 1888.

95. The Pension Bureau reviewed pension claims. Petitions to Congress were generally pension claims that had been rejected by the Pension Bureau. Petitions to the president from Congress were often vetoed by Cleveland.

96. Thomas Adams Upchurch, *Legislating Racism: The Billion Dollar Congress and the Birth of Jim Crow* (Lexington: Univ. Press of Kentucky, 2004), 11–12.

4. NEW YORK'S WORLD'S FAIR LOST: FIFTY-FIRST CONGRESS, 1888–1890

1. "Tariff Reform," *Boston Journal,* Dec. 29, 1888.

2. "All Stars: Big Banquet at the Hotel Vendome," *Boston Globe,* Dec. 29, 1888.

3. Ibid.

4. "The Tariff League: It Does Not Despair of Great Reform," *Boston Herald,* Dec. 29, 1888.

5. "Senatorial Stimulants," *Brooklyn Eagle,* Jan. 26, 1890.

6. "At Irving's Old Home," *New York Evening Sun,* July 23, 1889.

7. "Ashbel P. Fitch Serenaded," *Harlem Local Reporter,* Aug. 3, 1889.

8. Carl Schurz was a German immigrant, Civil War general, friend of Lincoln, senator, cabinet member in the Hayes Administration, editor of the *New York Evening Post* (1881–84), contributor to *Harper's Weekly* (1892–98), lawyer, and author.

9. "Who Will Take Mr. Cox's Seat?" *New York Herald,* Sept. 15, 1889.

10. Samuel W. McCall, *The Life of Thomas Brackett Reed* (Boston: Houghton Mifflin, 1914), 116.

11. Francis Barretto Spinola, born in 1921, was a harbor commissioner during the Civil War and was appointed brigadier general of the Volunteers in 1862. Turner, born in 1861, attended Columbia and went into the ice business before Tammany nominated him for Fiftieth Congress. Turner was not renominated for Congress but became doorkeeper of the House of Representatives for the Fifty-second Congress.

12. "Wanted—A Man: No Small Bore Statesman for Sam Cox's Seat," *New York Evening Telegram,* Sept. 28, 1889.

13. Ibid.

14. Roswell P. Flower, of Watertown, New York, was a two-term congressman (1881–83; 1889–91) and was governor of New York (1892–95). Flower was a successful investor through his firm R. P. Flower and Co.

15. "Who Will Take Mr. Cox's Seat?" *New York Herald,* Sept. 15, 1889.

16. "New York in Congress: One Able Representative in the Delegation," *New York Advertiser,* Aug. 5, 1890.

17. "1492: Let's Celebrate 1892, America's Discovery," *New York Herald,* July 10, 1889.

18. "Harlem's Building Boom," *New York Journal,* Feb. 10, 1889.

19. "1492: Let's Celebrate 1892, America's Discovery," *New York Herald,* July 10, 1889.

20. "Mayor Grant's Big Meeting," *New York Herald,* July 26, 1889.

21. "All for the Great Fair," *New York Sun,* July 23, 1889.

22. "Mayor Grant's Big Meeting," *New York Herald,* July 26, 1889.

23. "They Broke the Slate," *New York World,* Dec. 3, 1889.

24. Ibid.

25. "The Matter in a Nutshell," *New York World,* Dec. 6, 1889.

26. "We've Got to Work," *New York Morning Journal,* Dec. 7, 1889.

27. "New York Must Hustle," *New York Evening World,* Dec. 7, 1889.

28. "New York Won't Lobby," *New York Herald,* Dec. 10, 1889.

29. "Waiting for Congress to Act: No Lobbying for the World's Fair," *New York Tribune,* Dec. 10, 1889; "New York Won't Lobby: No Delegation to Go to Washington Just Yet to Work for the Fair in Congress," *New York Herald,* Dec. 10, 1889; "The World's Fair Bill: It Is Intrusted to the Care of Chauncey M. Depew: New York's Dignified Attitude," *New York Star,* Dec. 10, 1889.

30. Cummings served in the Fiftieth Congress but did not run for reelection. He was elected to fill Cox's unexpired term.

31. "A resolution offered in the House . . . ," *New York Herald,* Dec. 15, 1889.

32. "Mr. Handy's Letter: The Educational Advantages of the Members of the Senate and House," *Philadelphia North American,* Mar. 10, 1890.

33. "Ours! World's Fair Champions of New York and Chicago Meet in the National Capital: Now, We'll Surely Get It!" *New York World,* Jan. 12, 1890.

34. "In the Lead for the Fair," *New York Times,* Jan. 13, 1890.

35. "Brought Home the Fair," *New York World,* Jan. 14, 1890.

36. Ibid.

37. "New York's Bonds for the Big Fair," *New York Herald,* Jan. 11, 1890.

38. "New York Ahead," *New York Herald,* Jan. 18, 1890.

39. "The City of Harlem," *Harlem Reporter,* Jan. 18, 1890.

40. "'Me Too' Finds a Depew Waterloo," *New York Herald,* Feb. 18, 1890.

41. "Have Had Their Say," *Chicago Globe,* Feb. 22, 1890.

42. Ibid.

43. Ibid.

44. "A Boom for the Big Fair!" *New York Mail and Express,* Feb. 20, 1890.

45. Ibid.

46. "Won for Us," *New York World,* Feb. 21, 1890.

47. "New York's Solid Men!" *New York Mail and Express,* Feb. 22, 1890.

48. Ibid.

49. "Have Had Their Say," *Chicago Globe,* Feb. 22, 1890.

50. "The Banquet," *The New York Lumber Trade Journal,* Mar. 15, 1890.

51. Ibid.

52. Hill was mayor of Elmira, New York (1882), lieutenant governor (1883–85) and governor (1885–91) of New York, and United States senator from New York (1892–97).

53. "Look on This Picture and Then on This," *New York Sun,* Sept. 9, 1891.

54. "The Republican Fair," *New York Sun,* Sept. 16, 1891.

55. "Congressman Fitch, who is rapidly regaining . . . ," *Harlem Reporter,* Sept. 19, 1891.

56. The quotations in the succeeding several paragraphs that refer to the Flower demonstrations were taken from the following single source: "Harlem Ablaze," *Harlem Reporter,* Oct. 21, 1891.

5. REPUBLICAN OVERREACH, DEMOCRATIC MOMENTUM: FIFTY-FIRST CONGRESS, 1888–1890

1. "The Great Tariff Fight," *New York Sun,* May 18, 1890.

2. "McKinley a Sure Winner," *New York Tribune,* May 2, 1896.

3. "A Declaration of Independence," *New York Times,* May, 11, 1890.

4. "164 to 142—Tariff Bill Passes the House," *Boston Globe,* May 22, 1890.

5. Margaret Leech, *In the Days of McKinley* (New York: Harper and Brothers, 1959), 142.

6. Named for Senator John Sherman, Republican of Ohio and brother of Civil War general William Tecumseh Sherman.

7. "A Democratic Blunder," *Philadelphia Times,* July 2, 1890.

8. "Responsibility for executing the law was placed with nine federal circuit courts scattered across the country." Albie Burke, "Federal Regulation of Congressional Elections in Northern Cities, 1871–94," *American Journal of Legal History* 14, no. 1 (Jan. 1970): 18.

9. Upchurch, *Legislating Racism,* 165.

10. Nevins, *Grover Cleveland,* 2:460.

11. "Charles H. Turner, congressman from the Sixth District . . . ," *New York Sun,* June 26, 1890; "Charles H. Turner, the iceman . . . ," *New York Press,* June 29, 1890; "Want to Go to Congress," *New York Times,* June 30, 1890.

12. "Sailed for Europe," *Harlem Reporter,* July 5, 1890.

13. "New York in Congress. One Able Representative in the Delegation," *New York Advertiser,* Aug. 5, 1890.

14. "We hope that the tariff reformers . . . ," *New York Evening Post,* Sept. 23, 1890.

15. John R. Fellows (1832–1896) was born in upstate New York and moved to Arkansas in 1850, where he was admitted to the Arkansas bar in 1855. Fellows was a delegate to the Arkansas secession convention in 1861 and served in the Confederate Army at Shiloh and Vicksburg. He was a prisoner of war from 1863 to 1865. He moved to New York City in 1868 and joined Tammany Hall. He was

elected district attorney (1888–90) and elected to Congress (1890–93). He resigned at the end of 1893, when he was again nominated for district attorney and served in that office from 1894 until his death in December 1896.

16. "Congressman Fitch has returned . . . ," *New York Mail and Express,* Sept. 9, 1890.

17. "Considerable talk . . . ," *New York Star,* Sept. 14, 1890.

18. "For Congress," *New York Herald,* Sept. 14, 1890.

19. "Mr. Fitch's Ratification," *Harlem Reporter,* Oct. 29, 1890.

20. "Grant Writes to Noble," *New York Sun,* Oct. 22, 1890.

21. "An Indignant Protest," *New Haven Register,* Sept. 30, 1890. Fitch added, "The apportionment bill giving a representative to every 200,000 people seems to be part of the same conspiracy to defraud us. My own district up in Harlem polls a larger vote than the states of Nevada and Rhode Island combined. New York City has been kept out of her rights in the state legislature and now we are seeing the same policy carried out on a national basis by the Republicans." "Grant Writes to Noble," *New York Sun,* Oct. 22, 1890.

22. When the nation's first Congress met in New York City in 1789, the New York State delegation numbered six members. New York City alone sent eight members to the Fifty-second Congress which would assemble in Washington in December 1891. In raw terms, that appeared to reflect the growing importance of New York City to the nation's affairs. The ratio, however, of New York's members of Congress to the general population declined over the same period from one member for 33,000 people, to one member for 189,000 people in 1890. The under-representation of urban centers has been a successful cornerstone of southern and western political strategy since the nation's founding. "New York's Congressmen," *New York Sunday News,* Oct. 12, 1890.

23. "Public Improvements," *New York Morning Journal,* Oct. 19, 1890.

24. "An Indignant Protest," *New Haven Register,* Sept. 30, 1890.

25. Republicans McKinley (Ohio), Lodge (Massachusetts), and Dalzell (Pennsylvania) and Democrats Fitch (New York), McAdoo (New Jersey), and Clements (Georgia). "North American Review," *Boston Budget,* Nov. 2, 1890.

26. Ashbel P. Fitch, "What Congress Has Done," *North American Review,* Nov. 1890, 523–26.

27. Reed was born in Portland, Maine, in 1839 and graduated from Bowdoin in 1860. He served in Congress (1877–99); was Speaker of the House in the Fifty-first, Fifty-fourth, and Fifty-fifth Congresses; and was a presidential hopeful in 1896.

28. McCall, *Life of Thomas Brackett Reed,* 152.

29. Jim Brunelle, "Speaker of the House," *Down East,* Nov. 2005, 74–77.

30. McCall, *Life of Thomas Brackett Reed,* 158.

31. Fitch reported campaign expenses of $664.86. "Grant's Cash Outlay." *New York Herald,* Nov. 13, 1890.

32. The Fassett Committee, chaired by Republican Senator J. Sloat Fassett, was the Senate committee on cities that heard testimony regarding Tammany bribes and payoffs.

33. The four locations were Madison Square, Beaver and South William Streets, Broadway and Chambers Streets, and Fifth Avenue and Twenty-sixth Street. Lately Thomas, *Delmonico's: A Century of Splendor* (Boston: Houghton Mifflin, 1967), 225.

34. Historian Allan Nevins described Cleveland's honesty as "of the undeviating type which never compromised an inch." It seems unlikely that Cleveland would have referred lightly to Fitch as "one of his warmest friends." Nevins, *Grover Cleveland,* 1:4.

35. "Ashbel P. Fitch among Friends," *New York Times,* Dec. 14, 1890.

36. "Wouldn't Cheer for Him," *New York World,* Dec. 16, 1890.

37. "The Delmonico dinner . . . ," *Elmira Advertiser,* Dec. 19, 1890.

38. "Mr. Steinway's Speech," *New York Sun,* Dec. 18, 1890.

39. Organized in August 1881, the County Democracy was an amalgam of two earlier Democratic organizations led by Tilden, Hewitt, Whitney, and others who resisted Tammany's controlling corruption. The raison d'être of the County Democracy was that it was thoroughly democratic. Its nominating committee consisted of 678 members, one from each election district. It fought Tammany tooth and nail for nearly ten years, but by 1890 it was riven by splintered agendas and the weight of its own complex organization. Mark David Hirsch, *William C. Whitney: Modern Warwick* (New York: Dodd Mead, 1948), 164.

40. "End of Fusion Against Tammany," *New York Sun,* Dec. 20, 1890.

41. "Yesterday in Congress," *New York World,* Feb. 12, 1891.

42. "Gossip of Washington," *New York Evening Telegram,* Feb. 12, 1891.

43. "Fighting Ship Subsidies," *New York World,* Feb. 27, 1891.

44. "Club News and Gossip," *Harlem Reporter,* Mar. 5, 1891.

45. "Ashbel P. Fitch Honored," *Harlem Reporter,* Apr. 11, 1891.

46. "The bowl is one and a half feet high, and measures six feet in circumference. It weighs nearly thirty pounds Troy, or considerably more than three hundred silver ounces. The rim is supported by nine figures of mermaids and the exterior surface of the bowl is richly engraved. 'Presented to Ashbel P. Fitch by friends in the Thirteenth District in commemoration of his third election to Congress, November, 1890, by the largest majority ever given in New York to a candidate for that office, and in recognition of his distinguished services for Tariff Reform, in defence [*sic*] of the rights of the City of New York and in the cause of pure and impartial government for the People of the United States of America. Harlem. April 8th, 1891.' The bowl was made by Tiffany and Co. for the Paris Exhibition of 1888, where it took the prize. It is accompanied by a massive silver ladle." "Mr. Fitch and His Friends," *New York Times,* Apr. 9, 1891.

47. "Ashbel P. Fitch Honored," *Harlem Reporter,* Apr. 11, 1891.

48. In 2001 John Loring wrote erroneously for Tiffany and Co. that the bowl was presented by "anonymous citizens of Harlem." John Loring, *Magnificent Tiffany Silver* (New York: Harry N. Abrams, 2001), 152–53.

49. "Ashbel P. Fitch Honored," *Harlem Reporter,* Apr. 11 1891.

50. "A Quiet Fourth in Gotham," *Philadelphia Press,* July 4, 1891.

51. Nevins, *Grover Cleveland,* 2:482.

6. Silver Beckons: Fifty-Second Congress, 1890–1892

1. Nevins, *Grover Cleveland,* 2:482.

2. "Tammany Hall is now a factor . . . ," *Washington Post,* Nov. 17, 1891.

3. Ibid.

4. "Tammany Will Support Crisp," *New York Tribune,* Nov. 19, 1891.

5. "Seeking the Speakership," *New York Sun,* Nov. 18, 1891.

6. "The Next Speaker," *Harlem Reporter,* Nov. 21, 1891.

7. "The Speakership Canvass," *New York Evening Post,* Nov. 25, 1891.

8. "Not a Break!" *New York Mail and Express,* Dec. 7, 1891.

9. "Chasing Up Congressmen," *New York Sun,* Nov. 21, 1891.

10. "An Unfounded Rumor," *New York Times,* Nov. 13, 1891.

11. "No Choice for Speaker," *New York Tribune,* Dec. 6, 1891.

12. "The Speakership," *New York Times,* Dec. 7, 1891.

13. "Crisp Will Be Speaker," *New York Times,* Dec. 8, 1891.

14. "Crisp Named for Speaker," *New York Tribune,* Dec. 8, 1891.

15. "After a Hard Fight," *Washington Post,* Dec. 8, 1891.

16. "The Democrats of the Ways and Means Committee . . . ," *New York Herald,* Jan. 7, 1892.

17. In practice, Crisp's policy produced too many tariff bills, all hoped-for additions to the "free list." They included "bags for grain made of burlaps," "jute bagging, jute, iron ties and bagging twine," "binding twine made of istle or tampico fiber, manila, sisal grass," as well as more basic commodities such as "coffee, sugar, hides, lumber, salt, tin and tin plate," all items to which the tariff applied. And on it went. Fitch's bill included "casks and barrels of foreign manufacture." All in all there were 120 separate uncoordinated revenue bills introduced "within the last month," virtually insuring that the wheel of progress on tariff reform would grind to a halt. "Why Springer Halts," *New York Tribune,* Feb. 8, 1892.

18. "The *New York Times* wonders . . . ," *Harlem Reporter,* Dec. 12, 1891.

19. "The Brooklyn delegation will fare only tolerably well . . . ," *Brooklyn Standard Union,* Dec. 12, 1891.

20. "It looks to some of us as though Speaker Crisp . . . ," *New York Recorder,* Dec. 11, 1891.

21. "Lopping Off Expenses," *Washington Post,* Dec. 10, 1891.

22. "Cummings Slated for the Fisheries," *Chicago Times,* Dec. 10, 1891.

23. "Mr. Crisp Selects His Committee on Rules," *New York Herald,* Dec. 17, 1891.

24. "The Speaker has arranged his Committee . . . ," *New York Mail and Express,* Dec. 17, 1891.

25. "The membership of the Ways and Means Committee . . . ," *Boston Daily Traveler,* Dec. 17, 1891.

26. "The House Committees," *New York Times,* Dec. 1, 1891.

27. "New Yorkers Fixed," *New York Journal,* Dec. 20, 1891.

28. "Danger of Factional War," *New York Sun,* Dec. 22, 1891.

29. "Hard Times for Lobbyists," *New York Telegram,* Dec. 28, 1891.

30. "We Must Not Bully Chili," *New York Telegram,* Dec. 26, 1891.

31. The Committee on Private Land Claims was established in the early days of the Republic and held jurisdiction over private land claims to public land. In 1891, after concluding that political settlement of claims had corrupted the process, Congress created the United States Court of Private Land Claims. At that point, the committee had little to do. The committee was abolished in 1911. "Mr. Crisp's Committees," *New York Tribune,* Dec. 24, 1891.

32. "Speaker Crisp today announced the committees . . . ," *New York Sun,* Dec. 24, 1891.

33. "Mr. Crisp's Committees," *New York Tribune,* Dec. 24, 1891.

34. "Our New York Ledger," *Philadelphia Ledger,* Dec. 24, 1891.

35. Tammany Hall's "Big Four" were Richard Croker, Thomas Gilroy, Hugh Grant, and Bourke Cockran.

36. "New York On Congress Committees," *New York Press,* Dec. 24, 1891.

37. "Our Washington dispatches convey . . . ," *New York Times,* Dec. 22, 1891.

38. "Hill or Cleveland," *New York World,* Jan. 14, 1892.

39. "It is very clear . . . ," *New York Telegram,* Jan. 27, 1892.

40. "The Empire State Will 'Send' a Hill Delegation to Chicago," *Puck,* Feb. 10, 1892.

41. "Mr. Roger Quarles Mills's hands were well shaken, and then he was taken upstairs, with these gentlemen hovering about him: Louis Wundmuller, E. Ellery Anderson, Everett P. Wheeler, A. P.

Fitch, Charles S. Fairchild, St. Clair McKelway, Thomas G. Shearman, Walter S. Logan, Francis Lynde Stetson, and George Foster Peabody. These gentlemen were among the happy ones who were to dine with Mr. Mills before the reception, at which all Reform Clubmen were invited to do him honor." "The Champion of Free Trade a Guest at the Reform Club," *New York World,* Feb. 6, 1892.

42. Schurz was a committed reformer, Fairchild was Cleveland's secretary of the Treasury, and Stetson was Cleveland's personal attorney and law partner. "The Reform Club's Guest," *New York Times,* Feb. 6, 1892.

43. "R. Q. Mills Against the Senator," *New York Tribune,* Feb. 6, 1892.

44. "Congressman Fitch," *New York Telegram,* Feb. 11, 1892.

45. "Facts about Silver." *New York Mail and Express,* Feb. 29, 1892.

46. The act required government purchase at market prices of $2–4 million of silver bullion each month to be used to manufacture coins at a ratio of 16 oz. silver to 1 oz. gold.

47. Nevins, *Grover Cleveland,* 2:595.

48. "Opposing the Silver Bill," *New York Commercial Bulletin,* Apr. 3, 1890.

49. It was conceded by some that bimetallism might work in theory if all nations cooperated. No one thought that all nations would or even wanted to cooperate. And there were many who thought that it could not work whether or not all nations cooperated. "Free Coinage Denounced," *New York Times,* Feb. 12, 1891.

50. Fairchild referred to former secretaries of the Treasury Daniel Manning (1885–87) and William Windom (1889–91), under Cleveland and Harrison respectively.

51. "Against Free Coinage of Silver," *New York Sun,* Feb. 12, 1891.

52. Three other resolutions: (1) fixed relationships between gold and silver cannot be sustained (i.e., 16:1 silver to gold as expressed in the Bland-Allison Act of 1878); (2) free coinage of silver will drive gold from circulation (Gresham's Law); and (3) silver coinage cannot work without the cooperation of all nations. "Free Coinage Denounced," *New York Times,* Feb. 12, 1891.

53. The Bland-Allison Silver Purchase Act had become law in 1878. Subsequent unsuccessful free coinage efforts contributed to the passage of the Sherman Silver Purchase Act of 1890.

54. "The Silver Heresy," *New York Evening Post,* Feb. 12, 1892.

55. James McPherson, *Battle Cry of Freedom* (New York: Oxford Univ. Press, 1988), 53–54.

56. "The Silver Heresy," *New York Evening Post,* Feb. 12, 1892.

57. "The Bland Bill," *New York Times,* Mar. 25, 1892.

58. "Petition of the Chamber of Commerce of the state of New York to the Senate and the House of Representatives of the United States of America in Congress assembled" (Mar. 22, 1892). *Congressional Record,* 52nd Cong., 1st sess., 1892, vol. 23, 3:2431–33.

59. *Congressional Record,* 52nd Cong., 1st sess., 1892, vol. 23, 3:2431–33.

60. "If the 'Antis' Filibuster," *New York World,* Mar. 24, 1892.

61. "The Fight for Free Silver," *New York Sun,* Mar. 24, 1892.

62. "Disorder Reigns at a Night Session on the Silver Bill," *New York Herald,* Mar. 25, 1892.

63. *Congressional Record,* 52nd Cong., 1st sess., 1892, vol. 23, 3:2549.

64. "Details of the Debate," *New York Tribune,* Mar. 25, 1892.

65. The term "paired" refers to an arrangement between two congressmen who are opposed on a vote and who cannot attend, who agree not to attend and not to vote, thus canceling their votes without affecting the result.

66. *Congressional Record,* 52nd Cong., 1st sess., 1892, vol. 23, 3:2552.

67. "Silver Men Surprised," *New York Times,* Mar. 25, 1892.

68. "Bland Is Still Hopeful," *New York Times,* Mar. 26, 1892.

69. Ibid.

70. "No one will dispute . . . ," *Albany Argus,* Mar. 29, 1892; "It cannot but be gratifying . . . ," *New York World,* Mar. 26, 1892.

71. "Free Silver in the House," *New York Times,* July 7, 1892.

72. "Today Messrs. Fitch and Fellows . . . and one or two other anti-silver Democrats gave Mr. Reed a luncheon at the capital, during which the silver question was discussed with especial reference to the attitude of the Republicans." "Live Washington Topics," *New York Sun,* July 1, 1892.

73. Thomas G. Donlan, "The Dollar's Long Dive," *Barron's,* Oct. 2005.

7. NEW YORK AND THE ELECTION LAW IN CLEVELAND'S VICTORY: FIFTY-SECOND CONGRESS, 1890–1892

1. "A Talk with Mr. Fitch," *Washington Star,* May 13, 1892.

2. Ibid.

3. Whitney served as Cleveland's de facto campaign chairman.

4. Hirsch, *William C. Whitney,* 395.

5. Nevins, *Grover Cleveland,* 2:491.

6. "Harlem Democrats Solid," *New York Times,* June 25, 1892.

7. "Democrats All United," *Harlem Reporter,* June 29, 1892.

8. "Hostile to the Sundry Civil Bill," *New York Tribune,* May 27, 1892.

9. See Ackerman, *Boss Tweed,* 40–41.

10. The quotations in the succeeding several pages that refer to Shields, Davenport, and election laws in the southern district were taken from the following single source: *Congressional Record,* 52nd Cong., 1st sess., 1892, vol. 23, 5:4729–36.

11. Cummings's amendment "provided further that nothing herein contained shall apply to the clerks or the deputy clerks of the United States district or circuit court's for the Southern District of New York."

12. "In 1890, the number of federal officers at the polls in New York City alone was over ten thousand—nearly half the number of federal troops remaining in the South when reconstruction ended in 1877." Burke, "Federal Regulation of Congressional Elections," 17.

13. "Fitch for Mayor," *New York Evening Advertiser,* July 11, 1892.

14. The idea was that if Tammany nominated a Tammany man, a third-party candidate might emerge to split the Democratic vote. A Fitch candidacy might discourage a third candidate.

15. "Congressman Fitch Desires to Be Mayor," *New York Herald,* July 14, 1892.

16. "Ashbel P. Fitch for Mayor," *New York World,* July 14, 1892.

17. "Talk about A. P. Fitch for Mayor," *New York Tribune,* July 14, 1892.

18. "Congressman Ashbel P. Fitch . . . ," *Springfield (MA) Republican,* July 15, 1892.

19. "German Interests to Be Considered," *Baltimore Sun,* July 18, 1892.

20. "Fitch and the Mayoralty," *Harlem Reporter,* July 16, 1892.

21. "Politics in This City," *New York Globe,* July 23, 1892.

22. "The House and the World's Fair," *New York Evening Sun,* July 19, 1892.

23. Ibid.

24. Benjamin Butler was a former congressman, Civil War general, and Massachusetts governor and was noted for his harsh administration of New Orleans during the war.

25. "Except for New Orleans and St. Louis it was seldom used in the South. Throughout the twenty-three years that the law was in effect, the use of federal supervisors was concentrated in eight northern cities: Boston, New York, Brooklyn, Jersey City, Baltimore, Philadelphia, Chicago and San Francisco." Burke, "Federal Regulation of Congressional Elections," 17.

26. "The Election Supervisor," *New York Post,* Nov. 5, 1892.

27. "Force Bill Not a Sectional Measure," *Harlem Reporter,* Sept. 21, 1892.

28. Burke, "Federal Regulation of Congressional Elections," 17.

29. "To Block Davenport's Game," *Brooklyn Citizen,* July 20, 1892.

30. "To Investigate John I. Davenport," *New York World,* July 20, 1892.

31. Adlai E. Stevenson was vice president in the second Cleveland administration, postmaster general in the first Cleveland administration, and grandfather of the two-time Democratic candidate for president.

32. "Will Be a Grand Affair," *New York Times,* July 10, 1892.

33. "At the Manhattan Club," *New York Times,* July 21, 1892.

34. "The Sagamore Reception," *New York Times,* July 22, 1892.

35. "Harlem Honors the Men," *Harlem Reporter,* July 22, 1892.

36. The committee consisted of Chairman Fitch of New York, Geissenhainer of New Jersey, and DeForest of Connecticut, Democrats, and Ray of New York and Harmer of Pennsylvania, Republicans. "House of Representatives," *New York Sun,* Aug. 6, 1892.

37. "The Author of the Force Bill," *New Orleans Picayune,* Sept. 30, 1892.

38. Don Dickinson was Grover Cleveland's personal friend, political advisor, and postmaster general at the end of the first Cleveland administration.

39. "William C. Whitney gave last night . . . ," *New York Commercial Advertiser,* Sept. 7, 1892.

40. "To Let Light on John I.," *New York Evening Sun,* Sept. 7, 1892.

41. Ibid.

42. Ibid.

43. "William C. Whitney gave last night . . . ," *New York Commercial Advertiser,* Sept. 7, 1892.

44. "New York the Battle Ground," *Chicago Herald,* Sept. 11, 1892.

45. "Politics by Torchlight," *New York World,* Sept. 18, 1892.

46. M. C. Fitch, *Weekly Budget,* 480.

47. "To Investigate John I.," *New York World,* Sept. 23, 1892.

48. Ibid.

49. "Congressman Fitch's Committee to Begin Its Work Next Week," *New York World,* Oct. 6, 1892.

50. Ibid.

51. "He Will Not Be Present," *New York Morning Advertiser,* Oct. 14, 1892.

52. Ibid.

53. "Good for Davenport," *New York Mail and Express,* Oct. 14, 1892.

54. "Davenport Afraid," *New York News,* Oct. 14, 1892.

55. "Defied by John I.," *New York Evening World,* Oct. 14, 1892.

56. "The Congressional Committee . . . ," *New York Commercial Advertiser,* Oct. 14, 1892.

57. "The Congressional Committee Orders Another Subpoena to Be Served," *Philadelphia Evening Telegraph,* Oct. 14, 1892.

58. Ibid.

59. In addition to his tenured position as chief supervisor of elections, Davenport had been appointed a United States commissioner, which enabled him to sit as an examining magistrate. "An Incentive to Fraud," *New York Times,* Jan. 27, 1893.

60. "Davenport as an Object Lesson," *New York Times,* Oct. 15, 1892.

61. "The Latest Device of Tammany," *Rochester Chronicle,* Oct. 15, 1892.

62. "Harlemites Like Fitch," *New York World,* Oct. 23, 1892.

63. "Department of Public Works: Gilroy, Einstein, Quinn," *New York Sun,* Oct. 19, 1892.

64. "Congressman Fitch's Renomination," *Harlem Reporter,* Oct. 19, 1892.

65. "The Davenport Investigation," *Philadelphia Telegraph,* Oct. 19, 1892.

66. "Exposing Davenport," *New York Post,* Oct. 25, 1892.

67. "Still After Davenport," *New York Times,* Oct. 27, 1892.

68. "Davenport's Warrant Given to C. N. Bliss," *New York Herald,* Oct. 27, 1892.

69. "Davenport's Queer Ways," *New York Times,* "This Is Force-Bill Johnny," *New York Sun,* "Davenport Got Big Sums from Uncle Sam," *New York Herald,* "Davenport's Roll of Bills," *New York World,* all Oct. 26, 1892; "Davenport Warrant Given to C. N. Bliss," *New York Herald,* Oct. 27, 1892.

70. "Davenport Will Be Watched by Fitch's Committee," *New York Herald,* Nov. 6, 1892.

71. Determined by United States Circuit Judge Brewer "in the matter of the marshals." David Josiah Brewer was later named to the US Supreme Court by President Harrison. Ibid.

72. "Tammany Cowed," *New York Press,* Nov. 6, 1892.

73. Ibid.

74. "Davenport Will Be Watched by Fitch's Committee," *New York Herald,* Nov. 6, 1892.

75. Ibid.

76. "Fitch Foils the Republicans," *San Francisco Examiner,* Nov. 7, 1892.

77. Ibid.

78. General Emmons Clark, former commander of New York's Seventh Regiment. Ibid.

79. Ibid.

80. "Davenport as an Object Lesson," *New York Times,* Oct. 15, 1892.

81. "The Result in New York," *Philadelphia Evening Telegraph,* Nov. 11, 1892.

82. "Vote in New-York City," *New York Times,* Nov. 10, 1892.

83. The election results were: Fitch, 26,826, and Robinson, 15,847, for a plurality of 10,979. Ibid.

84. "Democratic Tidal Wave," *Harlem Reporter,* Nov. 12, 1892.

85. Henry Villard, a German immigrant, began his career as a *New York Tribune* correspondent covering the Civil War. He was a railroad magnate who helped finance Cleveland's 1892 presidential campaign. Villard's table that evening featured green turtle soup, saddle of lamb, risotto, terrapin, canvasback ducks, and other delicacies, washed down with Chablis, Moët and Chandon, and finally Château La Rose 1877. Ashbel P. Fitch archives.

86. Lawrence Godkin (*New York Evening Post*), J. P. Solomon (*Jewish Advocate*), Charles Miller (*New York Times*), and Oswald Ottendorfer (*Staats-Zeitung*).

87. *In Remembrance of the Dinner in Honor of President-elect Cleveland.* Nov. 17, 1892. Ashbel P. Fitch archives.

88. Ibid.

89. Ibid. Casting his own caution aside, Villard then said, "I trust and hope . . . that one of the fruits will be the formation and continuance in power, for a long time, of a great consolidated party of true progress." Little did he know that it would be twenty years before there would be another great national victory for the Democratic Party.

90. "Dined with Mr. Cleveland," *New York Sun,* Nov. 18, 1892.

91. "Reed, Lodge, Cockran," *New York Recorder,* Dec. 25, 1892.

92. "Davenport's Accounts," *Harlem Reporter,* Nov. 23, 1892.

93. "Davenport's Pay Will Not Be Withheld," *New York Herald,* Nov. 24, 1892.

94. Mitchell, when asked under oath if he examined Davenport's accounts, answered "that is a matter of accounting for the officers of the Treasury Department." "Mr. Fitch to Mr. Foster," *New York Times,* Nov. 27, 1892.

95. Ibid.

96. "Mr. Davenport's Accounts," *New York Times,* Dec. 1, 1892.

97. "No Attention Will Be Paid to Davenport's Request," *New York Herald,* Dec. 6, 1892.

98. "Against Honest Elections," *New York Tribune,* Jan. 30, 1893.

99. "The Tiger and the Ballot Box," *Albany Journal,* Jan. 27, 1893.

100. "The Doings of Davenport," *New York World,* Jan. 26, 1893.

101. "Davenport Evicted," *New York Evening World,* Aug. 24, 1893.

8. REPEAL OF THE ELECTION LAW AND SHERMAN ACT: FIFTY-THIRD CONGRESS, 1892–1894

1. Weisman, *Great Tax Wars,* 116–17.

2. Enacted in 1890, the Sherman Act required the federal government to issue treasury notes redeemable in gold for the purchase of four and a half million ounces of silver bullion every month.

3. "The Silver Danger," *New York Evening Post,* Jan. 21, 1893.

4. "The Sherman Act Stands," *New York Times,* Feb. 10, 1893.

5. "News From Washington," *New York Mail and Express,* May 5, 1893.

6. "President and Congress," *New York Times,* May 9, 1893.

7. "News from Washington," *New York Mail and Express,* May 5, 1893.

8. James Eckels became controller of the currency in the second Cleveland administration.

9. "Our Big Financial Problem," *New York Times,* June 12, 1893.

10. Nevins, *Grover Cleveland,* 2:527.

11. "Twenty-five of the leading anti-silver Democrats . . . ," *New York America,* Aug. 11, 1893.

12. "The Fight May Begin To-Day," *New York Times,* Aug. 11, 1893.

13. Ibid.

14. "Congressman Fitch, who has suffered . . . ," *New York America,* Aug. 11, 1893.

15. "Advocates of Repeal Still Plead: Congressman Fitch, of New York, Addressed the House Against the Silver Bill," *New York Telegram,* Aug. 23, 1893.

16. "Repeal Gaining Strength," *New York Times,* Aug. 24, 1893.

17. "Victory for Repeal," *Chicago Record,* Aug. 29, 1893.

18. "Over Two to One for Repeal," *New York Times,* Aug. 29, 1893.

19. Ratios of 16:1, 17:1, 18:1, 19:1, and 20:1 silver to gold that reflected gold's increasing value at ascending ratios.

20. "Over Two to One for Repeal," *New York Times,* Aug. 29, 1893.

21. "Cleveland Is Emphatic," unknown Washington newspaper, Sept. 9, 1893.

22. Tucker was the grandson of Henry St. George Tucker (1780–1848) and the son of John Randolph Tucker (1823–1897), both of whom served in the House of Representatives from Virginia. Tucker served intermittently until the Seventy-second Congress. He died in 1932. He was a professor of constitutional law and equity and dean of the Law School at Washington and Lee, dean of the School of Law and Diplomacy at George Washington University, and president of the American Bar Association in 1905.

23. "Election Law Repeal," *Washington News,* Sept. 11, 1893.

24. The Fifteenth Amendment to the United States Constitution guarantees that a citizen's right to vote cannot be denied on the basis of race, color, or previous condition of servitude.

25. "Cameron Out for Silver," *Philadelphia Record,* Sept. 12, 1893.

26. "A Raid," *Boston Journal,* Sept. 12, 1893; "The Election Laws," *Hartford Courant,* Sept. 12, 1893.

27. "Southerners Win," *New York Morning Advertiser,* Sept. 12, 1893.

28. "News from Washington," *New York Mail and Express,* Sept. 14, 1893.

29. "Crisp in Earnest," *Pittsburgh Dispatch,* Sept. 19, 1893.

30. "The Elections Repeal Bill," *New York Times,* Sept. 27, 1893.

31. "No Safeguards for Voters," *New York Tribune,* Oct. 6, 1893.

32. "Was Too Sweeping," *Indianapolis Journal,* Oct. 2, 1893.

33. "Those Election Laws," *Baltimore News,* Sept. 22, 1893.

34. "Nullify the Constitution," *New York Tribune,* Oct. 7, 1893.

35. "News from Washington," *New York Mail and Express,* Oct. 6, 1893.

36. "Getting Scared," *Detroit Tribune,* Oct. 9, 1893.

37. "Those Election Laws," *Baltimore News,* Sept. 22, 1893.

38. "Davenport's Doom," *New York World,* Oct. 10, 1892.

39. *Congressional Record,* 53rd Cong., 1st sess., 1893, vol. 25, 2:2359, app. 220.

40. "Congressman Fitch of New York . . . ," *Camden (NJ) Courier,* Oct. 11, 1893.

9. New York City's Watershed

1. Nevins, *Grover Cleveland,* 2:536.

2. "Feeding the Poor in New York City," *Philadelphia Inquirer,* Feb. 25, 1894.

3. H. Paul Jeffers, *Commissioner Roosevelt* (New York: John Wiley and Sons, 1994), 5.

4. Ibid.

5. For a detailed description of the events leading to Green's occupation of the controller's office, see Ackerman, *Boss Tweed,* 216–18.

6. New York City organization chart showing "Ashbel P. Fitch, Comptroller, '*appointed*' for four years." Morison, *Letters of Theodore Roosevelt,* chart 3, 480–81. Also, "Comptroller Ashbel P. Fitch . . . a Tammany man who had *somehow* missed being swept away by the Reform broom of 1894" (emphasis added). Jeffers, *Commissioner Roosevelt,* 228.

7. Mark Ash, *The New York City Consolidation Act as in force in 1891, with notes indicating the statutory sources, references to judicial decisions, and all laws relating to New York City, passed since January 1, 1882* (Albany: Weed, Parsons and Company, 1891), 14.

8. Ibid., 22.

9. The comptroller received a percentage of certain taxes collected, often 5 percent of the first $100,000, 3 percent of the second $100,000, and 1 percent of each additional $100,000. "Tax Law Valid," *New York Evening Advertiser,* Oct. 17, 1894.

10. "The head of the Finance department shall be called the comptroller of the City of New York . . . ," Ash, *New York City Consolidation Act,* 14. "The Finance Department shall have control of the fiscal concerns of the corporation." Ibid., 62.

11. "The executive power of the corporation shall be vested in the mayor and the officers of the departments. . . . The mayor shall be the chief executive officer of the corporation." Ibid., 13.

12. "The Most Important Office in the City Government," *New York Democrat,* Oct. 10, 1897.

13. Lewis, *Richard Croker,* 5.

14. "Croker—Who Will Be Dictator If Van Wyck Is Elected," *New York World,* Oct. 28, 1897.

15. Lewis, *Richard Croker,* 13–15.

16. The Sixty-seventh Street Station stands between Lexington and Third Avenues. The inscription reads: "A.D. 1886; Commissioners Henry D. Purroy, President, Richard Croker, Elward Smith; N. LeBrun and Son, Architect."

17. "A Source of Tammany Riches—Value of Controlling the Street Opening Board," *New York Post,* May 28, 1894.

18. Ibid.

19. "Croker Names His Candidates," *New York Mail and Express,* Oct. 18, 1893.

20. "Mr. Croker's List," *New York World,* Oct. 18, 1893.

21. "The Tammany Nominations," *New York Times,* Oct. 18, 1893.

22. "Not much need be said . . . ," *Philadelphia Bulletin,* Oct. 18, 1893.

23. "Tammany's Ticket," *Brooklyn Eagle,* Oct. 18, 1893.

24. "Mr. Croker's List," *New York World,* "Croker Names His Candidates," *New York Mail and Express,* Oct. 18, 1893. Frank Ehret was the son of Fitch's client George Ehret.

25. "Wants Myers for Controller," *New York Times,* Oct. 19, 1893.

26. Ibid.

27. "Hon. Ashbel P. Fitch, the Champion of New York City's Good Name," *New York Uptown Visitor,* Nov. 11, 1893.

28. "The Nominations," *New York News,* Oct. 18, 1893.

29. "Wm. R. Grace Is for Fitch," *New York Sun,* Oct. 21, 1893.

30. The City Club was founded in 1892 "to promote social intercourse among persons especially interested in the good government of the City of New York." *Club Men of New York* (New York: Republic Press, 1896), 11.

31. "Fitch Was Surprised, He Says," *New York Mail and Express,* Oct. 18, 1893.

32. "Wm. R. Grace Is for Fitch," *New York Sun,* Oct. 21, 1893.

33. "Tammany Candidates Accept," *New York Times,* Oct. 22, 1893.

34. "Controller-elect Ashbel P. Fitch . . . ," *Brooklyn Eagle,* Dec. 10, 1893.

35. "Unite on Myers," *New York Commercial Advertiser,* Oct. 20, 1893.

36. "Awaiting Myers's Exit," *New York Evening Post,* Nov. 25, 1893.

37. "New City Officials Take Charge," *New York Times,* Jan. 2, 1894.

38. "New City Officials," *New York World,* Jan. 1, 1894.

39. "Fitch Shakes Hands," *New York Recorder,* Jan. 2, 1894.

40. Ibid.

41. "Tammany's Sway," *Syracuse Journal,* Jan. 2, 1894.

42. "The Relief Fund from City Employes," *New York Tribune,* Jan. 16, 1894.

43. Six firms submitted architectural plans with the stipulation that they not be made public prior to the final selection. The mayor however, wanted to display the plans for public review prior to final selection. Comptroller Fitch said that the situation was a disagreeable one and that he thought it best that the commission adjourn to think it over. "Muddled Over City Hall Plans," *New York Times,* Jan. 19, 1894. The matter was resolved two years later. "Relic of Tammany Rule," *New York Tribune,* Feb. 18, 1896.

44. "Sinking Fund Business," *New York Evening Post,* Jan. 19, 1894.

45. "To Improve City Docks," *New York Herald,* Mar. 9, 1894.

46. "A Wise Comptroller," *New York Sun,* Feb. 23, 1894.

47. "Will Issue Bonds," *New York World,* Feb. 15, 1894.

48. The controller said, "the whole matter bristles with difficulties. The first question is as to the legality of the adjournment of the meeting on the day set for the opening of the bids and the opening of them on a subsequent day. Another question is whether bids can be accepted for a contract which it is intended to modify later." "The Speedway Question," *New York Mail and Express,* Jan. 26, 1894.

49. "The Comptroller Opposes Them," *New York Evening Sun,* Feb. 1, 1894.

50. "Liability of the Comptroller," *New York Sun,* Apr. 22, 1894.

51. "The Tiger Is After Fitch," *New York World,* Jan. 28, 1894.

52. Ibid.

53. "Are Croker and Fitch Out?" *New York World,* Feb. 3, 1894.

54. "Feeding the Poor in New York City," *Philadelphia Inquirer,* Feb. 25, 1894.

55. "The City to Provide Work," *New York Tribune,* Jan. 4, 1894.

56. "Work for Many More Men," *New York Sun,* Jan. 4, 1894.

57. "The City to Provide Work," *New York Tribune,* Jan. 4, 1894.

58. "Work for Many More Men," *New York Sun,* Jan. 4, 1894.

59. "The City to Provide Work," *New York Tribune,* Jan. 4, 1894.

60. Burrows and Wallace, *Gotham,* 1190.

61. "Plans for City Work," *New York Post,* "Work for Unemployed," *New York Evening Sun,* "Aid for More Employed," *New York News,* "The City to Provide Work," *New York Tribune,* all Jan. 3, 1894; "Work for Many More Men," *New York Sun,* Jan. 4, 1894.

62. "Asphalt and the Park Board," *New York Mail and Express,* June 7, 1894.

63. "Park Board Indictments," *New York Mail and Express,* Apr. 11, 1895.

64. "Heart Broken: Pathetic Fate of Judge Abraham B. Tappen," *New York Morning Advertiser,* July 6, 1896.

65. "Park Board Indictments," *New York Mail and Express,* Apr. 11, 1895.

66. "Statement of Nathan Straus," *New York Times,* Apr. 9, 1895.

67. "Heart Broken: Pathetic Fate of Judge Abraham B. Tappen," *New York Morning Advertiser,* July 6, 1896.

68. Ibid.

69. "To Vindicate Park Officials," *New York Times,* May 17, 1895.

70. Ibid.

71. Edwin Lawrence Godkin, *Triumph of Reform* (New York: Souvenir Publishing Company, 1895), 117.

72. Sheehan grew up in Buffalo, New York, where he was admitted to the bar; he moved to New York City in 1885 and joined Tammany Hall. In 1895, he was Richard Croker's chosen successor to lead Tammany Hall.

73. Joseph Choate successfully argued the first federal income tax case before the Supreme Court in 1895. He was later named ambassador to Great Britain.

74. "Choate's Tired Feeling," *New York Daily News,* Mar. 29, 1894.

75. Ibid.

76. "The Tiger's Diamonds," *New York Press,* Sept. 9, 1894.

77. According to historian Allan Nevins, Gilder was Grover Cleveland's most intimate friend. Nevins, *Grover Cleveland,* 2:452.

78. It is likely that Gilder and Fitch were acquainted because of their common interest in the passage of the international copyright law in 1891. Carole Klein, *Gramercy Park: An American Bloomsbury* (Boston: Houghton Mifflin, 1987), 172.

79. "Talked Against Tammany," *New York Herald,* Feb. 8, 1894.

80. "Result of a Bad Reputation," *Rochester Democrat and Chronicle,* July 30, 1894.

81. "Piling Up a Big City Debt," *New York Mail and Express,* July 20, 1894.

82. "The Controller's Explanation," *New York Tribune,* July 21, 1894.

83. "Increase in New York's Funded Debt," *New York Times,* July 21, 1894.

84. "Another Search for Frauds," *New York Times,* July 27, 1894.

85. Storrs said that Matthew O'Rourke had been dismissed from a clerkship in the Finance Department years before and blamed Storrs. O'Rourke warned each new comptroller since then to investigate Storrs. Ibid. O'Rourke first began reporting scandals in the Finance Department in 1871. Ackerman, *Boss Tweed,* 148.

86. "Old Charge Revived," *Bond Buyer,* July 27, 1894.

87. "Fitch's Books Wide Open," *New York World,* July 27, 1894.

88. "Mr. Fitch Ready for Investigation," *New York Times,* July 27, 1894.

89. "Mayoralty Gallery—Number 3," *New York Herald,* Aug. 24, 1894.

90. "Fitch Is Satisfied," *New York Mail and Express,* May 16, 1894.

91. "The City under Tammany," *New York Sun,* Oct. 23, 1894.

92. Ibid.

93. Godkin, *Triumph of Reform,* 131.

94. Roosevelt "proposed a Police Reorganization Bill to give the police board true power and authority to reform the department. The measure would [have] vest[ed] in the board the right to dismiss subordinates after a hearing . . . it was voted down." Jeffers, *Commissioner Roosevelt,* 72.

95. "More Room for Art," *New York Morning Advertiser,* Nov. 6, 1894.

96. "Opening the North Wing," *New York Herald,* Nov. 6, 1894.

97. Stanford White, a principal in the architectural firm of McKim, Meade & White, was a leading architect of the Gilded Age.

98. "The Art Museum Enlarged," *New York Times,* Nov. 6, 1894.

99. "A New Home of Art," *New York Commercial Advertiser,* Nov. 5, 1894.

100. "Before Strong Trouble Lies," *New York Herald,* Dec. 16, 1894.

101. "What Reform Can Do," *New York Commercial Advertiser,* Oct. 27, 1894.

10. REFORMERS IN CHARGE, 1895

1. "Tammany Crushed," *New York Evening Post,* Nov. 7, 1894.

2. Jeffers, *Commissioner Roosevelt,* 56–57.

3. In May 1894, Governor Flower signed the bill that submitted to the voters in November of that year the question of whether the five boroughs should be consolidated into a single Greater New York. The legislature had created a commission to study the issue four years before. Consolidation won by a margin of 44,188, which varied between 36,979 out of 156,897 votes cast "for" in Manhattan, and 277 out of 129,211 votes cast "for" in Brooklyn. Harold Coffin Syrett, *The City of Brooklyn, 1865–1898: A Political History* (New York: Columbia Univ. Press, 1944), 256–57.

4. "The new State constitution granted the city greater home rule, stating the legislature could 'act in relation to the property, affairs, or government of any city only by general laws which shall in terms and in effect apply to all cities.'" Jeffrey A. Kroessler, *New York Year by Year* (New York: New York Univ. Press, 2002), 146.

5. The three were Levi Morton, Ashbel Fitch, and Lemuel Quigg. "A Crushing Blow," *Albany Journal,* Jan. 31, 1894.

6. "Are Their Terms Extended?" *New York Tribune,* Nov. 16, 1894.

7. "What Strong Can Do," *New York Evening Sun,* Nov. 7, 1894.

8. Ibid.

9. "To Lose Their Pap," *New York Evening Advertiser,* Nov. 8, 1894.

10. "New York City Bonds," *Bond Buyer,* Dec. 1, 1894.

11. "The Bright Side of a Picture," *New York Mercury,* Dec. 18, 1894.

12. "Wore Kilt and Breeks," *New York Times,* Dec. 1, 1894.

13. "Earl of Aberdeen at St. Andrews Dinner," *New York Mail and Express,* Dec. 1, 1894.

14. Choate's xenophobic observations before an audience at Cooper Union are recounted in chapter 9 of this book.

15. "The instances I have given of his [Choate's] brilliant performances at the St. Andrew and St. Patrick Societies, illustrate perfectly that remarkable combination of audacious fun and satirical wit which he heaped good humoredly upon his entertainers with such remarkable tact as not to afford any just reason for offense." Theron G. Strong, *Joseph H. Choate* (New York: Dodd, Mead, 1917), 68–73.

16. Depew quoted Choate, "We Yankees used to be able to govern ourselves, but you Irish have come here and taken the government away from us. You have our entire city administration in your hands, and you do with us as you like." Chauncey M. Depew, *My Memories of Eighty Years* (New York: Charles Scribner's Sons, 1922), 382–83.

17. Ackerman, *Boss Tweed,* 138.

18. Ibid., 183.

19. "Before Strong Trouble Lies," *New York Herald,* Dec. 16, 1894.

20. Ibid.

21. "Legislature in Session," *New York Evening Post,* Jan. 2, 1895.

22. "Changing Places," *New York Daily Mercury,* Jan. 2, 1895.

23. Ibid.

24. "Shake, Lafayette!" *New York Journal,* Jan. 4, 1895.

25. "All to Be Investigated." *New York Times,* Jan. 5, 1895.

26. "Strong's Investigators," *New York Sun,* Jan. 13, 1895.

27. "Message of the Governor," *New York Herald,* Jan. 3, 1895.

28. "The New Mayor," *New York Evening Post,* Jan. 2, 1895.

29. Nelson, *Fighting for the City,* 80.

30. Elise Hancock, "100 Years of Manhattan's Garbage," *Johns Hopkins Magazine,* Apr. 1995.

31. "Streets Must Be Clean," *New York Times,* Jan. 12, 1895.

32. Jeffers, *Commissioner Roosevelt,* 57.

33. "Shake, Lafayette!" *New York Journal,* Jan. 4, 1895.

34. "Clean Street Problems," *New York Times,* Jan. 2, 1895.

35. Hancock, "100 Years of Manhattan's Garbage."

36. Mayor Strong said, "On Friday last [Waring and I] talked over the estimates for the Street Cleaning Department . . . and Mr. Andrews thought that additions ought to be made, or the efficiency of the department would be crippled. I advised that there should be no change in the appropriation, as I thought streets could be cleaned with $2.4 million. *If they can't be, we can get more money*" (emphasis added). "Mayor at Noon Today," *New York Sun,* Jan. 1, 1895.

37. "So the Money Goes," *New York Commercial Advertiser,* Jan. 29, 1895.

38. Through two long columns the *New York Times* pursued the spelling to Yale (*Scribner's Monthly,* Oct. 1879), to the English Philological Society, Shakespeare, *The Century Dictionary,*

Skeate's Etymological Dictionary, and numerous other educators and into the Middle Ages, "when Latin was the language of the Courts." "Controller Not Comptroller," *New York Times,* Nov. 1, 1896.

39. Ash, *New York City Consolidation Act,* 63.

40. "Could Not Sell Bonds," *New York Evening Advertiser,* Feb. 5, 1895.

41. "City Bonds to Be Gold," *New York Evening Sun,* Feb. 7, 1895.

42. Ibid.

43. "Mr. Morgan Calls," *New York Evening Sun,* Feb. 18, 1895.

44. The comparison is made using a "short-cut" method. Four percent (the coupon on the United States bonds) divided by 119 (the market price of the bond) equals 3.36 percent current yield; 3 percent (the coupon on the city bond) divided by 89 (the equivalent yielding price of the city bond) equals 3.37 percent. The assumed market price of the city bond (100) represents a 12 percent premium over 89 that would offer an equivalent yield to the Treasury bond. At issuance, the assumed comparable prices being 104.5 for a 4 percent rate of interest and 100 for a 3 percent rate, the premium was closer to 34 percent. Cleveland, Carlisle, and Morgan were criticized for their pricing of the Treasury bond. Nevins, *Grover Cleveland,* 2:663–64.

45. The Rapid Transit Act limited the total expenditure for the road to $50 million. "Now for Rapid Transit," *New York World,* Nov. 8, 1894.

46. "What Carlisle's Blunder Cost," *Philadelphia Press,* Feb. 28, 1895.

47. "The Fictitious Tax Rate," *New York Evening Post,* Mar. 7, 1895.

48. "Tax Rate Fictitious," *New York Morning Advertiser,* Mar. 7, 1895.

49. "Comptroller Fitch and the Tax Valuation," *New York Evening Post,* Mar. 9, 1895.

50. Nelson, *Fighting for the City,* 80.

51. "Fears Higher Taxes," *New York Evening Sun,* Apr. 2, 1895.

52. "The Mayor's Message," *New York Daily Mercury,* Apr. 3, 1895.

53. "Mayor Strong's Message," *New York Herald,* Apr. 2, 1895.

54. "Tammany's Financial Jugglery Exposed in Strong's Message," *Springfield (MA) Republican,* Apr. 3, 1895.

55. "From Mayor Strong," *Buffalo Express,* Apr. 3, 1895.

56. "Tammany's Financial Jugglery," *New York Tribune,* Apr. 3, 1895.

57. "Tammany's Financial Jugglery Exposed in Strong's Message," *Springfield (MA) Republican,* Apr. 3, 1895.

58. "A Mare's Nest," *New York Daily News,* Apr. 3, 1895.

59. The quotations in this and the following paragraph that refer to Fitch's response to Mayor Strong were taken from the following single source: "Defends the Bond Plan," *New York Times,* Apr. 4, 1895.

60. "Strong Drew Fitch Out," *New York Evening World,* Apr. 4, 1895.

61. "Pleased with Mr. Fitch's Reply," *New York Times,* Apr. 5, 1895.

62. "Consolation for the Mayor," *New York Daily News,* Apr. 4, 1895.

63. "Strong's Queer Message," *New York Sun,* Apr. 5, 1895.

64. "Says the Mayor Hurt Bond Sales," *Philadelphia Inquirer,* Apr. 6, 1895.

65. "Controller Fitch to the Mayor," *Bond Buyer,* Apr. 15, 1895.

66. "Comptroller Ashbel P. Fitch's Service to New York City," *Malone Franklin Gazette,* Apr. 19, 1895.

67. "Is Mayor Strong Dissatisfied?" *New York Times,* Sept. 1, 1895.

68. "It Pays—But Whom?" *New York Journal,* Sept. 1, 1895.

69. "Rumor Regarding Strong," *New York Press,* Sept. 1, 1895.

70. "Mr. Conkling on Boss Rule," *New York Times,* Jan. 2, 1895.

71. "Andrews Gives Up," *New York Herald,* Dec. 29, 1894.

72. Ibid.

73. Ibid.

74. "The Streets and the Controller," *New York Times,* June 27, 1895.

75. "Good Work with Snow," *New York Times,* Jan. 30, 1895.

76. Ibid.

77. "Really Cleaning Streets," *New York Tribune,* Jan. 30, 1895.

78. Oliver Teall had wanted to be deputy superintendent and was denied. "Waring Takes Hold," *New York Morning Advertiser,* Jan. 16, 1895.

79. A Hansom cab is a type of horse-drawn carriage, first designed and patented in 1834 by Joseph Hansom in England, that combined superior speed with maneuverability. The cab was introduced to the United States during the late nineteenth century and was most commonly used in New York City. Hansom Cab. *Wikipedia,* s.v. "Hansom cab."

80. "Waring Buys a Cab. The Street Cleaning Commissioner Orders the Hansom and the City Pays for It. Got a Beauty, Cost $828," *New York Herald,* Feb. 1, 1895.

81. "The New Street Cleaner, Waring's $828 Hansom," *New York Sun,* Feb. 2, 1895.

82. "Waring Has a Big Deficit," *New York Sun,* Feb. 6, 1895.

83. "A Case of 'Darn the Cost!'" *New York Recorder,* Feb. 6, 1895.

84. "Over Fitch's Protest," *New York Evening Sun,* Feb. 7, 1895.

85. "Waring Asks for More," *New York Sun,* Feb. 7, 1895.

86. "Roman Chariots and Trojan Horses," *New York Daily News,* Feb. 7, 1895.

87. "Money for Colonel Waring," *New York Press,* Feb. 21, 1895.

88. "Scolded Waring," *New York Evening Sun,* Feb. 27, 1895.

89. "Hard Raps for Waring," *New York Sun,* Feb. 28, 1895.

90. "$50,000 More for Waring," *New York Times,* Feb. 28, 1895.

91. "Hard Raps for Waring," *New York Sun,* Feb. 28, 1895.

92. "The Gentle Art of Making Enemies," *New York Daily News,* Apr. 23, 1895.

93. Ibid.

94. "Bummers, Not Bums," *New York Morning Advertiser,* Apr. 21, 1895.

95. "Big Deficit Says Waring," *New York Mail and Express,* Apr. 18, 1895.

96. "Probing," *New York Journal,* May 21, 1895.

97. "Waring May Have to Go," *New York Tribune,* May 22, 1895; "No Hope," *New York Journal,* May 24, 1895; "Waring's Doom Near," *New York Morning Advertiser,* May 26, 1895.

98. "At the waist there are loops through which pass a belt, fastened with a big buckle on which are the raised letters D. S. C. Then there is a cap . . . with a long visor. . . . A big badge is worn on the breast, giving the wearer's number and the words 'Sweeper, Department Street Cleaning.' The jacket is fastened with metal buttons." "Street Cleaners in White Suits," *New York Herald,* May 24, 1895.

99. Ibid.

100. Ibid.

101. "To Help Waring Out," *New York Evening Sun,* June 26, 1895.

102. Ibid.

103. Ibid.

104. "The Streets and the Controller." *New York Times,* June 27, 1895.

105. "Business Principles and Reform Administration," *New York Daily News,* June 27, 1895.
106. "Bids for City Gold Bonds," *New York Times,* July 4, 1895.
107. "New York City Bonds," *Bond Buyer,* July 8, 1895.
108. "The financial result of the 'reform' spasm . . . ," *New York Town Topics,* July 11, 1895.
109. "Higher Taxes Next Year," *New York World,* Oct. 3, 1895.
110. "Fitch Answers Mayor Strong," *Philadelphia Times,* Apr. 4, 1895.
111. Jeffers, *Commissioner Roosevelt,* 64.
112. Ibid., 66.
113. Ibid., 60.
114. Ibid., 135.
115. "Two Democrats," *New York Morning Journal,* July 4, 95.
116. "Ashbel P. Fitch," *New York World,* July 7, 1895.
117. "Slightly Wet," *New York Recorder,* July 9, 1895.
118. Ibid.
119. "Soda Water Next Sunday," *New York Sun,* July 19, 1895.
120. Ibid.
121. "Their July Fourth," *New York Journal,* July 20, 1895.
122. "Blue Sundays for a While," *New York Sun,* July 20, 1895.
123. "Their July Fourth," *New York Journal,* July 20, 1895.
124. "No All-Night Bars," *New York World,* July 20, 1895.
125. "Mayor Calls Up Mr. Roosevelt," *New York Herald,* Aug. 7, 1895.
126. Jeffers, *Commissioner Roosevelt,* 135.
127. "Liberal Army Marches To-Day," *New York Herald,* Sept. 25, 1895.
128. "'Teddy' Beamed on 'Em," *New York Recorder,* Sept. 26, 1895.
129. "A Home Rule Parade," *New York Morning Advertiser,* Sept. 26, 1895.
130. Ibid.
131. "'Teddy' Beamed on 'Em." *New York Recorder,* Sept. 26, 1895.
132. Ibid.
133. Ibid.
134. Jeffers, *Commissioner Roosevelt,* 145.
135. Ibid., 146.
136. Morris, *Rise of Theodore Roosevelt,* 513.
137. "Just What Did It," *New York World,* Nov. 7, 1895.
138. Morris, *Rise of Theodore Roosevelt,* 512–13.
139. "Just What Did It," *New York World,* Nov. 7, 1895.
140. Ibid.
141. Ibid.
142. "Taxes Too High," *New York Morning Advertiser,* Nov. 7, 1895.

11. A CRASH AND A BANG

1. "High Price of Reform," *New York Mercury,* "Want Six Millions," *New York Morning Advertiser,* both Oct. 18, 1895; "1896 Budget Grows," *New York World,* Oct. 19, 1895; "Millions for Schools," *New York Evening Sun,* Oct. 21, 1895; "Waring Wants More," *New York Journal,* "Vast Sums Apportioned," *New York Times,* both Oct. 23, 1895.

2. "Give Them What They Need," *New York Times,* Oct. 12, 1895.

3. "Pruning Knife at Work," *New York Tribune,* Oct. 12, 1895.

4. "The Estimates for 1896," *New York Times,* Oct. 17, 1895.

5. "Praise for the School Board," *New York Mail and Express,* Oct. 18, 1895.

6. Ibid.

7. "Reformers Dodging the Law," *New York Sun,* Nov. 28, 1895.

8. Ibid. The Rapid Transit Commission held that its workers were not employees of the city. Fitch held his ground, pointing to comparable circumstances in other departments. "I see no reason why your board should be exempt from the benefits and requirements of the laws which govern the expenditures of other city boards and departments." "Fitch Vexes the R.T. Board," *New York Sun,* "Not Civil Service Work," *New York Times,* Nov. 27, 1895.

9. "To Keep Streets Clean," *New York Times,* Dec. 28, 1895.

10. "Fitch Waring's Friend," *New York Journal,* Feb. 14, 1896.

11. "Go Slow, His Motto," *New York Press,* Jan. 11, 1896.

12. "Fitch Has a Motto, Too," *New York Evening Sun,* Jan. 13, 1896.

13. "Mr. Fitch Calls Waring Absurd," *New York Journal,* Oct. 25, 1896.

14. Ibid.

15. "Bigger, Better New York," *New York World,* Jan. 1, 1896.

16. "Mayor and Comptroller," *New York Evening Advertiser,* Mar. 7, 1896.

17. "To Shelve Roosevelt," *Syracuse Herald,* Nov. 8, 1895.

18. "Hot Talk in the Mayor's Office," *New York Morning Advertiser,* May 5, 1896.

19. "Snubs for Police Board," *New York Sun,* Dec. 18, 1895.

20. "One Year of Reform," *New York Mercury,* Jan. 8, 1896.

21. "Sought Mr. Fitch's Opinion," *New York Times,* Jan. 31, 1896.

22. Ibid.

23. Fitch contended that "the general spirit and purpose of the Consolidation Act is that unexpected balances of appropriations shall not be carried for years on the books to be ultimately used for some purpose entirely foreign to that for which the Board of Estimate originally made the appropriation. In the present instance the appropriation was made four years ago for a specific purpose which the Board of Police has refused or neglected to carry out." "Police Board Criticized," *New York Tribune,* Feb. 21, 1896.

24. The Police Board requested the Board of Estimate to transfer the sum of $7,500 from the 1892 appropriation for "Construction of a Station House" to the 1895 appropriation entitled "Contingent Expenses" to enable the treasurer to pay bills incurred by officers. "Expenses Were Illegal," *New York Times,* Feb. 21, 1896.

25. Ibid.

26. "The Police Board on the Gridiron," *New York Journal,* Feb. 21, 1896.

27. "Hundreds to the Wall Provisions of the Raines Liquor Law," *New York World,* Feb. 25, 1896.

28. "Maybe a Clash," *New York Recorder,* Feb. 27, 1896.

29. "Trouble in Transfers," *New York Times,* Mar. 5, 1896.

30. Ibid. Fitch offered three resolutions to the board, all aimed at clarifying transfer procedures. The first obligated the board to deny transfers to cover expenditures made in excess of appropriations, such as the Police Department was asking for, and that resolution failed. The second two were procedural, and they carried. The argument was left, therefore, where it began.

31. Syrett, *The City of Brooklyn,* 245.

32. Ibid., 262.

33. Roosevelt's part in the Tammany resurgence in New York City infuriated Platt. "A determined effort will be made to legislate Roosevelt out of office." "Platt's Big Schemes," *New York News,* Dec. 29, 1895.

34. "Now for the Charter," *New York World,* Apr. 26, 1896; Syrett, *The City of Brooklyn,* 265.

35. Fitch said, "The main objection to the consolidation of Brooklyn and New York arises from the difference which exists now in their financial standing. The valuation for taxation of real estate in Brooklyn . . . is exceedingly high. The valuation . . . in New York . . . is exceedingly low. The result of this is that . . . a property owner in Brooklyn pays very nearly twice as much . . . as a property owner in New York does on property of equal value." "Why Not Consolidate?" *New York World,* Dec. 7, 1895.

36. "They hate Mr. Platt. They oppose consolidation because he favors it." Syrett, *The City of Brooklyn,* 266.

37. Charles A. Schieren was the Republican mayor of Brooklyn (1894–95).

38. "Greater New York Wins," *New York Sun,* Apr. 23, 1896.

39. "Now for the Charter," *New York World,* Apr. 26, 1896.

40. "New York City Loans under New Conditions," *Bond Buyer,* Mar. 23, 1896.

41. "New York's Financial Plight," *Brooklyn Eagle,* "Went A-Begging," *New York Daily News,* "Bonds Not All Taken Up," *New York Times,* all Apr. 3, 1896; "Why Loan Failed," *New York Herald,* Apr. 4, 1896.

42. "Fitch on City Bonds," *New York Journal,* Apr. 4, 1896.

43. "Controller Fitch Not Hopeful," *New York Tribune,* Apr. 7, 1896.

44. "Offer Ten Times Amount," *New York Times,* May 5, 1896.

45. "No Money for Police Spies," *New York Daily News,* Mar. 4, 1896.

46. "Police Upheld," *New York Evening Advertiser,* Mar. 4, 1896.

47. "May Mandamus Fitch," *New York Mail and Express,* "To Mandamus Mr. Fitch," *New York Evening Post,* both Apr. 14, 1896; "May Mandamus Mr. Fitch," *New York Times,* Apr. 15, 1896.

48. "May Mandamus Mr. Fitch," *New York Times,* Apr. 15, 1896.

49. "Replies to Roosevelt," *New York Daily News,* Apr. 15, 1896.

50. Candice Millard, *The River of Doubt: Theodore Roosevelt's Darkest Journey* (New York: Doubleday, 2005), 58.

51. "Seeking to Have Mr. Fitch Indicted," *New York Tribune,* "A Boomerang," *New York Morning Advertiser,* both Apr. 26, 1896.

52. "Comptroller May Have to Answer," *New York Herald,* Apr. 28, 1896.

53. "Fitch and the Police Board," *New York Evening Sun,* Apr. 28, 1896.

54. "Come On, Says Fitch," *New York World,* Apr. 29, 1896.

55. "Dared Fitch to a Fight," *New York Sun,* May 6, 1896.

56. This quotation and quotations in the succeeding several paragraphs relating to the confrontation with Roosevelt are taken from "Fitch Said 'Pistols,'" *New York World,* May 6, 1896.

57. "Croton" refers to New York City's Croton Reservoir at Forty-second Street.

58. "Words, Not War," *New York Evening Sun,* May 6, 1896.

59. Morris, *Rise of Theodore Roosevelt,* 531.

60. "The Rivals—All-Star Cast," *New York Recorder,* May 7, 1896.

61. "Words, Not War," *New York Evening Sun,* May 6, 1896.

62. Roosevelt to Cabot Lodge, May 6, 1896. Morison, *Letters of Theodore Roosevelt,* 536.

63. The Board of Estimate, at a meeting that Fitch did not attend, "ordered the transfer of $11,000 from various non-expended balances to the contingency fund of the Police Department." These were not the unexpended balances from the 1892 building account, and Fitch expressed no opposition to the transfer. "Money for Roosevelt," *New York Mail and Express,* May 15, 1896.

64. The succeeding two quotations that refer to police expenses were taken from the following single source: "Bills of Police Spies," *New York Sun,* May 20, 1896.

65. Judge Roger A. Pryor was a former Confederate congressman and Confederate general. For more on Pryor, see David W. Blight, *Race and Reunion* (Cambridge, MA: Belknap Press of Harvard Univ. Press, 2001), 89–93.

66. "Hideous Bills from Detectives," *New York Tribune,* May 21, 1896.

67. "Spy Bill That Should Never Be Paid," *New York Recorder,* May 21, 1896.

68. "Police Expenses Must Be Paid," *New York Commercial Advertiser,* Oct. 23, 1896.

69. Ibid.

70. "Richard A. Storrs Dead," *New York Times,* May 12, 1896.

71. "Veteran in City Service," *New York Times,* May 10, 1896.

72. "Storrs Is Dead," *New York Daily News,* May 11, 1896.

73. "Croker's Parting Words," *New York Sun,* Feb. 19, 1896.

74. "Tammany's Advice Is Not Wanted," *New York Herald,* May 24, 1896.

12. SILVER AND THE NEW YORK ELECTIONS OF 1896 AND 1897

1. Republicans: former secretary of the Navy General Benjamin F. Tracy, former judge of the United States Circuit Court John F. Dillon, former lieutenant governor Steward L. Woodford, former state superintendent of public works Silas B. Dutcher, district attorney of Richmond County George M. Pinney, county judge of Queens County Garrett J. Garrettson; Democrats: New York City controller Ashbel P. Fitch, former corporation counsel of Brooklyn William C. Dewitt; Independent: Seth Low.

2. Republicans: state engineer Campbell W. Adams, New York State attorney general Theodore E. Hancock, New York mayor William L. Strong, Brooklyn mayor Frederick W. Wurster; Democrats: president of the Greater New York Commission and former New York City comptroller Andrew H. Green and mayor of Long Island City Patrick J. Gleason.

3. "To Draft a Charter," *New York World,* June 10, 1896.

4. "Wise Men All," *New York Morning Advertiser,* June 10, 1896.

5. "No Weak Points in the Commission," *New York Recorder,* June 11, 1896.

6. "Representative Men," *New York Evening World,* June 9, 1896; "Wise Men All," *New York Morning Advertiser,* "Remarkable," *New York Journal,* both June 10, 1896.

7. "Citizens May Frame the City's Charter," *New York Journal,* June 11, 1896.

8. "Fitch a Misfit in a New Berth?" *New York Press,* June 12, 1896.

9. Fitch questioned whether drafting a charter was the equivalent of an "office" within the meaning of the law. He said "the Court of Appeals has decided several times that where an office is created without limit as to time and with a single purpose, such as this Commission, it can be held by a public official without sacrificing his original office." "Fitch Can Serve," *New York Mail and Express,* June 12, 189610. "Mr. Fitch Declines," *New York Mail and Express,* June 23, 1896.

11. Ibid.

12. "Gout in the City Hall," *New York Sun,* June 30, 1896.

13. John Peter Altgeld was governor of Illinois (1893–97).

14. William Jennings Bryan was a Nebraska congressman and the Democratic presidential nominee in 1896, 1900, and 1908.

15. "Free Silver Is a Reef," *New York World,* June 11, 1895.

16. Leech, *In the Days of McKinley,* 79.

17. "On October 27, 1890, he [McKinley] had written the Farmers' Alliance: 'I am in favor of the use of all the silver product of the United States for money as circulating medium. I would have silver and gold alike.'" Hirsch, *William C. Whitney,* 487.

18. Leech, *In the Days of McKinley,* 83.

19. "The issue quickly lifted the Treasury's gold reserve, which had fallen as low as $44.5 million to a high point of $128.7 million." Nevins, *Grover Cleveland,* 2:688.

20. "Talks with Harlem Delegates," *Harlem Reporter,* July 4, 1896.

21. "Whitney a Delegate," *New York World,* "New York May Not Vote," *New York News,* July 7, 1896.

22. Hirsch, *William C. Whitney,* 501.

23. Ibid., 502.

24. "Cannot Support the Ticket," *New York Times,* July 14, 1896.

25. "The Silver Heresy," *New York Evening Post,* Feb. 12, 1892.

26. "Bolting Democrats," *New York Tribune,* July 15, 1896.

27. "Fitch Backed by Democrats," *New York Morning Advertiser,* July 22, 1896.

28. "Fitch's Firm Stand," *New York Evening Advertiser,* "Congratulate the Comptroller," *New York Times,* "Mr. Fitch's Stand Approved," *New York Tribune,* all July 21, 1896. The *Evening Advertiser* and the *Tribune* were Republican newspapers, and the *Times* was Democratic.

29. "A Democratic Opinion Worthy of the Consideration of Democrats," *North Adams (MA) Transcript,* July 23, 1896.

30. Leech, *In the Days of McKinley,* 90.

31. Marcus Alonzo Hanna was an industrialist and Republican politician from Ohio. After the presidential campaign Hanna became United States senator from Ohio.

32. Thomas Beer, *Hanna* (New York: Alfred A. Knopf, 1929), 111.

33. "Hanna and Platt Will Soon Meet," *New York Evening Advertiser,* July 30, 1896.

34. "Hanna Hustles Like Ten Men," *New York Press,* July 31, 1896.

35. "City Bonds Redeemed," *New York Evening Post,* July 2, 1896.

36. "Bids for City Bonds Too Low," *New York Recorder,* Aug. 18, 1896.

37. "Will Sell When Bryan's Beaten," *New York Sun,* Sept. 27, 1896.

38. "Proposed Sale of City Bonds," *New York Journal of Commerce,* Oct. 26, 1896.

39. Ibid.

40. Ibid.

41. Senator John M. Palmer of Illinois was nominated for president by the National Democratic Party, a sound-money party. Nevins, *Grover Cleveland,* 2:707.

42. Hirsch, *William C. Whitney,* 509.

43. Nevins, *Grover Cleveland,* 2:712.

44. "The Vote in the City," *New York Evening Sun,* Nov. 4, 1896.

45. Nevins, *Grover Cleveland,* 2:712.

46. "Great City Bond Sale," *New York Times,* Nov. 9, 1896.

47. "Eager for City Bonds," *New York Mail and Express,* Nov. 7, 1896.

48. "A Wonderful Success," *New York Tribune,* Nov. 10, 1896.

49. "Fitch Is Zealous," *New York Morning Advertiser,* Dec. 5, 1896.

50. "Millions for the Police," *New York Herald,* Dec. 15, 1896.

51. "Charities Budget Cut," *New York Sun,* Dec. 18, 1896.

52. "Taking Over for Wright," *New York Sun,* Dec. 23, 1896.

53. "Annual Budget Increased," *New York Times,* Dec. 30, 1896.

54. "Tax Rate Jumps Thirty Points," *New York Morning Advertiser,* Dec. 30, 1896.

55. "The Increased Budget," *New York Times,* Dec. 31, 1896.

56. Ibid.

57. "At War Over Budget," *New York Herald,* Jan. 1, 1897.

58. Ibid.

59. "Tammany Anxious to Forget the Silver Craze," *New York Post,* Dec. 5, 1896.

60. It is curious that such a letter would have been written by a reader not possessing more than ordinary interest and knowledge of the subject. Over the next several months several unusually well-written letters (and some corresponding editorials) appeared in the *Commercial Advertiser* from alleged "Republicans" who endorsed Fitch for controller. The *Brooklyn Eagle* also carried several similar letters arguing that Fitch should remain as controller of the consolidated New York.

61. "Good Words for Mr. Fitch," *New York Commercial Advertiser,* Nov. 30, 1896.

62. Lewis, *Richard Croker,* 340.

63. In 1891 the Republican vote in Brooklyn was larger than that of Vermont, almost equal to that of Maine, and double that of Oregon. Syrett, *The City of Brooklyn,* 235.

64. The quotations in this paragraph were taken from the following single source: "Mayor's Message an Explanation," *New York Journal,* Jan. 13, 1897.

65. "Greater City Mayor," *New York Commercial Advertiser,* Jan. 23, 1897.

66. "The Candidates for Mayor," *New York Times,* Feb. 16, 1897.

67. "Mr. Fitch Doesn't Want to Be Mayor," *New York Sun,* Jan. 23, 1897.

68. "Would Be Mayor," *New York Daily News,* Jan. 24, 1897.

69. "For the Hall of Records: Mayor Talks about Tweed," *New York Times,* Mar. 27, 1897.

70. "Admires Tweed," *New York News,* Mar. 26, 1897.

71. "Admires Tweed," *New York News,* Mar. 26, 1897; "Strong Praises Boss Tweed," *New York Morning Journal,* Mar. 27, 1897; "Praise of Tweed Arouses Critics," *New York Herald,* Mar. 28, 1897.

72. "Praise of Tweed Arouses Critics," *New York Herald,* Mar. 28, 1897.

73. "Pernicious Tributes to Tweed," *New York Times,* Mar. 28, 1897.

74. "Wigwam Lays Plans," *New York World,* Apr. 4, 1897.

75. "Party Leaders Are Fixing Up Fences," *New York World,* Apr. 25, 1897.

76. "Solid for the Controller," *New York Tribune,* May 13, 1897.

77. "Roosevelt on Himself," *Auburn (NY) Bulletin,* Aug. 25, 1897.

78. Ibid.

79. Lewis, *Richard Croker,* 341.

80. Ibid., 339–41.

81. "Croker Sails Tuesday," *New York World,* Aug. 29, 1897.

82. "Waiting for Croker," *New York Post,* Sept. 4, 1897.

83. "Comptroller Fitch Back," New York *Commercial Advertiser,* Sept. 7, 1897.

84. Two things had changed. First, "the legal investments for Savings Banks of New York State had been extended to include thirty-two of the richest cities of the country," which naturally cut into demand for the city's bonds. Second, owing to reform spending and city legislation in Albany, "many

millions of bonds had been authorized," thereby increasing their supply. In combination it seemed clear that the city would have to pay more for its money. "City Controller Ashbel P. Fitch," *Bond Buyer,* July 26, 1897.

85. "A bill was introduced in the Senate . . . ," *New York Times,* Apr. 24, 1897.

86. "Greater New York's Accounts," *New York Financial News,* May 25, 1897.

87. "Finances of Greater New York," *Albany Argus,* July 2, 1897.

88. "In Support of Controller Fitch," *New York Tribune,* Sept. 24, 1897.

89. "Ten years ago last Friday . . . ," *New York Times,* Sept. 19, 1897.

90. "Prominent Figures in the Municipal Campaign," *New York Times Illustrated Magazine,* Oct. 3, 1897.

91. "Morgan Failed as a Politician," *New York Herald,* Oct. 6, 1897.

92. "Croker Makes Up a Slate," *New York Sun,* Sept. 28, 1897.

93. "All in Harmony," *New York Press,* Sept. 29, 1897.

94. "Mr. Fitch Is on the Right Ticket," *New York Sun,* Oct. 1, 1897.

95. "Sheehan's Knife Out for Croker," *New York Herald,* Sept. 30, 1897.

96. "Controller Fitch's Acceptance," *New York Tribune,* Oct. 1, 1897.

97. "Tammany in Tatters," *Rochester Democrat Chronicle,* Oct. 2, 1897.

98. The quotations in this paragraph were taken from the following single source: "Whitney Forsakes Political Strife," *Philadelphia Press,* Oct. 5, 1897.

99. "Fitch May Run on Three Tickets," *New York Herald,* Sept. 24, 1897.

100. "Kings County Declares War," *Brooklyn Citizen,* Sept. 24, 1897.

101. "Brooklyn Will Get Neither the Mayor Nor Comptroller," *Brooklyn Times,* Sept. 23, 1897.

102. "Tracy Will Be Named," *Chicago Inter-Ocean,* Sept. 26, 1897.

103. "Tiger Beset on Every Side," *New York Herald,* Sept. 28, 1897.

104. "Croker Deceived Him," *New York World,* Sept. 25, 1897.

105. Ibid.

106. Ibid.

107. "Croker Is Not with Sheehan," *Brooklyn Times,* Sept. 27, 1897.

108. Lewis, *Richard Croker,* 338.

109. "Croker Is Not with Sheehan," *Brooklyn Times,* Sept. 27, 1897.

110. "Croker Shy on Brooklyn," *New York Evening Sun,* Oct. 15, 1897.

111. "Cits Have Made a Slate," *New York Sun,* Sept. 30, 1897.

112. "Citizens to Name Fitch," *New York Tribune,* Sept 28, 1897.

113. "Cits Have Made a Slate," *New York Sun,* Sept. 30, 1897.

114. Ibid.

115. "Fairchild Won't Withdraw," *New York Sun,* Oct. 14, 1897.

116. "Opposed by Mr. Low," *New York Commercial Advertiser,* Nov. 11, 1897.

117. "Platt Names General Tracy," *Philadelphia Times,* Sept. 24, 1897.

118. "The City Convention," *New York Tribune,* Sept. 29, 1897.

119. "Full Platt Ticket Named: Clean and Finished Performance," *Brooklyn Eagle,* Sept. 29, 1897.

120. "General Benjamin F. Tracy has agreed to accept . . . ," *New York Press,* Sept. 25, 1897.

121. "All in Harmony," *New York Press,* Sept. 29, 1897.

122. "Convention Opened," *New York Evening Sun,* Sept. 28, 1897.

123. "Republican Unity Bothers Croker," *Philadelphia Press,* Sept. 30, 1897.

124. "Republican Slate Ready," *New York Times,* Sept. 28, 1897.

125. "Tracy, Fitch, Appleton: No Excitement Over Fitch," *New York Times,* Sept. 29, 1897.

126. "Chaos Reigns in George Camp," *New York Daily News,* "George Smashes Things," *New York Herald,* Oct. 9, 1897.

127. "George Wants Dayton," *New York Herald,* Oct. 12, 1897.

128. "Waring Off the George Ticket," *Philadelphia Press,* Oct. 13, 1897.

129. "Dayton Is Ready to Fight Bossism," *New York Herald,* Oct. 13, 1897.

130. Alfred Henry Lewis, "His Column," *New York Journal,* Oct. 16, 1897.

131. "Dayton Intends to Run," *New York Evening Journal,* Oct. 12, 1897.

132. Lewis, "His Column," *New York Journal,* Oct. 16, 1897.

133. De Lancey Nicoll was a lawyer, Tammany Hall politician, and New York district attorney.

134. "Richard Croker left his real estate office . . . ," *New York Journal,* Oct. 14, 1897.

135. "May Fight Over Ruppert's Place," *New York Herald,* Oct. 9, 1897.

136. "Tammany Calls Dayton a Stalking Horse for Fitch," *Brooklyn Eagle,* Oct. 13, 1897.

137. "Coler's Fate—Dayton's Acceptance Makes Him a Dead Bird in the Pit. Leaders Plunged in Gloom," *Brooklyn Standard Union,* Oct. 14, 1897.

138. "Mr. Dayton for Controller," *New York Commercial Advertiser,* Oct. 14, 1897.

139. "Disastrous to Tammany," *New York Evening Sun,* Oct. 14, 1897.

140. "Tracy Will Sweep All," *New York Evening Sun,* Oct. 27, 1897.

141. "Tracy Is Ahead," *New York Press,* Oct. 27, 1897.

142. "Mr. Croker Got the Tip," *New York World,* Sept. 28, 1897.

143. "'Twixt' Devil and Deep Sea." *Albany Journal,* Sept. 3, 1897.

144. Lewis, "His Column," *New York Journal,* Oct. 21, 1897.

145. Ibid.

146. "Croker Expresses Belief in Victory," *New York Evening Telegram,* Oct. 14, 1897.

147. "Thousands to Bet; Million to Bluff," *New York Evening Telegram,* Oct. 20, 1897.

148. Alfred Henry Lewis, "His Column," *New York Journal,* Oct.21, 1897.

149. "As has been previously set forth in these columns . . . ," *Leslie's Weekly,* Nov. 4, 1897.

150. "The Controller," *Boston Traveler,* Nov. 1, 1897.

151. "How Candidates Cast Their Ballots," *New York Herald,* Nov. 3, 1897.

13. PASSAGE

1. "Tammany Leaders at Police Headquarters," *New York Telegraph,* Nov. 3, 1897.
2. "Fitch Takes the Result Cheerfully," *New York Tribune,* Nov. 4, 1897.
3. "Mayor Strong Talks Out," *New York Times,* Nov. 4, 1897.
4. "Everyone Is Now Roasting Platt," *Philadelphia Inquirer,* Nov. 4, 1897.
5. "Mr. Fitch's Breakfast," *New York Telegraph,* Nov. 8, 1897.
6. "Work of Consolidation," *Brooklyn Eagle,* Nov. 23, 1897.
7. "Comptroller's Clerks Safe," *New York Evening Sun,* Dec. 20, 1897.
8. "New Issue of City Bonds," *New York Telegraph,* Dec. 8, 1897.
9. "High Bids for City Bonds," *New York Times,* Dec. 15, 1897.
10. "A Remarkable Bond Sale," *Bond Buyer,* Dec. 15, 1897.
11. "Sons of Oneida," *Utica Herald,* Mar. 16, 1898.
12. "The last official act . . . ," *New York Herald,* Jan. 1, 1898.
13. "Comptroller Ashbel P. Fitch," *New York Herald,* Jan. 1, 1898.

14. "Controller in Office," *New York Herald,* Jan. 2, 1898.

15. New York City's outstanding debt was limited by law to 10 percent of the city's assessed valuation.

16. "Richard Croker's Unworthy Mayor," *Philadelphia Press,* Mar. 27, 1898.

17. "Debt Limit Passed," *New York Mail and Express,* Apr. 2, 1898.

18. "Not Scared by Croker," *New York World,* Apr. 5, 1898.

19. Ibid.

20. "Good King Dick Virtuously Angry," *New York Press,* Apr. 3, 1898.

21. Ibid.

22. "A Tammany Game," *New York Mail and Express,* Apr. 4, 1898.

23. "Debt Limit of the City," *New York Post,* Apr. 4, 1898.

24. Ibid.

25. Ibid.

26. "$50 Millions Excess Debt," *New York Sun,* Apr. 29, 1898.

27. "City Debt Limit Passed," *New York Post,* Apr. 28, 1898.

28. "$50,000,000 Over Debt Limit," *New York Telegraph,* Apr. 29, 1898.

29. "Debt Limit Ties Up $708,000 Pay," *New York Journal,* May 3, 1898.

30. "The Manufactured Debt Limit," *New York World,* "Coler the Wrecker," *New York Press,* both Apr. 30, 1898; "A Partisan Report," *New York Mail and Express,* "A New View of Municipal Debt," *Newark (NJ) News,* both Apr. 29, 1898.

31. "Why New York Seems Insolvent," *Philadelphia Press,* Apr. 30, 1898.

32. "Fitch Replies to Coler," *New York Tribune,* May 3, 1898.

33. "The 'Fake' Debt Limit," *New York World,* May 3, 1898.

34. "Settle This Debt Question," *New York Mail and Express,* May 4, 1898.

35. "Fitch Says Coler Has Erred about Debt Limit," *New York World,* May 3, 1898.

36. "Fitch Replies to Coler," *New York Tribune,* May 3, 1898.

37. "Contractors See Coler," *Brooklyn Eagle,* May 3, 1898.

38. "Hard Luck," *New York Post,* May 5, 1898.

39. "Standing from Under," *New York Tribune,* May 13, 1898.

40. "Amount to Be Raised by Taxes," *New York Tribune,* June 10, 1898.

41. "New York City Bond Award," *Boston Financial News,* Aug. 11, 1898.

42. "Trust Company of America," *New York Times,* June 24, 1899.

43. "Wealthy Men in a Trust Company," *New York Herald,* June 25, 1899.

44. "Trust Company of America," *New York Times,* June 24, 1899.

45. "Trust Company of America Ready for Business," *New York Commercial,* June 26, 1899.

46. "The Silver Heresy," *New York Evening Post,* Feb. 12, 1892.

47. "Intentions of Gold Democrats," *New York Evening Post,* July 10, 1900.

48. "Gold Democrats' Action No Surprise," *New York Morning Journal,* July 26, 1900.

49. "Mr. Fitch Not a Candidate," *New York Times,* Sept. 10, 1901.

50. "Ashbel P. Fitch, ex-comptroller and ex-congressman . . . ," *New Yorker,* May 22, 1901.

51. "Ashbel P. Fitch Dead," *New York Tribune,* May 5, 1904.

52. "A. P. Fitch Dead," *New York Globe and Commercial Advertiser,* May 4, 1904.

53. Charles Dayton to Lizzie, May 4, 1904, Ashbel P. Fitch archives.

54. "Death of Ex-Comptroller Ashbel P. Fitch," *New York Vigilant,* May 7, 1904.

55. "We sincerely regret . . . ," *Lexington (KY) Herald,* May 7, 1904.

56. "Ashbel P. Fitch," *Harlem Reporter,* May 7, 1904.

57. "Ashbel P. Fitch Is Dead," *New York Sun,* May 5, 1904.

58. "Ashbel Fitch Dies," *New York Evening Sun,* May 4, 1904.

59. "Ashbel P. Fitch," *Harlem Reporter,* May 7, 1904.

60. The story was known to have appeared in the *Boston Post, Kansas City Journal, Washington Post,* and *Cincinnati Enquirer.* "Newsboy's Limited Permission," *Washington Post,* May 22, 1904

61. "Ashbel P. Fitch Dead," *Malone (NY) Palladium,* May 12, 1904.

62. Lewis S. Burchard to Lizzie, Feb. 11, 1907, Ashbel P. Fitch archives.

CONCLUSION

1. Morton Cross Fitch, *History of Ragged Lake* (privately printed, 1933), 174.

2. "Controller Fitch," *New York Press,* Nov. 15, 1897.

Bibliography

The primary source for Fitch's papers is the Ashbel P. Fitch archives, a privately held collection of approximately three hundred letters written by Ashbel P. Fitch to his wife, Elizabeth Cross Fitch. It also contains miscellaneous family papers and forty-six volumes of newspaper clippings relating to Mr. Fitch's career. The clippings were assembled (labeled, dated, and entered) by Mr. Fitch's clerks for twenty-one years (1884–1904).

Ackerman, Kenneth D. *Boss Tweed*. New York: Carroll and Graf, 2005.

Armstrong, John. *Love, Life, Goethe*. New York: Farrar, Straus and Giroux, 2007.

Ash, Mark. *The New York City Consolidation Act as in force in 1891, with notes indicating the statutory sources, references to judicial decisions, and all laws relating to New York City, passed since January 1, 1882*. Albany: Weed, Parsons and Company, 1891.

Barry, David S. *Forty Years in Washington*. Boston: Little, Brown, 1924.

Beer, Thomas. *Hanna*. New York: Alfred A. Knopf, 1929.

Binder, Frederick M., and David M. Reimers. *All the Nations Under Heaven*. New York: Columbia Univ. Press, 1995.

Blight, David W. *Race and Reunion*. Cambridge, MA: Belknap Press of Harvard Univ. Press, 2001.

Boritt, Gabor. *The Gettysburg Gospel: The Lincoln Speech That Nobody Knows*. New York: Simon and Schuster, 2006.

Brunelle, Jim. "Speaker of the House." *Down East*, Nov. 2005.

Budeit, Janice, ed. *Papers of William H. Seward*. Woodbridge, CT; Reading, UK: Research Publications, 1983.

Burke, Albie. "Federal Regulation of Congressional Elections in Northern Cities, 1871–94." *American Journal of Legal History* 14, no. 1 (Jan. 1970): 18.

Burrows, Edwin C., and Mike Wallace. *Gotham*. New York: Oxford Univ. Press, 1999.

Carlyle, Thomas. *Essay on Goethe's Faust*. Introduction by Dr. Richard Schroeder; translated by Ashbel P. Fitch. New Rochelle, NY: Knickerbocker Press, 1900.

Caulkins, Frances Manwaring. *History of Norwich, Connecticut, 1866*. Chester, CT: Pequot Press, 1976.

Club Men of New York. New York: The Republic Press, 1896.

Depew, Chauncey M. *My Memories of Eighty Years*. New York: Charles Scribner's Sons, 1922.

Donlan, Thomas G. "The Dollar's Long Drive." *Barron's,* Oct. 2005.

Ehret, George. *Twenty-five Years of Brewing with an illustrated history of American beer, dedicated to the friends of George Ehret.* New York: Gast Lithograph and Engraving Company, 1891.

Faust, Albert Bernhardt. *The German Element in the United States.* 2 vols. Boston: Houghton Mifflin, 1909.

Fitch, John T. *Puritan in the Wilderness: A Biography of the Reverend James Fitch, 1622–1702.* Camden, ME: Picton Press, 1993.

Fitch, Morton Cross. *The Fitch Family at Mooers, New York.* Monograph, 1932.

———. *History of Ragged Lake.* Privately printed, 1933.

———. *The Weekly Budget after Thirty Years.* Privately printed, 1920.

Fitch, Roscoe Conkling, comp. *History of the Fitch Family,* A.D. *1400–1930, A Record of the Fitches in England and America, including "pedigree of Fitch" certified by the College of Arms, London, England.* 2 vols. Published privately by the Fitch family, 1930.

Godkin, Edwin Lawrence. *Triumph of Reform.* New York: Souvenir Publishing Company, 1895.

Hancock, Elise. "100 Years of Manhattan's Garbage." *Johns Hopkins Magazine,* Apr. 1995.

Hirsch, Mark David. *William C. Whitney: Modern Warwick.* New York: Dodd, Mead, 1948.

Holzer, Harold. *Lincoln at Cooper Union.* New York: Simon and Schuster, 2004.

Homberger, Eric. *Historical Atlas of New York City.* New York: Henry Holt and Company, 1994.

Hurd, Duane Hamilton. *History of Clinton and Franklin Counties, New York with illustrations and biographical sketches of its prominent men and pioneers.* Philadelphia: J. W. Lewis and Co., 1880.

Jeffers, H. Paul. *Commissioner Roosevelt.* New York: John Wiley and Sons, 1994.

Josephson, Matthew. *The Robber Barons.* New York: Harcourt, Brace, 1934.

King, Moses, *Notable New Yorkers, 1896–1899.* New York: The Orr Press, 1899.

Klein, Carole. *Gramercy Park: An American Bloomsbury.* Boston: Houghton Mifflin, 1987.

Kroessler, Jeffrey A. *New York Year by Year.* New York: New York Univ. Press, 2002.

Leech, Margaret. *In the Days of McKinley.* New York: Harper Brothers, 1959.

Lewis, Alfred Henry. *Richard Croker.* New York: Life Publishing, 1901.

Loring, John. *Magnificent Tiffany Silver.* New York: Harry N. Abrams, 2001.

Mason, Louis B. *The Life and Times of Major John Mason.* New York, London: G. P. Putnam's Sons, 1935.

McCall, Samuel W. *The Life of Thomas Brackett Reed.* Boston: Houghton Mifflin, 1914.

McElroy, Robert. *Grover Cleveland, the Man and the Statesman.* Introduction by Elihu Root. New York: Harper and Brothers Publishers, 1923.

McPherson, James. *Battle Cry of Freedom.* New York: Oxford Univ. Press, 1988.

Millard, Candice. *The River of Doubt: Theodore Roosevelt's Darkest Journey.* New York: Doubleday, 2005.

Morison, Elting E., ed. *Letters of Theodore Roosevelt.* Cambridge, MA: Harvard Univ. Press, 1951.

Morris, Edmund. *The Rise of Theodore Roosevelt.* New York: Coward, McCann and Geoghegan, 1979.

Mushkat, Jerome. *Tammany: The Evolution of a Political Machine, 1789–1865.* Syracuse: Syracuse Univ. Press, 1971.

Nelson, William E. *Fighting for the City.* New York: New York Law Journal, 2008.

Nevins, Allan. *Grover Cleveland: A Study in Courage.* 2 vols. New York: Dodd, Mead, 1932.

Parmelee, Ashbel B. *Biography of Rev. Ashbel Parmelee, D.D.* Philadelphia: J. W. Lewis and Co., 1880.

Reitano, Joanne. *Restless City.* New York: Routledge, 2006.

———. *The Tariff Question in the Gilded Age: The Great Debate of 1888.* University Park: Pennsylvania State Univ. Press, 1994.

Riordon, William L. *Plunkitt of Tammany Hall.* New York: E. P. Dutton, 1963. Reprinted, New York: Meridian, a division of Penguin Books, 1991.

Rybczynski, Witold. *A Clearing in the Distance: Frederick Law Olmstead and America in the Nineteenth Century.* New York: Scribner, 1999.

Silver, Nathan. *Lost New York.* New York: Schocken Books, 1967.

Strong, Theron G. *Joseph H. Choate.* New York: Dodd, Mead, 1917.

Syrett, Harold Coffin. *The City of Brooklyn, 1865–1898: A Political History.* New York: Columbia Univ. Press, 1944.

Thomas, Lately. *Delmonico's: A Century of Splendor.* Boston: Houghton Mifflin, 1967.

Upchurch, Thomas Adams. *Legislating Racism: The Billion Dollar Congress and the Birth of Jim Crow.* Lexington: Univ. Press of Kentucky, 2004.

US Congress. *Congressional Record.* 1888–93. Washington, DC.

Weisman, Steven R. *The Great Tax Wars.* New York: Simon and Schuster, 2002.

Wood, Gordon S., *Empire of Liberty.* Oxford; New York: Oxford Univ. Press, 2009.

Index